MORE WITH MORE

More with More
Investing in the Energy Transition

2025 European Public Investment Outlook

Edited by Floriana Cerniglia and Francesco Saraceno

OpenBook
Publishers

https://www.openbookpublishers.com

©2025 Floriana Cerniglia, Francesco Saraceno
Copyright of individual chapters is maintained by the chapters' authors

Open Reports Series vol. 14 | ISSN Print: 2399-6668 | ISSN Digital: 2399-6676

Paperback: 978-1-80511-743-8
Hardback: 978-1-80511-744-5
PDF: 978-1-80511-745-2
HTML: 978-1-80511-747-6
EPUB: 978-1-80511-746-9

DOI: 10.11647/OBP.0499

Cover image: A close up of a wind turbine. Photo by Kamran Abdullayev (2023), https://unsplash.com/photos/a-close-up-of-a-wind-turbine-with-a-sky-background-GpWz5_3Ac2w

Cover design: Jeevanjot Kaur Nagpal

The publication of this book was supported by CRANEC—Centro di ricerche in analisi economica e sviluppo economico internazionale, Università Cattolica del Sacro Cuore, Milan; F2i SGR; and OFCE-Sciences Po Paris

UNIVERSITÀ CATTOLICA del Sacro Cuore

CRANEC
Centro di ricerche in Analisi economica
e sviluppo economico internazionale

F2i SGR

ofce

Contents

List of Figures

List of Tables

Acknowledgements

The *European Public Investment Outlook* is the result of a joint effort by several economists belonging to a wide range of academic institutions and policy institutes; they all wrote in their own personal capacity.

The work was coordinated by Floriana Cerniglia and Francesco Saraceno with logistical and financial support by CRANEC—Centro di ricerche in analisi economica e sviluppo economico internazionale, Università Cattolica del Sacro Cuore—Milan; and OFCE-Sciences Po Paris.

The authors are affiliated to the following institutions:

- Accademia Nazionale dei Lincei (Rome, Italy)
- Complutense Institute for International Studies (ICEI-UCM)—Universidad Complutense de Madrid (Madrid, Spain)
- Copenhagen School of Energy Infrastructure (CSEI)—Copenhagen Business School (Copenhagen, Denmark)
- CRANEC—Centro di ricerche in analisi economica e sviluppo economico Internazionale, Università Cattolica del Sacro Cuore (Milan, Italy)
- DISEIS—Dipartimento di Economia internazionale, delle istituzioni e dello sviluppo—Università Cattolica del Sacro Cuore (Milan, Italy)
- Eco-union (Barcelona, Spain)
- EIB—European Investment Bank (Luxembourg)
- ENEA—Agenzia nazionale per le nuove tecnologie, l'energia e lo sviluppo sostenibile (Rome, Italy)
- Enel Foundation (Rome, Italy)
- ETUI—European Trade Union Institute (Brussels, Belgium)
- Florence School of Regulation—European University Institute (Florence, Italy)
- IMK—Macroeconomic Policy Institute (Germany)
- Institut d'Etudes Politiques de Paris—Sciences Po (Paris, France)
- IVIE—Instituto Valenciano de Investigaciones Económicas (València, Spain)

- Luiss Institute for European Analysis and Policy—LEAP, Università Luiss Guido Carli (Rome, Italy)

- JDI—Jacques Delors Institute (Paris, France)

- Neoma Business School (Mont-Saint-Aignan, France)

- Observatoire français des conjonctures économiques, OFCE-Sciences Po (Paris, France)

- RGI—Renewable Grid Initiative (Berlin, Germany)

- Saïd Business School, University of Oxford (United Kingdom)

- Technology, Innovation and Society Research Group, Department of Industrial Engineering and Innovation Sciences—Eindhoven University of Technology (Eindhoven, the Netherlands)

- UAM—Universidad Autónoma de Madrid (Madrid, Spain)

- Universitat de València (València, Spain)

Our thanks go first and foremost to the chapter authors, who offer countless insights into the challenges and policy options related to the energy transition.

We also want to acknowledge the logistical and financial support of our institutions: CRANEC—Centro di ricerche in analisi economica e sviluppo economico internazionale, Università Cattolica del Sacro Cuore—Milan; and OFCE-Sciences Po Paris. The respective presidents, Alberto Quadrio Curzio and Xavier Ragot have been behind this project from its outset.

The help of Giovanni Barbieri in assembling the manuscript, as well as the amazing work of Alessandra Tosi and of all the Open Book Publishers staff in the editing and typesetting process, is gratefully acknowledged.

Last, but absolutely not least, we are grateful to Renato Ravanelli and to F2i SGR, Fondi italiani per le infrastrutture, for the financial support that enormously facilitates the production and dissemination of the *Outlook*.

Floriana Cerniglia

Francesco Saraceno

Preface

Alberto Quadrio Curzio and Xavier Ragot

More with More: Investing in the Energy Transition is the 2025 issue of the *European Public Investment Outlook*. It continues the remarkable effort to keep public investment at the centre of the European policy debate, at a moment in which the EU is looking for a way to cope with an unstable geopolitical environment and with the backlash against the green transition.

The sixth volume of the *European Public Investment Outlook* series, devoted to the energy transition, could not be timelier. Energy sits at the crossroads of two urgent priorities: the accelerating ecological transition and the need for the EU to safeguard its strategic autonomy in an increasingly confrontational (when not outright hostile) international arena.

The common thread linking the different chapters of the 2025 *Outlook* is the necessity of tackling the challenges of the energy transition at the European level. While, as the chapters of the first part of the *Outlook* show, national policies matter, energy remains intrinsically a European public good, for which common policies, or at least strong cooperation, are needed.

The other message that emerges from the impressive roster of contributors to the volume is that, while it is of course important to improve the quality of public investment in an environment of high debt and limited resources, no energy transition nor structural transformation is possible without a substantial increase of public and private investment. The European Union needs to do more with more.

With the 2025 *European Public Investment Outlook,* Floriana Cerniglia and Francesco Saraceno are consolidating the cooperation of our institutions (CRANEC— Università Cattolica del Sacro Cuore, Milan and OFCE-Sciences Po, Paris) and continuing in the creation of a network of European researchers working on the topic of public investment.

We commend the effort by the editors of the *Outlook* to renew the collaboration between our institutions every year and to keep alive the attention of policymakers and economists on the topic of public investment, especially at a juncture when the temptation of fiscal consolidation is strong, and risks jeopardizing our common future.

    https://doi.org/10.11647/OBP.0499.15

Introduction:
Energy Transition in the EU—The Need for a Governance Revolution

Floriana Cerniglia[1] and Francesco Saraceno[2]

The theme of *More with More: Investing in the Energy Transition* is closely linked to two earlier volumes of the *European Public Investment Outlook* (Cerniglia and Saraceno 2022, 2024). A consistent theme across those reports—and one that continues in this volume—is the acknowledgement of public investment as a crucial driver of structural transformation. Moreover, the energy transition stands among the most pressing and complex challenges confronting contemporary societies. It deserves to be at the very top of the political agenda, while also serving as a cornerstone of industrial policy seen as a multidimensional strategy—one that combines innovation, sustainability, and competitiveness— aimed at fostering the structural transformation of the European economy.

Energy is pivotal in all the dilemmas faced by the EU. First, and foremost, the ecological transition is essential in reducing emissions and attaining climate goals: 60% of total investment classified as "green" is energy related; therefore, there cannot be an energy transition without an energy transition. Then, energy is a key element in the quest for strategic autonomy in an increasingly uncertain global environment, both economically and geopolitically. Last, but not least, energy and energy prices are going to be one of the main pieces of the strategy the EU will have to put in place to close the productivity gap with the US.[3] These are structural challenges that the contingent factors (the trade war, the invasion of Ukraine, Israel's war in the Middle East) compound and make it more urgent to address.

The energy transition is inherently linked to industrial policy, as the shift toward sustainable energy entails a fundamental restructuring of production systems,

---

1   CRANEC—Università Cattolica del Sacro Cuore.
2   Observatoire français des conjonctures économiques (OFCE) Sciences Po Paris and Luiss Institute for European Analysis and Policy (LEAP).
3   "EU companies still face electricity prices that are 2-3 times those in the US. Natural gas prices paid are 4-5 times higher" (Draghi 2024, p. 14).

                    https://doi.org/10.11647/OBP.0499.00

technological pathways, and labour markets. Yet, EU Member States exhibit divergent interests and policy approaches, reflecting the reliance on distinct energy mixes and different stages of progress toward the green transition. This heterogeneity is shaped by geography, historical trajectories, and the availability of domestic energy resources, as discussed in the country chapters in the first part of this *Outlook*. Within this fragmented landscape, the European Union should assume a pivotal role in reconciling national priorities with collective European objectives and in fostering the potential efficiency gains associated with a more integrated energy market.

In the current geopolitical and economic context, the energy transition fosters a set of interdependent policy objectives. Accelerating the deployment of renewable energy, electrification, and energy efficiency measures is essential to meeting climate commitments, while simultaneously reducing Europe's dependence on fossil fuel imports, an imperative underscored by recurrent supply shocks and mounting geopolitical tensions. Over the medium to long term, lower fossil fuel dependence is also expected to contribute to a decline in overall energy costs, thus fostering productivity and competitiveness. The clean energy transition, therefore, not only supports environmental sustainability but also enhances Europe's economic resilience and strategic autonomy by strengthening control over critical infrastructures and technologies.

Not surprisingly, the Letta (2024) and Draghi (2024) reports highlight the need for market-enabling reforms (completing the single market, a savings and investment union, etc.) that are a precondition for the full exploitation of the large scale of the European economy; advocating for these reforms is, after all, business as usual. But there is an important novelty in the Draghi report, in that that it does not stop there and is unambiguous about the fact that reforms are far from being sufficient. It is in fact impossible to imagine that the digital and energy transitions and the catching up in terms of productivity and growth can be implemented without massive investments. The team working on the Draghi report quantified these resources at around €800 billion per year (around 5% of EU GDP), of which a substantial part would have to come from public investment.[4] While it may seem obvious among academics and the EU scholars who have been working on the green transition,[5] this clear call for the mobilization of new resources as a complement to other instruments is an important and welcome step forward for EU policymakers. The report has two further merits. The first is its emphasis on the urgency of the situation. It is hard to disagree with the former European Central Bank (ECB) President when he states that this is the last call for the European Union. Without a radical change in priorities and public policies, the EU will not only fail to be a main character of the ecological and digital transitions;

---

4   It is useful here to recall that for all major OECD economies, the share of public investment on GDP has declined significantly and steadily since the peaks of the 1970s. This trend accelerated further in the wake of the 2008 financial crisis (Bubbico et al. 2020).

5   See Cerniglia and Saraceno (2022), in particular Baccianti (2022).

it will eventually be doomed to irrelevance and stagnation. The second merit—that is central to the topic of energy and a recurrent theme in the previous instalments of the *European Public Investment Outlook*—is highlighting that closing the growth and productivity gap requires a wide spectrum of policies.

The "New" Industrial Policy

The ever-ongoing debate on markets vs the state (Saraceno 2018) has shaped discussions on industrial policy as well, with those arguing the need for the public hand to steer the economy towards socially desirable long-term goals opposed to those who claim that the state is particularly inefficient in "picking the winners", a task that should be left to markets. After three decades in the closet, since 2008, fiscal policies have returned to the toolbox of policymakers (Saraceno 2022). The most recent discussion on fiscal policy has centred on industrial policy and public investment: in the short term, to tackle the disruption of the global economy caused by the pandemic, by inflation, by the reorganization of global value chains and by repeated geopolitical shocks (Bontadini et al. 2024); in the long run, as documented by the previous issues of the *European Public Investment Outlook*, to facilitate and guide the long-term ecological and digital transitions.

An increasing number of economists argue today that industrial policy is particularly relevant in periods of structural transformation, well beyond dealing with market failures, as it helps shape the economy in the long term. Mariana Mazzucato's "Entrepreneurial state" (Mazzucato 2013) has in fact some characteristics that private entrepreneurs lack. Firstly, it does not aim to maximize profit, but social welfare; it also has an indefinite time horizon (the state does not "die") and can be patient, waiting long periods to reap the benefits of investments; last, it has deep pockets, and borrowing capacities superior to those of private operators. These characteristics allow the entrepreneurial state to go beyond markets not only in dealing with standard market failures but also, and equally importantly, in exploring productive possibilities that are not accessible to private actors and implementing public policies that lay the groundwork for (private and public) long-term investment, both tangible and intangible.

In fact, a "new" doctrine[6] of industrial policy is emerging (for details, see Aiginger and Rodrik 2020, Juhász et al. 2024, and the chapters of Cerniglia and Saraceno 2024) that emphasizes precisely how industrial policy cannot be reduced simply to regulation, or to enabling markets, for example by "levelling the playing field" and reducing rents; nor can it aim solely to push for the creation of large oligopolistic conglomerates to compete on international markets. Instead, industrial policy must be a *multidimensional*

---

6 We put "new" between quotes, because this theory of industrial policy is a revival of the policies followed in the post-WWII period (*les trente glorieuses*) to foster the development of Europe and of the United States.

strategy that fosters structural transformation, reduces bottlenecks in strategic sectors, and facilitates the process of creative destruction, reallocating resources from low-productivity activities to sectors that are strategic either for economic or for geopolitical reasons. Recognizing the multidimensional aspect of industrial policy also challenges the idea that an optimal institutional and political architecture for capitalist economies exists. The remarkable performance of China in the race for global hegemony is the latest example of the capacity of capitalism to prosper under different institutional settings (Freeman 2000).

Compared to the initial phase of the Green Deal—which had a strong focus on limiting emissions, and was relatively less interested in industrial, security, and social policy dimensions—it has now become evident that, in the energy domain, the European Union must confront a complex set of interrelated and often conflicting objectives and constraints. The Union is simultaneously striving to combat climate change through more ambitious emission-reduction targets and a profound transformation of the energy mix; to revitalize European competitiveness, which is increasingly challenged by the structural effects of the green transition on European industry and by the growing advantages of major global competitors such as the United States and China in clean technologies, energy costs, and innovation capacity; and to ensure energy security, a goal that became an urgent priority in the aftermath of Russia's invasion of Ukraine, highlighting the need to rapidly reduce dependence on Russian fossil fuels.

These objectives are, however, constrained by two critical factors. First, social consensus, which has weakened in recent years due to the uneven territorial and social impacts of policies for the green transition and the redistributive consequences of rising energy prices. Second, the availability of financial resources and investment capacity—both public and private—which remain essential to sustaining the energy transition and achieving strategic objectives.

These interdependencies generate complex short- and medium-term policy trade-offs, particularly in relation to competitiveness. Key challenges remain unresolved: ensuring affordable energy prices for firms and households; completing the single European energy market; and diversifying energy supply sources and interconnection infrastructures, notably through deeper strategic partnerships with Africa and the Middle East.

More with More: Investing in Energy Transition, like its predecessors, is divided into two parts. Part I presents country experiences in critical domains pertinent to the energy transition. A general overview of EU policies can be found in Chapter 1, while Chapters 2 to 5 offer more detailed analysis on France, Germany, Italy, and Spain, the four largest economies of the European Union. Reading the chapters of Part I, it emerges that these countries are extremely heterogeneous regarding their energy mix and their dependency on imports. The differences in the energy mix among countries show how difficult it is to implement a single European policy for the energy transition that can work for all Member States and, consequently, to find a path that suits everyone regarding strategic autonomy in the energy sector. The authors highlight that strategies to decarbonize energy are in place in all these countries, and analyze their state of advancement. The role of regulation, public procurement, and investment—both public and private—is also a common thread. In addition, the chapters provide updates on the National Energy and Climate Plans, to offer a prospective view on the destination of public investment in support of the energy transition.

Chapter 1, by A. Brasili, B. Magné, E. Öndeş, D. Revoltella, and A. Tueske, argues that maintaining the EU's climate ambitions demands clear direction, collaboration between stakeholders, and efficient use of limited public resources. While investment needs for achieving long-term climate goals are well established, there is a lack of detailed data on current investment levels, creating uncertainty about the EU's climate trajectory. To improve decision-making, the authors emphasize the need for more detailed and systematic data on climate and energy progress, as well as allocated resources. They also stress the importance of an improved regulatory framework and increased public financing, along with a clearer strategy outlining the roles of the public and private sectors, and the EU and Member States in this transition.

In Chapter 2, P. Malliet, M. Plane, F. Saraceno, and A. Saumtally document the past behaviour of French public investment, highlighting that the state of public capital remains overall better than in other EU countries, even if, since the sovereign debt crisis, net investment has been mostly negative. The authors then focus on the energy sector. Since 2005, greenhouse gas emissions have decreased by 33%, but current choices will be crucial in achieving France's decarbonization goals by 2030, as well as by 2050, the target date for reaching carbon neutrality. Today, France is at a crossroads. The reduced fiscal space and a missing medium-term energy transition plan coalesce to threaten the continuity and stability of investment in the energy transition. The chapter concludes with recommendations on how to strengthen the French energy transition policies but warns that a European effort is essential for success in the energy and green transition.

Chapter 3, by T. Bauermann, examines the progress of the energy transition in Germany, with a focus on the electricity sector and on the gradual expansion of renewable energies. The policy support under the Renewable Energy Act (EEG)—notably operating cost subsidies—has played a pivotal role in shaping this trajectory. These subsidies made it possible for initially expensive and risky technologies to establish themselves on the market, but the author critically assesses the limitations of this funding model, whereas a publicly funded infrastructure model—common in many other European countries—would be significantly more cost-effective.

In Chapter 4, G. Barbieri, F. Cerniglia, and A. Pronti document that Italy is aligned with the EU's 2030 climate goals, aiming to cut greenhouse gas emissions by 55% compared to 1990 levels. Progress remains too slow to meet the target. The National Recovery and Resilience Plan (NRRP) allocates €69 billion to green investments until mid-2026. Despite this, a €175 billion investment gap remains between 2024 and

2030. Achieving climate goals demands yearly investments close to 5% of GDP. Since public support will soon decline, making private sector engagement is essential, but the increasing heterogeneity of regulations and authorization procedures adopted by different regions is a significant obstacle to a homogeneous and quick development of renewable sources in Italy.

In Chapter 5, I. Álvarez and J. Uxó show that Spain has a relative advantage in its capacity to produce energy from renewable sources, which is already translating into lower prices than the European average. In the energy transition framework, Spain has set ambitious targets, specifically for renewable energies in electricity production. Meeting them requires substantial investment. PERTE is a valuable instrument in developing investments and an important novelty in applying Next Generation EU (NGEU) funds. The main question, however, is whether this investment effort will be sustained once these funds are no longer received, especially in a context marked by the return of fiscal rules and pressure to increase security spending.

Part II (Chapter 6 to 14) delineates priority areas and challenges for public intervention in the energy transition, in the context of increasing competition among EU policy objectives to tap into public resources; in the next few years, the pressure to increase investment in other categories, such as defence, will required increased vigilance to protect the energy transition investment. Although, in recent years, much more attention has been paid to the crucial role of public investment in promoting growth and productivity (Cerniglia and Saraceno 2024), there are other critical aspects of public intervention related to the energy transition which are the focus of the chapters that make up the second part of the *Outlook*.

Part II can be divided in two further sub-parts. The first (Chapters 6 to 11) is devoted to the broad topic of how the energy transition is linked to competitiveness. In Chapter 6, F. Gracceva and D. Palma evaluate the EU's current underperformance relative to its 2030 targets, and then they assess whether the current strategy can truly serve as an effective development policy—one capable of revitalizing the European economy and contributing to global decarbonization. They argue that the "European competitiveness obsession" tends to overlook the trade-offs between increasing domestic production and maintaining economic efficiency and it falls short in addressing the structural weaknesses of Europe's industrial base, also because of the relative scarcity of science-based activities. They propose a "cooperative mission-oriented" strategy: a new model of productive globalization based on collaboration rather than competition.

EU industrial competitiveness is also the main topic of investigation of Chapter 7, by M. Armiento and A. Villa, who invoke the need for a coherent policy approach that must account for the interaction between efforts to decarbonize the energy mix and measures that support the adoption of end-use clean technologies in the industrial sector. They highlight the complexities of technologies inherent in different pathways towards transition and, moreover, emphasize that manufacturing industries are highly exposed to international competition, making them particularly sensitive to trade policies. Therefore, a comprehensive policy framework should prioritize effective use of EU funds and ensure stable regulatory conditions. A coherent EU-wide framework to support industrial electrification is imperative.

F. Alkemade, W. Klok, and F. Pasimeni in Chapter 8 discuss how a systems-based research and innovation (R&I) approach is essential to address the complexity of integrating renewables, managing sociotechnical change, and ensuring economic and social sustainability. Special attention is given to the role of small and medium-sized enterprises (SMEs), energy communities, and sustainable finance mechanisms as critical drivers of bottom-up innovation and structural transformation. The chapter also offers recommendations for policymakers seeking to realign R&I strategies in support of a transformative, inclusive, and competitive European energy transition, to highlight how climate objectives, economic resilience, and social cohesion are increasingly interconnected.

Chapter 9, by A. Battaglini and C. Sikow-Magny, examines the central role of electricity grids in Europe's energy transition toward climate neutrality, energy security, and sustainability. Well-designed grids are the backbone of a just, secure, and efficient European energy transition. The Iberian blackout of 2025 highlights the risks of underinvestment, lack of flexibility and the issues of interconnection between networks. The authors analyze EU regulatory frameworks—especially the National Energy and Climate Plans (NECPs) and the Trans-European Networks for Energy (TEN-E)—and identify key investment needs, flexibility technologies, and optimization strategies.

The last two chapters of this sub-part focus on specific issues related to the energy transition, critical raw materials, and green hydrogen. R. Zoboli, in Chapter 10, emphasizes that the procurement of critical raw materials (CRM) risks becoming a major barrier to the development of clean-tech and net-zero manufacturing in the EU, thus jeopardizing the achievement of key EU self-sufficiency objectives in the energy transition. The EU policy framework includes several measures introduced in 2024 and 2025 to promote both clean-tech manufacturing and the security of CRM supply, within the EU Competitiveness Compass and the Clean Industrial Deal of 2025. The "criticality" of materials is defined as a combination of "economic importance" and "supply risk". While there are significant investments that could boost manufacturing autonomy, they may not keep up with the fast-growing demand and strong external competition, especially from China.

Green hydrogen is the focus of Chapter 11 by R. Fernández and C. García. They observe that the EU's strategy for green hydrogen (GH2) combines regulatory tools and investor-state mechanisms to address challenges in scaling up this emerging industry. While hydrogen is key to Europe's decarbonization goals, its adoption is hindered by high costs, price risks, and uncertain demand. To address these issues, the EU has introduced new instruments to manage price and volume risks. Without additional fiscal innovation or coordinated planning, Europe risks missing its hydrogen targets, jeopardizing its broader industrial and climate goals.

The second sub-part, the last three chapters of the *Outlook*, deals with the distributional issues of the energy transition. The evolving concept of a just transition is explored by F. Cots, J. Fosse, and Diana Mangalagiu in Chapter 12. The authors examine the EU's Just Transition Mechanism (JTM), and highlight the sociopolitical, cultural, and economic barriers to transition. They argue that, in addition to technological and financial solutions, addressing local identities and narratives—in coal-dependent regions—is key to ensuring legitimacy and success. Energy communities are seen as crucial for democratizing the energy transition, encouraging local ownership, and overcoming resistance in coal-reliant regions. The chapter contains policy recommendations to enhance regulatory frameworks, protect community integrity, and support citizen-led initiatives, positioning energy communities as essential for achieving a just, inclusive low-carbon future in Europe.

Social acceptance of energy transition is the focus of Chapter 13 by A. Eisl and P.-V. Nguyen. This chapter discusses the introduction of a CO_2 price for housing and mobility as a key measure for the EU to meet its climate goals. However, without proper compensation and investment measures, additional costs for citizens could become socially unacceptable and potentially reverse climate policies. The chapter recommends ways to design accompanying policies for the expansion of the EU Emissions Trading System (ETS2). It draws lessons from carbon taxation schemes in France, Germany, and Austria, analysing their redistribution and investment measures. The chapter stresses the importance of ensuring the visibility of support measures, and effectively targeting citizens with redistribution mechanisms, while balancing compensation with investment tools.

B. Galgóczi and A. Watt, in Chapter 14, argue that the green energy transition offers substantial benefits, but it involves significant upfront costs and disruptions, with benefits realized only after a delay. For a fair distribution of these benefits and burdens, effective and inclusive governance is essential. The risk is that increasing defence spending and geopolitical instability might limit investment in climate and social initiatives. The growing emphasis on competitiveness, especially against the backdrop of China's dominance in transition sectors, further complicates the transition.

Adapting EU Institutions to the Newly Found Role of Industrial Policy

A common message that emerges from the chapters of this *Outlook* is that, together with regulation, coherent strategies, and coordination of national policies, public investment is paramount both for implementing the energy transition and for adapting social capital and dealing with its distributional consequences. Furthermore, many of the chapters plead for truly European solutions, from investment to public procurement, regulation, and so on. The question then arises of whether European institutions are fit to enable the development and implementation of industrial and fiscal policies for the structural transformation of the economy. There is little room for optimism.

The introduction of Next Generation EU, the most innovative instrument introduced by the EU in decades, seemed to finally break through the stubborn refusal of European policymakers to imagine common tools both to address crises and manage structural transformations (see Saraceno 2021, 2022). In the wake of its introduction, a stimulating debate began on the need to complement the common management of the single currency with a Central Fiscal Capacity to stabilize the economy and finance European public goods more effectively and at lower costs than national policies, while also making transnational investment projects easier and more stable to finance (see, e.g., Buti et al. 2023).

Unfortunately, however, the momentum from the collective and solidarity-based reaction to the pandemic, that led to Next Generation EU, quickly dissipated. Germany's return to its obsession with frugality (Rietlzer and Watt 2024) leaves little room for optimism on the front of common policies.[7] The draft proposal for the Multiannual Financial Framework, the EU budget for 2028–2034, while having some merits, on one side is facing substantial opposition from frugal countries; on the other, it fails to mobilize the resources to close the investment gap, most notably in the decarbonization of the economy.

Therefore, while efforts at creating new tools for common action or reinforcing existing ones are to be acknowledged and encouraged, realism calls for the renewed attention to fiscal space at the national level: although it is not optimal, this is where most of the additional investment will likely have to come from in the short-to-medium term. There are two issues: the first is that the Stability Pact prevents, even in its reformed version and even for the most virtuous countries, the implementation of investment plans of the necessary size. The second is that the high public debt inherited from past crises risks exposing countries to market pressure and therefore limits the fiscal space. These two problems must be tackled simultaneously, aiming for a coherent institutional framework.

Protect Public Investment with an "Augmented Golden Rule" of Public Finances

As is now widely acknowledged, the new EU fiscal rule, in force since 2024, restricts fiscal and industrial policies. In the coming months, the flaws of the new rule will unfortunately become increasingly evident, even for countries like Germany that wanted and imposed it (see Steinbach and Zettelmeyer 2025). Discussions on the

---

7   One may wonder whether Germany is still a frugal country, after its government in the Spring of 2025 has launched a massive investment plan and significantly softened the constitutional debt brake. What is certain is that, at least so far, this increased domestic flexibility has not translated into a softer stance on EU governance.

architecture of fiscal rules in Europe should therefore resume, to allow for a meaningful protection of public investment.

We have long called for an "Augmented Golden Rule" that excludes investment (in a broad sense) from the 3% deficit limit (Saraceno 2017, Cerniglia and Saraceno 2020). The logic would not be very dissimilar from the recent exemption of defence expenditure from the Stability Pact limits proposed by the Commission. But contrary to that, it would not be based on an exceptional activation of the suspension clause, with validation ex post by the Parliament; rather, it would be institutionalized and rooted into an ex ante democratic process: the Council and the Parliament might periodically agree on the policy priorities to increase the stock of (tangible and/or intangible) capital and allow countries to raise debt to finance these priorities.

It goes without saying that allowing borrowing to finance investment expenses would lead to an increase in debt. This is where a second pillar of the renewed institutional architecture would have to come into play.

While the continuing savings glut and globally low interest rates do not pose a problem of sustainability for the EU as a whole, in the current context of fragmentation, individual countries may still face restricted access to market financing. Nevertheless, if debt is sustainable at the European level, addressing the public finances problems of a single country becomes a purely technical problem. And that is what the second pillar is for: a European Debt Agency (EDA), which would operate as a stabilizing intermediary between national governments and financial markets, enhancing market discipline while safeguarding systemic stability (Amato et al. 2021; Amato and Saraceno 2022).

To conclude, the European Union is currently confronted with three pivotal objectives that shape its energy policy framework: combating climate change, revitalizing European competitiveness, and ensuring energy security. In pursuing these objectives, the EU must take into consideration the inherent trade-offs among them, as well as the binding constraints of social sustainability, the need for consensus among Member States, and the new rules of the Stability and Growth Pact. This *Outlook* seeks to shed light on several of these dimensions, offering operational insights into the policy measures required to achieve these goals.

We argue that the development of a coordinated strategy that integrates the green transition with industrial policy—one that ensures the economic sustainability of the transformation of the energy mix—would necessarily require a profound rethinking of the EU governance framework. First, while it is hard to imagine, under current conditions, the implementation of a Central Fiscal Capacity, the European Union should at minimum finance projects of common interest (for example, interconnection infrastructures); second, increasing the fiscal space of Member States through an augmented golden rule and the creation of a European Debt Agency should help attain the necessary stronger coordination between national energy transition programs and EU-wide objectives, including through the establishment of common-interest investment initiatives.

References

Aiginger, K., and D. Rodrik (2020) "Rebirth of Industrial Policy and an Agenda for the Twenty-First Century", *Journal of Industry, Competition and Trade* 20.2, 189–207, https://doi.org/10.1007/s10842-019-00322-3

Amato, M., E. Belloni, P. Falbo, and L. Gobbi (2021) "Europe, Public Debts, and Safe Assets: The Scope for a European Debt Agency", *Economia Politica* 38.3, 823–861, https://doi.org/10.1007/s40888-021-00236-6

Amato, M., and F. Saraceno (2022) "Squaring the Circle: How to Guarantee Fiscal Space and Debt Sustainability with a European Debt Agency", *OFCE Working Paper* 2022–02 (January), https://leap.luiss.it/wp-content/uploads/2022/06/WP1.22-Squaring-the-circle-How-to-guarantee-fiscal-space-and-debt-sustainability-with-a-European-Debt-Agency.pdf

Baccianti, C. (2022) "The Public Spending Needs of Reaching the EU's Climate Targets", in F. Cerniglia and F. Saraceno (eds), *Greening Europe: 2022 European Public Investment Outlook*. Cambridge, UK: Open Book Publishers, pp. 107–128, https://doi.org/10.11647/OBP.0328.08

Bontadini, F., V. Meliciani, M. Savona, and A. Wirkierman (2024) "Nearshoring and Farsharing in Europe within the Global Economy", *Luiss LEAP Working Paper* 16/2024 (August), https://leap.luiss.it/wp-content/uploads/2024/09/WP16.24-Nearshoring-and-Farsharing-in-Europe-within-the-Global-Economy.pdf

Bubbico, R. L., P. B. Brutscher, and D. Revoltella (2020) "Europe Needs More Public Investment", in F. Cerniglia and F. Saraceno (eds), *A European Public Investment Outlook*. Cambridge, UK: Open Book Publishers, pp. 17–32, https://doi.org/10.11647/OBP.0222.01

Buti, M., A. Coloccia, and M. Messori (2023) "European Public Goods", in F. Cerniglia et al. (eds), *Financing Investment in Times of High Public Debt: 2023 European Public Investment Outlook*. Cambridge, UK: Open Book Publishers, pp. 191–200, https://doi.org/10.11647/obp.0386.11

Cerniglia, F., and F. Saraceno (2020) "Introduction", in F. Cerniglia and F. Saraceno (eds), *A European Public Investment Outlook*. Cambridge, UK: Open Book Publishers, pp. 1–14, https://doi.org/10.11647/OBP.0222.11

Cerniglia, F., and F. Saraceno (eds) (2022) *Greening Europe: 2022 European Public Investment Outlook*. Cambridge, UK: Open Book Publishers, https://doi.org/10.11647/OBP.0328

Cerniglia, F., and F. Saraceno (eds) (2024) *Investing in the Structural Transformation. 2024 European Public Investment Outlook*. Cambridge, UK: Open Book Publishers, https://doi.org/10.11647/OBP.0434

Draghi, M. (2024) *The Future of European Competitiveness*. Brussels: European Commission, https://commission.europa.eu/topics/eu-competitiveness/draghi-report_en

Freeman, R. B. (2000) "Single Peaked Vs. Diversified Capitalism: The Relation Between Economic Institutions and Outcomes", *National Bureau of Economic Research Working Paper Series* No. 7556, https://papers.ssrn.com/sol3/papers.cfm?abstract_id=214910

Juhász, R., N. Lane, and D. Rodrik (2024) "The New Economics of Industrial Policy", *Annual Review of Economics* 16.1, 213–242, https://doi.org/10.1146/annurev-economics-081023-024638

Letta, E. (2024) "Much More than a Market", *Report Prepared for the European Council*, https://www.consilium.europa.eu/media/ny3j24sm/much-more-than-a-market-report-by-enrico-letta.pdf

Mazzucato, M. (2013) *The Entrepreneurial State*. London: Anthem Press, https://demos.co.uk/wp-content/uploads/files/Entrepreneurial_State_-_web.pdf

Rietlzer, K., and A. Watt (2024) "Germany: Additional Investment Needs Require Reform of the Debt Brake", in Cerniglia F. and F. Saraceno (eds), *Investing in the Structural Transformation. 2024 European Public Investment Outlook*. Cambridge, UK: Open Book Publishers, pp. 45–58, https://doi.org/10.11647/obp.0434.04

Saraceno, F. (2017) "When Keynes Goes to Brussels: A New Fiscal Rule for the EMU?", *Annals of the Fondazione Luigi Einaudi* 51.2, 131–158. https://www.annalsfondazioneluigieinaudi.it/images/LI/R28201702_E-3817-Saraceno.pdf

Saraceno, F. (2018) *La Scienza Inutile. Tutto Quello Che Non Abbiamo Voluto Imparare Dall'economia*. Rome: Luiss University Press.

Saraceno, F. (2021) "Europe After COVID-19: A New Role for German Leadership?", *Intereconomics* 59 (March/April), 65–69, https://doi.org/10.1007/s10272-021-0955-z

Saraceno, F. (2022) "The Return of Fiscal Policy. The New EU Macroeconomic Activism and Lessons for Future", *ILO Working Paper* 59 (April), https://ideas.repec.org/p/ilo/ilowps/995179893402676.html

Steinbach, A., and J. Zettelmeyer (2025) "Germany's Fiscal Rules Dilemma", 24 April, *Bruegel Analysis*, https://www.bruegel.org/analysis/germanys-fiscal-rules-dilemma

1. An EU-wide Perspective on Public Investment in the Energy Transition

Andrea Brasili,[1] Bertrand Magné,[2] Ege Öndeş,[3]
Debora Revoltella,[4] and Annamaria Tueske[5]

Staying the course on EU climate ambitions in a context of competitiveness, strategic autonomy concerns, and rising geopolitical tensions implies a fostered deployment of cleaner and more secure energy sources. This requires clarity on the path forward, concerted efforts among stakeholders, and a wise and timely usage of scarce public resources. While investment needs to reach mid- to long-term targets are well documented, details on current investment levels are lacking, thus creating uncertainty about the path on which the EU is embarking. Beyond existing data sources, more systematic and granular data collection on the state and pace of climate and energy transitions and on allocated resources is needed to boost the effectiveness of decision-making. More conducive regulatory frameworks and financing contributions are amongst the priority areas for immediate public intervention. Further, a clearer strategy establishing the respective role of the public and the private sector, but also of the EU and Member States, is key.

1.1 Introduction

Staying the course on EU climate ambitions in a context of rising geopolitical tensions and pressing concerns around competitiveness and strategic autonomy implies a fostered deployment of cleaner and more secure energy sources, thereby alleviating the exposure of EU consumers to volatile energy markets.[6] This requires clarity on the path forward, concerted efforts among stakeholders, and a wise and timely usage of scarce public resources. The ratio of public investment to GDP in the EU has increased

---

1   European Investment Bank (EIB).
2   EIB.
3   EIB.
4   EIB.
5   EIB.
6   The monthly EU energy trade balance has been on average €-34.5 billion over 2021–2025 (March), compared to €-21.9 billion over the preceding 2003–2020 period.

https://doi.org/10.11647/OBP.0499.01

since the pandemic and is now established at historically high levels. These levels need to be further increased and should also stimulate greater private investment to ensure the successful delivery of the green transition, in line with other EU policy objectives.

While investment needs to reach mid- to long-term targets are well documented, details on current investment levels are lacking, thus creating uncertainty surrounding the path on which the EU is embarking, and impeding further investment decisions. In what follows, recent dynamics on public investment and capital transfers are highlighted to shine a light on the status of the energy transition and inherent supporting actions. Some emphasis is given to two areas involving both public and private resources: investments in more interconnected power networks, which are crucial for the European single market and the integration of renewable electricity capacities, as well as support to research and development (R&D) in strategic areas such as clean-tech manufacturing.[7] The revised National Energy and Climate Plans developed by EU Member States and recently assessed by the European Commission provide some elements on the relative contributions of the public and private sectors expected in the coming years, another key area of policy uncertainty.

1.2 The Recent Dynamics of Public Investment in Europe

Public investments in Europe are sustained at high levels, with a potential to support the energy transition. As documented in previous reports in this series, public investment in the EU, supported by the Recovery and Resilience Facility (RRF), has returned to levels (as a share of GDP) comparable to those observed prior to the 2008 Global Financial Crisis.[8] According to official data available through Q4 2024, public investment in the EU is estimated to remain at around 3.5% of GDP in 2024, similar to the level recorded in 2023. Capital transfers, which represent a second key component of public intervention in the capital stock, also remained elevated, albeit slightly lower than the record high reached in 2023. Taken together, these two components have exceeded 5% of GDP for the fourth consecutive year in 2024.

Disaggregating the data by macro-regions[9] reveals that the recent increase in capital investment is a shared trend across all three country groups. This pattern holds for capital transfers as well, though the increase is particularly pronounced in the South-Eastern (SE) region, where the extensive use of subsidies and the implementation of other capital-support measures was reported in the aftermath of the pandemic.

---

7   This extends our contribution to last year's EPIO edition (https://doi.org/10.11647/OBP.0434) in which we took account of the evolution of R&D expenditures from public sources pertinent to the energy transition, arguing that R&D is a European public good.

8   And before the public finances consolidation wave that started during the EU sovereign crisis in 2012–2013.

9   Central and Eastern Europe, including Bulgaria, Croatia, Czechia, Estonia, Hungary, Latvia, Lithuania, Poland, Romania, Slovakia, and Slovenia. Southern Europe, including Cyprus, Greece, Italy, Malta, Portugal, and Spain. Western and Northern Europe, including Austria, Belgium, Denmark, Finland, France, Germany, Ireland, Luxembourg, the Netherlands, and Sweden.

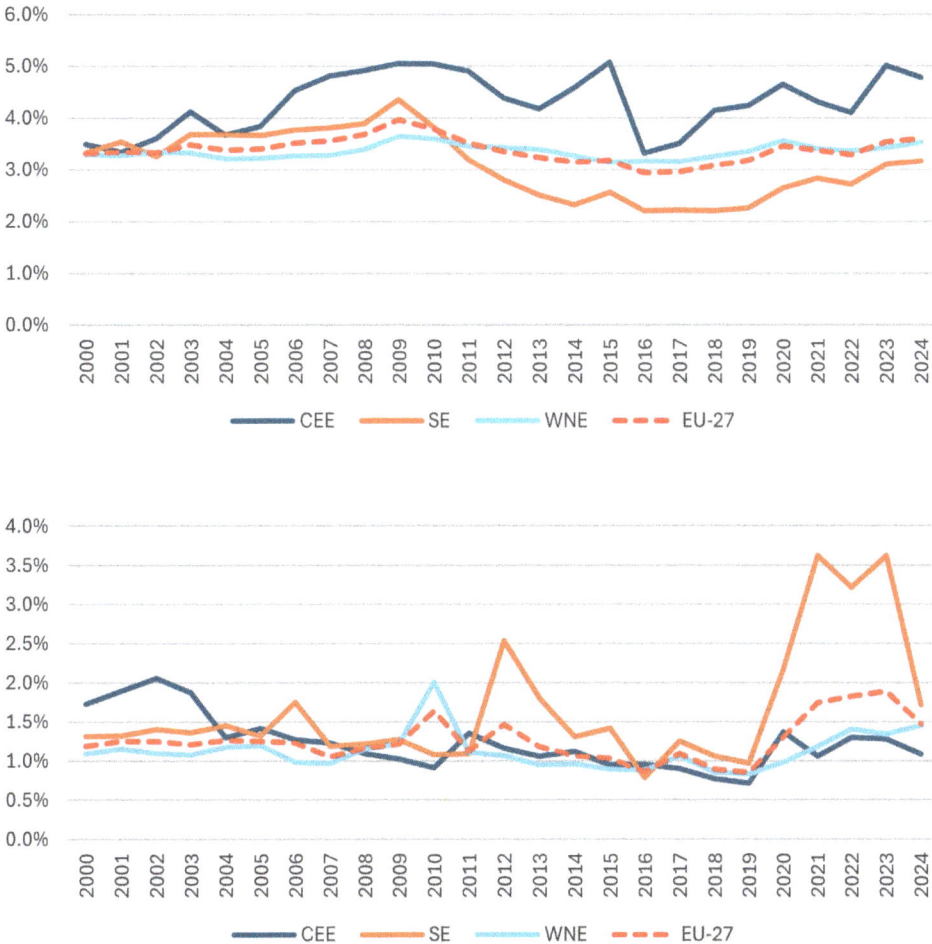

Fig. 1.1 (a) Public investment as a % share of GDP (above); (b) Capital transfer as a % share of GDP (below). *Source:* EIB on Eurostat data.

Data for Figs. 1.1–1.8 are available at
https://hdl.handle.net/20.500.12434/43fd843e

The RRF has played a significant role in accelerating public investment, all the more so in recent years (see Table 1.1). In the last two years, its impact has been especially notable in several Central and Eastern European (CEE) and South-Eastern (SE) countries. In 2024, public investment financed through the RRF accounted for 0.66% of GDP in Croatia, compared to 0.33% in 2023. For Latvia, the figures were 0.65% in 2024 and 0.28% in 2023. In Spain, RRF-funded public investment reached 0.28% of GDP in

2024 and 0.24% in 2023, while in Italy it amounted to 0.47% and 0.31%, respectively. RRF-financed capital transfers were also substantial. In Greece, they represented 0.76% of GDP in 2024 and 0.65% in 2023. For Croatia, the figures were 0.54% and 0.28%; for Italy, 0.18% in 2024 and 0.73% in 2023; and for Portugal, 0.40% and 0.33%.

Table 1.1 The role of RRF in supporting public investment and capital transfer *Source:* EIB on Eurostat data. *Note:* the table represents the share of public investment and capital transfer financed through the RRF.

Public Investment				
	CEE	SE	WNE	EU-27
2021	0.2%	0.7%	0.2%	0.3%
2022	0.5%	2.3%	0.7%	1.0%
2023	2.1%	8.4%	0.9%	2.7%
2024	5.6%	11.5%	0.4%	3.7%
Capital Transfer				
	CEE	SE	WNE	EU-27
2021	0.0%	0.0%	0.1%	0.1%
2022	0.1%	3.6%	6.8%	4.8%
2023	5.1%	14.7%	3.5%	8.9%
2024	8.8%	15.7%	2.8%	7.0%

The RRF is expected to continue its significant contribution to public investment in the second half of its implementation period and it is likely that actual expenditures will continue for a while after the official conclusion date, fixed at the end of 2026. In addition, the slow start of the spending of the Multiannual Financial Framework (MFF) 2021–2027 suggests that the spending based on the EU budget will be a bit more concentrated in the period 2025–2027.

1.3 Public Investment Details According to COFOG Categories

This section focuses on public sector support for the energy transition, whether through direct public investments or capital transfers designed to incentivize private investment. In this regard, the Draghi report emphasized the need to scale up investments aimed at advancing the energy transition. However, growing demands for increased defense and security expenditures are challenging for this objective as they intensify pressure on already limited fiscal resources. Assessing how much of current public investment is allocated to energy transition-related areas is difficult. While Eurostat provides data on government expenditures by function through the COFOG[10] classification system, these categories were not designed to specifically capture the concepts and needs of the green transition. Moreover, detailed functional data lags behind headline figures by about one year and is currently available only up to 2023.

Focusing on the COFOG categories most likely to encompass energy transition-related spending, namely "Environmental protection" and "Fuel and energy", expenditures

---

10   Classification of the Functions of Government (COFOG).

in these areas have broadly tracked overall public investment trends in recent years. Specifically, spending under "Environmental protection" has remained roughly aligned with total investment growth, while the "Fuel and energy" category shows slightly lower growth in investment, but higher growth in capital transfers. Nevertheless, as the figures below indicate, both categories account for only a small share of total public investment, and their relative share declined over the period 2000–2015.

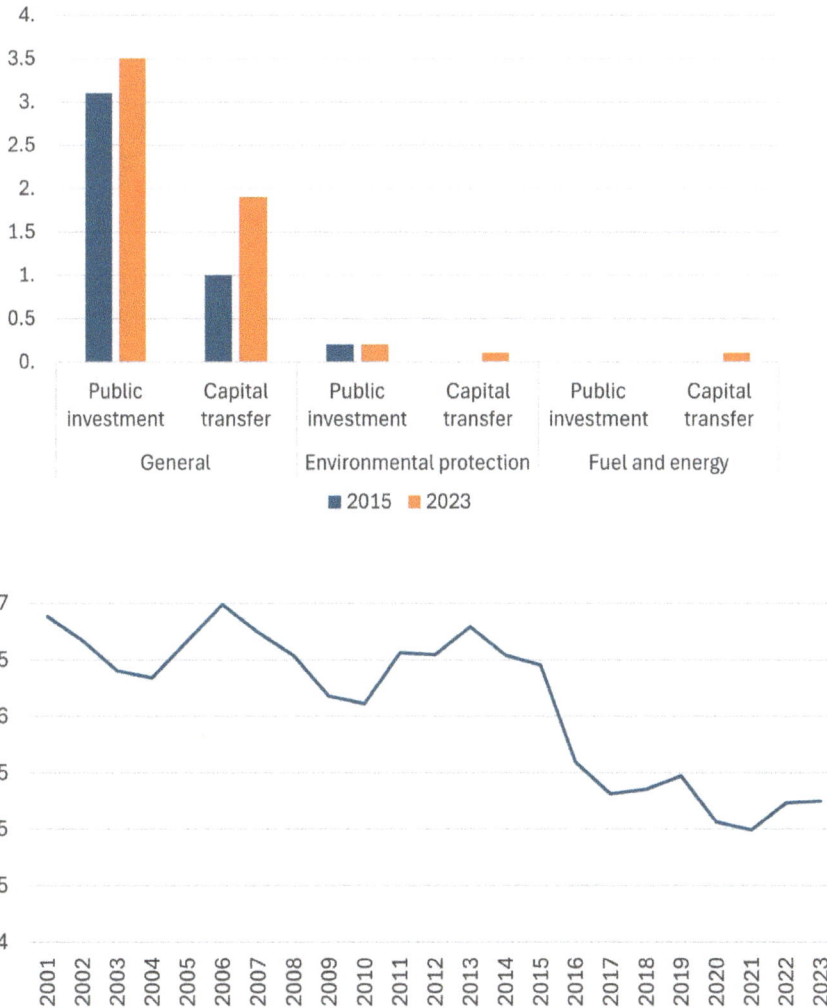

Fig. 1.2 (a) Public support by COFOG categories of interest (above); (b) Share of total investment (below). *Source:* EIB calculations based on Eurostat data.

Data for Figs. 1.1–1.8 are available at
https://hdl.handle.net/20.500.12434/43fd843e

1.4 Public Support for the Energy Transition through Cohesion Policy

To analyze public support for the energy transition, project-level data regarding expenditures linked to cohesion policy can complement Eurostat. The Kohesio dataset includes all approved projects under the 2014–2020 MFF and is continuously updated with data on new projects and beneficiaries under the 2021–2027 programming period.[11] Leveraging the detailed information available at the project level, we identified projects explicitly aimed at supporting the energy transition and grouped them by sector of intervention and financial instrument. While the Kohesio database contains a vast amount of granular information, it also includes keywords and project-level descriptions that enable this type of categorization and analysis. However, project timelines are only presented as overall implementation periods, with no breakdown of annual spending. As a result, only the total project duration can be considered, and figures must be interpreted as yearly averages.

The dataset reflects the full envelope of resources allocated through the MFF for structural funds and cohesion policy. For the 2014–2021 period, this amounts to €404 billion.[12] The share specifically allocated to energy transition-related projects accounts for approximately 9% of this total. More precisely, EU funding covers around €36 billion in energy transition-related expenditures, which, including national co-financing, rises to approximately EUR 65 billion over the full MFF period. Figure 1.3 presents a breakdown of these allocations by country, as well as a thematic disaggregation of supported interventions.

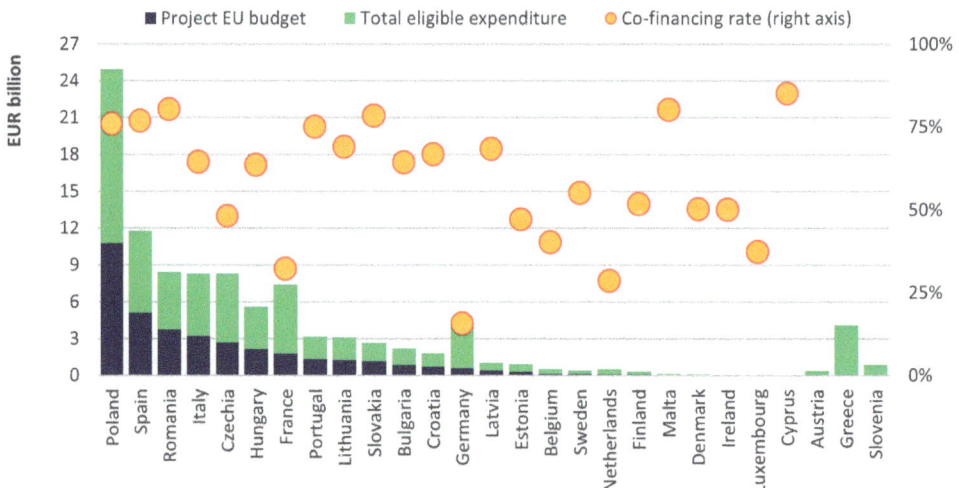

---

11   Kohesio includes projects that are funded through different instruments: the European Regional Development Fund (ERDF), the Cohesion Fund (CF), and the European Social Fund (ESF). By Q2 of 2025, there were almost two million projects listed. The database can be filtered for countries, regions, policies, and themes. It can also be filtered by fund, programme type, programme, priority axis, total budget, EU contribution, and intervention field.

12   In the period 2021–2027, the total envelope should be €368 billion.

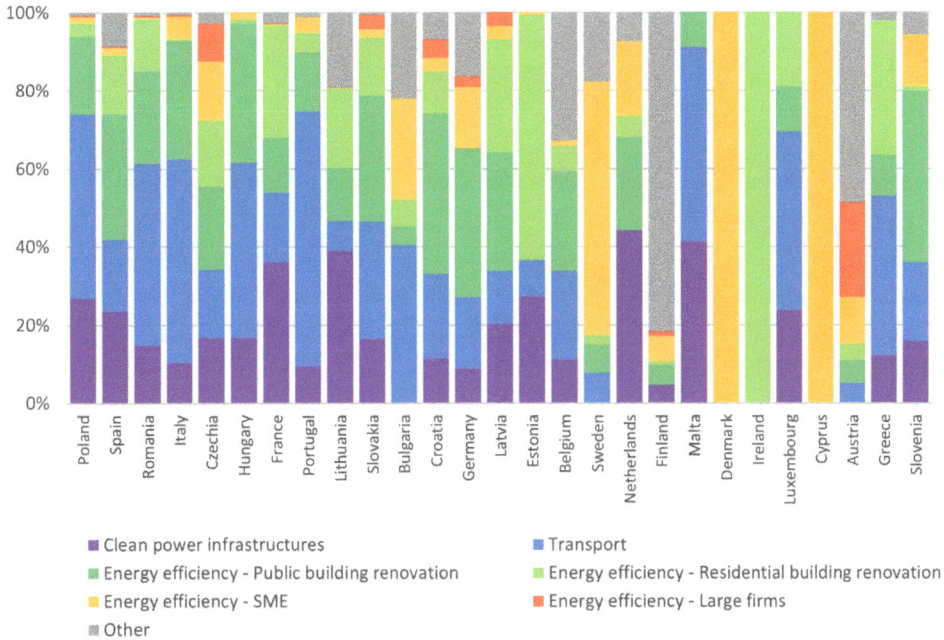

Fig. 1.3 (a) Total resources of cohesion policy devoted to the energy transition (first image) and (b) to their decomposition by themes (second image). *Source:* EIB analysis based on Eurostat, Kohesio database. *Note:* Total resources combine EU budgets and co-financing with national resources.

Data for Figs. 1.1–1.8 are available at
https://hdl.handle.net/20.500.12434/43fd843e

The total allocation remains relatively modest, considering that it encompasses both public investment and capital transfers. In terms of sectoral distribution, transport receives the largest share, accounting for 34% of the total. Clean power infrastructure follows, absorbing 20% of the allocated resources. Projects targeting energy efficiency collectively represent 42% of the total. Within this category, 23% is directed toward energy efficiency improvements in public buildings, 12% toward residential buildings, 5% to small and medium-sized enterprises (SMEs), and 2% to large firms.

1.5 Catalyzing Power Grid Investment with Public Support

Electrification needs require substantial upgrades of European power networks to accommodate the large and decentralized capacities of solar and wind energy. According to the International Energy Agency, power grid investments in Europe stood at €76 billion in 2024 (including energy storage investments),[13] with 40% of capital mobilized in the sector stemming from European Investment Bank financing (€8.5 billion in 2024, mainly in the form of loans). The majority of grid investment remains financed by operators' revenues without direct public provisions and it has to meet profitability criteria.

Contrary to distribution network operations, the natural monopoly nature of transmission networks leaves more space for public involvement. The ownership structure of EU transmission system operators (TSOs),14 often state-owned companies, allows for the alignment of corporate investment strategies with public interest. Investments are expected to reach €85 billion in 2025 (+11%), following the accelerating trend initiated a few years ago (Fig. 1.4). At least 40% of spending made by European TSOs between 2020 and 2023 occurred in 2023, signalling the growing strategic importance of modernized and reliable grids to ensure the security of electricity supply.

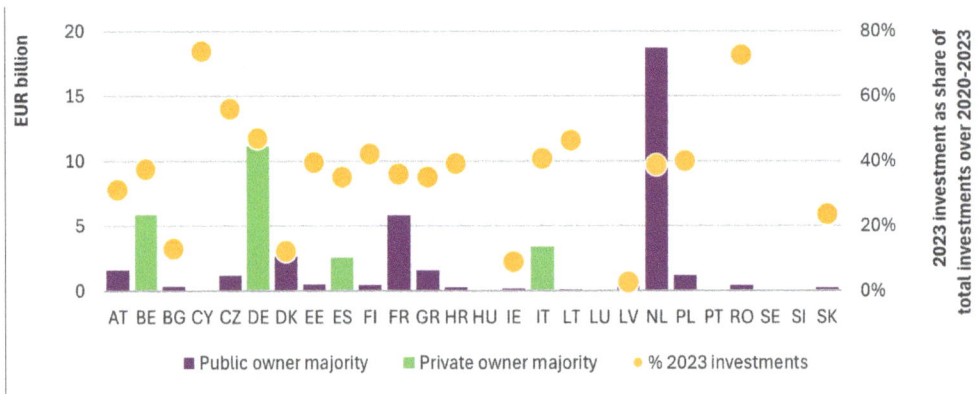

Fig. 1.4 Cumulative TSO investments by EU Member State, 2020–2023 and 2023 share of investment relative to the period 2020–2023. *Source:* EIB analysis based on TSOs' financial statements for 2023 fiscal year. *Note:* Investments for selected TSOs based on ENTSO-E membership (Malta has no TSO). Investment made by the various TSOs operating in Germany and Austria are grouped together.

Data for Figs. 1.1–1.8 are available at
https://hdl.handle.net/20.500.12434/43fd843e

More interconnected power grids are indispensable to the single market integration and the security of energy supply and are thus at the centre of European energy and competitiveness policy objectives (Draghi 2024). Investing in inter-country connectivity of power networks requires the implementation of harmonized incentives for TSOs and coordination among Member States. The European Commission assessment of National Energy and Climate Plans (European Commission 2025d)

---

13   Investments in battery storage doubled between 2022 and 2023, reaching €7.6 billion (I4CE 2025).

14   The thirty corporates operating in the EU (and members of the ENTSO-E) have heterogeneous ownership structures, ranging from 100% government-owned and not listed, to listed with the majority control in private (and even non-EU) hands.

highlights domestic levels of electricity interconnectivity (defined as import capacity over installed generation capacity) as well as the progress realized between 2020 and 2024. Some countries still fall below the EU-wide interconnectivity target of 15%, while a larger group saw their interconnectivity levels decreasing since 2020 (Fig. 1.5).

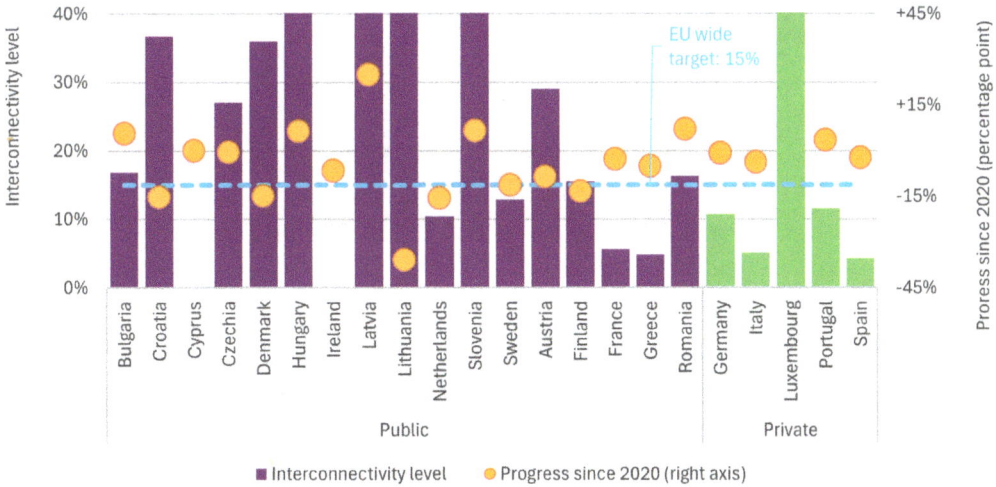

Fig. 1.5 Interconnectivity level by country and ownership structure relative to EU target, 2024 and progress since 2020. *Source:* EIB analysis based on National Energy and Climate Plans.

Data for Figs. 1.1–1.8 are available at
https://hdl.handle.net/20.500.12434/43fd843e

Current levels of investments are expected to be extended to at least 2030 (European Commission 2025b; I4CE 2025), before diminishing slightly (ECA 2025). According to the European Commission, enhancing transmission infrastructures requires €472 billion of investments until 2040, completed by €730 billion of investments directed to power distribution networks (European Commission 2025a). Lengthy planning, including the difficulty to align EU and national strategies, and permitting procedures are often identified as impediments to timely grid infrastructure developments (ECA 2025; I4CE 2025). Finally, as large monopolistic firms, TSOs play a key role in the adoption of innovative products. More harmonized standards put in place by Member States can foster clean-tech adoption, including digital solutions to optimize power network management.

1.6 Public Support for Energy Innovation

Closing the innovation gap with its global competitors is at the heart of the bloc's strategy to revive EU competitiveness (Draghi 2024; EIB 2025). The innovation race is particularly intense for EU clean-tech manufacturers, which are critical to the delivery of more secure supplies of strategic technologies and consumer goods (e.g., renewable energy, energy storage, hydrogen, heat pumps, and electric vehicles).

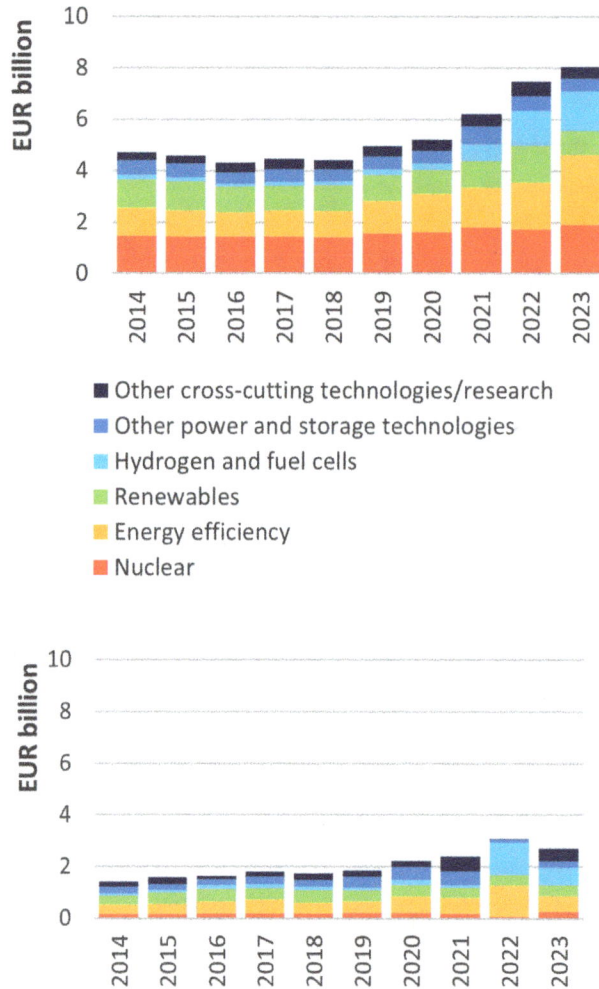

Fig. 1.6 EU- and national-level public R&D expenditure in low carbon technologies, 2014–2024. (a) National public R&D budgets (above); (b) European Union public R&D budgets (below). *Source:* IEA Energy Technology RD&D Budgets, May 2025 update. *Note:* National budgets for twenty EU Member States that are also IEA Member Countries. EU budgets include provisions from Horizon 2020, Horizon Europe, Innovation Fund (small-scale project) funding programmes.

Data for Figs. 1.1–1.8 are available at
https://hdl.handle.net/20.500.12434/43fd843e

Energy innovation in Europe is largely driven and funded by corporates but the inflow of public resources, combining national budget allocations and dedicated EU funds, including Horizon Europe and the Innovation Fund, grew significantly in the aftermath of the pandemic (Fig. 1.6). The pandemic brought to light the resilience and competitiveness of low carbon energy. In 2023, the relevance of energy saving measures prompted the allocation of sizeable provisions to energy efficiency R&D, as well as hydrogen-based technologies. National-level support to energy R&D reached €8.8 billion. EU budgets for energy innovation have been increasing more steadily in the last decade, with more focus on energy storage solutions and cross-cutting technologies. Acknowledging the financing gap for disruptive innovation, the TechEU programme proposed by the Commission, bringing together the European Investment Bank and private investors, aims to strengthen domestic industrial capacities and boost the scale up of clean-tech supply chains, including critical raw material supplies (European Commission 2025c).

Note that the EU gap in terms of R&D with the largest global innovators is mainly on the business R&D portion. On the public side, the resources devoted to clean energy, as the figure above shows, has grown more than two times faster than total public R&D Expenditures.[15]

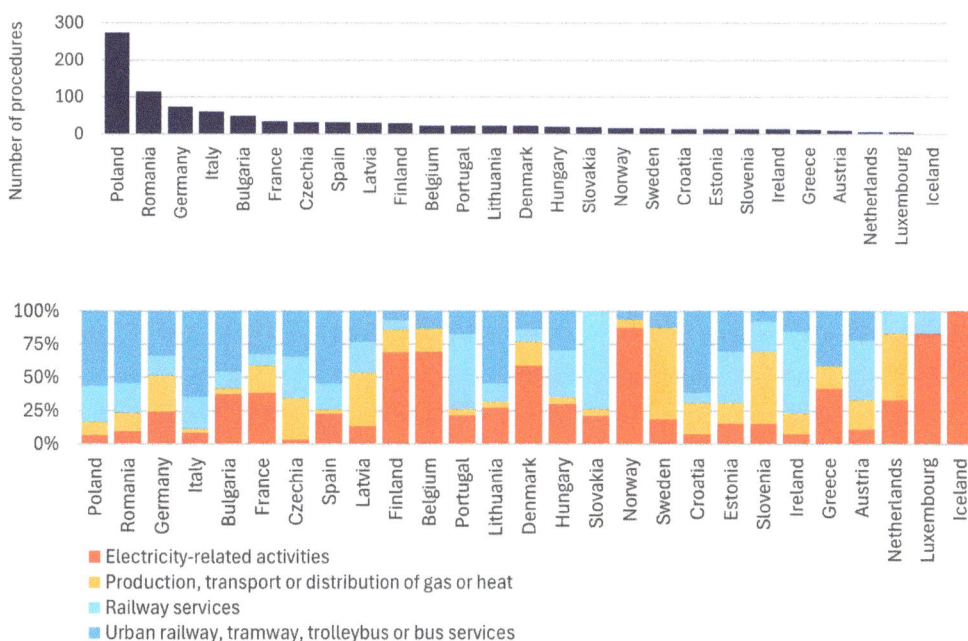

Fig. 1.7 (a) Number (above) and (b) breakdown (below) of public procurement procedures for selected buyer types by country, 2021–2025. *Source:* EU Tenders Electronic Daily (TED) database.

Data for Figs. 1.1–1.8 are available at
https://hdl.handle.net/20.500.12434/43fd843e

---

15   In nominal terms, total public R&D performed by the government sector increased 33% in the period 2014–2023, 41% including the higher education sector. While R&D in clean energy rose close to 80% in nominal terms in the period 2014–2024.

Public procurements (accounting for about 14% of EU GDP each year) offer vast opportunities to boost innovation and foster the uptake of clean technologies and green products across the board (Draghi 2024). However, they remain largely underutilized, notably due to lack of standardized low-carbon criteria in procurement rules. Around one thousand tenders were issued by energy utilities and rail transport companies across the EU since 2021 (Fig. 1.7). Half of the reported procedures were initiated in Poland, Romania, Germany, and Italy, often by public undertakings or bodies governed by public law providing rail transport services.

1.7 The Role of the Public Sector in the Financing of Long-term Clean Energy Transformations

The National Energy and Climate Plans (NECPs) offer a complementary and prospective view of investment needs until 2030.[16] Nineteen Member States provided a sectoral breakdown of total investment needs, while ten of them have documented public contributions.[17] The availability of reliable estimates, pertaining to the aforementioned factors, is essential to identify the full role of public finance, the ways in which policy tools in disposal can be employed, and how they can take effect at s sectoral level (I4CE 2025).

The assessment concludes that the full implementation of existing and planned policies sets the EU to achieve its energy and climate targets for 2030 (European Commission 2025e). The extent of investment needs in the EU, concerning full implementation of the policy mix, has had several estimates. In its accompanying Communication, the Commission reiterates investment needs in the energy system as a projected 3.3% of the GDP at €5.7 trillion over this decade (European Commission 2025f). Additional investment needs for the green transition are estimated at €2.25 trillion over the next five years (Draghi 2024). In comparison, the aggregation of total investment needs contained in NECPs bring cumulative investment needs to €4.7 trillion with the existing policy mix and to €6.7 trillion when taking additional measures into account. As current projections stand, these figures translate into 2.7% and 3.9% of the GDP (IMF 2025).18 The aggregation of NECPs appears to align with previous estimates, though unidentified investment needs from Member States and

---

16   Twenty-three Member States submitted their updated plans and received the European Commission's assessment. Slovakia submitted in April, pending an assessment. Belgium, Estonia, and Poland are yet to submit. Cyprus and Slovakia submitted the two plans that fully addressed the previous round of Commission recommendations in terms of investment needs, allowing for the identification of potential financing gaps (European Commission 2025d).

17   When lacking corresponding estimates, outlined national budgets and EU contributions are aggregated.

18   Currency conversion respects the IMF assumption that the 6 March–3 April 2025 level stays constant.

further additional spending needs, particularly in the transport sector,19 may still drive the aggregated investment needs upward (European Commission 2024).

In addition to the derivation of aggregate investment needs, the analysis of NECPs also allows for exploring the national projections regarding the share of investments, in terms of sectors and the role of the public sector. Based on Member States' NECPs that provide information relevant to these breakdowns, Figure 1.8 outlines the sectoral distribution of investment needs and the share of public investment in fulfilling them.

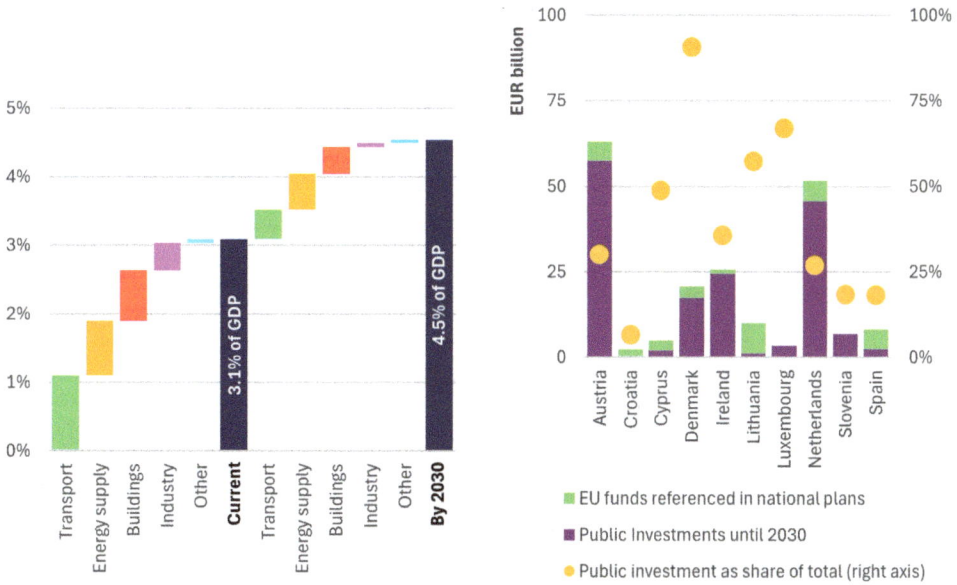

Fig. 1.8 (a) Sectoral investment levels as share of GDP (current, 2030) (left); (b) Public budgets and EU funds from domestic plans (right). Investment needs by sector to 2030 (% GDP); public budgets and EU funds (EUR billion). *Sources*: EIB analysis based on National Energy and Climate Plans, IMF World Economic Outlook (April 2025). *Note*: 2024 and 2030 GDP levels at current prices as forecast by the IMF.

Data for Figs. 1.1–1.8 are available at
https://hdl.handle.net/20.500.12434/43fd843e

The relevant NECPs imply that transport, energy supply, buildings, and industry gather the largest investment needs. Taking additional measures into account, a third of total needs pertains to transport while energy supply makes up for 29%. Investment needs in residential, commercial, and government buildings add up to a quarter of

---

19 Incorporating transport would lead to more than doubling the initial estimate of the European Commission.

the total. Industrial transformations require 10% of total investment needs, with the remaining sectors primarily corresponding to agriculture and waste. Figure 1.8(a) provides the same breakdown in terms of GDP shares and policy scenarios. Based on the Member States which provide information relevant to these breakdowns,[20] total investment needs until 2030 may equal up to 4.5% of their combined GDP (IMF 2025).

The national plans underline large contributions from public investment, generally accounting for a third of total investment efforts. Significant variation at the country level is observed (Fig. 1.8). Data availability partly explains the range of different outlooks in the role of the public sector—in Denmark's case, private investment also contributes to projects initiated with public funding from the national budget, potentially inflating the role of public sector. On the other hand, a notable portion of NECPs explicitly project an indispensable role for the public sector. In Cyprus, Lithuania, and Luxembourg, public investment constitutes most of the financing at 49%, 57%, and 67% in the current policy mix. The first two projections, which Spain can complement, further highlight the importance of EU funding for realizing such levels of public investment, not least for its key role in these plans.

The national plans extend to funding targets on research and innovation, with a view to public investment in R&D by 2030. Ireland reiterates the goal of 2.5% GNI, the Netherlands targets 3% of GDP while Slovenia's ambition level is set at 3.5% of GDP, specifically targeting clean energy technologies.

1.8 Conclusion

Public contributions are indispensable to meet EU climate targets, address specific investment needs, and mobilize corporate investments. The chapter rests on available data to take stock of current levels of public spending in critical domains pertinent to the green transition. The chapter also delineates priority areas for further public intervention in the near term, in a context of increasing competition among EU policy objectives to tap into public resources.

The level of public spending seen in the aftermath of the COVID-19 pandemic, boosted by RRF provisions and a strong commitment from the European Commission, is expected to remain unchanged. However, the analysis of government expenditures, both national and EU wide, such as the EU Multiannual Financial Framework expenditures, points to insufficient amounts devoted to climate action and the energy transition. Beyond existing data sources, more systematic and granular data collection on the state and pace of climate and energy transitions and on allocated resources is needed to boost the effectiveness of decision-making and the implementation of transformations at the required scale.

---

20   The European Commission's assessment deems some country estimates of total or sectoral investment as inconsistent, leading to the change of sampled countries in Fig. 1.8, and different GDP share estimates as a result.

More conducive regulatory frameworks and financing contributions are amongst priority areas for immediate public intervention. Enhanced and interconnected power network infrastructures and a strong support for innovation will boost the bloc's clean-tech manufacturing capacities, which are key to the future of European competitiveness and the bloc's strategic autonomy. Given the sizeable weight of public procurements in the economy, a revision of procurement rules incorporating more explicit and consistent obligations for bidding companies in terms of low carbon content has the potential to accelerate the green transition.

National budgets and domestic climate action plans feature the green transition as a policy priority, but the anticipated level of support remains context dependent. A review of up-to-date National Energy and Climate Plans offers a prospective view on the destination of public investments in support of the energy transition, as foreseen by EU Member States. These domestic assessments shine a light on the public-private allocation of investment efforts up to 2030, including at a sectoral level in some cases. The comparison with the top-down Commission's investment assessment underpinning the EU climate target setting points to a progressive alignment between EU-level ambitions and national budgets, more likely to deliver an orderly and effective energy transition. Further, a clearer strategy establishing the respective roles played by the public and the private sector, and also that of the EU and Member States, is key (I4CE 2025).

Staying the course on climate ambitions is essential while other pressing issues—and associated expenses—are capturing the attention of policymakers. The green transition entails large investment needs but also growth opportunities for the EU that require strong partnerships and shared resources between public and private stakeholders. The catalytic financing provided by the European Investment Bank is key to mobilize the large amounts of capital required for the energy transition, in partnership with private investors. In 2024, 60% of EIB financing was deployed for climate action and environmental sustainability. The €31 billion backing EU energy security measures, including energy efficiency, renewables, storage, and electricity grids, represented 8.5% of overall EU investment in energy transition. Renewables (€13.8 billion) are followed by investment support to the transport sector (€8.2 billion), energy efficiency (€7.5 billion) and research, development, and innovation (€1.1 billion), together expected to support over €100 billion in private investment.

References

Draghi, M. (2024) *The Future of European Competitiveness*. Brussels: European Commission, https://commission.europa.eu/topics/eu-competitiveness/draghi-report_en

European Investment Bank (2025) *Investment Report 2024–2025: Innovation, Integration and Simplification in Europe*. Luxembourg: EIB, https://www.eib.org/attachments/lucalli/20240354_investment_report_2024_en.pdf

European Commission (2024), "EU Climate Action Progress Report", COM(2024) 498 final, https://eur-lex.europa.eu/legal-content/EN/TXT/?uri=celex:52024DC0498

European Commission (2025a) "Guidance on Anticipatory Investments for Developing Forward-looking Electricity Networks", Commission Notice (2025) 3291 final, https://energy.ec.europa.eu/publications/commission-notice-guidance-anticipatory-investments-developing-forward-looking-electricity-networks_en

European Commission (2025b) "Investment Needs of European Energy Infrastructure to Enable a Decarbonised Economy", Commission-Trinomics, DG ENER, https://strategicenergy.eu/wp-content/uploads/2025/02/investment-needs-of-european-energy-infrastructure-MJ0125020ENN.pdf

European Commission (2025c) "A Competitiveness Compass for the EU", COM(2025) 30 final, https://eur-lex.europa.eu/legal-content/EN/TXT/?uri=celex:52025DC0030

European Commission (2025d) "EU-wide Assessment of the Final Updated National Energy and Climate Plans: Delivering the Union's 2030 Energy and Climate Objectives", SWD(2025) 140 final, https://eur-lex.europa.eu/legal-content/EN/TXT/?uri=celex:52025SC0140

European Commission (2025e) "EU Closing in on the 2030 Climate and Energy Targets, According to National Plans", Press Release IP/25/1337, https://ec.europa.eu/commission/presscorner/detail/en/ip_25_1337

European Commission (2025f) "EU-wide Assessment of the Final Updated National Energy and Climate Plans: Delivering the Union's 2030 Energy and Climate Objectives", COM(2025) 274 final, https://eur-lex.europa.eu/legal-content/EN/TXT/?uri=celex:52025DC0274

European Court of Auditors (ECA) (2025) "Making the EU Electricity Grid Fit for Net-zero Emissions", https://www.eca.europa.eu/ECAPublications/RV-2025-01/RV-2025-01_EN.pdf

Institute for Climate Economics (I4CE) (2025), *The State of Europe's Climate Investment*. Paris: I4CE, https://www.i4ce.org/wp-content/uploads/2025/06/The-State-of-Europes-Climate-Investment-2025-edition_V2.pdf

International Energy Agency (IEA) (2025) *World Energy Investment 2025*. Paris: IEA, https://www.iea.org/reports/world-energy-investment-2025

International Monetary Fund (IMF) (2025) *World Economic Outlook 2025*. Washington, DC: IMF.

2. France: Preserving Investment in the Energy Transition in an Unstable Policy Environment

Paul Malliet,[1] Mathieu Plane,[2] Francesco Saraceno,[3] and Anissa Saumtally[4]

This chapter begins by assessing the situation of public capital and investment in France. We show that public capital is overall less degraded in France than in other EU countries, even if, since the sovereign debt crisis, net investment growth has been sluggish. We then focus our attention on the energy sector, important both for the green transition and for strategic autonomy. Since 2009, greenhouse gas emissions have decreased by 33%, nevertheless the decarbonization of the energy mix in recent years has stalled. Today, France is at a crossroads; the coming years will be crucial in achieving France's decarbonization goals for 2030 and for 2050, the target date for reaching carbon neutrality. Past choices regarding public finances (entailing a reduced fiscal space), and a missing medium-term energy transition plan concur in threatening the continuity and stability of investment in the energy transition. The chapter concludes with recommendations on how to strengthen the French energy transition policies but warns that a European effort is essential to succeed in the energy and green transition.

2.1 Introduction

The energy transition relies on a mix of complementary tools aimed at reducing emissions while ensuring energy security and economic viability. These include energy sufficiency and reducing consumption through behavioural and systemic changes; incentives, such as tax credits, subsidies, and feed-in tariffs; regulatory

---

1   Observatoire français des conjonctures économiques (OFCE) Sciences Po Paris.
2   OFCE Sciences Po.
3   OFCE Sciences Po and Luiss Institute for European Analysis and Policy (LEAP).
4   OFCE Sciences Po.

    https://doi.org/10.11647/OBP.0499.02

tools—including emissions standards—carbon pricing, and phase-out mandates; and last, but not least, public and private investment in renewable energy infrastructure, grid modernization, and low-carbon technologies. While France has acted (alone or as a part of the EU) on all these levers, this chapter will focus specifically on public investment, the theme of the broader *European Public Investment Outlook* series.

Mario Draghi (2024) offers the latest of many reports documenting the chronic shortage of public investment in the EU (this *Outlook* series has also highlighted this dynamic for several years). The investment gap in the energy transition—estimated at €477 billion per year by the European Commission (2023, p. 43)— if not tackled seriously, risks compromising the 2030 targets and, more importantly, moving the EU further away from the possibility of achieving carbon neutrality by 2050.

France is not in a better position than other countries. Since 2005, greenhouse gas emissions have decreased by 33%, but the decarbonization of the energy mix in recent years has remained slow. Figure 2.1 shows the evolution of the French energy supply mix between 2019 and 2024. While the energy mix is overall already low carbon due to the strong reliance on nuclear energy (around two thirds of electricity production comes from nuclear), and thus progress is necessarily low, the share of low-carbon energy sources has progressed by only 5 percentage points between 2019 and 2024. We'll see in the following that COVID-19 and the policy response to the inflation crisis have played a role in this.

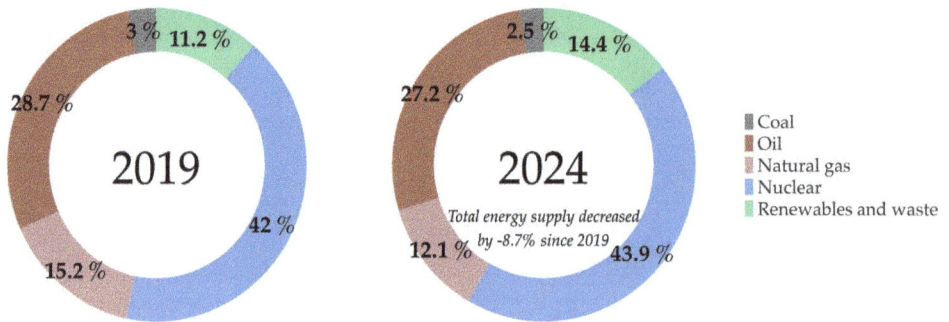

Fig. 2.1 Evolution of the French Energy Supply Mix, 2019-2024. *Source:* IEA. Figure created by the authors.

Data for Figs. 2.1–2.6 are available at
https://hdl.handle.net/20.500.12434/cacfec49

In the remainder of the chapter we will, first give a descriptive account of the evolution of public investment and capital since the 1970s. Then, in Section 2.3, we will focus on investment in the energy transition, highlighting how France today lacks both a medium- to long-term coherent framework and a sufficient fiscal space. We will then conclude with some policy recommendations.

2.2 Public Investment in France: State of the Art

2.2.1 The Historical Evolution of Public Investment

After a long period of sustained growth (5.6% of GDP on average in the 1960s and then 5% during the 1970s and 1980s; see Fig. 2.2), public investment in France declined substantially in the past three decades. The first break took place in the mid-1990s, when deficit reduction to meet the Maastricht criteria and join the euro became the priority. Since then, public investment has been consistently below 4.5% of GDP and was further reduced following the sovereign debt crisis: when the fiscal stance turned restrictive, a substantial part of the fiscal adjustment was achieved by reducing capital expenditure. The share of public investment to GDP from 2015 to 2018 fell below 4%. A mild recovery began in the two years before the COVID-19 crisis, mostly because of the political cycle and local elections. It is in fact important to note that public investment remains mainly the responsibility of local authorities (54% of the total in 2024, see Fig. 2.2) even though local public expenditure barely represents 20% of total public expenditure.[5]

The 2017 uptick was short-lived because of the pandemic; after the drop in early 2020, public investment recovered quickly, despite other lockdowns, to remain flat thereafter. The government introduced in September 2020 a €100 billion recovery plan (*France Relance*, see Plane and Saraceno 2021), partially financed (€40 billion) with funding from the Next Generation EU program. Moreover, a new €54 billion investment plan, 'Build the France of 2030', announced in October 2021, is focused on the green transition, through massive investment in energy, automotive, aeronautics, and space. Despite these major announcements, public investment has remained surprisingly flat, with even a drop of more than 2% between the end of 2020 and mid-2022. The pre-COVID level was only reached three and a half years after the beginning of the crisis. By contrast, it took only one year for private investment and 7 quarters for GDP. Since mid-2022, public investment is more dynamic, at least more than private investment and GDP, and it is, for the first quarter of 2025, 6% above its pre-COVID level, while GDP and private investment are respectively 5% and 4% above.

---

5   The State and social security represent respectively 36% and 45% of the total public expenditure.

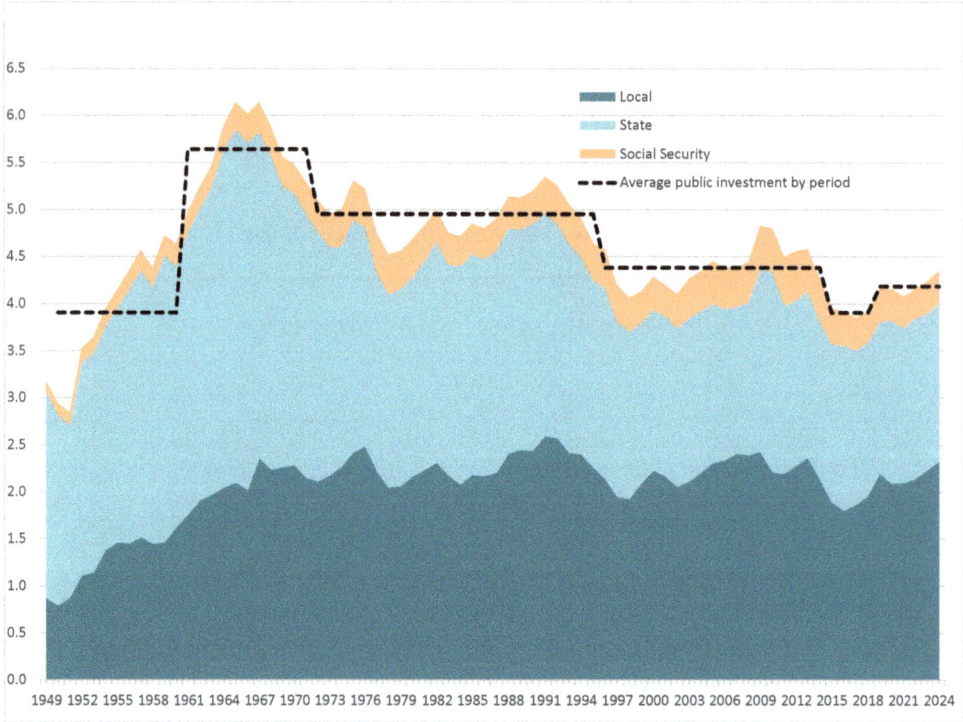

Fig. 2.2 Public investment by administrative category in % of GDP. *Source:* Insee. Figure created by the authors.

Data for Figs. 2.1–2.6 are available at
https://hdl.handle.net/20.500.12434/cacfec49

2.2.2 Net Investment Recently Increased, but the Pace of Public Capital Accumulation Is Still Low

To assess the dynamics of the capital stock it is useful to focus on the net flow of fixed assets (net investment), i.e., on gross investment minus the depreciation of capital (consumption of fixed capital, CFC, in national accounts nomenclature).

France's general government net investment broadly follows the same patterns as gross investment: from the late 1970s to the first half of the 1990s it was strong, averaging significantly more than 1% of GDP per year (Fig. 2.3). From 1993 to 1998, general government net investment declined sharply, reaching 0.5% of GDP in 1998, again because of the effort to meet the Maastricht criteria: the cyclically adjusted deficit for France decreased from 4.6% of GDP in 1993 to 1.8% in 1998, and investment was the main adjustment variable. Net investment recovered in the next phase, then fluctuated between 0.7% and 1.1% of GDP over the 2000–2010 period, without ever returning to the levels observed during the 1980s and the early 1990s. After 2011 and the Global

Financial Crisis, net investment has been at its lowest level since the late 1970s, when wealth accounts were introduced.

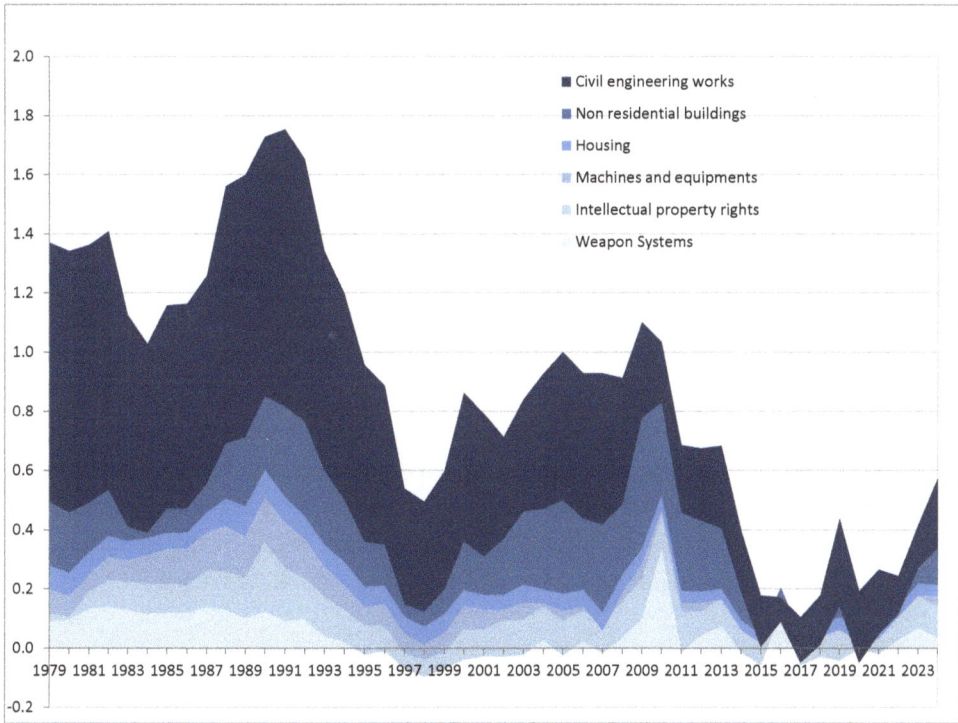

Fig. 2.3 Net general government investment by component as a % of GDP. *Source:* Insee. Figure created by the authors.

Data for Figs. 2.1–2.6 are available at
https://hdl.handle.net/20.500.12434/cacfec49

The average level from mid-1980s to mid-1990s, of 1.4 percentage points of GDP by year against 0.3 percentage points over the last ten years, corresponds to approximately the necessary amount of additional public investment per year to achieve carbon neutrality in 2050.[6] The recent recovery of 2023–2024 is visible for net investment (0.5 percentage points of GDP in average) but this rate of investment remains well below the levels it had before the turn to austerity of 2013. The fiscal adjustment program for 2026 of €44 billion announced in the summer of 2025 by the Prime Minister of the time, which does not spare investment aid and local authorities, risks undermining the slight recovery in public investment observed in recent years.

---

6   Pisani-Ferry and Mahfouz (2023) estimate the need for additional financing for the energy transition to meet French climate commitments to be €67 billion per year, of which €34 billion would be public investment (1.2 pp of GDP).

A comparison of the evolution of non-financial assets' net flows in relation to primary net financial flow (financial assets—financial liabilities—interest expenses), which we consider here as a proxy of the net worth, clearly reveals the emergence of two sub-periods (see Fig. 2.4). The first, which runs from 1996 to 2008, can be seen as a period in which the additional public net financial debt (excluding interest expense) was more than offset by the accumulation of non-financial assets, leading to a positive net worth. This means that the general government stock of wealth increased in value over this period, even abstracting from price effects. The second period, which runs from 2009 to 2024, displays a new pattern in which the net financial debt increase is no longer offset by an increase in public non-financial capital, generating a deterioration in government net worth. In summary, during the recent period of strong public debt accumulation, there was a corresponding disinvestment in public assets, which ultimately led to a sharp reduction in the net asset value of public administrations. In 2024, the primary net lending of the government is 3.7% of GDP while the net investment represents only 0.7% of GDP.

The Global Financial Crisis and the sovereign debt crisis led to a sharp increase in public debt. Fiscal consolidation began in 2011 and it partly reduced public capital accumulation, causing a collapse of the net asset value of general government (for more details, see Charlet et al. 2024). The strong reduction in public net worth casts doubt on the effectiveness of fiscal consolidation in strengthening the public finances outlook for France.

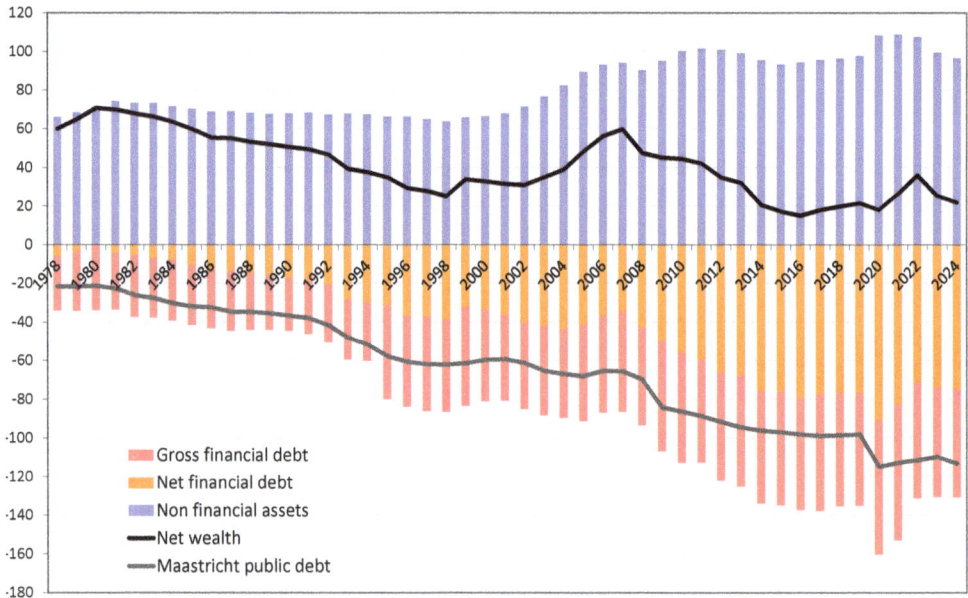

Fig. 2.4 Evolution of general government net wealth as a percentage of GDP. *Source:* Insee. Figure created by the authors.

Data for Figs. 2.1–2.6 are available at
https://hdl.handle.net/20.500.12434/cacfec49

2.3 The Energy Transition at a Crossroads

The revision introduced by the "Fit for 55" package, increasing the emissions reduction target for 2030 (compared to 1990 levels) to 55% from 44%, translates for France into an emissions reduction target of 47.5% compared to 2005, significantly more ambitious than the previously envisaged 37% reduction (see Fig. 2.5).[7]

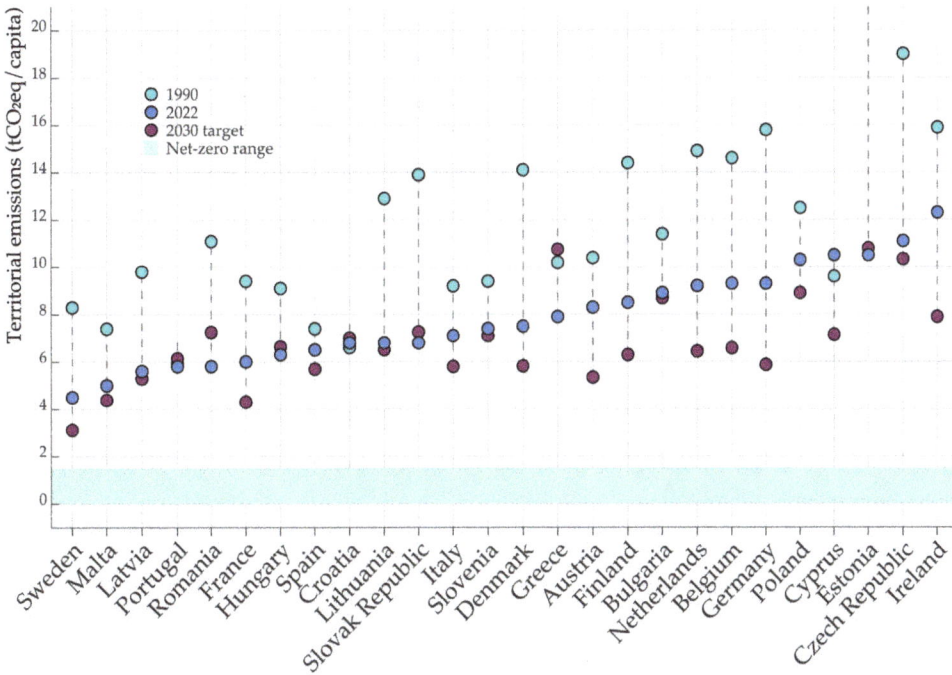

Fig. 2.5 Emissions per capita and fit for 55 targets across Member States. *Reading*: In 1990 and 2022, the EU's territorial emissions stood at 11.8 tCO_2eq/inhabitant and 7.8 tCO_2eq/inhabitant, respectively. The 2030 target translates to 4.62 tCO_2eq/inhabitant. *Note*: Countries are ranked by their current per-capita emission levels. Since the carbon neutrality target depends on other factors—such as the absorption capacity of natural sinks—we provide a range here between 0 and 1.5 tCO_2eq/inhabitant. *Source*: Eurostat. Figure created by the authors.

Data for Figs. 2.1–2.6 are available at
https://hdl.handle.net/20.500.12434/cacfec49

This change necessitates a revision of the transition scenarios considered so far, and consequently, of the yearly investment needs for the decarbonization of economic activity. The overview of low-carbon transition financing published by I4CE (2025)

---

7   Regulation of the European Parliament and of the Council amending Regulation (EU) 2018/842 on binding annual greenhouse gas emission reductions by Member States from 2021 to 2030 contributing to climate action to meet commitments under the Paris Agreement, and Regulation (EU) 2018/1999.

highlights a constant deficit in the amounts allocated to the energy transition. Although a notable acceleration has been observed since 2020, with over €100 billion spent in 2023 (against amounts inferior to €75 billion in previous years), additional efforts are still necessary. The government estimates in its multi-year financing strategy for the ecological transition that low-carbon investment will need to double by 2030 to align with carbon neutrality trajectories (DG Trésor 2024).

The two main sectors requiring the most investment are transport and housing, with identified needs of €43 billion and €39 billion per year respectively, of which €14 billion and €21 billion would be the additional needs for decarbonization.

This translates into increased efforts to move away from fossil fuels. Until 2019, investments in brown technologies still amounted to nearly €100 billion per year (DG Trésor 2024). Although they have fallen significantly since 2020 (to €77 billion), this level remains too high and must be reduced to €35 billion per year by 2030.

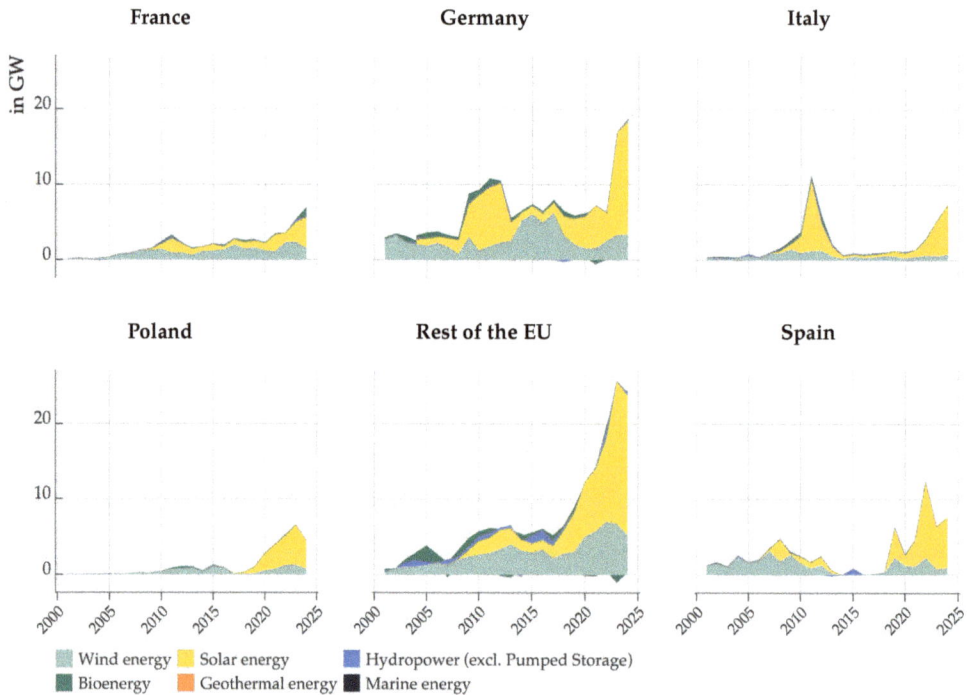

Fig. 2.6 Annual installations of renewable energy production capacities. *Sources*: Renewable capacity statistics 2025, IRENA.

Data for Figs. 2.1–2.6 are available at
https://hdl.handle.net/20.500.12434/cacfec49

In the current geopolitical context, the low-carbon transition has become an essential element for the EU to strengthen its energy sovereignty, a necessary building block of its strategic and geopolitical autonomy. The acceleration in the deployment rate of renewable energies in the Member States illustrates this paradigm shift (Fig. 2.6).

However, France stands out from other major European countries with a relatively slow pace, having installed less than 7GW in 2024 (against, e.g., more than 15GW for Germany). The predominance of nuclear energy in the French energy mix, which already makes it one of the least emitting countries in Europe, does not completely explain this difference.

2.3.1 Unfinished Business

The beginning of 2025 has been marked by a reduced engagement of the government from the goal to drive and plan the decarbonization of the economy. Energy and the green transition were declared national priorities in 2022, with the Prime Minister overseeing this issue and with the creation within the government of a national secretariat for ecological planning responsible for interministerial coordination and the development of a French National Strategy for Energy and Climate (SFEC). Nevertheless, the resignation of its president on February 2025, and more importantly the fact that a replacement has not yet been found, marks a break with the stated ambitions. The French strategy is based on three main texts: the Multi-Year Energy Program (PPE), which sets the guidelines for the evolution of the energy mix and the resulting investment choices; the National Low-Carbon Strategy (SNBC), which allocates efforts among the different sectors of the economy; and the National Climate Change Adaptation Plan (PNACC), which guides actions to adapt local realities to the transition. The third version of the SNBC, intended to define the decarbonization effort within the carbon budget framework for the period 2025–2030, is being finalized after a public consultation on November 2024. This text is essential as it must indicate to what extent France is meeting its intermediate emissions reduction target, that as mentioned above was increased by the European "Fit for 55" package. Similarly, while it was initially scheduled for publication in 2023, the PPE 3, for which public consultation ended on April 2025, is still awaiting a decision. The Bayrou government had announced its publication before the end of the summer without further details on the nature of the final text or the exact timeline; there has been no news since then.

It is essential for the government to quickly publish these texts to provide the necessary information and clarity to the economic actors in the sectors concerned. While most of the investment effort needs to come from the private sector, the public sector must play an essential supporting role. France Stratégie (Belle-Larant et al. 2024) estimates that to make investment choices economically viable for private agents, €9 billion in yearly direct financing (e.g., subsidies) will be needed between 2024 and 2030 in the transport and housing sectors (which alone represent more than 80% of the necessary investments). The continuing hesitations of the executive, with the proposed suspension of several key instruments such as *MaPrimeRénov'* (a public subsidy instrument for buildings' thermal renovation expenses, which was ultimately maintained), and more generally the almost exclusive focus on the objective of controlling public debt, constitute additional obstacles to this effort. As we write (September 2025), a newly named Prime Minister is trying to gather consensus on a budget law and there is almost no discussion in the public debate on priorities other than deficit reduction. The current degraded fiscal situation is of course a challenge, but the recent choices seem to indicate that the French political class has reduced its commitment to safeguarding expenditure for the low-carbon transition.

2.4 The Shrinking Fiscal Space and the Risk of a Change in Priorities

On paper, France's commitment to the energy transition is well asserted. Nevertheless, the actions (or lack of) in recent years speak of different policy priorities when push came to shove. The last two crises, first the pandemic, then (somewhat paradoxically) the energy crisis, created major setbacks for public investment in the green transition by prioritizing support to households and businesses, often to the detriment of ecological concerns. In addition, in the recent past, several unfinanced fiscal policy choices (such as, but not limited to, the tax cuts of President Macron's first term; see Heyer et al. 2025) have increased structural deficits and public debt to a level that jeopardizes the capacity for future investment. If, on top of that, come new geopolitical priorities (e.g., defence), the risk of a shrinking fiscal space for the energy transition becomes tangible.

These choices were compounded by the unprecedented measures to support firms' revenues and households' purchasing power during the COVID-19 shock.[8] In the heat of urgency, not only were no expenses spared, but also no financing scheme other than increasing public debt was set in place. The policy did succeed in helping households weather the storm; however, the price tag for public finances was very large: the primary deficit for 2020 reached 8.9% of GDP, and public debt went from 98.2% of GDP at the end of 2019 to 114.9% of GDP at the end of 2020.

To support the post COVID-19 economic recovery, the government then put in place a large-scale package, *France Relance*: around €100 billion over the course of three years to be spent on fostering the recovery of the economy, ranging from employment subsidies to private investment support and new public investment (see Plane and Saraceno 2021). A third of this amount was allocated to the green transition in

---

8   The IMF compiled a detailed database of country measures: see https://www.imf.org/en/Topics/imf-and-covid19/Fiscal-Policies-Database-in-Response-to-COVID-19. For France, the Cour des Comptes estimates the cost to be around €79 billion between 2020 and 2022 (see https://www.ccomptes.fr/sites/default/files/2025-01/20250109-Les-mesures-daide-exceptionnelles-une-sortie-de-crise-a-achever-pour-le-budget-de-lEtat.pdf)

accordance with Next Generation EU funding conditionalities; nevertheless, most of this investment remained one-shot and was not made long-term.

The economic recovery was, however, very soon impeded by the energy crisis that started in late 2021. This shock affected the whole economy: energy bills for households increased, while businesses faced increased production costs throughout the supply chain, fuelling a price inflation that for the Eurozone in October 2022 peaked at 10.6% (against 7.1% in France) and strongly set back the recovery effort.

The French government once again came through to mitigate the consequences of the shock on the economy. Price caps for household gas and electricity were in place until 2023, limiting the increase to 4% in 2022 and 15% in 2023. This price control was achieved by removing some of the taxes on energy goods and by introducing a compensation to energy suppliers for the loss incurred when applying the caps. Additional measures were taken such as price caps at the pump for petrol or subsidies for heating fuels for households. The most recent estimated costs by the government for the energy "price shield" are €47.4 billion for gas and electricity alone between 2021 and 2023 (Malliet and Saumtally 2025).

The measures worked in protecting households' purchasing power, as inflation in France remained low in comparison to its European neighbours (6.7% in 2022, against an EU average of 10.4%). Nevertheless, the policy design raises questions about the efficiency of public spending and, even more importantly, about the commitment to the energy transition. For ease of implementation in the face of the emergency, price cap measures were not means-tested and placed no limit on consumption, unlike for example Germany, where only 80% of the previous year's energy consumption was subsidized. This raises some economic and ecological quandaries. The choice to subsidize high-income households, who have a lower price elasticity and could have borne part of the burden, is certainly questionable. In addition, while the government accompanied these policies with calls to energy sufficiency (*la sobriété*) under the threat of energy shortages, in practice, there were no clear incentives for households to follow suit. On the opposite, the price caps shrouded the signal price and prevented a moderation of energy consumption that could also have reduced the cost for the public purse. The 2022 car fuel rebate at the pump is yet another example of a problematic policy, costing €7.7 billion. The intent was to lower the impact of increased fuel prices for car-dependent, rural, low-income households, but a side effect was that it also subsidized unessential car travel for higher-income urban households. The French Ministry of Finance, in its Green Budget assessment[9] (Direction du Budget 2024), considered that those emergency policies have been detrimental to the energy transition.

Furthermore, the cost for the government was dependent on volatile market gas price fluctuations. Gas and oil prices in 2022 fell faster than expected, due to a stabilization of supply and to a mild winter putting less strain on demand. The estimation of the cost

---

9   This is a report published yearly since 2020, evaluating the impact of each public spending item on the green transition.

has thus been subjected to revisions throughout different fiscal exercises. In October 2022, the total estimated cost for the gas and electricity price shields was €72.3 billion for the years 2021 to 2023. The latest estimates (April 2025) have revised it to €47.4 billion, almost one third less (DG Trésor 2025). Albeit welcome, this revision shows two shortcomings of these measures; first, had prices increased instead of falling, the impact on public finances would have been calamitous. Second, there was a crowding-out effect, as a more accurate forecast would have allowed for better resource allocation, specifically towards more long-term measures to compensate for the brown nature of price caps, such as expanding low-carbon transition investments.

The end of extraordinary measures in 2024 could not provide the expected public finance relief, as the primary deficit increased by 0.9 percentage points of GDP during the year (OFCE 2025a), mostly due to a decrease in fiscal revenues. In addition, disappointing growth did not compensate through revenues a fiscal stance that remained broadly expansionary. As a result, government deficit in 2024 increased to 5.8%, and is projected to be at 5.4% in 2025 (OFCE 2025b).

Public debt, which like in most other countries had increased sharply following the pandemic, is not receding. The debt-to-GDP ratio increased of 1.9 and 2.1 percentage points of GDP in 2023 and 2024 respectively. According to the latest government forecasts, debt is not expected to decrease before 2028, reaching 118.1% of GDP in 2027. While interest rates that remain reasonably low do not put immediate pressure on public finance (Blot et al. 2024), the public debt drift in France has triggered the excessive deficit procedure as soon as the reformed version of the Stability Pact came into force, in June 2024. The new EU fiscal rule requires Member States that have a debt ratio above 90% of GDP a 1 percentage point decrease per year during the adjustment period. For France, this implies a restrictive fiscal stance in the medium term, to bring government deficit to below 3% by 2029. OFCE (2025b) estimates that this corresponds to a fiscal effort of around €20 billion (0.6–0.7 percentage points of GDP) for 2026 alone, and around €110 billion in total until 2029.

This need for debt consolidation has a bad timing. While the already quoted report by Pisani-Ferry and Mahfouz estimates that €66 billion of total investment per year (half of which should be public) are needed to achieve the 2030 climate objectives, the trend has been in the opposite direction. As mentioned above, energy transition programs have not been spared from budgetary cuts, with popular and impactful programs (such as *MaPrimeRénov'*, that helps households improve the energy efficiency of their homes) being suspended, reduced in coverage, or outright suppressed.

The socioeconomic environment poses another serious challenge. The recent succession of economic shocks has arguably left households more vulnerable economically than they were prior to 2019. As a result, the population may be less receptive to environmental issues, echoing the "Yellow Vests" movement of late 2019 when a planned increase in carbon tax was scrapped following social unrest due to increased energy costs and the strong perception of unfairness of the measure.

While economic shocks are perceived immediately, climate change effects are slower to materialize, albeit with more nefarious consequences. Pulling back on the low-carbon transition efforts to focus on short-run solutions popular with voters, as was the case for the energy crisis, is therefore not a good choice. Ageing and the sustainability of the French pension and social security systems may also divert attention away from ecological and green energy issues, given their impact on public finances and the space they take in the public debate.

On the geopolitical scale, as revealed by the war in Ukraine and the disruption in the world multilateral order brought in by the Trump administration, there is more than ever a need for more strategic European independence. Achieving energy sovereignty is now a key part of the European Green Deal. The question of a European defence, a sector where France is a key player, has also become a priority and competes with environmental and energy issues for public resources. This is already a reality: in the latest budgetary exercise, the defence sector budget has been expanded, from 2% to at least 3% of GDP and locked-in until 2030, while the budget for the transition has not.

2.5 Conclusion

Regardless of whether it is exaggerated or not, the place that public debt has taken in the public debate critically reduces the fiscal space; therefore, decisions on public investments constitute a tricky political puzzle that requires a careful assessment of the priorities. New concerns arise every day, for example, the questions surrounding technological sovereignty and AI (the discussion of which is beyond the scope of this chapter). Amid competing demands, there is a real risk that the critical issue of climate change (whose costs, it's worth repeating it, will mostly appear in the future) may be overshadowed, potentially delaying essential transition efforts. To ensure that France stays on track to meet its climate goals and commitments at the national, European, and global levels, it is crucial to secure a consistent and reliable stream of public investments dedicated to the green transition.

First, it is crucial that the government renews its commitment to the energy and green transition by, for example, naming an authoritative president for the national secretariat for ecological planning and, even more importantly, not delaying any longer the release of the framework documents necessary to clarify the medium-term strategy (the PPE, the SNBC, and the PNACC, all discussed above).

Second, and even more important, the French government needs to preserve investment in the transition from the pressure of public finances' consolidation. The economic and geopolitical instability that is likely to persist in the foreseeable future requires a clear statement of the government's investment priorities, among which the green and energy transition needs to have a paramount place. Not only for environmental sustainability, but also for strategic autonomy.

This could be achieved by adopting a multi-year financing law for investments in the transition to a low-carbon economy, ensuring that the resources are consistent with the objectives set out in the various medium-term strategy documents. The SNBC, that is already based on five-year carbon budgets, provides a suitable time frame. While the publication of the Climate, Clean Air, and Ecological Transition Strategy (SCAPTE) marks a first step in this direction, only legislative action will provide sufficient impetus and, above all, help to make public finances more predictable.[10]

Nevertheless, both sustainability and strategic autonomy have little meaning at the national level; this is why, while France must do its own homework, this needs to be framed in a much wider EU effort. The scale of resources needed for a successful energy transition is colossal. According to Commission estimates cited by the Draghi report (2024), Europe must mobilize an additional 5% of its GDP annually (around €800 billion) for the twin transitions—green and digital—with a substantial part of that coming from public investment. More specifically, the already quoted figures from the European Commission (2023) put the investment gap for the green transition at almost €500 billion. These are not marginal adjustments but structural shifts that require deep transformation across sectors, territories, and value chains. National budgets, already under pressure from aging populations, defence spending, and social demands, are ill-equipped to carry this burden alone. Even countries like France, with relatively robust industrial policies, face limits in financing such an ambitious overhaul exclusively through national means.

That is why the French effort must be placed within the broader framework of a genuine European energy policy. Let's be clear, such a comprehensive strategy exists, as shaped by the many EU documents and decisions of the recent past. Nevertheless, because of the strong emphasis on fiscal consolidation that pervades the European debate, this strategy mostly relies on the mobilization of private financing (e.g., European Commission 2023). Now, one of the merits of the Draghi report (2024), paradoxically quite emphatically endorsed by all EU policymakers, is that none of the challenges the EU faces will be met without a substantial increase in *public* investment. A continental-scale industrial policy for the transition—an "EU IRA" inspired by the American Inflation Reduction Act—is necessary. While it relies on several levers, the IRA is backed by a massive public spending effort, be it in the form of infrastructure investment, incentives and tax breaks, or demand-pull measures. A similarly designed EU-IRA must be backed by a new round of common borrowing, as was the case with the Recovery and Resilience Facility after the COVID-19 pandemic. Only common financing can guarantee an adequate flow of investment across Member States, especially in countries with more limited fiscal space. Moreover, it would help avoid

---

10 In its latest report on the issue, published in September 2025, the Court of Auditors (*la Cour des comptes*) stresses that it is essential to better align climate programming with public finance planning (see https://www.ccomptes.fr/fr/publications/la-transition-ecologique).

fragmentation of the single market, where wealthier countries outspend others in state aid and industrial subsidies, undermining the level playing field.

This approach would serve not only economic and climate goals but also financial stability. The issuance of common European debt on a sustained basis would provide global markets with a credible and liquid alternative to US Treasury bonds at a time when the dollar's role as the world's dominant safe asset is increasingly questioned. A green/energy European safe asset would anchor confidence in European institutions, channel global savings into strategic investment, and help shield the euro area from external shocks. The energy transition is too important to be made on a shoestring.

References

Belle-Larant, F., G. Claeys, and A. Durré (2024) "Investissements Bas Carbone : Comment Les Rendre Rentables", *La Note d'analyse de France Stratégie* 144, October, https://www.strategie-plan.gouv.fr/files/files/Publications/Rapport/fs-2024-na144-investissements_bas_carbone_0.pdf

Blot, C., J. Créel, H. Kempf, S. Levasseur, X. Ragot, and F. Saraceno (2024) "Sailing in All Weather Conditions the Next 25 Years: Challenges for the Euro", Paper Presented at the European Parliament ECON Committee Monetary Dialogue, February, https://www.europarl.europa.eu/thinktank/en/document/IPOL_STU(2024)747835

Charlet, V., M. Plane, and F. Saraceno (2024) "Public Investment and Industrial Policy in France", in F. Cerniglia and F. Saraceno (eds), *Investing in the Structural Transformation: 2024 European Public Investment Outlook*. Cambridge, UK: Open Book Publishers, pp. 31–44, https://doi.org/10.11647/OBP.0434.03

DG Trésor (2024) "Stratégie pluriannuelle des financements de la transition écologique et de la politique énergétique nationale", October, https://www.tresor.economie.gouv.fr/Articles/c7e0b977-a0a6-482c-b5b2-730f67fb4be8/files/5e32f3fc-ecab-4e90-86c0-8df657551343

DG Trésor (2025) "Rapport d'avancement Annuel 2025", 16 April, https://www.tresor.economie.gouv.fr/Articles/2025/04/16/publication-du-rapport-d-avancement-annuel-2025

Direction du Budget (2024) "Rapport sur l'impact environnemental du budget de l'État 2024", https://www.budget.gouv.fr/documentation/documents-budgetaires/exercice-2024/projet-loi-finances-les/budget-vert-plf-2024

Draghi, M. (2024) *The Future of European Competitiveness*. Brussels: European Commission, https://commission.europa.eu/topics/eu-competitiveness/draghi-report_en

European Commission (2023) "Investment Needs Assessment and Funding Availabilities to Strengthen EU's Net-Zero Technology Manufacturing Capacity", Commission Staff Working Document, SWD(2023) 68, https://single-market-economy.ec.europa.eu/publications/staff-working-document-investment-needs-assessment-and-funding-availabilities-strengthen-eus-net_en.

Heyer, É., M. Plane, X. Ragot, R. Sampognaro, and X. Timbeau (2025) "Quelles trajectoires pour les finances publiques de la France ?", *OFCE Policy Brief* 146, https://www.ofce.sciences-po.fr/pdf/pbrief/2025/OFCEpbrief146.pdf

I4CE (2025) *Panorama des financements climats*. Paris: I4CE, https://www.i4ce.org/publication/panorama-financements-climat-edition-2025/

Malliet, P., and A. Saumtally (2025) "The Macroeconomic Effects of the Energy Price Cap: An Evaluation Conducted Using the ThreeME Multisectoral Model", September, *Economie et Statistique / Economics and Statistics*, www.insee.fr/fr/statistiques/8641095

OFCE (2025a) "France : l'incertaine croissance. Perspectives 2025-2026 pour l'économie française", *OFCE Policy Brief* 144, April, https://www.ofce.sciences-po.fr/prev/prev2503/france/intro.html

OFCE (2025b) "France : Perspectives 2026-2027 pour l'économie française", forthcoming.

Pisani-Ferry, J., and S. Mahfouz (2023) "Les Incidences Économiques de l'action Pour Le Climat", May, *France Strategie, Rapport à La Première Ministre*, https://www.strategie-plan.gouv.fr/files/files/Publications/Rapport/2023-incidences-economiques-rapport-pisani-5juin.pdf

Plane, M., and F. Saraceno (2021) "From Fiscal Consolidation to the Plan de Relance", in F. Cerniglia, F. Saraceno, and A. Watt (eds), *The Great Reset. 2021 European Public Investment Outlook*. Cambridge: Open Book Publishers, pp. 33–43, https://doi.org/10.11647/OBP.0280.02

RTE (2024) *Bilan prévisionnel Édition 2023. Futurs énergétiques 2050*. Paris: RTE, https://assets.rte-france.com/prod/public/2024-07/2024-05-27-principaux-resultats.pdf

3. The Role of Public Support for the Energy Transition in Germany: Past and Future Tasks

Tom Bauermann[1]

This chapter examines the progress of the energy transition in Germany, with a focus on the electricity sector. Attention is paid here to the significant expansion of renewable energies. Political support under the Renewable Energy Act, particularly the operating cost subsidies, has played a decisive role in shaping this development. This chapter highlights both the advantages and disadvantages of this financing model. It also describes the future tasks associated with the expansion of renewable energies. A central issue of the upcoming energy transition in Germany, which is linked to the further development of renewables, is the urgent need for expansion investments in the electricity grid. There is a notable risk of (further) privatization of the electricity grid, which could lead to higher costs for consumers. This jeopardizes the socioecological transition. As will be shown, a publicly financed infrastructure model and greater government involvement in the expansion of clean energy would be significantly more cost-efficient and offer additional advantages.

3.1 Introduction

Germany has set the goal of achieving climate neutrality by 2045. Despite these ambitions, fossil fuels continue to dominate Germany's gross final energy consumption, accounting for 78% in 2024 compared to 22% from renewable sources. Due to the decommissioning of the remaining power plants, nuclear energy no longer plays a role. Energy from renewable sources has grown since 2005, when its share was only 7.5%, but the development was uneven. Renewables now play a leading role in electricity, covering 54% of gross electricity consumption in 2024. In contrast, their contribution remains modest in heating (18.1%) and transport (7.2%) of the final energy consumption, where natural gas still prevails in the heating sector (>40%) and oil in transport sector (>90%). The share of green energy is growing only slowly

---

1   Macroeconomic Policy Institute (IMK).

https://doi.org/10.11647/OBP.0499.03

in these sectors, as its share in heating and cooling processes was 14% in 2014 and around 6% in the transport sector (UBA 2025b). Achieving a climate-neutral economy requires a fundamental transformation in energy generation and consumption. Central to this transition is the electrification of key sectors (i.e., manufacturing, transport, and buildings) leading to a near doubling of electricity demand. The foundation for a climate-neutral economy therefore lies in a decarbonized electricity sector. Germany aims to make its electricity supply climate-neutral by 2035 in order to create the basis for the decarbonization of other sectors. This target presents a dual challenge. First, it requires climate-neutral electricity generation. Second, it demands comprehensive modernization and expansion of the electricity grid to prepare it for further expansion of renewable electricity supply and electrification.

This chapter analyzes the German electricity sector and power grids. It highlights both the progress made so far in the transition to clean electricity and the challenges that remain. A particular focus is placed on the government's role in the development and diffusion of renewable energy, as well as its involvement in shaping the electricity grid during this transition. The analysis focuses on the publicly accessible electricity grid, defined as the infrastructure used for the general distribution of electricity, which excludes private grids and privately generated electricity for own use. This means that the grid is not necessarily operated by a public company, but that it is open to electricity suppliers who want to feed into the grid for the general public. The chapter is structured as follows: In the next subsection, the current status of renewables in the electricity sector is presented. Afterwards, the main drivers behind their expansion are examined, with particular attention to public support schemes. This is followed by an analysis of the current condition of the grid and an assessment of the government's role, especially its retreat from active grid development. The chapter concludes with a summary and an outlook.

3.2 The Development of Renewable Electricity

As can be seen in Figure 3.1, the installed capacity of renewable electricity in the publicly accessible grid grew markedly in the recent decades. The overall net installed capacity grew from nearly 115 GW installed capacity in 2002 to roughly 260 GW in 2024. At the same time, the capacity of renewable electricity grew from 20 GW to 190 GW such that the share of green installed capacity is now nearly 73% of the overall installed capacity. The installed capacity of fossil-fired power plants remained more or less the same. However, their composition changed. Hard coal and lignite fell from 52 GW at the beginning of the century to 31 GW in 2024, while the less emission-intensive gas-fired power plants increased from 20 GW to 37 GW in the same period. The installed capacity of nuclear power plants decreased from 24 GW to 0 GW due to the fact that the then centre-right government planned the nuclear phase-out in 2012 after the incident in Fukushima in 2011 (Hasselbach 2021). The most important pillars of renewable energies are photovoltaics (100 GW), land-based wind energy (64 GW), and offshore wind energy (9 GW). Hydropower, biomass, renewable waste and geothermal electricity are less relevant for electricity generation.

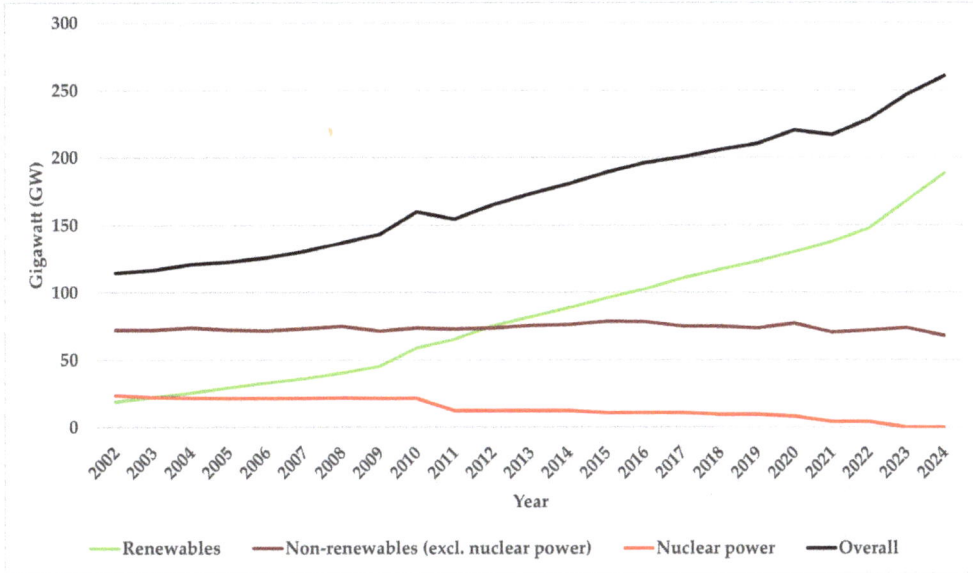

Fig. 3.1 Installed capacity (GW). *Source:* Fraunhofer ISE (2025a). *Note:* The figure depicts the installed capacity of various electricity sources which feed into the public electricity grid.

Data for Figs. 3.1, 3.2 and 3.4 are available at
https://hdl.handle.net/20.500.12434/fcd06753

Figure 3.1 does not provide any information on the actual share of renewable energies in total electricity generation in the publicly accessible grid. Figure 3.2 shows more clearly how the share of renewable energies in net public electricity generation has risen, while the share of non-renewable electricity has fallen. The share of electricity from renewables rose from 8% in 2002 to 63% in 2024. Overall, there were 413 terawatt hours (TWh) net public electricity generated in 2024 and nearly 260 TWh from renewables. The most important sources of electricity from renewables in 2024 were offshore wind energy (26 TWh), land-based wind energy (110 TWh), and photovoltaics (59 TWh). Lignite, hard coal, and natural gas are the most important resources for non-renewable electricity generation. Over the years, the less emission-intensive gas-fired power plants have partially replaced electricity generation from hard coal. While in 2002, 111 TWh of electricity from fossil fuels came from hard coal and 40 TWh from natural gas, in 2024 it was 24 TWh from hard coal and 47 from natural gas. In contrast to hard coal-fired power plants, gas-fired power plants can usually be ramped up more quickly, making them more flexible and better complementing more volatile renewable energy sources. Electricity generated from lignite decreased from 141 TWh to 71 TWh in the same period (Fraunhofer ISE 2025b).

Germany's nuclear power generation fell from 156 TWh in 2002 to zero by 2024. A phase-out deal was first reached in 2000 and formalized in 2002, but reversed in 2010 by Chancellor Merkel's government. After the 2011 Fukushima disaster, the decision was quickly overturned by the same government, with a new goal to exit nuclear energy by 2022. Due to the energy crisis, the final shutdown was delayed until 2023, with no major push to reverse it from the providers (Naschert and Blackburne 2024). Given that nuclear power is a rather expensive source of energy it seems economically reasonable (Fraunhofer ISE 2024).

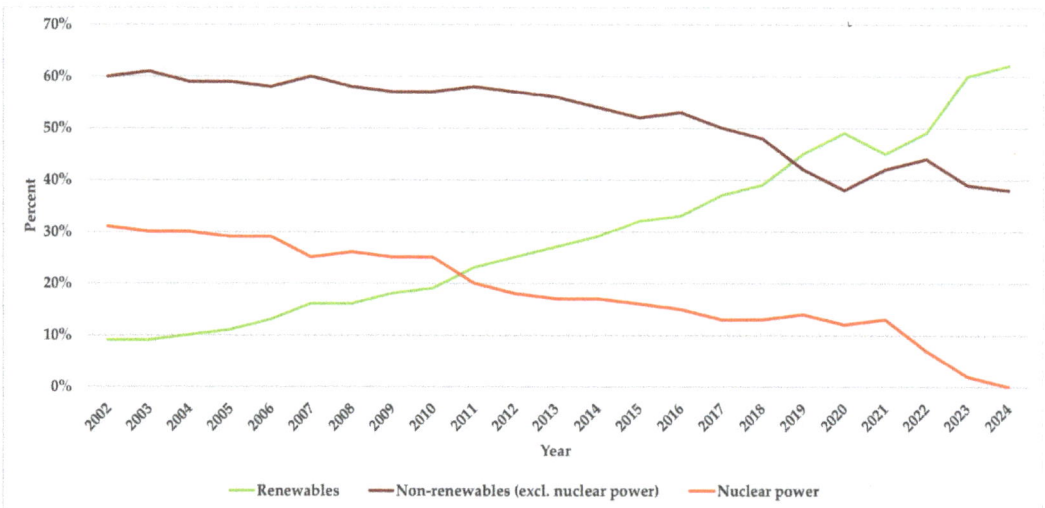

Fig. 3.2 Share of renewables in public net electricity production (in %). *Source:* Fraunhofer ISE (2025b). *Note:* The figure shows the share of the respective electricity source in the total public net electricity generation. Privately generated electricity for own consumption is not shown.

Data for Figs. 3.1, 3.2 and 3.4 are available at
https://hdl.handle.net/20.500.12434/fcd06753

3.3 The German Remuneration: The Pros, the Cons, and the Tasks

As it was shown above, the share of renewable electricity grew over time from below 10% at the beginning of the 2000s to now over 60% of the net public generated electricity. Between 2000 and 2024, total greenhouse gas emissions of the German economy fell from 1.04 million to 0.65 million tons of carbon dioxide equivalents per year.[2] The electricity sector contributed over 40% to the overall reduction in emissions. This was by far the largest contribution compared to other sectors such as manufacturing (13%), buildings (17%), and transport (10%) (UBA 2025a). The main driver of the renewable electricity development and the drop in emissions was the Renewable Energy Act (Schäfer 2019; AGORA 2023). Apart from granting feed-in priority and obligating grid operators to connect renewables, the act primarily provided for the subsidization of operating costs for renewable energy systems.

The way in which operating costs were subsidized under the Renewable Energy Act has changed over time. In the beginning, renewable energy systems were mainly subsidized through a fixed feed-in tariff. It guaranteed a fixed payment per kilowatt hour (kWh) of electricity generated by renewable energy producers for twenty years. To incentivize a more market-oriented approach to renewable energy, Germany switched from a fixed feed-in tariff to a variable remuneration model known as the one-sided sliding market premium. In addition, most new renewable energy producers must take part in competitive auctions in which bidders propose the remuneration they require per kilowatt hour. The projects with the lowest bids are awarded contracts, helping to limit overall subsidy costs. Under this system, the support payment per kilowatt hour equals the difference between the awarded bid price and a reference market price, typically the average spot market price over a defined period. This creates a "one-sided" premium, which means that producers receive support when market prices are below their awarded price, but do not have to return money if market prices rise above it. Thus, producers receive at least the market price and, if it is below the awarded price, the market premium. The remuneration is therefore variable and depends on market prices but guarantees producers a minimum price per kilowatt hour for a period of up to twenty years. Fixed feed-in tariffs are now limited to small systems and old ones from before 2012.

Figure 3.3 shows the annual public expenditure to finance the above-mentioned support programs under the Renewable Energy Act and thus to promote green electricity. Until 2022, the costs of this support scheme were largely borne by electricity consumers through a levy on every kilowatt hour consumed. This meant that households and companies financed the transition, with energy-intensive industries benefitting from partial exemptions. The levy was abolished in mid-2022. Since then, renewable energies have been financed directly from the federal budget. By the end of 2024, around €422 billion in public spending went towards financing renewable energies. Participation in this support program was very high. Of all the green electricity generated in 2023, 80% was subsidized through the remuneration scheme. As already mentioned, the level of financial support has been linked to spot market prices for more than a decade, which means that high electricity prices mean low

---

2   These are the greenhouse gas emissions excluding emissions from land use, land-use change, and forestry (LULUCF).

subsidies. After the decline in 2022 due to the high spot market prices, expenditure increased as spot market prices also rose.

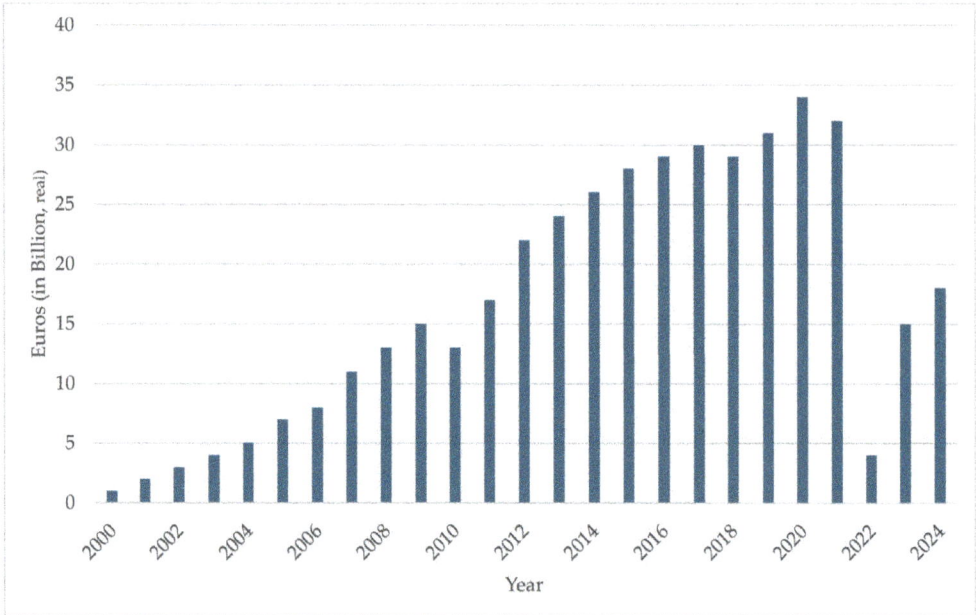

Fig. 3.3 Financial support for renewable electricity (in billion euros). *Source:* Statistisches Bundesamt (2025) and own calculations. *Note:* The figure depicts the public funding of renewable energy support schemes with the help of the levy on consumers and, later on, the federal budget. Values are noted in prices of 2024.

The slightly more than €420 billion seem to be a worthwhile investment in general but have some downsides. The support has been a major driver of climate protection. As already mentioned, a large share of Germany's reduction in greenhouse gas emissions were made by the electricity sector. This success is closely tied to renewable energy subsidies. By granting stable prices per unit of green electricity generated and setting favourable regulations (e.g., feed-in priority for green electricity), the government reduced the risks for private investments in green technologies (Couture and Gagnon 2010). As a result, investors felt more confident to invest in carbon-free electricity and to build-up capacity (Angelopoulos et al. 2016). In contrast, the impact of carbon pricing via the European Emission Trading System I (ETS I) is rather questionable. Schäfer (2019), Rogge, Schneider, and Hoffmann (2012), and Schmidt et al. (2012) showed that the ETS I had a rather negligible impact on the uptake of low- and zero-carbon technologies, i.e. due to a lack of stringency and predictability.

However, predictability is important when introducing new technologies, especially because twenty years ago the new zero-carbon technologies were very expensive compared to conventional technologies, like lignite-fired power plants. The increasing demand for renewable energies induced by the support schemes and the regulatory framework as well as the competition between manufacturers worldwide led to a significant cost degression of green technologies (Mercure et al. 2014). In 2010, the average cost of generating one kilowatt hour of electricity from utility scale photovoltaics was more than 20 cents (ct), expressed in prices from 2024. For onshore wind it was 10 ct/kWh. The costs were significantly higher than the 7 ct/kWh of fossil-fired power plants (Fraunhofer ISE 2010). In 2024, the average levelized costs were around 6 ct/kWh for photovoltaics and 6–7 ct/kWh for onshore wind power, and thus significantly lower than the costs of fossil fuel power plants (Fraunhofer ISE 2024).

Further, the public support scheme had positive impacts on building up new industries. Since the early 2000s, employment in the renewable energy sector has quadrupled and now employs 400,000 people. Still, Germany is one of the largest producers of wind turbines worldwide. Also, since the early 2000s more than €550 billion, primarily from private sources, has been invested in the deployment of renewable energies (ZSW 2025).

German support for renewable energies was considerable, even by European standards. However, it was less extreme than it is often portrayed by conservatives and some economists (Bojanowski 2024). Firstly, compared to other EU countries, German support per kilowatt hour ranks in the mid-range rather than at the top end. For example, the Czech Republic, the Netherlands, and Italy offer significantly higher support per kilowatt hour (CEER 2023, p. 28). The average subsidy for renewable energies in Germany has also already fallen from 20 ct/kWh in 2009 to around 7 ct/kWh now, as the lower subsidy is necessary for producers due to the lower costs. Secondly, this support has led to remarkable results: While the share of renewable electricity in Germany has increased from under 10% to over 60%, the average share among EU countries has risen from just over 10% to 47% (Eurostat 2025). Thirdly, the promotion should be compared with the promotion of other energy sources. Around €300 billion were spent on promoting nuclear energy during the operating phase. When external costs are added, the costs would even increase significantly (FÖS 2020). Thus, renewables do not seem excessively supported.

Nonetheless, the design of the renewable support mechanism is not without criticism. As it was written above, to refinance the support schemes, a levy was charged on households and firms on electricity consumed until mid-2022. The levy disproportionately burdened low-income households, as it was charged per kilowatt hour consumed regardless of income. In absolute terms, electricity costs are only slightly higher in the upper income deciles than in the lower income groups. But, in relation to their income, the costs for the levy were higher for low-income households than for upper-income groups. An analysis of the IW (2013) showed that almost 1% of the income of the bottom 10% of earners was used to finance renewable energy subsidies. For the top 10% of earners, this proportion was significantly lower, at just 0.17%.

There is also room for improvement from an industrial policy perspective. Germany initially developed a strong solar manufacturing sector due to generous support of renewables in the beginning of the century. However, the support was not sufficiently focussed on R&D investments and innovation. Therefore, Germany's share in global photovoltaic manufacturing was eventually overtaken by Chinese competitors due to a lack of technological progress compared to China and insufficient political support (Wen et al. 2021).

Another point of criticism is the heavy reliance on private capital. The remuneration of the renewable energies was mainly a derisking for private capital. Thus, it took risks from competing on the market. At the same time, the deployment of renewable energies became largely dependent on private capital investments. While profits were privatized, the risks were borne by the public (Gabor 2023). The dependence on private investments had further disadvantages. When the support mechanism changed in 2011, the investments in renewables dropped and the growth rates slowed down. Hence, greater state involvement, e.g., more direct build up of renewables, or direct public investment could have ensured a fairer distribution of risk and taken advantage of lower government borrowing costs.

The experiences from the Renewable Energy Act offer important lessons for the future. Overall, the remuneration by the Renewable Energy Act has significantly contributed to emission reductions, technological advancement, employment, investments, and the establishment of renewable energy in Germany. At the same time, future support instruments need to be more targeted, equitable, and strategically coordinated. The design of support schemes should ensure a fair distribution of costs between the public and operators, and between income groups. The latter could be achieved by aligning the refinancing of remuneration with income tax. In addition, direct public investment would be more effective as governments face lower interest rates on their investments and reduce dependence on private venture capitalists. Public funding should also be more closely linked to research and development and the development of sustainable industries.

Looking ahead, one of the key challenges will be ensuring the continued expansion of renewable energy in the coming years. Current projections suggest that Germany is partly on track to meet its targets for providing enough renewable electricity to enable a carbon-free power supply by 2035 (Dullien et al. 2025). While capacity goals of photovoltaics will likely be achieved, land-based and offshore wind energy may fail to achieve their goals (EWI and BET 2025). Compared to the current one-sided market premium, the announcement of the transition to a two-sided market premium is a step in the right direction. It guarantees a minimum price for renewables and, in contrast to the current premium, redistributes windfall profits to consumers when spot market prices exceed the awarded price. However, the effects of some of the announced changes to the support scheme for renewable energies are still uncertain. The German government also announced a plan to shift from an operating cost-based support model to one that focuses solely on investment cost subsidies (Du and Teng

2023). However, in the past such changes affected the growth dynamics of renewables negatively. It remains to be seen how such a reform works out in the future.

3.4 Power Grids and the Energy Transition—Challenges and Potential Solutions

The expansion of electricity grids plays a central role in the energy transition. In addition to the continuous increase in renewable energy, a significantly stronger electrification is also expected in the future. For example, the manufacturing sector will switch from fossil fuels to electricity. According to forecasts, the electrification will increase electricity consumption from the roughly 400–500 TWh to nearly 1100 TWh per year by 2045 (50Hertz Transmission GmbH et al. 2023). The growth of renewables and electrification therefore requires expansion of the power grid.

The German electricity grid consists of transmission and distribution grids. While the transmission grids transport the electricity over long distances, the distribution grids deliver the electricity regionally to the end consumers. In the course of the liberalization of the electricity market at the beginning of the century, the transmission grid was divided into four parts, which are now operated by four operators. TenneT TSO GmbH manages about 36% of the transmission network and is owned by the Dutch state. Amprion GmbH operates about 30% and is mainly privately owned. 50Hertz Transmission GmbH covers about 28% of the network. The Kreditanstalt für Wiederaufbau (KfW), a public investment bank owned by the German government and the federal states, holds a 20% stake. TransnetBW GmbH manages about 6% and is majority-owned by public companies in the state of Baden-Württemberg. The federal government, through the KfW, holds a 25% stake. Summed up, the federal government is only involved in the smaller transmission operators, while private actors play a significant role. Distribution networks are often publicly owned, but the private company E.ON, through various forms of corporate involvement, has a significant position, being involved in nearly 50% of the German distribution network. The structure of the transmission and distribution grid reflects decades of political decisions and contrasts with most European countries, where at least the transmission grids are almost exclusively state-owned. Given that electricity networks are natural monopolies, public ownership is economically justified.

Figure 3.4 shows past replacement and expansion investments (gray bars) of transmission system operators (TSOs) and transmission distribution operators (DSOs), as well as their planned investments (green bars) for a power grid that is capable of a climate-neutral electricity supply. The expansion measures will particularly concentrate in the next decade to prepare the grid for the electrification of the economy. Bauermann, Kaczmarczyk, and Krebs (2024) estimate investments up to 2045 to be nearly €650 billion.

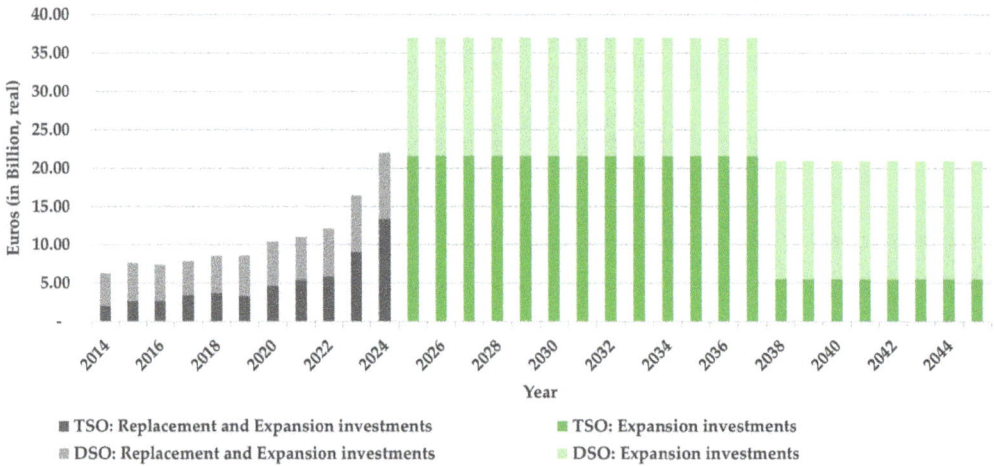

Fig. 3.4 Actual and planned grid investments (in € billion). *Source:* Bauermann, Kaczmarczyk and Krebs (2024). *Note:* The figure shows the investments in the transmission and distribution grid. The grey bars show the investments up to 2024. The green bars show the planned expansion investments for a carbon-neutral grid. The figure has been updated and recalculated in prices of 2024.

Data for Figs. 3.1, 3.2 and 3.4 are available at
https://hdl.handle.net/20.500.12434/fcd06753

The operating costs and investments of electricity grid operators, including expansion investments, are financed by grid fees, which are paid by electricity consumers (i.e., households and companies). The level of these grid fees is monitored and set by the Bundesnetzagentur, a German regulatory authority. The Bundesnetzagentur decides which costs transmission and distribution system operators are allowed to pass on to consumers. These regulated costs include the permissible return on equity and interest on borrowed capital. The expansion investments shown in Figure 3.4 will not be refinanced immediately through the grid fees, but over decades, probably into the 2080s. However, as the planned expansion investments require more capital, they lead to higher expenses for interest on debt and equity for the grid operators. These additional costs will ultimately be passed on to consumers in the form of higher grid fees. However, the increase depends on the capital structure.

With the current capital structure, which largely dispenses with state (public) capital, the permissible capital costs will surely rise. A central problem is that grid operators need to raise more equity to meet the massive investment needs in the grid expansion. Without increasing equity, they risk or have already experienced credit rating downgrades (e.g., Moody's 2024). Operators are therefore already seeking additional investors, and private investors like Blackrock may enter. This could significantly increase grid fees for consumers, as private investors apply a high risk premium and demand correspondingly high returns of 8–10% for the provision of private capital—about 6–7 percentage points above the risk-free government bond rate (KPMG 2025). In order to accelerate grid expansion, the Bundesnetzagentur has already raised the permissible return on equity to over 7% and the return on debt to almost 4%. Instead, public investments could fall back on the low bond interest rates from Germany and provide capital relatively cheaply, as the public sector is legally obliged to serve the common good and not profit.

Regarding the necessary expansionary investments from above, Kaczmarczyk and Krebs (2025) calculated two scenarios for Germany to compare private with public investments. In the scenario, which focuses on the further expansion of private investments, the capital costs would be 6%.[3] In the second scenario, which envisages public investments, the federal and the state governments take a stake in the transmission and distribution grid operators, e.g., via a fund that provides equity to grid operators, and thus effectively invest in the grid infrastructure themselves. The cost of capital would be around 3%, which corresponds to the yield of German twenty-year-bonds. Based on grid fees of around 5 ct/kWh, which correspond to the average of recent decades, this would lead to a 30% increase in grid fees for consumers (around 1.7 ct/kWh) in the case of public expansion investments. Private financing, as in the first scenario, would lead to an increase of 50% (around 3 ct/kWh). This means a considerable difference for consumers. The public investment model could save around €14 billion annually compared to a private solution. This strongly supports public involvement in grid expansion.

In summary, grid expansion is a key element of the energy transition. The current path, characterized by extensive privatization and state withdrawal, is increasingly reaching its limits. The return expectations of private investors would lead to significantly higher costs for consumers. This jeopardizes the socioecological transition if the costs lead consumers to avoid switching from fossil fuels to electricity. Greater public participation could help to make the energy transition more cost-effective and reliable for society. Considering the enormous investment amounts and the strategic importance of power grids, a paradigm shift toward increased public responsibility is therefore not only reasonable but necessary in Germany.

3.5 Summary and Conclusions

By adopting a support scheme that aimed to de-risk private investments, the share of renewables in the German electricity sector grew enormously, along with a remarkable job creation and growth in clean-tech manufacturing. To a certain extent, the Renewable Energy Act was an effective industrial policy tool. However, the support scheme

---

3   Here, we consider the concept of the weighted average costs of capital (WACC). WACC indicate the weighted average cost of capital from equity and debt capital. It is assumed that 40% equity, with a rate of return of 9%, and 60% debt with a rate of return of 5%, are used. The WACC are around 7%.

also had notable shortcomings. For example, insufficient investment in research and development has contributed to Germany's loss of competitiveness worldwide as a manufacturer of photovoltaic systems. In the case of power grid development, the privatization of critical energy infrastructure creates serious challenges. While the grid must be upgraded, relying too much on private investment will be costly and inefficient. Overall, when it comes to deploying renewable electricity and building the necessary grid infrastructure, the transition so far has demonstrated a clear need for stronger government intervention—particularly in the form of industrial policy and public infrastructure investment. It offers several advantages, as it helps achieve societal goals such as climate protection, strengthens the economy and employment, and is less expensive for the general public, including households and businesses. Looking to the future, the active involvement of the public sector is essential to ensure a successful and affordable socioecological transition.

This lesson also applies to hydrogen. So far, the approach to hydrogen development in Germany has been mainly market-oriented, with the vision of a privately operated hydrogen grid. However, this strategy is likely to fail. Private investors have shown limited interest in building the hydrogen grid, and the production targets for 2030 are unlikely to be met with the current model, and grid fees might explode (Dullien et al. 2025). Government intervention, for example, as an operator, is therefore necessary to ensure an efficient hydrogen grid. Hydrogen production, including operating costs, should also be better supported, as prices are still too high for customers and potential producers are reluctant to engage in hydrogen production. The provision of equity capital could also be an option to reduce capital costs and thus prices.

References

50Hertz Transmission GmbH, Amprion GmbH, TenneT TSO GmbH, and TransnetBW GmbH (2023) *Netzentwicklungsplan Strom 2037/2045.* Dortmund: Bundesnetzagentur, https://www.netzentwicklungsplan.de/en/nep-aktuell/netzentwicklungsplan-20372045-2023

AGORA—AGORA Energiewende (2023) *Der CO2-Preis für Gebäude und Verkehr. Ein Konzept für den Übergang vom nationalen zum EU-Emissionshandel.* Berlin: AGORA, https://www.agora-energiewende.de/publikationen/der-co2-preis-fuer-gebaeude-und-verkehr

Angelopoulos, D., R. Brückmann, F. Jirouš, I. Konstantinavičiūtė, and P. Noothout (2016) "Risks and Costs of Capital for Onshore Wind Energy Investments in EU Countries", *Energy and Environment* 27.1, 82–104, https://doi.org/10.1177/0958305X16638573

Bauermann, T., P. Kaczmarczyk, and T. Krebs (2024 "Ausbau der Stromnetze: Investitionsbedarfe", *IMK Study* 97, https://www.imk-boeckler.de/fpdf/HBS-009011/p_imk_study_97_2024.pdf

Bojanowski, A. (2024) "Wir erleben jetzt hautnah, wie Klimapolitik die Basis unseres Wohlstands bedroht", 16 October, *Welt*, https://www.welt.de/wissenschaft/plus253820512/Energiewende-Wir-erleben-hautnah-wie-Klimapolitik-die-Basis-unseres-Wohlstands-bedroht.html?utm_source

CEER—Council of European Energy Regulators (2023) "Status Review of Renewable Support Schemes in Europe for 2020 and 2021", https://www.ceer.eu/publication/status-review-of-renewable-support-schemes-in-europe-for-2020-and-2021/

Couture, T., and Y. Gagnon (2010) "An Analysis of Feed-in Tariff Remuneration Models: Implications for Renewable Energy Investment", *Energy Policy* 38, 955–965.

Du, Y., and M. Teng (2023) "From FIT to FIP: Assessing the Impact of Feed-in Policies on Renewable Development in Germany", *Applied Economics Letters* 30, 2597–2606.

Dullien, S., T. Bauermann, A. Herzog-Stein, C. Paetz, K. Rietzler, U. Stein, S. Stephan, S. Tober, S. Watzka (2025) "Modell Deutschland neu justieren - Nachfrage und Innovationen stärken. Wirtschaftspolitische Herausforderungen 2025", *IMK Report* 194, https://www.imk-boeckler.de/de/faust-detail.htm?sync_id=HBS-009025

Eurostat (2025) "Electricity from Renewable Sources Reaches 47% in 2024", 19 March, *Eurostat*, https://ec.europa.eu/eurostat/web/products-eurostat-news/w/ddn-20250319-1

EWI—Energiewirtschaftliches Institut an der Universität zu Köln and BET—BET Consulting GmbH (2025) "Energiewende. Effizient. Machen. Monitoringbericht zum Start der 21. Legislaturperiode", https://www.bet-consulting.de/fileadmin/redaktion/PDF/Veroeffentlichungen/2025/Energiewende.Effizient.Machen.pdf,

FÖS—Forum Ökologisch Soziale Marktwirtschaft (2020) *Gesellschaftliche Kosten der Atomenergie in Deutschland*. Berlin: FÖS, https://foes.de/publikationen/2020/2020-09_FOES_Kosten_Atomenergie.pdf

Fraunhofer ISE—Fraunhofer-Institut für Solare Energiesysteme (2010) "Stromgestehungskosten Erneuerbare Energien", https://www.ise.fraunhofer.de/content/dam/ise/de/documents/publications/studies/DE2010_ISE_110706_Stromgestehungskosten_mit%20DB_CKost.pdf

Fraunhofer ISE—Fraunhofer-Institut für Solare Energiesysteme (2024) "Stromgestehungskosten Erneuerbare Energien", https://www.ise.fraunhofer.de/de/veroeffentlichungen/studien/studie-stromgestehungskosten-erneuerbare-energien.html

Fraunhofer ISE—Fraunhofer-Institut für Solare Energiesysteme (2025a) "Net Installed Electricity Generation Capacity in Germany", https://www.energy-charts.info/charts/installed_power/chart.htm?l=en&c=DE,

Fraunhofer—Fraunhofer-Institut für Solare Energiesysteme (2025b) "Public Net Electricity Generation in Germany", https://www.energy-charts.info/charts/energy/chart.htm?l=de&c=DE&interval=year&year=2024&source=public

Gabor, D. (2023) "The (European) Derisking State", *Stato e mercato, Rivista quadrimestrale* 1, 53–84.

Hasselbach, C. (2021) "Fukushima Triggered Germany's Nuclear Phaseout", 3 October, *Deutsche Welle*, https://www.dw.com/en/how-fukushima-triggered-germanys-nuclear-phaseout/a-56829217

IW—Institut der deutschen Wirtschaft Köln (2013) "Unerwünschte Verteilungswirkungen", 12 February, *Umwelt-Service*, https://www.iwkoeln.de/studien/hubertus-bardt-unerwuenschte-verteilungswirkungen.html

Kaczmarczyk, P., and T. Krebs (2025) "Finanzierungsoptionen für den Stromnetzausbau und ihre Auswirkungen auf die Netzentgelte", *IMK-Study* 98, 1–36.

KPMG (2025) "Marktrisikoprämie und Basiszins", 30 September, https://atlas.
kpmg.com/de/de/deal-advisory-services/kapitalkosten-und-multiplikatoren/
marktrisikopraemie-und-basiszins

Mercure, J.-F., H. Pollitt, U. Chewpreecha, P. Salas, A. M. Foley, P. B. Holden, and N. R.
Edwards (2014) "The Dynamics of Technology Diffusion and the Impacts of Climate Policy
Instruments in the Decarbonisation of the Global Electricity Sector", *Energy Policy* 73,
686–700.

Moody's (2024) "TenneT Holding B.V. Update to Credit Analysis", https://tennet-drupal.
s3.eu-central-1.amazonaws.com/default/2024-06/04-06-2024%20Credit%20Rating%20
Moody%27s%20TenneT%20Holding%20B.V..pdf

Naschert, C., and A. Blackburne (2024) "German Utilities Say No Way Back for Nuclear
Power", 15 November, *S&P Global*, https://www.spglobal.com/commodity-insights/en/
news-research/latest-news/electric-power/111524-german-utilities-say-no-way-back-for-
nuclear-power-despite-market-hype

Rogge, K. S., M. Schneider, and V. H . Hoffmann (2012) "The Innovation Impact of the EU
Emission Trading System—Findings of Company Case Studies in the German Power
Sector", *Ecological Economics* 70, 513–523.

Schäfer, S. (2019) "Decoupling the EU ETS from Subsidized Renewables and Other Demand
Side Effects: Lessons from the Impact of the EU ETS on CO2 Emissions in the German
Electricity Sector", *Energy Policy* 133, https://doi.org/10.1016/j.enpol.2019.06.066

Schmidt, T. S., M. Schneider, K. S. Rogge, M. J. Schuetz, and V. H. Hoffmann (2012) "The
Effects of Climate Policy on the Rate and Direction of Innovation: A Survey of the EU ETS
and the Electricity Sector", *Environmental Innovation and Societal Transitions* 2, 23–48.

Statistisches Bundesamt (2025), *EEG-Umlage*, https://www.destatis.de/DE/Themen/
Gesellschaft-Umwelt/Umwelt/UGR/_inhalt.html

UBA—Umweltbundesamt (2025a) "Emission von Treibhausgasen nach den Sektoren des
Klimaschutzgesetzes (KSG)", https://tinyurl.com/2d56uyxx

UBA—Umweltbundesamt (2025b) "Endenergieverbrauch nach Energieträgern
und Sektoren", https://www.umweltbundesamt.de/daten/energie/
energieverbrauch-nach-energietraegern-sektoren

Wen, D., W. Gao, F. Qian, Q. Gu, and J. Ren (2021) "Development of Solar Photovoltaic
Industry and Market in China, Germany, Japan and the United States of America Using
Incentive Policies", *Energy Exploration and Exploitation* 39, 1429–1456.

ZSW—Zentrum für Sonnenenergie- und Wasserstoff-Forschung Baden-Württemberg (2025)
*Wirtschaftliche Impulse durch Erneuerbare Energien. Zahlen und Daten zum Erneuerbaren-Ausbau
als Wirtschaftsfaktor.* Stuttgart: ZSW, https://www.bundeswirtschaftsministerium.de/
Redaktion/DE/Downloads/Energie/kurzdokumentation-wirtschaftl-impulse-ee-2024.
pdf?__blob=publicationFile&v=4

4. Energy Transition and Public Investment in Italy

Giovanni Barbieri,[1] Floriana Cerniglia,[2] and Andrea Pronti[3]

Italy is aligned with the EU's 2030 climate goals, aiming to cut greenhouse gas emissions by 55% compared to 1990 levels. Although emissions dropped from 9 to 6 tons per capita by 2023, progress remains too slow to meet the target. Still, renewables alone are not enough to fully decarbonize the energy sector. Most solar systems are small-scale and concentrated in the North, leaving the sunnier South underused. The updated 2024 National Energy and Climate Plan (NECP) sets a 43.7% economy-wide emission cut by 2030. Meeting this goal requires faster deployment of renewables, energy efficiency, and electrification. The National Recovery and Resilience Plan (NRRP) allocates €69 billion to green investments until mid-2026. Despite this, a €175 billion investment gap remains between 2024 and 2030. Achieving climate goals demands considerable amounts of yearly investment. Public intervention will soon decline, making private sector engagement essential. Italy's green transition might necessarily hinge on stronger policies and a joint public-private effort.

4.1 Introduction

In 2024, Italy's energy transition continues its path at a stronger pace than in the recent past, but still not enough to meet the trajectory required by the National Energy and Climate Plan (NECP) drafted by the Italian Ministry of the Environment and Energy Security in 2019 and then finally updated in 2024 (NECP 2024). Meeting this trajectory requires substantial resources, both public and private.

In Italy, in 2024, CO_2 emissions were sharply reduced; however, rising temperatures continue with significant economic effects. Based on the latest BES[4] report (MEF 2024a), total emissions of CO_2 and other greenhouse gases (GHG) in Italy in 2023 fell

---

1   CRANEC—Università Cattolica del Sacro Cuore.
2   CRANEC—Università Cattolica del Sacro Cuore.
3   DISEIS—Università Cattolica del Sacro Cuore.
4   Indicatori di Benessere Equo e Sostenibile (i.e. Fair and Sustainable Well-being Indicators) that are published every year.

https://doi.org/10.11647/OBP.0499.04

sharply, by 5.3% from the previous year, due to increased use of renewables and lower industrial energy consumption due (from 2022) to declining production demand. From 2019, the overall reduction was 7.7%

Reconfiguring Italy's energy mix remains essential, though sectoral inertia persists. Fossil fuels, largely imported, still account for about 75% of energy supply, with oil (37%) and natural gas (36%) prevailing as major sources. Renewables cover roughly 20% of national energy consumption, but their importance increased over years in the last decade (Terna 2024). Their share in electricity generation increased from 15% in 2007 to 44% in 2023. Among renewable energy sources (RES), hydro dominates, accounting for 35%, while solar and wind have become increasingly central to Italy's energy transition with a share of 26% and 20% respectively, reflecting both technological advances and supportive policies. Bioenergy (14%) and geothermal (5%) remain more stable contributors (GSE 2024).

Analysis contained in the 2024 European Climate Risk Assessment show that in 2022 Italy was among the countries with the greatest increase in deaths related to abnormal heat waves, experiencing, along with France and Spain, substantial economic damage from drought and extreme heat (European Environment Agency 2024, p. 151).

Southern European regions, including Italy, show greater climate vulnerability due to a combination of high temperatures, high unemployment, and socioeconomic fragility, which are especially present in southern Italy. Regarding manufacturing activities, climate, as well as demographics,[5] affects investment choices and business structures. In warmer areas of the country, rising temperatures would appear to slow the growth of active businesses, due to a lower business birth rate. Therefore, the impact of global warming could widen the already significant disparities between warmer and more temperate climate areas, which in Italy also show demographic and production gaps.[6]

In this chapter we present the main features of the Italian strategy to promote the energy transition, and we mainly address the role of public intervention to boost such transition.

4.2 NRRP and Public Intervention to Accelerate the Green Transition

In 2024, Italy's GDP grew by 0.7%, driven by both domestic and net foreign demand, but this growth was lower than that of the European Union for the first time since 2021. In 2024, the deficit (-3.36% of GDP) decreased compared to the previous year (-7.2%) mainly due to lower effects of the Superbonus; it was also lower than anticipated due to

---

5   According to the Svimez report (2023), by 2080 there will be an estimated loss of 8 million residents in southern Italy, which would become the oldest area in the country.

6   For example, Cascarano et al. (2025) identify long-term effects of high temperatures on the size and composition of Italian business firms.

higher-than-expected revenues. The primary balance turned positive again after four years (+0.5% of GDP). With reference to expenditures, capital expenditures were also higher than expected by €2 billion. Within the latter, investment subsidies (or grants) to firms were lower than expected by €2.3 billion (reflecting, among other things, lower spending on the Transition 4.0 and Transition 5.0 incentives (see Section 4.4) while both investment and other capital expenditures recorded higher-than-expected amounts of €1.9 billion (equally divided between central and local governments) and €2.4 billion (attributable almost exclusively to central government).

The following figure shows the dynamics of capital expenditure and public investment (a component of capital expenditure) in Italy in recent years. The strong push in capital expenditure between 2020 and 2024 is due to an extraordinary increase in general government grants.[7]

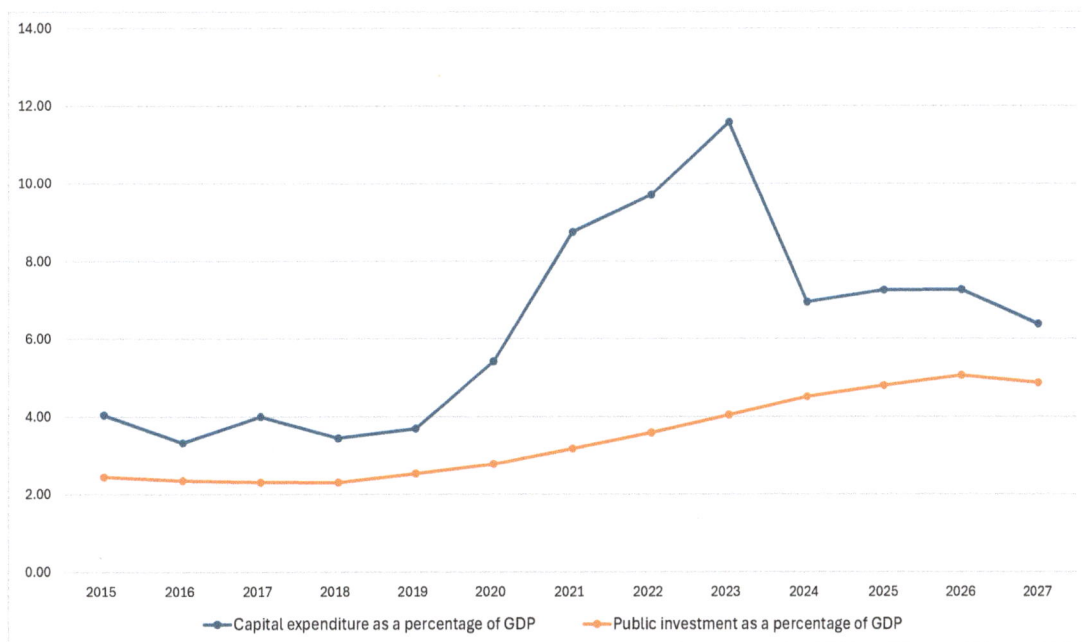

Fig. 4.1 Capital expenditure and public investment over GDP. *Source:* own elaboration based on data from Istat and PSB 2025–2029 (MEF 2024b).

Data for Figs. 4.1–4.10 are available at
https://hdl.handle.net/20.500.12434/a92c7fa5

---

7   In particular, as a result of the so-called Superbonus: the 110% Superbonus is an incentive measure (via tax credit) introduced on 19 May 2020 by the Conte II government. It consists of a series of facilitation mechanisms, deductions, and refunds for interventions of a building nature, with the aim of modernizing buildings and infrastructures by improving their energy efficiency. This measure still exists in 2025, but with reduced rates as for tax credits and different rules than in the past.

In the coming years, concern will grow over the dynamics of public investment once the National Recovery and Resilience Plan (NRPP) phase comes to an end, given the new constraints of the Stability Pact for Italy.

As we documented in the previous editions of the *Outlook*, the NRPP is expected to play a crucial role in stimulating public investment and growth in Italy.[8] It is worth recalling that the NRRP allocates over €194.4 billion (including €122.6 billion in loans and €71.8 billion in grants). Mission 2 of the NRPP (entitled "Green Revolution and Ecological Transition") includes €55.52 billion (28.56% of the Plan) plus €9.17 billion from the Complimentary Fund, dedicated to achieving the country's green, ecological, and inclusive transition by promoting the circular economy, the development of renewable energy sources and more sustainable agriculture. Details of Mission 2 are in Table 4.1 which follows.

Table 4.1 Breakdown of NRRP's Missions 2 and 7. *Source:* own elaboration on data from https://www.italiadomani.gov.it/content/sogei-ng/it/it/il-piano/Risorse/le-risorse-per-la-crescita.html

Mission	Component	NRRP Amount	Complimentary Fund Amount	% NRRP
2. Green revolution and ecologic transition	2.1 Circular Economy and Sustainable Agriculture	€8.11bn	€1.20bn	28.56
	2.2 Renewable Energies, hydrogen, networks and sustainable mobility	€21.97bn	€1.40bn	
	2.3 Energy efficiency and buildings' upgrading	€15.57bn	€6.56bn	
	2.4 Protection of land and water resources	€9.87bn	€ 0	
Mission 2 Total		**€55.52bn**	**€9.16bn**	
7. REPowerEU	7.1 REPowerEU	€11.8bn	€0	5.75
Mission 7 Total		**€11.8bn**	**€0**	

---

8   See Barbieri, Cerniglia, Gori, and Lattarulo (2022); Barbieri, Cerniglia, and Dia (2023); Barbieri, Cerniglia, and Mosconi (2024).

However, in these years of implementation, NRRP has been the subject of proposals for amendments (both for reforms and investments) by the Italian government, and which have been accepted by the Commission. Particular attention has been paid to strengthening investments aimed at promoting Italy's competitiveness and resilience, as well as the green and digital transition, and affects sectors such as renewable energy, green supply chains, and railways.

Compared to the original text, the amended NRRP increases overall the resources allocated to measures that accelerate the green transition to 39.5% instead of the initial 37.5%: it accelerates the deployment of renewable energy through more streamlined permitting procedures, and includes as additional goals for the reduction and revision of environmentally harmful subsidies, increased biomethane production, and intensified provision and adoption of the skills needed for the green transition. Investments include electricity grid efficiency upgrades, new measures to increase hydrogen production, and strengthening the zero-emission rail and local public transport network. The new reforms include rationalizing business incentives, streamlining procedures for renewable energy through a unified regulatory framework, and revising policies to promote territorial cohesion.

A key component of the strategy to accelerate the green transition is the REPowerEU chapter, introduced as Mission 7 within the NRRP. This autonomous mission amounts to €11.18 billion (representing 5.75% of the NRRP, as shown in Table 4.1). In particular, Mission 7 comprises five reforms and seventeen investments, twelve of which are new and the remaining five strengthen (scale up) existing NRRP investments.

As for REPowerEU, the five reforms are as follows: i) the first, the simplification of authorization procedures for renewable energy at the central and local levels, establishes a unified regulatory framework (the "Single Text") consolidating all primary regulations governing the construction of energy production facilities from renewable sources; ii) the second reform aims to reduce environmentally harmful subsidies listed annually in the "Catalog of Environmentally Harmful Subsidies" published by the Ministry of Environment and Energy Security; iii) the third reform, reducing connection costs of biomethane production facilities, aims to improve the integration of biomethane production facilities into the national energy grid; iv) the fourth reform, mitigating financial risk associated with renewable energy PPA agreements, establishes a guarantee system aimed at mitigating the financial risk associated with renewable energy power purchase and sale (PPA) agreements; v) the fifth reform, the new skills transitions plan, seeks to update the training regulatory framework by operationalizing tools to counter the mismatch between skills supply and demand.

To date, the total amount of resources that have been effectively committed to the two missions is equivalent to €43.4 billion for Mission 2 and €2.5 billion for Mission 7[9] (Camera dei Deputati 2025).

---

9 ReGiS database (actualized 1 July 2025). Data for Mission 2 includes, in addition to regionalized funding and projects, non-regionalized funding and projects identified in the ReGiS database as "national" projects. Data for Mission 7 refers only to projects and interventions currently in the ReGiS database compared to the total resources available for Mission 7.

Also, for the 2024–2025 period, the NRRP allocated €6.3 billion to a new tax credit scheme for companies making new investments in production facilities located in Italy, to support private sector investments aligned with this twin transition (both digital and green transition). These resources are allocated through the Transition 5.0 plan, an investment from the new Mission 7 (REPowerEU) of the NRRP which acts in a complementary manner to the previous Transition 4.0 plan.[10] Transition 5.0 supports the transformation of production processes towards an energy-efficient, sustainable, and renewable-based model. The allocated resources consist mainly of incentives for enterprises to modernize industrial processes and enhance energy efficiency, thereby addressing the key challenges of digital and green transitions. These incentives are organized into three modules: Energy Efficiency, Self-Consumption and Self-Production, and Training.

In conclusion, in recent years, a substantially greater volume of public resources has been allocated to promote firms' investments in the green transition compared to previous periods. Nevertheless, a systematic assessment of the impact of these resources remains absent, which is essential to ensure the efficient and productive use of public funds.

4.3 Designing the Energy Transition in Italy

Italy's decarbonization targets are aligned with the European Union's enhanced climate ambition, as formalized in the European Climate Law,[11] which establishes a legally binding objective of reducing net greenhouse gas emissions by at least 55% by 2030, compared to 1990 levels. This revision strengthens the EU's initial commitment under the 2015 Paris Agreement, which had originally aimed for a 40% reduction relative to 1990 levels, as reflected in the first round of Nationally Determined Contributions (NDCs).

The commitment of successive Italian governments to reducing carbon emissions has been consistent over the past decades, yielding significant results. Starting from an emission level of approximately 9 tons of greenhouse gas (GHG) emissions in CO_2 equivalent per capita in 1990, Italy has achieved an average annual reduction rate of 1.37%, reaching 6 tons per capita by 2023. This places Italy below the EU27 average, which stood at 7 tons per capita in the same year (Fig. 4.2).

Since the second decade of the 2000s, Italian GHG emissions have been reduced at an average rate of -3% per year, a figure slightly higher than the EU27 average of -2% per year over the same period (Fig. 4.3). Most of the GHG emission reduction occurred between 2007 and 2014, driven by lower emissions intensity and economic contraction, but progress has slowed since 2014 due to the economic recovery and limited further gains in emissions efficiency (OECD 2024).

---

10   The Transition 4.0 plan was financed with €6.4 billion and supported the digital transformation of companies by incentivizing private investment in technologically advanced capital goods, innovation and skills upgrading activities. Further details for Transition 4.0 and Transition 5.0 are found in Barbieri, Cerniglia, and Mosconi (2024).

11   Regulation (EU) 2021/1119 of the European Parliament and of the Council of 30 June 2021 establishing the framework for achieving climate neutrality and amending Regulations (EC) No 401/2009 and (EU) 2018/1999 ("European Climate Law").

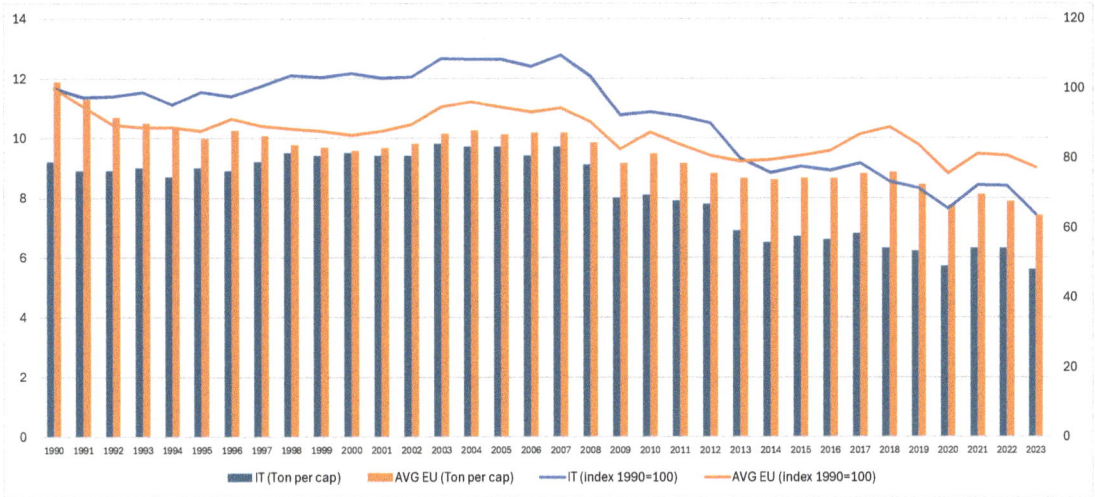

Fig. 4.2 Italy's carbon emissions between 1990–2023 in ton per capita (left-hand side), using 1990 year index (right-hand side). *Source:* own elaboration on Eurostat (2025a).

Data for Figs. 4.1–4.10 are available at
https://hdl.handle.net/20.500.12434/a92c7fa5

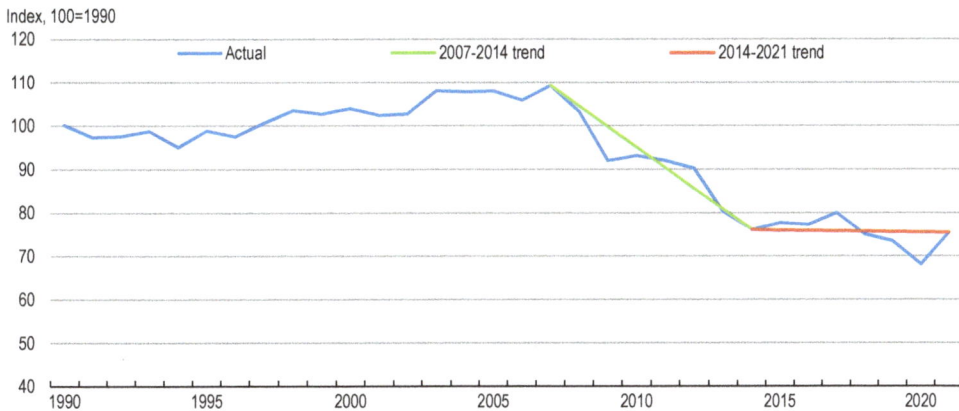

Fig. 4.3 Emission reduction in Italy since 1990 (index: 1990=100). *Source:* OECD 2024.

Data for Figs. 4.1–4.10 are available at
https://hdl.handle.net/20.500.12434/a92c7fa5

The largest reductions were observed in electricity generation and manufacturing, the most polluting sectors, reducing their overall emissions by -42% and -53%, respectively, between 2008 and 2023. Meanwhile, buildings and transport showed the least progress. Overall, total GHG emissions in Italy decreased by -36% during this period (Eurostat 2025b). This reflects the enhanced carbon intensity efficiency of the Italian industrial sector, which has achieved a relative decoupling of environmental impacts driven by eco-innovations and technological improvements that have significantly reduced GHG emissions of manufacturing and energy productions (OECD 2024). Figure 4.4 depicts the trend in GHG reduction that occurred in Italy from 2008 to 2023 by principal economic sectors.

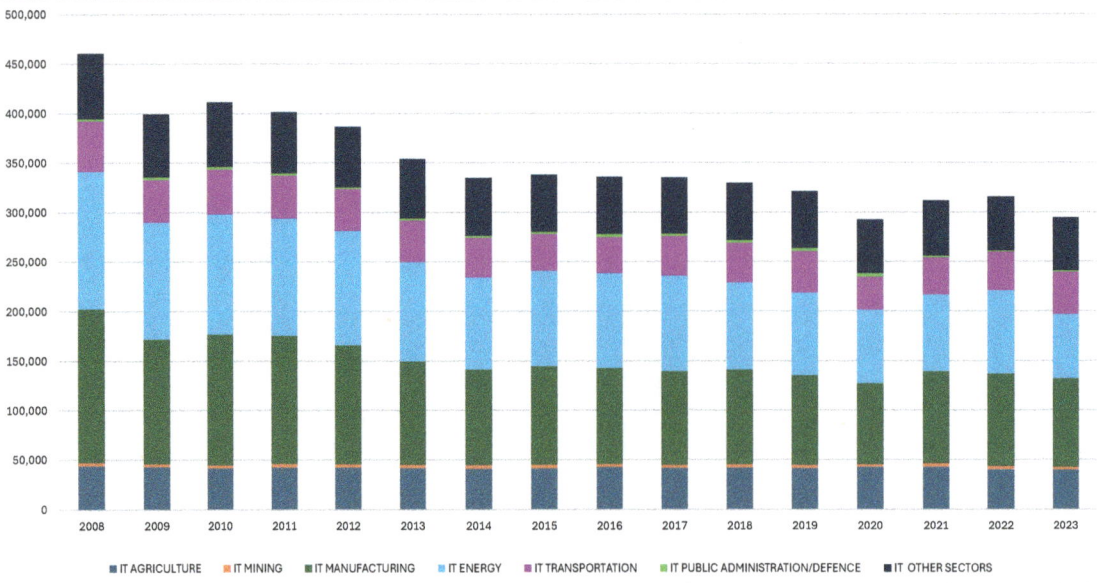

Fig. 4.4 GHG emissions in Italy by sectors in thousand tons. *Source:* own elaboration on Eurostat (2025b).

Data for Figs. 4.1–4.10 are available at
https://hdl.handle.net/20.500.12434/a92c7fa5

Italy is far from meeting its 2030 climate targets and must significantly accelerate emissions cuts. Between 1990 and 2021, emissions fell by 25%, well below the 55% target for 2030. Reaching this goal would require reducing emissions intensity over five times faster than the 2014–2021 pace (OECD 2024).

Structural changes in the economy, particularly in the energy mix, are on the agenda, but the inertia of Italy's energy sector remains a major challenge to overcome. Fossil fuels supply nearly 75% of Italy's energy, almost entirely through imports.[12] Renewables cover about 20% of the national energy consumption, which is still mainly powered from oil (37%) and natural gas (36%) (Terna 2024). According to the national energy services operator (Gestore Servizi Energetici—GSE), over the past decade the share of renewable energy sources (RES) in Italy's gross electric energy production has increased from 15% in 2007 to 44% in 2023 (GSE 2024). Among RES, solar energy has gained a growing role, accounting for 26% of renewable electricity generation in 2023, following hydro (35%) and ahead of wind (20%), bioenergy (14%), and geothermal (5%) (Fig. 4.5).

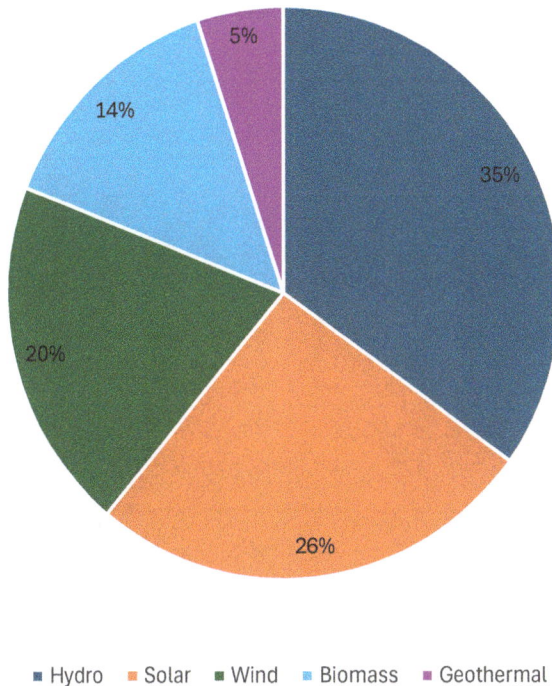

■ Hydro   ■ Solar   ■ Wind   ■ Biomass   ■ Geothermal

Fig. 4.5 National distributions of Renewable Energy Sources for power generation in Italy in 2023.
Source: own elaboration on GSE (2024).

Data for Figs. 4.1–4.10 are available at
https://hdl.handle.net/20.500.12434/a92c7fa5

---

12   Natural gas is the main source (over 40%), followed by oil, with coal playing a minor role. The reliance on fossil energy imports is still an important vulnerability in Italy's economy both, in geopolitical and productive terms. As highlighted by the 2024 Draghi report, high energy cost is one of the most impactful factors contributing to the loss of competitiveness between European firms and their US and Chinese competitors.

By the end of 2023, Italy had reached over 30 GW of installed solar capacity (up from just 0.48 GW in 2008), with nearly 1.6 million photovoltaic (PV) systems in operation. This growth is due not only to policy support but also to the increasing cost-competitiveness of solar PV.[13] The average scale of installed photovoltaic systems in Italy is relatively small, at around 19 kW per system (Fig. 4.6). Yet since 2024 the relative share of large-scale plants has been increasing while overall deployment continues to grow (Terna 2025, p. 13).

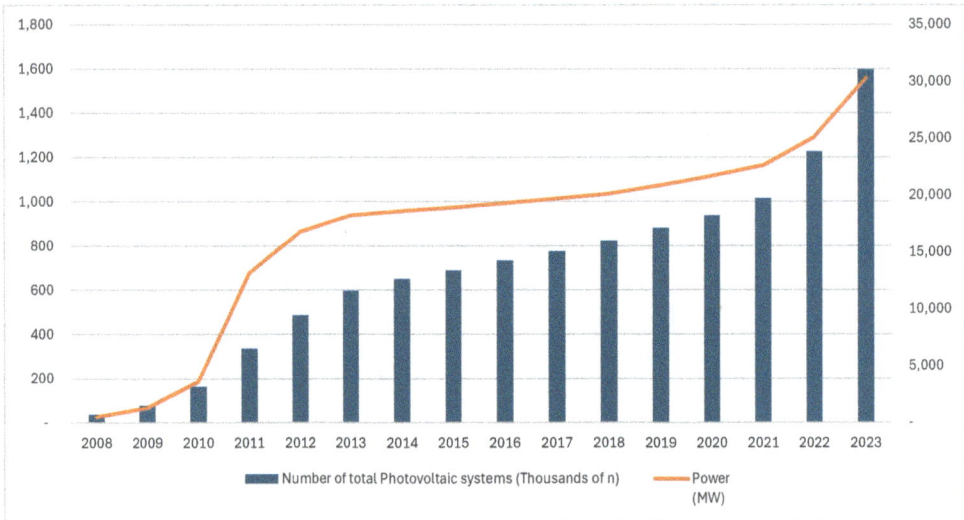

Fig. 4.6 Deployment of photovoltaic systems in Italy from 2008 to 2023. Blue bars indicate number of installations, orange line marks the total cumulated power installed. *Source:* own elaboration on GSE (2024).

Data for Figs. 4.1–4.10 are available at
https://hdl.handle.net/20.500.12434/a92c7fa5

As with many other socioeconomic aspects of the Italian system, there are significant regional disparities in photovoltaic systems deployment, both in terms of the number of systems and total installed capacity. According to data from the GSE, 41% of all PV

---

13   The expansion of solar PV began in earnest with the launch of the *Conto Energia* in 2005, a feed-in tariff scheme that strongly incentivized installation across both residential and industrial sectors, pushing installed capacity beyond 18 GW by 2014. Although direct incentives were gradually reduced after 2013, support continued through mechanisms like net metering (*Scambio sul Posto*) and tax deductions for building renovations and energy efficiency (*Superbonus 110*). Small-scale installations (≤20 kW) account for about 94% of the total number of systems but contribute only 29% of total installed capacity. In contrast, medium- and large-scale systems, which represent just 6% of installations by number, account for 71% of total capacity (GSE 2024).

systems are located in just three northern regions (Lombardy, Veneto, and Emilia-Romagna) highlighting the concentration of small-scale installations in the Centre-North compared to the South. In terms of installed capacity, the Centre-South generally lags behind the North, with the notable exception of the Apulia region (*Puglia*), which alone accounts for 10.9% of national PV capacity.[14] A clear North-South divide emerges.[15] This is particularly noteworthy given that Southern regions benefit from higher solar efficiency due to better exposure conditions and thus greater potential productivity. This raises important questions about the underlying causes of such a disparity (Alpino et al. 2025). Figures 4.7 and 4.8 illustrate the geographic distribution of PV systems and solar irradiation by region.

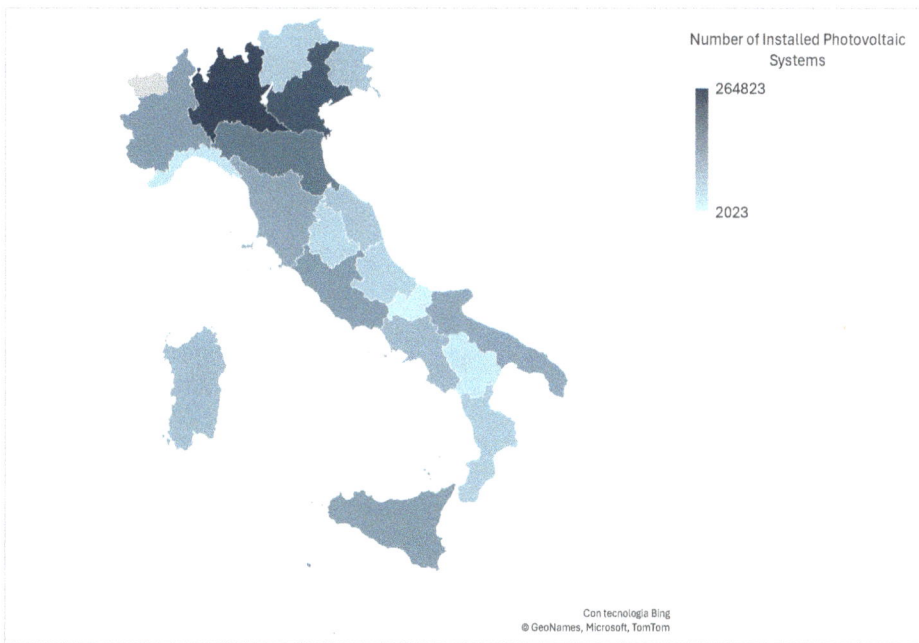

Fig. 4.7 Installations of photovoltaic systems by regions (number of systems). *Source:* own elaboration on GSE (2024).

Data for Figs. 4.1–4.10 are available at
https://hdl.handle.net/20.500.12434/a92c7fa5

---

14   Other leading regions include Lombardy (13.35%), Veneto (10.45%), Emilia-Romagna (9.99%), Piedmont (8.46%), and Sicily (7.14%).

15   The North-South divide is one of Italy's bottlenecks that we have consistently highlighted in previous chapters on Italy in the *Outlook* series, and is one of the reasons why the NRRP allocates 40% of its resources to the South.

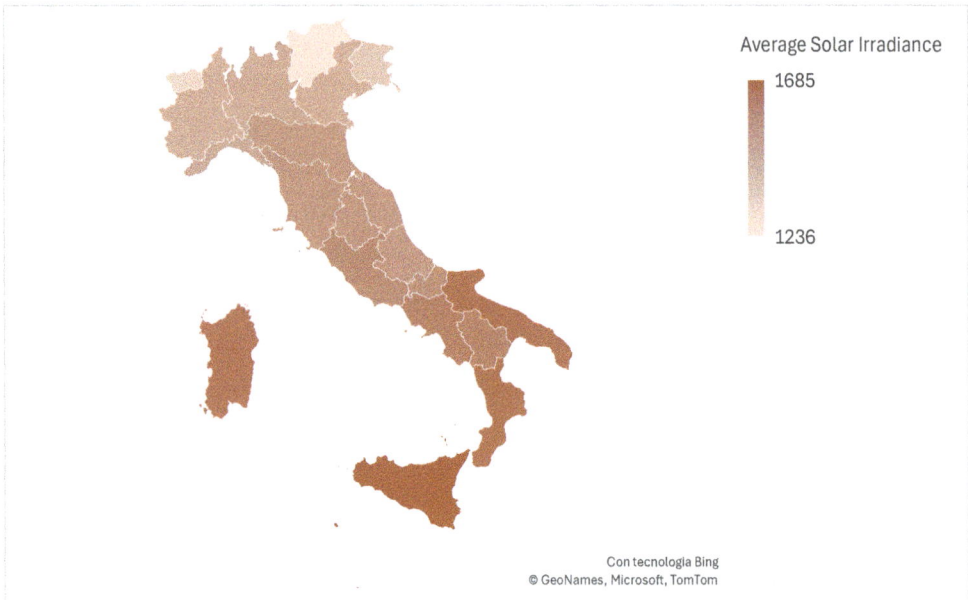

Fig. 4.8 Solar irradiation by regions (Kwh). *Source:* own elaboration on RSE (2024).

Data for Figs. 4.1–4.10 are available at
https://hdl.handle.net/20.500.12434/a92c7fa5

Italy's updated National Energy and Climate Plan (NECP) sets ambitious targets, aiming for a 43.7% reduction in economy-wide emissions for the sectors not included in the Emissions Trading System (ETS) by 2030 (compared to 2005). However, meeting these goals requires a much faster pace than recent trends and current policies can deliver. Stronger action is needed to accelerate renewable energy deployment, improve energy efficiency, and advance electrification (NECP 2024).

4.4 The Investment Needs in Italy

The NRRP is one of the main instruments to bridge the investment gap needed for the energy transition. The main mission dedicated to this purpose is Mission 2—"Green Revolution and Ecological Transition"—which, as already mentioned, allocates €64.68 billion to green objectives focusing on renewable energy, energy efficiency, sustainable mobility, and the circular economy, to be spent by mid-2026. The NRRP thus supports infrastructure modernization, biodiversity protection, and simplification of permitting procedures, investments which are essential to accelerate decarbonization, reduce fossil fuel dependence, and bring Italy closer to its climate commitments. However, they are still insufficient to close the gap toward 2030 targets, highlighting the need for stronger and more sustained policy efforts beyond 2026 (OECD 2024).

The investment of the NRRP complements the Italian NECP,[16] which was updated in June 2024, revising the initial version submitted in 2019 and covering the years 2024–2030. In its latest update, the Italian Ministry for the Environment and Energy Security (Ministero dell'Ambiente e della Sicurezza Energetica) reassessed investment needs in light of the events that occurred after 2019 (i.e., COVID-19 and the Russia-Ukraine War), considering ongoing policies and the partial revision of EU targets under the "Fit for 55" package and the REPowerEU plan. As a result, the Ministry had to increase resources compared to the levels initially planned in 2019 in order to bridge the investment gap and to account for the new context and updated climate targets.

These data are shown in Table 4.2. In the period 2024–2030, over €174 billion of additional cumulative investments (column 3 of Table 4.2) will be required to fill the gap with the current scenario (i.e., without the additional increases foreseen in the new revision of the NECP in 2024), corresponding to a 27% increase over the period considered.[17] These investments would be directed towards solutions with high technological and innovative content.

It should be noted that a cumulative investment requirement of around €824 billion over the period considered would require annual investments of approximately 5% of GDP.[18] Notice that the main sector facing an investment gap is transport, which requires around €60 billion to replace old thermal vehicles with electric ones (an additional 2.82% of GDP). Another key sector is electricity generation, with an estimated €35.7 billion investment gap (an additional 1.68% of GDP) between 2024 and 2030. The residential sector follows closely, with €34.6 billion (an additional 1.63% of GDP) needed for energy and thermal efficiency upgrades in housing. The tertiary sector also shows a significant shortfall, requiring €25 billion of additional investments (an additional 1.18% of GDP). Other sectors with comparatively smaller gaps include electricity networks (€7.4 billion), the industrial sector, particularly for environmental sustainability and energy efficiency (€4.8 billion), energy storage systems (e.g., batteries) (€4.5 billion), and electrolyzers (€2 billion). In terms of annual investment

---

16 NECP (National Energy and Climate Plan) is the English acronym for PNIEC (Piano Nazionale Integrato per l'Energia e il Clima). The PNIEC was prepared by the Ministry of Economic Development, Environment, and Infrastructure and Transport, and covers the period 2024–2030 (see https://www.mase.gov.it/portale/-/pubblicato-il-testo-definitivo-del-piano-energia-e-clima-pniec-).

17 The first column of Table 4.2 shows the first assessment of investment needs done in the first version of the NECP in 2019. The second column shows the new requirements/needs forecasted by the 2024 revision of the Plan. The third column shows the Investment Gap in terms of the difference between the new investment requirements made in 2024 and the first assessment of the NECP done in 2019. Column four shows the same difference (investment gap) in terms of % of GDP (current prices in 2023). The columns from 5 to 7 represents the annual total investment needs assessed in 2024, the annual investment gap (NECP 2024–NECP 2019) and the annual investment gap in terms of GDP.

18 This percentage, along with the other annual gap estimates, have been calculated by dividing the total amount of investment needs by GDP and then spreading the result evenly over the time period of 2024–2030 length (n=7).

needs for the period 2024–2030, the residential sector will require €4.94 billion per year (an additional 0.23% of GDP per year), while the tertiary sector will need €3.59 billion annually (an additional 0.17% of GDP per year). The transport sector will demand the largest yearly investment, with €8.59 billion (an additional 0.40% of GDP per year), followed by the electricity generation sector, which will require €5.10 billion per year (an additional 0.24% of GDP per year).

Table 4.2 Investments in technologies, processes, and infrastructure necessary for the evolution of the energy system. Cumulative costs (2024–2030), € billion. *Source:* own elaboration from NECP (2024) data.

	(1) Investments needs (first version NECP 2019)	(2) Investments needs (revision NECP 2024)	(3) Investment gap (additional investment needs)	(4) Investment gap (% GDP)	(5) Investments needs for the NECP 2024 (Annual)	(6) Investment gap (Annual additional investment needs)	(7) Investment gap (% GDP per year)
Residential	59	93.6	34.6	1.63	13.37	4.94	0.23
Tertiary	37.2	62.3	25.1	1.18	8.90	3.59	0.17
Industry	8.2	13.1	4.8	0.23	1.87	0.69	0.03
District heating (distribution only)	0.04	0.06	0.02	0.00	0.01	0.00	0.00
Transport (vehicles only)	468.7	528.8	60.1	2.82	75.54	8.59	0.40
Electricity sector (generation)	46.1	81.8	35.7	1.68	11.69	5.10	0.24
Electricity system (networks)	22.6	30	7.4	0.35	4.29	1.06	0.05
Storage systems (batteries, pumping)	7.5	12	4.5	0.21	1.71	0.64	0.03
Electrolyzers	1	3	2	0.09	0.43	0.29	0.01
Total	650.3	824.7	174.4	8.20	117.81	24.91	1.17

Considering the electricity generation system sector (€35.7 billion of additional investment), the main area in which investment will be needed is photovoltaic systems, given the almost €20 billion gap between the first and the latest version of the NECP needed between 2024 and 2030. Other areas of the electricity generation sector with relevant additional investment needs are shore wind and offshore wind respectively, with an additional investment gap of €8.3 billion and €5.4 billion in the same period (Table 4.3 and Fig. 4.10).

Table 4.3 Investments in RES electricity generation technologies needed for the evolution of the energy system. Cumulative costs (2024–2030), € billion. *Source:* own elaboration from NECP (2024) data.

	(1)	(2)	(3)
	Investments needs (first version NECP 2019)	Investments needs (revision NECP 2024)	Investment gap (additional investment needs)
Bioenergy	0.7	2.1	1.4
Hydropower	0.3	0.3	0
Geothermal energy	1.1	1.6	0.5
Photovoltaics	26.1	45.9	19.8
Concentrated solar power	0	0.3	0.3
Shore wind	15.8	24.1	8.3
Offshore wind	0.1	5.5	5.4
Fossils	2	2	0
Total	46.1	81.8	35.7

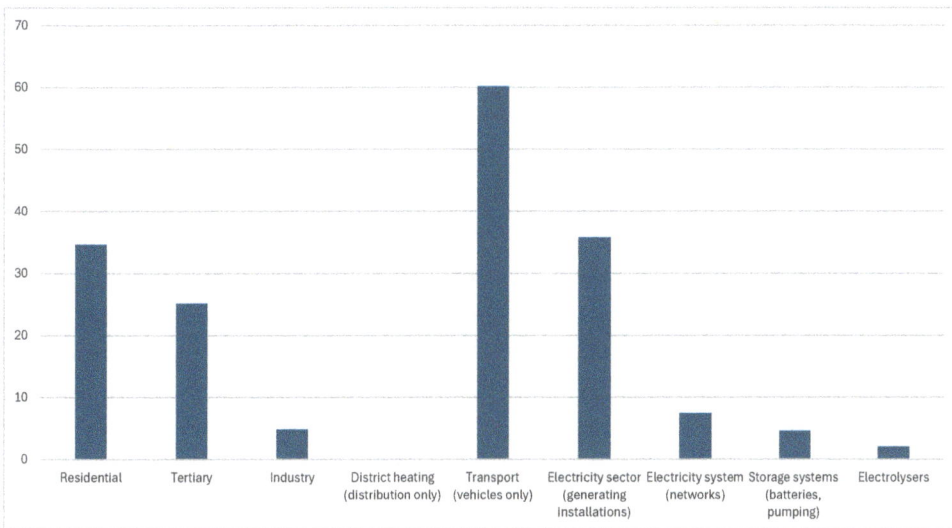

Fig. 4.9 Additional investment needs for the period 2024–2030 for technology process and infrastructure by main sectors, in € billion. *Source:* own elaboration on NECP (2024).

Data for Figs. 4.1–4.10 are available at
https://hdl.handle.net/20.500.12434/a92c7fa5

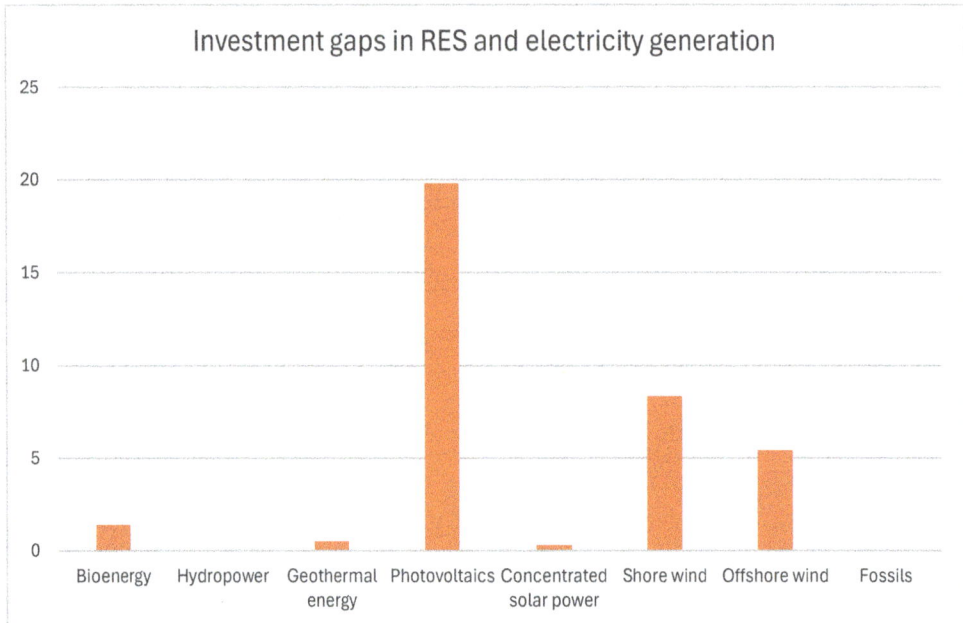

Fig. 4.10 Additional investment needs for the period 2024–2030 for renewable energy sources (RES) and electricity generation by main areas, in € billion. *Source:* own elaboration on NECP (2024).

Data for Figs. 4.1–4.10 are available at
https://hdl.handle.net/20.500.12434/a92c7fa5

Achieving these investment targets for Italy's green transition will require an important contribution from the private sector, and this will also apply to financing the main investments just outlined, considering that NRRP funding will no longer be available after mid-2026. Consumers, firms, banks, and other financial institutions will become the main actors, investing and boosting the green transition with the help of public authorities. This will sustain the process of structural change for the economy within the framework designed by the European Commission.

4.5 Conclusion

In the coming years, Italy will face the pressing challenge of securing the investments (both public and private) needed to bridge the existing infrastructure gaps in order to meet climate targets. The green transition could be an opportunity for Italy to relaunch its economy and industry. In this perspective, the environmental and energy security process must be pursued in tandem with the relaunch of industrial competitiveness. Climate change policies must be intertwined with industrial and technological policies.

In the Italian case, in particular, a new phase of industrial and institutional policy is needed, capable of simplifying and harmonizing authorization procedures, offering operators clear, stable and proportional instruments, and finally—given the nature of multi-level government, with competences in energy matters distributed also between the state and regions—effectively coordinating actions between the state, regions, and network operators. The increasing heterogeneity of regulations and authorization procedures adopted by different regions is one of the most significant obstacles to a homogeneous development of renewable sources in Italy; technical criteria, timing, and procedural burdens often vary significantly from one territory to another, generating uncertainty for operators and investors and multiplying administrative litigation.

References

Alpino, M., L. Brugnara, M. G. Cassinis, L. Citino, F. David, A. Frigo, G. Papini, P. Recchia, and L. Sessa (2025) "Il recente sviluppo delle energie rinnovabili in Italia (Going Green: The Recent Development of Renewable Energy Sources in Italy)", *Bank of Italy Occasional Paper* 908, http://dx.doi.org/10.2139/ssrn.5248242

Barbieri, G., F. Cerniglia, G. F. Gori, and P. Lattarulo (2022) "NRRP—Italy's Strategic Reform and Investment Programme: Sustaining an Ecological Transition", in F. Cerniglia and F. Saraceno (eds), *Greening Europe: 2022 European Public Investment Outlook*. Cambridge, UK: Open Book Publishers, pp. 55–70, https://doi.org/10.11647/OBP.0328.04

Barbieri, G., F. Cerniglia, and E. Dia (2023) "Italy's Public Investments. The NRRP and Beyond", in Cerniglia, F., F. Saraceno, and A. Watt (eds), *Financing Investment in Times of High Public Debt: 2023 European Public Investment Outlook*. Cambridge, UK: Open Book Publishers, pp. 69–84, https://doi.org/10.11647/obp.0386.04

Barbieri, G., F. Cerniglia, and F. Mosconi (2024) "Italy, NRRP and Industrial Policy", in F. Cerniglia and F. Saraceno (eds), *Investing in the Structural Transformation. 2024 European Public Investment Outlook*. Cambridge, UK: Open Book Publishers, pp. 59–76, https://doi.org/10.11647/obp.0434.05

Camera dei Deputati (2025) "Monitoraggio del Piano Nazionale di Ripresa e Resilienza. I traguardi e gli obiettivi per il conseguimento dell'VIII rata. Focus sui profili finanziari del Piano e la programmazione nelle Regioni", *Servizio studi della Camera*, https://documenti.camera.it/leg19/dossier/pdf/DFP28j.pdf

Cascarano, M., F. Natoli, and A. Petrella (2025) "Entry, Exit, and Market Structure in a Changing Climate", in *European Economic Review* 176, https://doi.org/10.1016/j.euroecorev.2025.105027

European Environment Agency (2024) *European Climate Risk Assessment*, EEA Report 01/2024. Luxembourg: EU, https://www.eea.europa.eu/en/analysis/publications/european-climate-risk-assessment

Eurostat (2025a) "Domestic Net Greenhouse Gas Emissions", http://ec.europa.eu/eurostat/databrowser/view/sdg_13_10__custom_16974382/default/table

Eurostat (2025b) "Air Emissions Accounts by NACE Rev. 2 Activity", https://ec.europa.eu/eurostat/databrowser/view/env_ac_ainah_r2__custom_16976659/default/table

GSE (2024) "Rapporto Statistico 2023. Solare Fotovoltaico", Rapporto Statistico 2023 Gestore Servizi Energetici, Ufficio Statistiche e Monitoraggio Target, May 2024.

MEF (2024a) "Relazione sugli Indicatori di Benessere Equo e Sostenibile", *Ministero dell'Economia e delle Finanze*, https://www.dt.mef.gov.it/export/sites/sitodt/modules/ documenti_it/analisi_progammazione/documenti_programmatici/Relazione-BES-2024_ finale.pdf

MEF (2024b) "Italia 2025-2029. Piano strutturale di bilancio di medio termine", *Ministero dell'Economia e delle Finanze*, https://www.dt.mef.gov.it/export/sites/sitodt/modules/ documenti_it/analisi_progammazione/documenti_programmatici/psb_2024/Piano- strutturale-di-bilancio-e-di-medio-termine-Italia-2025-2029.pdf

NECP (2024) "NECP, 2024. National Integrated Plan for Energy and Climate, Italy", *Italian Ministry of the Environment and Energy Security*, https://commission. europa.eu/energy-climate-change-environment/implementation-eu-countries/ energy-and-climate-governance-and-reporting/national-energy-and-climate-plans_en

OECD (2024) *OECD Economic Surveys: Italy 2024*. Paris: OECD Publishing, https://doi. org/10.1787/78add673-en

Presidenza del Consiglio dei Ministri (2025) "Sesta relazione al Parlamento sullo stato di attuazione del Piano Nazionale di Ripresa e Resilienza", Struttura di Missione del PNRR, https://www.strutturapnrr.gov.it/it/documenti/relazioni-al-parlamento/ sesta-relazione-al-parlamento-sullo-stato-di-attuazione-del-pnrr/

RSE (2023) *Ricerca sul Sistema Energetico*, https://www.rse-web.it/.

SVIMEZ (2023) *Rapporto Svimez 2023. L'Economia e la Società del Mezzogiorno. Cittadinanza, lavoro, imprese: l'inclusione fa crescere, Capitolo 5. Il gelo demografico*. Bologna: Il Mulino.

Terna (2024) "Dati statistici sull'energia elettrica in Italia 2023", *Terna*, https://www.terna.it/it/ sistema-elettrico/statistiche/pubblicazioni-statistiche

Terna (2025) "Prospettive di sviluppo del sistema energetico 2050. Copertura della domanda elettrica", Terna, https://download.terna.it/terna/Terna_Prospettive_Sviluppo_Sistema_ Energetico_2050_Copertura_domanda_elettrica_8de15802728e7d1.pdf

UPB (2025) "Audizione della Presidente dell'Ufficio parlamentare di bilancio nell'ambito delle audizioni preliminari all'esame del Documento di finanza pubblica 2025", *Ufficio Parlamentare di Bilancio*, https://www.upbilancio.it/wp-content/uploads/2025/04/UPB_ Audizione-DFP-2025.pdf

5. Investment in the Energy Transition in Spain

Ignacio Álvarez[1] and Jorge Uxó[2]

As part of its energy transition framework, Spain has set ambitious targets to increase the share of renewable energies in electricity production. Meeting them requires substantial investment. Although the context of public investment until the pandemic was unfavourable, Next Generation EU has changed the situation with a significant increase in funds for the energy transition. The PERTE, a valuable instrument in developing a new active industrial policy, is an important innovation in applying these funds. Spain has a relative advantage in its capacity to produce energy from renewable sources, which is already translating into lower prices than the European average. It can use this advantage to improve competitiveness and promote a reindustrialization process, attracting industrial projects that choose to set up in Spain because of the access to cheap and stable energy. The main question, however, is whether this investment effort will be sustained once these funds are no longer received, especially in a context marked by the return of fiscal rules and pressure to increase security spending.

5.1 Introduction

The first sentence of the Integrated National Energy and Climate Plan of Spain (MITECO 2024) is crystal clear: "the opportunity of the ecological transition". Indeed, it is widely accepted that the energy transition represents an opportunity for transforming the Spanish economy, and that, in addition to its contribution to decarbonization and the fight against climate change, it can have very positive economic effects. These benefits will potentially be greater than in other countries precisely because of Spain's historical dependence on fossil fuel imports and its high availability of natural resources associated with electricity generation from renewable sources (sun and wind).

In fact, the recent transformation of Spain's energy mix clearly reflects the energy transition process that the country is undergoing. In 2024, almost 57% of all electricity

---

1   Universidad Autónoma de Madrid (Madrid, Spain).
2   Universidad Complutense de Marid (Madrid, Spain).

https://doi.org/10.11647/OBP.0499.05

produced in Spain came from renewable energy sources such as wind, sun, or water, which is 22 percentage points more than in 2019, as we can see in Figure 5.1.

2019

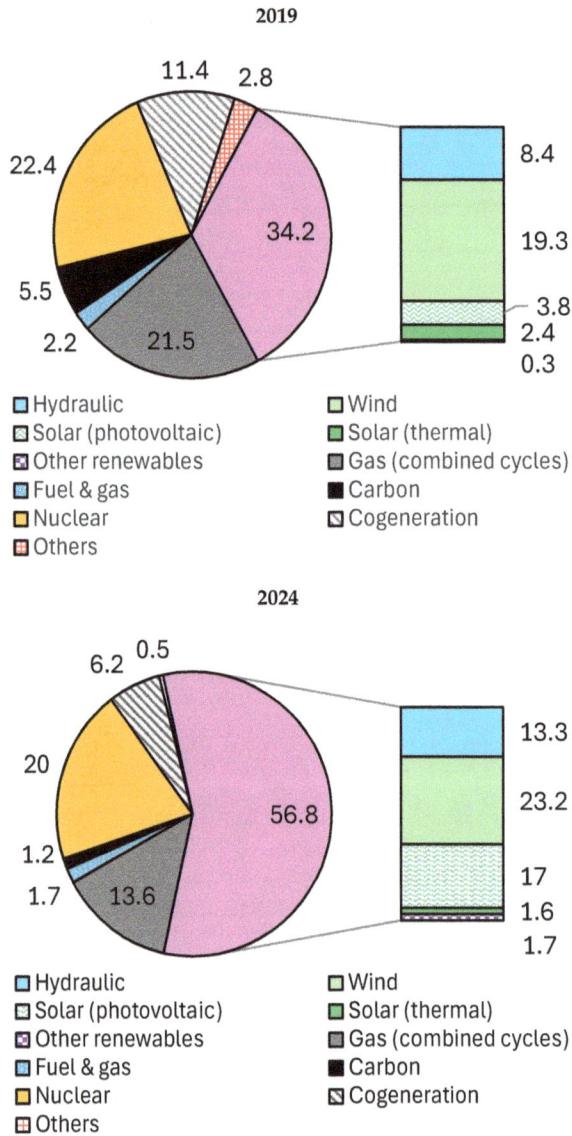

2024

Fig. 5.1 Spanish energy mix (electricity produced, 2019–2024). *Source:* Red Eléctrica (2024).

Data for Figs. 5.1–5.3, Table 5.1 and Table 5.2 are available at https://hdl.handle.net/20.500.12434/074fa1a7

In the next section, we will present some of the main features of the Spanish strategy to promote this energy transition, with a particular focus on the leading role of renewable energies. Next, we will analyze the development of public investment and emphasize the fundamental role of European funds in the recent boost experienced by this investment. In the fourth section, we focus on the most significant economic effect that this process may have: the possibility of using lower electricity prices to improve competitiveness, attract investment, and reindustrialize the country. The fifth section summarizes the conclusions.

5.2 The Design of the Energy Transition in Spain and the Role of Renewable Energies

Two fundamental documents for the design of the ecological transition in Spain are the Long-Term Decarbonization Strategy and the Integrated National Energy and Climate Plan (PNIEC), both drawn up in 2020, coinciding with the launch of the European Green Pact. While the former aims to achieve climate neutrality by 2050, the latter focuses on more targeted measures for the current decade.[3] The Climate Change and Energy Transition Act, passed in 2021, incorporates the main objectives of both documents. Additionally, the Just Transition Strategy seeks to manage the consequences that the transition may have on territories or people especially linked to affected or displaced activities. Lastly, some of the main measures included in the PNIEC have been specified in strategic documents and sectoral roadmaps.

The revision of the PNIEC was strongly conditioned by the approval of the Recovery, Transition, and Resilience Plan (PRTR, which we will analyze in the next section) and by the Russian invasion of Ukraine in February 2022. This event accelerated the energy transition, as the rising cost of fossil fuels added to the need to respond to the climate emergency, and the vulnerability of external energy dependence became even more evident. Securing supply has become a priority objective, and the best guarantee for achieving this is a system based on a combination of renewable technologies and greater energy efficiency.

The PNIEC has also adapted to the increased ambition of European climate targets:

- The greenhouse gas emission reduction target for 2030 has been set at 55% compared to 2005, which is 32% compared to 1990 (in the initial version of the PNIEC, it was 23%). This will be achieved mainly by increasing energy efficiency, rising the share of renewable energies in electricity generation, and further electrifying the economy.

- Regarding energy efficiency improvement, a 43% improvement in energy end-use has been targeted relative to the projections of a baseline scenario without measures (42% in the previous version).

---

3   The European Commission approved its update in 2024. In this chapter, we will refer to this version.

- The increase in wind and solar capacity should raise the share of renewables in electricity generation to 81% in 2030 (from 37% in 2019) and to 48% of final energy use. The previous targets were 74% and 42%, respectively. It is also proposed to boost self-consumption to 19 GW installed, equivalent to 11% of demand, and to strengthen energy storage up to 22.5 GW. This is necessary to ensure a more secure integration of renewables in electricity generation and to take full advantage of the increase in installed renewable capacity. In recent years, renewable capacity has grown above its end-use, partially due to the lack of such storage infrastructure.

- The electrification rate of the economy, which is key to the decarbonization of the Spanish economy, should rise to 35% of the final energy demand by 2030 (it currently stands at around 22%).

To achieve these objectives, the PNIEC includes 110 measures structured around five dimensions (decarbonization of the economy and progress in renewables; energy efficiency; energy security; energy market; and research, innovation, and competitiveness) plus a transversal component.

One of this strategy's central elements is deploying renewable energies. Currently,[4] oil-based fuels are still the prominent source of energy in Spain, even above the European average (46% of the total final consumption compared to 33%), followed by electricity (25% in both cases) and natural gas (which represents a lower percentage in Spain, 17% compared to 22% in Europe). The high share of oil-based fuels in total final consumption is mainly explained by the transportation sector, which is highly intensive in oil products.

Regarding the penetration of renewable energies in electricity generation, installed capacity has grown by 40% between 2019 and 2023, mainly due to the progress recorded in photovoltaic solar energy. Furthermore, wind power capacity increased also by 20% in those years. Currently, renewable energies already represent 65% of Spain's total installed electricity capacity. The IRENA ranking[5] places Spain in 2024 as the second country in the EU in terms of installed renewable capacity, after Germany, and the seventh in the world. According to the PNIEC, Spain accounts for around 20% of the renewable hydrogen projects announced worldwide in 2022, only behind the United States.

This evolution of installed capacity has led to an increase in the share of renewable energies in electricity production to 51% (17% in 2000). With this increase, it is 10 points above the European average. This growth has been driven by the sharp fall in the levelized cost of electricity (LCOE) of new solar and wind installations in Spain, which benefits from the high number of hours of sunshine and wind. According to

---

4   Cubero et al. (2025).
5   See https://www.irena.org/Data/View-data-by-topic/Capacity-and-Generation/Country-Rankings

IRENA (2024), the LCOE of new solar and wind installations in Spain is at the same level as in the United States, below France and Germany, and only China has lower values.

This development of renewables has not taken place continuously over the last twenty-five years, with the regulatory policies of the different governments having a significant influence. After robust growth between 2000 and 2008 (especially in wind energy), this process was drastically interrupted thereafter, both by the economic crisis and by the suspension by the authorities of the 'renewable premiums' in 2012, which guaranteed a sufficient return on these investments. From 2019 onwards, energy policy substantially boosted the installation of renewable capacity, which has mainly been reflected in photovoltaic solar energy.

5.3 Public Investment and the Role of European Funds

Achieving the energy transition objectives requires a significant investment effort, both private and public, which the PNIEC estimates at €308,000 million in the period 2021–2030. 37% would be allocated to renewable energies, 28% to energy efficiency, and 17% to boosting electrification. Another 17% will be invested in improving networks.

The private sector is expected to make 82% of these investments, so public investment should reach €55 billion in a decade (0.3% of Spanish GDP in 2024).

The context of public investment in Spain until the pandemic was not very favourable for this, with a truly lost decade due to austerity policies (Álvarez and Uxó 2024). However, the Recovery, Transition, and Resilience Plan (PRTR) approved in the Next Generation EU programme framework has been a game changer, with a significant increase in funds earmarked precisely for the energy transition.

In a first phase, the PRTR funds for Spain amounted to € 69 billion in transfers. Subsequently, in October 2023, a second phase, known as the 'addendum' to the PRTR, was approved, adding a further €10 billion in transfers and up to a maximum of €84 billion in loans.

Of this €163 billion, the Ministry for Ecological Transition and the Demographic Challenge (MITECO 2023) estimates that half, almost €83 billion, contributes to climate objectives, articulated around six principal axes. As shown in Table 5.1, the amount of investment planned in the field of energy transition accounts for two thirds of this planned investment, with €25.6 billion earmarked for improving energy efficiency (31%), €14.6 billion for enhancing sustainable mobility (18%), €9.6 billion for renewable energy generation (12%), and €2.14 billion for improving energy storage capacity (3%).

Table 5.1 Climate and environmental investment in the PRTR. *Source: MINECO (2023)*

Axes and objectives			Bill. €	%
Axes linked to ecological transition	Biodiversity and ecosystems	Nature conservation	1.649	2.0
		Water management	9.100	11.0
		Climate change adaptation	0.958	1.2
	Climate change and energy transition	Energy efficiency	25.589	31.0
		Sustainable mobility	14.659	17.8
		Renewable energy	9.569	11.6
		Storage	2.140	2.6
	Pollution, waste management, and circular economy	Pollution reduction	3.014	3.6
		Waste management and circular economy	4.950	6.0
Transversal axes	Green employment		0.378	0.5
	Green research		9.192	11.1
	Sustainable production systems		1.386	1.7
TOTAL			**82.584**	**100**

Data for Figs. 5.1–5.3, Table 5.1 and Table 5.2 are available at https://hdl.handle.net/20.500.12434/074fa1a7

The Strategic Projects for Economic Recovery and Transformation (PERTE, in Spanish) constitute an important novelty in the design of this type of public investment. They are an instrument that can be useful for developing a new active industrial policy following the idea of 'missions' proposed by M. Mazzucato (García Tabuenca et al. 2024). The PERTE are inspired to some extent by the Important Projects of Common European Interest (IPCEI), and they are a new instrument for collaboration between the different public administrations, companies, and research centres in strategic, complex projects with high pulling power and strong multiplier effects. Each PERTE identifies a key area for the future of the economy, which are selected based on several criteria:

- Relevance for growth and employment: sectors that can significantly contribute to economic growth and have a combination of knowledge, experience, resources, and actors that can address market failures or societal challenges, as well as innovative character and added value in R&D&I.

- Quantitative or qualitative importance: sectors where a high technological or financial risk is identified, that allow the integration and growth of small- and medium-sized enterprises, and projects with disruptive and ambitious research and innovation phases followed by a first industrial deployment.

The PERTEs were created in the framework of the PRTR but are intended to be permanent beyond this timeframe. So far, twelve PERTEs have been approved, four of which have environmental objectives ("Green PERTE"):

- Development of the electric and connected vehicle. Its main objective is the creation of the necessary ecosystem and infrastructures for the development and production of electric and connected vehicles to respond to new mobility. The aim is to turn Spain into a European hub for electromobility.

- Renewable energies, renewable hydrogen and storage (ERHA). This project focuses on areas associated with the energy transition where Spain is well positioned (renewable energies, power electronics, storage, and renewable hydrogen) but also aims to strengthen other areas where it has less presence. It has implemented twenty-five measures aimed at developing technology, industrial capacities, new business models and their implementation in the country's productive system; seventeen accompanying, training, and capacity-building measures for the adaptation of industries to new technologies; and a system for monitoring, evaluating, and analyzing the impact on the energy transition value chain. It also includes investments aimed at reinforcing the security and flexibility of the electricity system.

- Industrial decarbonization: within the framework of the objective of climate neutrality by 2050, this PERTE aims to support industry transition towards more environmentally friendly models and processes. It is structured around four measures: aids for decarbonization (electrification of processes and incorporation of hydrogen, integrated energy management of industrial processes, reduction in the use of natural resources or carbon capture); aids to companies participating in the IPCEI on the industrial chain of hydrogen from renewable sources; study of a fund to support contracts for carbon differences and implementation of a pilot project; and support for the development of new highly efficient and decarbonized manufacturing installations that use the best decarbonization technology in their sectors.

- Circular economy: in this case, the aim is to contribute to a sustainable economy that is more efficient in the use of resources and generates less waste. It is also an opportunity to promote new niches of activity and employment (recycling or repair, for example). It includes actions in key sectors (textiles, plastics, and capital goods for the renewable energy industry) and other transversal actions to promote the circular economy in companies.

The 12 PERTE were initially endowed with €14 billion, representing 20% of all transfers included in the first phase of the PRTR. Subsequently, the €10.3 billion transfers included in the addendum and €17 billion of the loans were used to reinforce the PERTE. Therefore, their financing reached €41.2 billion (25% of the total investment linked to the PRTR), divided between transfers by €24.5 billion (31% of the total) and loans by €16.7 billion (20% of the total).

As shown in Table 5.2, the "Green PERTE" are endowed with €16.179 billion in transfers, representing 66% of the total transfers allocated to the PERTEs, and €2.7 billion in loans (16% of the loans allocated to the PERTEs). Another €2 billion are also available for loans to businesses and households related to the ecological transition projects (ICO-Green line). Considering the private investment expected to be mobilized around these Green PERTE, the final investment figure would be €53.12 billion.

Table 5.2 Public investment in Green PERTE (billions euros). *Source:* PRTR. *Note:* * = Chip (Microelectronics and semiconductors), Advanced healthcare, Agrifood supply chain, New language economy, Digitization of the water cycle, Social and care economy, Aerospace industry, Shipbuilding industry.

PERTE	Transfers, 1st phase	Transfers, addendum	Loans, addendum	RePower	Total
Development of the electric vehicle	2.870	0.250	1.000		4.120
Renewable energy, hydrogen, and storage	6.600	1.557		2.640	10.797
Industrial decarbonization	0.450	1.020	1.700		3.170
Circular economy	0.192	0.600			0.792
Other PERTE*	4.093	4.225	13.986		22.304
Total	**14.205**	**7.652**	**16.686**	**2.640**	**41.183**

Data for Figs. 5.1–5.3, Table 5.1 and Table 5.2 are available at https://hdl.handle.net/20.500.12434/074fa1a7

A fundamental issue that has generated some doubts in the first years of the PRTR is the capacity to quickly implement such a large volume of funds due to limitations associated with the capacity of public administrations to manage them or the absorption capacity of the economic sectors involved.

The most recent data (up to January 2025, provided by Hidalgo, Galindo, and Martínez 2025) show that, of the funds committed up to that date, 94% had already been tendered, and 61% had been awarded to specific projects. In the case of the Green PERTE, this execution level seems somewhat higher. According to official data, calls for tenders already resolved (or being close to) reach an amount equivalent to €13,456 million, 74% of the planned public investments. The highest execution percentages are recorded for the electric vehicle PERTE (93%) and renewable energies (78%), while the decarbonization of industry has a very low execution level (25%).

5.4 Reducing Electricity Prices as a New Strategy to Increase Competitiveness and Boost Re-industrialization in Spain

As we have said, the energy transition is seen in Spain as an opportunity with important economic and environmental effects.

For example, Pollin, Chakraborty, and Garrett-Peltier (2015) presented a decade ago a clean energy investment programme in Spain to, in their own words, "making three major contributions to advancing broadly-shared well-being in Spain: 1) Producing dramatic reductions in carbon dioxide emissions generated within the Spanish economy; 2) Dramatically reducing Spain's current level of oil import dependency; and 3) Generating hundreds of thousands of new jobs throughout the Spanish economy".

The PNIEC also estimates the economic effects expected from its implementation. First of all, they take the form of an increase in GDP and employment, derived directly from the investments to be made, but also from other indirect effects, such as energy savings (which frees up resources for other types of expenditure)[6] and the shift of part of the expenditure associated with energy imports towards the domestic renewables sector. Compared to a baseline scenario (without PNIEC), GDP would increase by 3.2% and employment by 2.8% in 2030.

The combination of increased energy efficiency, more installed renewable capacity, and electrification of sectors such as transport, construction, and parts of industry will reduce energy imports. This not only strengthens strategic autonomy and security of supply but also contributes to reducing the balance of goods deficit and energy dependence. In particular, the PNIEC estimates that this will be reduced to 50% by 2030 (the average in recent years has been 72%). In fact, the volume of crude oil imports at the end of 2024 was 5% lower than it was in 2019, before the pandemic, and the volume of gas imports was 20% lower.[7]

Related to this, one of the main opportunities that the energy transition can bring for Spain is to turn lower electricity prices into an advantage for its domestic industry's competitiveness and attract investment.

Overall, this is a key issue for the future of European industry. Heussaff (2024) points out that the European economy has a competitiveness problem stemming from the higher price it must pay for its energy, mainly because of its dependence

---

6   In 2019, household energy expenditure accounted for 7.8% of household income, but with the PNIEC measures it is expected to fall to 5.7% by the end of the decade.

7   See https://www.cores.es/es/estadisticas

on imported fossil fuels (two thirds of its energy consumption in 2022 depended on these foreign purchases). According to his data, in 2024, the wholesale price of gas was almost five times higher in the EU than in the US, and the price of electricity for European industry was two and a half times higher than in the US.

With these figures, it is reasonable to see the energy transition in Europe as an opportunity to improve its industry's competitiveness, and this is especially relevant for a country with Spain's conditions.

The influence of the growing weight of renewables on electricity prices is determined by the marginal pricing mechanism ("merit order mechanism"). Technologies with the lowest marginal costs (renewables) are the ones that cover demand first. However, the price of all the electricity consumed is set by the most expensive technologies needed to fully satisfy demand. In this context, the increase in electricity generation capacity with solar and wind installations, with lower production costs, affects prices in two ways. Firstly, their presence in the market increases competition and puts downward pressure on the offers of other more expensive technologies; secondly, when the supply of electricity from renewable sources increases sufficiently, it can cover the entire demand for more hours per day and fix the price.

The investment required for installing solar panels and windmills has been substantially reduced in recent years, making them more competitive than traditional technologies. Producing electricity today with renewable energies, including the cost of this investment, is substantially cheaper. However, it should be noted that increasing the capacity to produce electricity with renewable sources also increases other fixed costs, such as batteries, grid extension, or maintaining sufficient reserve capacity. As Gasparella et al. (2023) point out, these investments are necessary to prevent dependence on weather conditions from becoming a source of supply-demand imbalances and grid instability: "The growing share of renewable electricity with low marginal costs will exert an increasing downward pressure on wholesale electricity prices. [...] However, rising variable renewable generation will expose market prices to intermittent production profiles and climate volatility, which will increase market instability if not counterbalanced by adequate growth in electricity storage, system flexibility and cross-border interconnectivity".

These authors model the evolution of electricity prices in Europe between 2022 and 2030, taking into account all these effects, and conclude that, indeed, "2030 simulated wholesale electricity prices present, on average, lower values compared to 2022 levels due to lower expected gas prices and the rising share of renewable energy sources in the EU generation mix" and add that "this scenario is likely to evolve in later years when renewable generation will start to exceed total EU demand for multiple hours per day, pushing average electricity prices to lower values. The combination of a higher renewable energy share paired with increasing storage and flexibility resources is expected to bring price stability and overall reductions in electricity costs in the following decade".

Cevik and Ninomiya (2022), using panel data from twenty-four European countries between 2014 and 2021, also agree that there is good reason to believe that the price of electricity will fall with increased penetration of renewables. Specifically, their results are that, in the EU as a whole, for every point by which the share of renewables in electricity production increases, the price reduces by 0.6 points on average. However, this effect does not occur linearly: the more the share of renewables increases, the greater the effect on prices because the hours in which this technology determines the price increase more than proportionally.

In the case of Spain, Cubero et al. (2025) use a two-stage model to analyze the effect of the expansion of renewable electricity generation on electricity prices. First, they estimate the relationship between electricity prices and the factors that traditionally determine them. In their case, they use the international price of gas, the price of CO_2 emission rights, and the Tax on Electricity Production. The interest in this first stage is to obtain the residuals of this regression to see in a second stage to what extent this part, not explained by the traditional factors, is related to the share of renewables in electricity generation.

Their results confirm that the increase in renewables reduces the price of electricity. On average, each percentage point increase in their share in the technologies producing electricity reduces its price by 0.74 percentage points. Furthermore, this influence is non-linear. The number of hours in which renewable energies set the market price begins to grow when their share reaches 60%. Between 60% and 80%, however, the predominant effect on prices occurs through increased competition between technologies, forcing the more expensive ones to lower their prices. Once 80% is reached, according to this model, the effect of renewables on prices is mainly due to their ability to set the market price more frequently.

Transferring their results to the evolution of renewables in Spain, he finds that the increase in renewable energies from 45% to 60% between 2021 and 2023 has reduced the wholesale price of electricity by 12.5%. However, the effect of the increase to 65% in 2024 has had a proportionally much larger additional effect, reducing the price by another 7.5% in the last year. In total, the cumulative reduction would already be 20%. Finally, if the PNIEC targets are met in 2030 (a further 15 percentage points increase in the share of renewables), an additional 20% reduction in electricity prices in Spain could be expected.

Quintana (2024) performs a similar exercise, confirming that "increasing the share of renewables in electricity generation could have a profound impact on price dynamics in wholesale electricity markets". To measure this, he also estimates a two-stage model.

According to their results, if renewables' weight had remained at the same level as in 2019, prices would have been 25% higher in 2023 and almost 40% higher in 2024. With the PNIEC targets for 2030, an additional reduction of 50% (over 2024 prices) could take place. In short, this author concludes that "in addition to contributing to the green transition, renewable energies play a key role in bringing down wholesale electricity prices and will foreseeably become even more important in this respect in the future".

Therefore, expanding renewables can lead to lower and more stable electricity prices and a more secure supply, which can be an important element of competitiveness for the economy as a whole. Moreover, a new regulation of the marginal pricing mechanism to prevent the most expensive technology from systematically setting the remuneration of all the other technologies would bring energy prices down even faster. This was in fact temporarily done in Spain during the 2022 energy crisis, with the so-called "Iberian exception", and allowed prices in the Iberian wholesale electricity market to be up to three times lower than in the rest of the EU markets.

In fact, wholesale electricity prices in Spain have already gone from higher than the European average to below. Spanish households and companies have started to enjoy lower electricity prices, as shown in Figure 5.2 and Figure 5.3. For example, in the case of industry, the price of electricity is currently 20% lower than the European average, when in the previous expansionary phase (2014-2019), it was 25% higher.

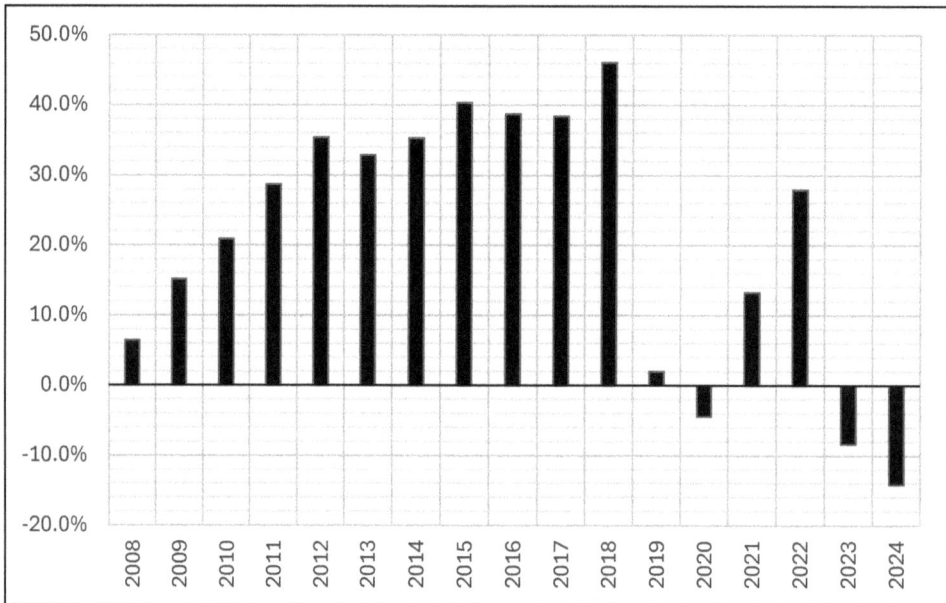

Fig. 5.2 Households electricity prices (Spain vs EU). Excluding taxes and levies. *Source:* Eurostat.

Data for Figs. 5.1–5.3, Table 5.1 and Table 5.2 are available at https://hdl.handle.net/20.500.12434/074fa1a7

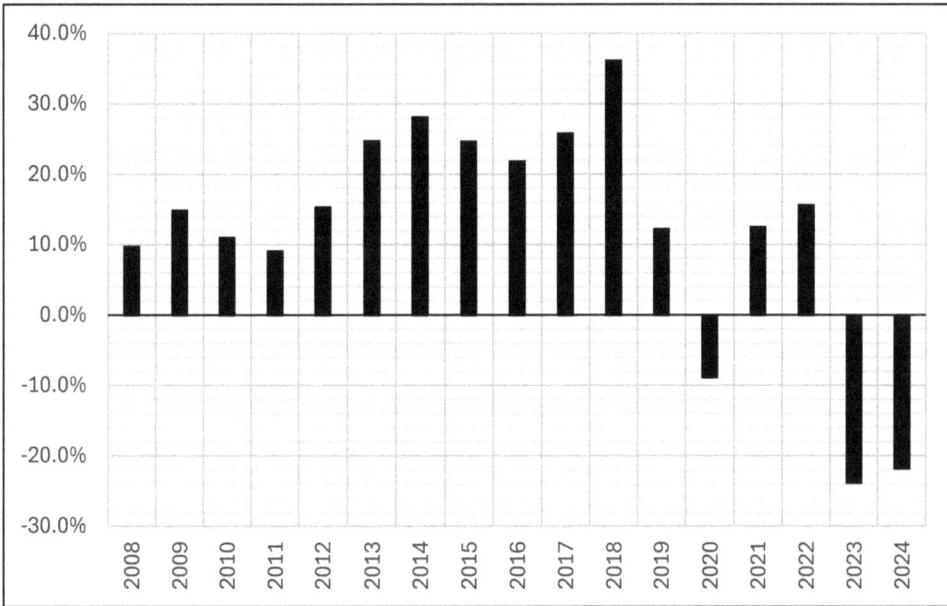

Fig. 5.3 Industrial electricity prices (Spain vs EU). Excluding taxes and levies. *Source:* Eurostat.

Data for Figs. 5.1–5.3, Table 5.1 and Table 5.2 are
available at https://hdl.handle.net/20.500.12434/074fa1a7

This change is due both to the reduced exposure to natural gas from Russia and
to Spain's competitive advantages in electricity generation with solar and wind
technology. As the latter derive mainly from favourable climatic and geographic
conditions (more extended hours of sunshine and wind, as well as large extensions
of land with low population density that facilitate their installation), they can become
structural if accompanied by the necessary investments.

Heymann (2025) estimates the effects of a change in electricity prices on the growth
of manufacturing value added and finds that a 10-cent increase in the price per kWh
reduces this growth by 2.0 to 2.7 pp. In other words, energy prices have a significant
influence on manufacturing performance. Transferring this to Spain's price differences
with the eurozone, the higher prices recorded up to 2018 would have meant a negative
differential in the growth of manufacturing in Spain of 0.6 points, and the lower prices
in 2024 had a positive differential effect of 1 percentage point. This would explain an
important part of the differences observed in the evolution of manufacturing in both
zones over the last two decades.

5.5 Conclusions

Regarding energy transition, Spain is one of the European countries that has set the most ambitious goals. Its natural conditions position it as an international leader in renewable energy, representing an opportunity for the transformation of its economy. In particular, the possibility of producing cheap and safe energy can be the basis of a strategy to relaunch its competitiveness and reindustrialize its economy. This could happen in three ways: lowering the costs of its current industry, attracting industrial investments that choose to locate in Spain to benefit from this advantage, and boosting the value chain associated with renewables (currently, it already can produce 90% of wind and 60% of solar equipment).

This requires substantial investment (private and public) and appropriate regulation. The PRTR and the Green PERTEs are driving this process within the framework of a new industrial policy. The main question, however, is whether this investment effort will be sustained once these funds are no longer received, especially in a context marked by the return of fiscal rules and pressure to increase security spending.

References

Álvarez, I., and J. Uxó (2024) "Public Investment and Structural Transformation in Spain", in F. Cerniglia and F. Saraceno (eds), *Investing in the Structural Transformation—2024 European Public Investment Outlook*. Cambridge, UK: Open Book Publishers, pp. 91–112, https://doi.org/10.11647/OBP.0434.06

Cevik, S., and K. Ninomiya (2022) "Chasing the Sun and Catching the Wind: Energy Transition and Electricity Prices in Europe", *IMF Working Paper*, WP/22/220.

Cubero, J. J., P. Más, R. Ortiz, and P. Ruíz (2025) *Reaping the Benefits of Renewable Energy in the Spanish Economy*. Madrid: BBVA.

García-Tabuenca, A., M. Gálvez del Castillo, and J. C. Díez (2024) *Reindustrialización y PERTE en España. Industria y política industrial en la transición verde*. Madrid: Catarata.

Gasparella, A., D. Koolen, and A. Zucker (2023) "The Merit Order and Price-Setting Dynamics in European Electricity Markets", *Science for Policy Brief*, Joint Research Centre, European Commission, https://publications.jrc.ec.europa.eu/repository/handle/JRC134300

Heussaff, C. (2024) "Decarbonising for Competitiveness: Four Ways to Reduce European Energy Prices", *Policy Brief* 32, https://www.bruegel.org/sites/default/files/2024-12/PB%2032%202024_0.pdf

Hidalgo, M., J. Galindo, and J. Martínez (2025) "Evolución de los Fondos NextGen EU en España", *EsadeEcPol Brief* 48, https://www.esade.edu/ecpol/es/publicaciones/nextgeneu-tracker-evolucion-de-los-fondos-nextgen-eu-en-espana/

IRENA (2024) *Renewable Power Generation Costs in 2023*. Abu Dabhi: IRENA, https://www.irena.org/-/media/Files/IRENA/Agency/Publication/2024/Sep/IRENA_Renewable_power_generation_costs_in_2023.pdf

MITECO (2023) *Transición Ecológica en el Plan de Recuperación, Transformación y Resiliencia. Informe de ejecución*, https://www.prtr.miteco.gob.es/content/dam/prtr/es/obligaciones-medioambientales/I%20Informe%20de%20Transici%C3%B3n%20Ecol%C3%B3gica%20en%20el%20PRTR.pdf

MITECO (2024): *Plan Nacional Integrado de Energía y Clima, 2023-2030. España*, https://www.miteco.gob.es/es/energia/estrategia-normativa/pniec-23-30.html

Pollin, R., S. Chakraborty, and H. Garrett-Peltier (2015) "An Egalitarian Clean Energy Investment Program for Spain", *PERI Working Papers Series* 390, https://peri.umass.edu/wp-content/uploads/2025/01/WP390.pdf

Quintana, J. (2024) "The Impact of Renewable Energies on Wholesale Electricity Prices", *Economic Bulletin* 2024/Q3, https://www.bde.es/f/webbe/SES/Secciones/Publicaciones/InformesBoletinesRevistas/BoletinEconomico/24/T3/Files/be2403-art09e.pdf

6. Tackling the Drawbacks of Past and Current EU Energy Transition Policies: The Need for a Cooperative, Mission-oriented Industrial Strategy

Francesco Gracceva[1] and Daniela Palma[2]

This chapter examines the main challenges of the EU's energy transition. It first provides a comprehensive assessment of the EU's performance against the objectives of the Energy Union, the EU's most explicit attempt to address the so-called energy trilemma. Based on a set of indicators, structured around the five dimensions of the Energy Union, the analysis shows that the EU's energy system is today in a weaker position than ten or even five years ago. The chapter then evaluates whether the EU's current strategy can serve as an effective development policy, capable of revitalizing the European economy and contributing to global decarbonization. The growing emphasis on strategic autonomy—amid rising geopolitical tensions—reflects a view of global interdependence as conflictual rather than cooperative. This inward-looking stance risks undermining the international cooperation essential for a successful energy transition, while the narrow solution space of the energy trilemma is further constrained by Rodrik's new climate trilemma. It also reflects what Krugman termed the "competitiveness obsession", overlooking trade-offs between domestic production and economic efficiency, and failing to address Europe's industrial weaknesses. As an alternative, the chapter advances a "cooperative mission-oriented" strategy: a new model of productive globalization based on collaboration rather than competition. Its dual objectives are to reduce global inequality and combat climate change, through industrial policies that promote innovation without resorting to protectionism, and through international cooperation that can foster the global development of green technologies and services and expand the clean economy. Such a strategy could improve allocative efficiency while ensuring Europe secures a fair share of the benefits.

---

1   ENEA—Agenzia nazionale per le nuove tecnologie, l'energia e lo sviluppo sostenibile.
2   ENEA—Agenzia nazionale per le nuove tecnologie, l'energia e lo sviluppo sostenibile.

https://doi.org/10.11647/OBP.0499.06

6.1 Introduction

Since the beginning of the century, the European Union's energy policy has been shaped by the overall objective of balancing the goals of sustainable energy use, competitiveness and security of supply (EC 2000; EC 2006; EC 2025), that is by the triple challenge that has been framed as the "energy trilemma" (WEC 2010; IEA 2023). However, more than focusing on the potential tensions that can arise between the three goals—as progress in one area can come at the expense of another—the energy strategy adopted by EU policymakers to address this trilemma has been rooted in the belief that the transition to a low-carbon economy not only "ensures competitive and affordable energy for all consumers" (EC 2014), but is even "necessary in order to provide jobs, growth and investment opportunities for present and future generations of Europeans". Moreover, "if the EU does not maintain and exploit its first mover advantage when fostering renewable energy, energy efficiency and competing on the development of other low carbon technology markets globally, other regions will" (EC 2016).

Over time this vision has been progressively reinforced. Europe has set out the ambition to lead the way to climate neutrality (EC 2018) and, with the launch of the Green Deal (EC 2019), committed to becoming the world's first climate-neutral continent by 2050, while at the same time achieving the objectives of "boosting the economy, improving people's health and quality of life, caring for nature, and leaving no one behind".

Then, in just a few years the EU has faced two major global shocks—the COVID-19 pandemic and the war in Ukraine—that have placed unprecedented strain on its economic and energy systems: in 2020, the Eurozone's GDP contracted by 6% and energy consumption fell by 9%; in 2022, gas and electricity prices surged to five times their long-term averages (on annual basis). In response, European policymakers further reinforced their strategy to revive economic growth by advancing environmental sustainability: the updated EU Nationally Determined Contribution (NDC), submitted in December 2020 to the UNFCCC, raised its 2030 emissions reduction target from -40% to "at least -55%" (compared to 1990 levels); then, in 2022, the REPowerEU package introduced new targets for renewable energy sources (RES) and energy efficiency, effectively setting the EU on a trajectory toward a 2030 emissions reduction exceeding 57% relative to 1990. The driving idea behind this acceleration is that the sequence of the two unprecedented crises can act as opportunities to fast-track the decarbonization of the European economy, because the interaction between external shocks and internal policy responses can lead not merely to temporary adjustments, but to deep, structural transformations.

In short, the issue of energy transition has acquired new and more complex centrality, becoming the cornerstone of the path Europe must follow—not only to revive an economy increasingly marked by a long-term trend of stagnation, but also to reshape its development model. The Green Deal is no longer just a climate policy—it has become the EU's *de facto* growth strategy.

This chapter aims to explore Europe's energy transition in depth, by addressing three key questions:

- What is the current state of the EU's transition, and how effective has the strategy been so far?

- Can this strategic vision truly serve as a development policy capable of revitalizing the European economy?

- To what extent does the EU's recent shift toward strategic autonomy in critical clean energy technologies and materials represent a viable strategy for ensuring a successful transition? And can it offer an effective response to rising geopolitical tensions between advanced and emerging economies in an increasingly fragmented and multipolar global order?

6.2 A Short, Comprehensive Assessment of the EU Energy Transition So Far

As a result of the two crises of 2020 and 2022, by the middle of 2025 the European energy system is significantly more decarbonized and less energy-intensive than it was in 2019: CO_2 emissions in the Eurozone are estimated to have fallen by 16%, and by more than 30% compared to 1990 levels; primary energy consumption is down by around 12% (reaching the lowest level recorded since the mid-1980s). Notably, this decarbonization has occurred despite a net increase in GDP, which is now over 3 percentage points above its 2019 level.

However, a closer look reveals that the recent trajectory of the energy system has been shaped not only by "virtuous" structural transformations, but also by temporary or non-structural factors. The structural component of the reductions in energy use and emissions is largely concentrated in electricity generation. Here, the shift from coal and natural gas to renewables has produced a twofold benefit: it has lowered the carbon intensity of electricity and, by eliminating the conversion losses typical of fossil-fuel-based thermal generation, has also reduced primary energy consumption. The discrepancy between the drop in primary energy use (−12%) and final energy use (−6%) over the past five years suggests that changes in power generation alone account for roughly half of the decline in primary energy demand.

In contrast, the much smaller decrease in energy consumption across end-use sectors—that is industry, transport, residential, and services—highlights the rigidity within these areas of the energy system. Two key temporary or non-structural factors help explain this limited decline: first, the mild winters of the past three years, which sharply reduced gas demand for heating; and second, the unprecedented high levels of gas and electricity prices, which dampened energy consumption both directly and through their recessionary effects, particularly on energy-intensive industries.

As the Energy Union represents the European Union's most explicit attempt to systematically address the synergies and trade-offs of the so-called energy trilemma,[3] a comprehensive assessment of the EU energy transition can be grounded in the methodology developed by the Commission, designed "to develop a sound, robust monitoring tool that provides a factual snapshot of the situation across the EU" in relation to the Energy Union's objectives. Notably, the availability of reliable, independent, and transparent evaluation methods is crucial to ensure that public policy follows a flexible, adaptive approach grounded in "iterative learning". This entails the continuous adjustment of objectives and instruments as new evidence emerges and observed outcomes are systematically assessed (Rodrik and Stiglitz 2024).

This methodology developed by the Commission is based on a set of indicators structured around five interrelated dimensions: (i) security, solidarity and trust; (ii) a fully integrated internal energy market; (iii) energy efficiency; (iv) climate action and the decarbonization of the economy; and (v) research, innovation and competitiveness. The examination of the temporal evolution of the selected indicators over the period 2015–2025, taking as a starting point the first 2030 EU strategy (EC 2014), highlights a first important general finding: in almost all respects the current position of the European energy system is worse than it was ten or five years ago (Table 6.1). More specifically:

- Achieving the 2030 decarbonization target now requires an average annual CO_2 emissions reduction of approximately 7% between 2025 and 2030, the steepest rate recorded in the entire time series: indeed, until 2021—when the EU raised its 2030 target from -40% to -55% compared to 1990—achieving the goal would have required an average annual reduction of around 2%. Remarkably, even if the -55% target had already been in force ten or five years ago, the implied average annual reduction would have been on the order of 5%, thus still much lower than what is required today.

- A similar acceleration applies to RES: until 2021, achieving the 32.5% target set for 2030 required an average annual increase of around 1%. Today, however, meeting the new target (raised to 42.5%) necessitates an average annual increase of more than 3%.

- In short, even though according to the European Commission (2025) the EU is on track to reach the targets on CO_2 and RES—but provided the full implementation and effectiveness of Member States' existing and additional policies and measures—in both cases the current situation is clearly much more challenging than ten years ago, or even just five years ago.

---

3   Indeed, the stated objective of the Energy Union is to ensure "that European consumers—both households and businesses—have secure, affordable and clean energy" (EC 2015a).

- In terms of final energy consumption, the necessary annual decrease between 2025 and 2030 now exceeds 3%. In this case, the increased gap relative to the past is attributable entirely to the higher level of ambition embedded in the revised target, as the energy consumption projected for 2025 remains below the threshold established by Directive 2018/2002 on energy efficiency.

- Regarding energy security, despite the significant growth in renewable energy production, the overall energy dependence (net imports of all primary sources relative to total consumption) remains slightly higher than ten years ago. However, gas supply has become more diversified, supplier political stability—measured by an OECD indicator—has improved, and substantial European investments in gas storage have enhanced system resilience. Notably, these gas-related indicators are the only ones in the entire set considered that show a clear net improvement compared to a decade ago.

- The trade balance in low-carbon technologies has worsened significantly since 2015, even though 2024 saw a marked narrowing of the deficit. But this reduction was primarily due to a sharp drop in photovoltaic module prices in global markets, not to a substantial change in the volumes of trade.

- Despite targeted policy efforts to mitigate the energy crisis, prices for both households and businesses remain at historically high levels following the peaks reached in 2022.

- Unsurprisingly, energy-intensive industries—such as steel, basic chemicals, paper, and non-metallic minerals—are experiencing a profound crisis. In 2025, their output levels have fallen to their lowest point in three decades, nearly 20% below what they were three years ago. This trend stands in stark contrast to the broader manufacturing sector, which, while still sluggish, has not contracted as severely.

Table 6.1 A comprehensive assessment of the EU energy transition through a set of indicators. *Note:* 2024 and 2025 data are authors' estimations; the 2025 data refer to the first half of the year, calculated on a rolling twelve-month basis.

	2015	2016	2017	2018	2019	2020	2021	2022	2023	2024*	2025**
Decarbonization											
Total CO2 emissions - Mt CO2	3,063	3,073	3,099	3,042	2,907	2,555	2,735	2,737	2,507	2,434	2,430
Total CO2 emissions - CAGR to 2030 target	-2.2%	-2.3%	-2.6%	-2.7%	-2.5%	-1.5%	-2.4%	-6.1%	-5.8%	-6.3%	-7.4%
Share of RES on Final Energy Consumption - %	17.8%	18.0%	18.4%	19.1%	19.9%	22.0%	21.9%	23.1%	24.6%	25.4%	25.7%

	2015	2016	2017	2018	2019	2020	2021	2022	2023	2024*	2025**
Share of RES on Final Energy Consumption - Annual change to reach 2030 target	1.6%	1.8%	1.9%	2.0%	2.1%	2.0%	2.3%	2.4%	2.6%	2.8%	3.4%
Efficiency											
Final Energy Consumption - Mtoe	940	959	971	974	969	891	948	921	894	889	886
Final Energy Consumption - CAGR to reach 2030 target	1.1%	1.0%	1.0%	1.1%	-0.1%	0.7%	0.1%	0.5%	1.0%	-2.5%	-3.0%
Energy security											
Energy dependency - %	55.8%	56.7%	57.9%	58.1%	59.4%	58.0%	57.5%	60.7%	58.5%	57.8%	57.8%
Gas - Political stability of suppliers (IEA index, range 1-7)	4.8	5.2	5.4	5.3	4.5	3.8	3.6	3.5	1.8	2.3	1.9
Trade balance low-carbon technologies - mln €	-	-	-1,693	-4,860	-11,291	-7,263	-15,042	-39,419	-42,196	15.279 prelim.	-
Volatility electricity prices - index	0.163	0.145	0.155	0.127	0.152	0.224	0.172	0.167	0.288	0.433	0.544
Energy markets and energy poverty											
% population unable to keep home adequately warm (%)	9.6	9.0	8.1	7.6	6.9	7.5	6.9	9.3	10.6	9.2	-
Energy prices and competitiveness											
Electricity prices (Eurostat Band IB) - €/MWh	142	138	140	138	147	151	161	218	241	226	225
Gas prices (Eurostat Band I2) - €/GJ	12.2	10.8	10.5	11.1	11.5	11.1	12.7	21.7	25.3	22.4	22.6
Industrial production of energy intensive sectors - index 2021=100	97.7	96.1	100.5	99.6	96.9	91.2	100.0	94.6	83.0	83.1	82.8

Complete version of Table 6.1 available at
https://hdl.handle.net/20.500.12434/2ccf34bc

It is noteworthy that European policymakers have not succeeded in shielding the euro area economy from the negative effects of the energy system's recent evolution—despite having, at times, prioritized economic support and energy security over long-term decarbonization goals. According to the IEA's *Government Energy Spending Tracker*, which monitors OECD government expenditures on "clean energy investment" and "affordability measures", Europe's spending was heavily concentrated on making energy more affordable. This stands in sharp contrast to the approaches of the world's two other major economies, the United States and China, which channeled the bulk of their resources into low-carbon technology investments (Fig. 6.1).

These data reveal the largely defensive nature of the EU's policy response during the twin crises. Policy efforts were focused primarily on cushioning the immediate impact of surging energy prices caused by macroeconomic and geopolitical turmoil, rather than on promoting structural transformations in energy demand or industrial production systems. Given the limited effectiveness of EU measures to curb energy prices (see Table 6.1), reductions in energy consumption were mainly due to price pressures—more than to efficiency improvements—and were largely the result of lower production levels, posing a serious risk to the competitiveness of Europe's industrial sector, particularly the more energy intensive industries.

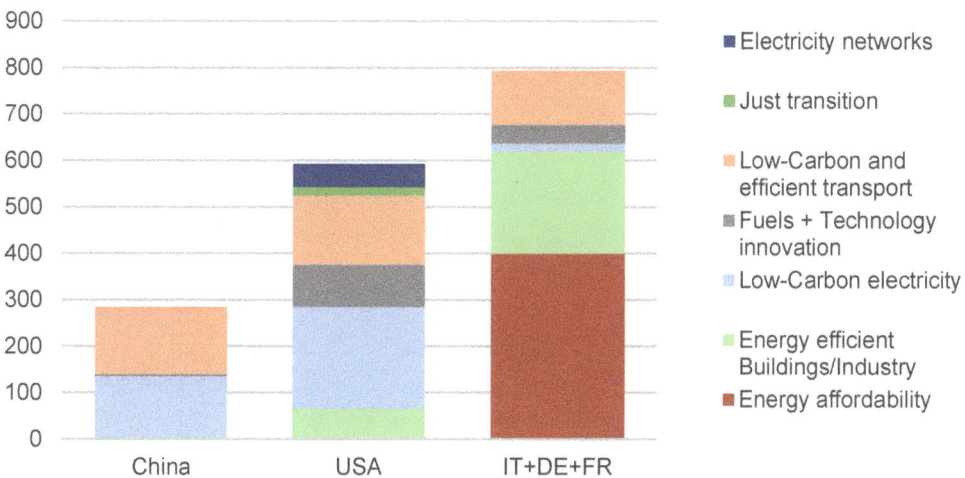

Fig. 6.1 Government expenditures for "clean energy investment support" and "consumer energy affordability measures"—China, USA and three main European countries (Germany, Italy, France), 2018–2024 (billion $). *Source:* IEA.

Data for Fig. 6.1 are available at
https://hdl.handle.net/20.500.12434/7f849ee4

6.3 Recent Revisions in the EU's Green Strategy Approach

In recent years, against the background of increasing geopolitical tensions, policy strategies around the world have been marked by what has been described as a move from universalism to neo-mercantilism and the "abandonment of neoliberal globalization", through rising tariffs, formation of trade blocs, restrictions on technology transfer and the use of economic coercion—driven both by geostrategic competition and the adverse effects of the second wave of globalization on the Western middle class (Milanovic 2024).

In Europe, the fading of "the previous global paradigm"—namely, the erosion of "three external conditions in trade, energy, and defence that supported Europe's growth after the Cold War" (Draghi 2024), has multiplied the concerns over the vulnerability of the industrial system, with the fear of de-industrialization and of missing out on the growth opportunities of cleantech manufacturing. Even more dramatically, the underlining premise is that "turning brown jobs into green jobs represents an essential condition for Europe to maintain and strengthen its socioeconomic model—and welfare state—while meeting its decarbonisation goals" (Tagliapietra et al. 2023).

In this context, industrial policy has gained momentum, particularly in advanced economies, driven by concerns on competitiveness, climate mitigation, supply chain resilience, geopolitical and national security considerations (Ilyina et al. 2024). A renewed approach to industrial policy aims to address the dual challenge of strengthening economic competitiveness while enhancing the resilience and autonomy of the productive supply chain and a substantial regain of "technological sovereignty". Indeed, Europe's economic policy has undergone a significant and gradual shift, marked by a growing emphasis on the concept of strategic autonomy. Whereas strategic autonomy was originally restricted to defence matters, it is now explicitly mentioned in other sectors and has increasingly become a central element of the current green industrial strategy.[4] Since 2020, as consequence of the COVID-19 pandemic, the US IRA, the war in Ukraine, and growing geopolitical tensions, an increasing number of EU policy documents explicitly set a strategic autonomy objective. However, strategic autonomy is an evolving and ambiguous concept, which can be interpreted in different ways and is often used interchangeably with terms like sovereignty and independence. Even though the concept of *open* strategic autonomy is often advocated, there is clearly inherent tension between the twin aims of strategic autonomy and preserving an open economy. Open strategic autonomy is actually a "balancing act on a spectrum ranging

---

4   The Green Deal communication (2019) still didn't include any mention of the term "autonomy", let alone of "strategic autonomy", while access to resources—in particular, critical raw materials—was seen as a security of supply issue, to be addressed "by diversifying supply", and the EU "will work to facilitate trade in environmental goods and services, in bilateral and multilateral forums, and in supporting open and attractive EU and global markets for sustainable products. It will work with global partners to ensure the EU's resource security and reliable access to strategic raw materials" (EC 2019a).

from absolute self-sufficiency or autarky to full dependence" (Paleari 2024), therefore much depends on its actual operationalization.

It seems that European policymakers have increasingly adopted the view that global interdependence is now a source of conflict, not harmony (Youngs 2021). Indeed the Net-Zero Industry Act (NZIA), and the Critical Raw Materials Act (CRMA), the two main legal instruments of the Green Deal Industrial Plan (2023), which aims to boost the EU's clean-tech industry and strengthen its competitiveness in the global green transition, set fixed rigid targets for the domestic production of a set of "critical" net-zero technologies—solar PV and solar thermal, onshore and offshore wind, battery/storage, heat pumps, geothermal, electrolyzers and fuel cells, sustainable biogas/biomethane, carbon capture and storage, grid technologies, nuclear—as well as raw materials. The launch of the "Competitiveness Compass" in January 2025 has further reinforced this strategic direction.

But this increased emphasis on strategic autonomy, amid a landscape of parceled regionalism, rising nationalism, and the primacy of domestic political interest and so-called security concerns (Milanovic 2025), poses a range of critical challenges, especially in a global economy increasingly viewed as a zero-sum game.

6.3.1 The Global Dimension Deficiency

The inward-looking approach characterizing the EU strategy and the lack of attention paid to the global dimension of decarbonization pose an existential threat to the viability of the global energy transition. Indeed, a wide literature underlines that robust international cooperation, including the transfer of technology, is a key prerequisite for a successful global energy transition (Rodrik 2024), while on the contrary strategic autonomy implies a range of "risks and trade-offs, such as further fragilizing multilateralism, higher barriers for cross-border trade and investment (with negative impacts especially on developing countries)" (Paleari 2024). Protectionism policies undermine the current trading system and cross-border investment, particularly in globalized supply chains, with "the effect of slowing down globalization, increasing the cost of deployment of clean technologies, dampening technological cooperation and limiting the diffusion of innovation and knowledge spillovers" (Fattouh 2025, p. 7).

Moreover, the already challenging energy trilemma (see above) risks being intertwined with the new climate trilemma identified by Rodrik (Fig. 6.2), which highlights the potential trade-offs between the three objectives of global decarbonization, global poverty reduction, and supporting the middle class in advanced economies (Rodrik 2024). In particular, policies in more industrialized countries aimed at protecting the middle class—such as protectionist measures and the restructuring of global value chains through reshoring and friendshoring (Guerrieri and Padoan 2024), even in the absence of comparative advantages—may be perceived by emerging economies as "an assault on their development prospects" (Rodrik 2024).

Yet, achieving climate neutrality on a worldwide scale is clearly impossible without their active cooperation.

In short, the already narrow solution space of the energy trilemma is further constrained by the complex challenge of resolving the climate trilemma.

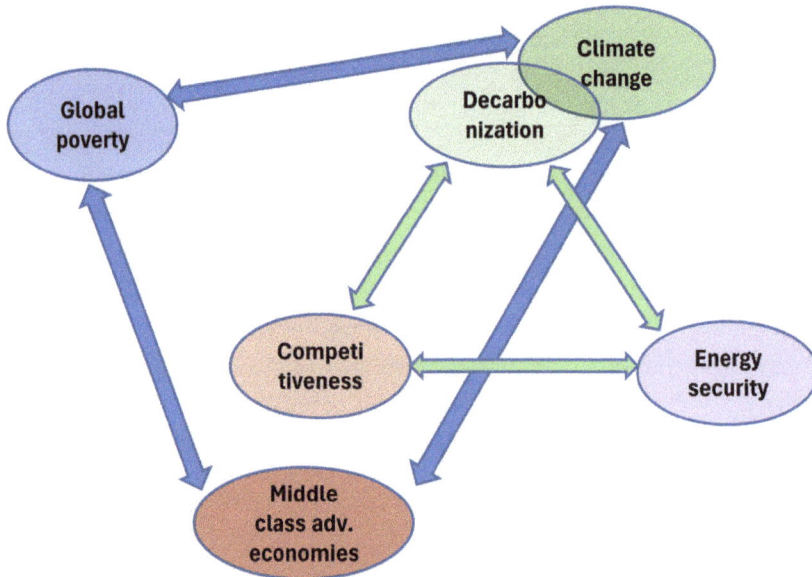

Fig. 6.2 Two intertwined trilemmas: energy and Rodrik's climate trilemma. *Source:* own graphic elaboration of the concept of climate trilemma by Rodrik (2024).

A range of empirical studies provide further support for this conclusion:

- According to the IEA (2024), trade in clean energy technologies has expanded quickly over the last ten years, helping to drive the energy transition. Without trade, much of today's deployment of clean technologies would not be possible.

- According to Wood Mackenzie, excluding Chinese-made clean-tech products from global markets could result in a 20% increase in capital expenditure between 2023 and 2050, adding an additional $6 trillion to the overall cost of the global energy transition. In short, "a successful net zero global economy will only be possible through international collaboration, pragmatism, and innovation between US, Europe, China and others. This will be essential to achieve the scale required at an optimum cost and value for all" (McCarthy 2024).

- According to an IMF scenario analysis (Alvarez et al. 2023), fragmentation in commodity markets could hinder the global energy transition. In a hypothetical scenario where trade of critical minerals between blocs is disrupted, investment in renewable energy and electric vehicles could fall by as much as 30% by 2030, compared to a more integrated global market.

This could slow progress toward mitigation of climate change, because demand for minerals is expected to rise sharply in the coming years, while economically viable deposits are concentrated in a limited number of countries. Trade becomes essential to guarantee access to these resources.

6.3.2 The Competitiveness Obsession

Prioritizing *strategic autonomy* in green technologies as the foundation of the transition is based on the premise that a country's economic success is primarily determined by its ability to compete effectively in the global market. Indeed, the president of the European Commission presented the Competitiveness Compass stating that "Europe has everything to succeed in the race to the top. But [...] we must fix our weaknesses to regain competitiveness" (EC 2025a).

However, as argued by Nobel Prize winner Paul Krugman (1994), applying the concept of competitiveness to nations is misleading and potentially harmful, because a country's prosperity is not determined by its ability to "win" against other countries in international markets, but primarily by the growth of its internal productivity. An obsession with competitiveness can drive misguided economic policies, such as protectionism or ineffective investments in so-called "strategic" sectors, while masking underlying domestic economic issues. A clear example is Europe's export-led growth model over recent decades, which relied on the competitiveness of specific manufacturing sectors achieved through cost-cutting, wage restraint, and the suppression of domestic demand (Saraceno 2025). By contrast, EU underinvested in the technological and manufacturing aspects of the transition, letting innovation scale in the US and manufacturing expertise and capacity develop in China.

Now, the main EU legal instrument to promote clean-tech manufacturing—the Net-Zero Industry Act—implements strategic autonomy by setting a uniform and rigid self-sufficiency benchmark: a 40% domestic production target across all selected technologies, without any evaluation of the costs involved compared to cheaper imports. At least for some technologies, this target is a major increase from current levels: in the case of solar PV, investments to increase EU manufacturing would need to be fifteen times higher than those projected under currently stated policies, even though "EU solar PV production supply chain remains less competitive than those in most other regions" (IEA 2024a, p. 217). And similar conclusions apply to batteries. Moreover, it is worth noting that for both solar PV and batteries, the levelized cost of production depends significantly on whether components are produced domestically or imported, with domestically manufactured PV components costing 25% to 100% more than those imported from China.

Far from being a solution to competitiveness problems, boosting internal production of clean technologies, without considering international comparative advantages, and disregarding the dividends of trade, risks imposing costs to the EU industry.

The objective of strategic autonomy—to reduce the risk of trade dependencies on unreliable partners or potential adversaries—inevitably involves a trade-off with the goals of an economically efficient transition and even the competitiveness of the EU industry. Contrary to the implicit assumption that one policy can kill two birds with one stone, this situation actually illustrates the "Tinbergen Rule": a single policy instrument can effectively address only one objective, which in the case of NZIA is strategic autonomy, but there is no guarantee that it doesn't have unintended negative consequences on other goals, which require instead a separate, dedicated policy tool.

Moreover, other criticisms have focused on the apparent arbitrariness of the criteria set out in the NZIA for selecting the set of strategic net-zero technologies, which are described as the result of a "vertical, top-down, picking winners type of industrial policy" (Veugelers et al. 2024, p. 15), lacking proper evaluation of the projects to be supported and offering a limited scope for exploiting relevant technological opportunities.

A further major weakness of the current approach lies in the lack of adequate EU funding instruments and financial resources, leading to growing technological disparities between countries and, consequently, to a loss of innovation synergies at the EU scale (D'Amato et al. 2024). Due to the EU's limited budgetary capacity, national state aid has become increasingly pivotal in driving investment in net-zero technologies and, owing to the fiscal discipline imposed by the Stability and Growth Pact, the scope for such interventions has largely depended on the available fiscal space at the country level, giving greater leeway to Member States with healthier public finances. As a consequence, Europe remains far "from having a full-fledged EU integrated green industrial policy", as "it has at best a multitude of green industrial policy initiatives at EU level, adding to the multitude of policy initiatives at Member State or regional level [...] generally not coordinated – if not even conflicting" (Veugelers et al. 2024, p. 7).

6.3.3 Structural Weaknesses

A thorough reappraisal of the impact of recent energy price shocks on the European manufacturing system could provide deeper insights into the more structural weaknesses inherent in the current approach to green industrial policy. The energy crisis—closely linked with rising geopolitical tensions—has in fact brought to light significant flaws in European competitiveness, notably the prominence of energy-intensive sectors and, conversely, the lack of adequate production capacity in science-driven industries, whose development—particularly in digital and communication technologies—has played a decisive role in driving growth in global manufacturing markets. In this respect, low energy import costs have long prevented the EU industry from suffering heavy losses in competitiveness despite delays in adapting production structures to major technological shifts.

Thus, prioritizing "strategic autonomy" in green technologies fails to adequately address the systemic weaknesses of the European innovation ecosystem, while the industrial base continues to suffer from a persistent technological gap that is likely to widen due to growing disparities between core and peripheral countries. In this context, even calling for improved coordination between national and EU-level industrial policies should be seen as part of a broader, integrated innovation strategy that accounts for sectoral disparities across EU regions while aiming for carbon neutrality and energy security.

In the same vein, recent calls for increased public investment appear questionable unless clearly aimed at a structural transformation of the production system consistent with decarbonization goals. This issue has gained prominence following the publication of the Draghi report, which, while rightly drawing attention to the central role of public investment in addressing Europe's innovation challenges and enhancing competitiveness, also raises several concerns regarding the design of industrial policies for the energy transition, identified as a top priority in the document. Critics argue the report takes an overly optimistic view of the competitive advantage the EU could derive from innovation in key clean energy technologies—fields where China already leads—and overlooks the burden of high energy costs for energy-intensive industries, offering only support measures in response (Furfari 2024; Zachmann 2024). In this light, the acceleration of decarbonization, which the report assumes to be a driving force for the energy transition and the recovery of competitiveness, may risk hindering the necessary adaptation of Europe's industrial system rather than strengthening it. At its core, the report appears to echo the defensive logic that informed past responses to economic and energy crises, while providing neither a comprehensive assessment of industrial needs—particularly in energy-intensive sectors—nor a strategic vision for low-carbon innovation in the face of growing global competition.

6.4 A Cooperative, Mission-oriented Strategic Approach

An alternative strategic approach towards an effective energy transition, one that achieves climate goals and enhances EU economic growth, should start from the key issues discussed in the previous paragraph, to identify a narrow path that combines industrial policies, promoting innovation and a broader structural transformation of the productive system—without resorting to protectionism—with international cooperation supporting the global development of green goods and services and thereby optimizing allocative efficiency in their production.

6.4.1 A Mission-oriented Approach

A profound reversal in green strategy—whereby the achievement of climate and energy targets is linked to an overall structural transformation of the production system—is essentially aligned with a mission-oriented approach to industrial policy, designed to tackle the grand challenges of modern societies. Mission-oriented policies are in fact characterized by clear directionality in policy action and aim to catalyze industrial transformation by leveraging technological innovation (Mazzucato 2013; Mazzucato 2021). This approach entails prioritization, but within an ecosystem that enables bottom-up experimentation and competition among technologies, leaving room for pluralism and bottom-up discovery (i.e., multiple technological paths can be explored in pursuit of the same mission).

Within this framework, all productive sectors of the economy are involved in the innovation process, which implies that "instead of using vertical policies to 'pick' sectors or technologies, the vertical aspect of missions picks the problem" (Mazzucato 2018, p. 12), while horizontal policies are tasked with ensuring adequate investment to enhance innovation capabilities across sectors. Accordingly, industrial policy should not be seen merely as a tool to correct market failures, but rather as an activity aimed at creating new market opportunities aligned with mission goals. This, in turn, requires a revamped role for government intervention—not only in assuming the high entrepreneurial risks associated with the extreme uncertainty surrounding innovation processes but also in bringing about "the most radical, path-breaking types of innovation" (Mazzucato 2013, p.62) that underpin the creation of new markets through "new forms of partnership between the public sector, the private sector, and civil society organizations" (Mazzucato 2018, p. 12). In this way, the traditional dichotomy between the state and the market is overcome, giving rise to more collaborative interactions, while simultaneously marking a clear departure from the regulatory approach that has characterized European industrial policy since the Green Deal, in continuity with classical market-oriented policies of the past three decades.

However, the effectiveness of mission-oriented innovation policies depends on its actual implementation, which is far from straightforward: the failure of Northvolt (Milne 2025)—once a symbol of the EU's clean-tech ambitions and its goal of developing a competitive domestic battery value chain—offers a revealing lens through which to evaluate the potential shortcomings of mission-oriented innovation policies. Northvolt was by far Europe's best-funded private start-up—with $15 billion in equity, debt, and subsidies from investors and governments, backed financially by Volkswagen, BMW, Siemens, and investors including Goldman Sachs and BlackRock, and $55 billion of orders—and some aspects of the policy intervention aligned with mission-oriented principles. But a critical shortcoming was the lack of systemic strategy, as it largely focused on a single firm rather than nurturing a broader ecosystem of innovation, supply chains, and skills development.

6.4.2 A Cooperative Approach to Industrial Policies

Moreover, in order to take into account the global dimension of the climate challenge, the mission-oriented approach discussed so far should also stick to the cardinal rule of industrial policy: not to stray too far from an economy's comparative advantages, but rather to help them evolve in the desired direction (Hausmann and Ahuja 2023). According to Hausmann and Ahuja a "Europe first" strategy to climate neutrality—becoming the first continent to reach net-zero emissions and building the industry of the future within Europe—may raise the costs of critical green technologies, lead to inefficient capital allocation, and contribute little to global decarbonization. Hence, rather than focusing narrowly on domestic leadership, the EU should support global decarbonization efforts by allowing green goods and services to be produced where it is most efficient so as to maximize the size of the clean economy, and take a fair share of it for Europe, while preventing harmful industrial rivalries that risk undermining common climate goals.

When comparative advantages are clearly lacking, a potential strategy, instead of fixing rigid targets, could be partnering with foreign players ("derisking by embracing"), building strategic partnerships, and offering market access. This is a "location over ownership" approach, keeping production within Europe but regardless of ownership(Tagliapietra and Trasi 2024).

Thus, what emerges from this view is a cooperative approach in which strategic competition between countries is considered only after optimal positioning within global value chains has been identified and achieved through coordinated efforts. This process cannot be entrusted to market forces alone—given their inherent limitations—but requires public intervention aimed not only at constructing more efficient value chains, but also at reinforcing them in the most promising areas for development. In this context, the targeted role of the state, as envisioned in the mission-oriented approach, finds its fullest expression, as it outlines a new model of productive globalization, where countries "resist the temptation to slide into green protectionism by prioritizing their own carbon-neutral development over global cooperation that prioritizes equity and progress toward global climate goals" (Mazzucato 2024, p. 43).

In short, industrial policies must acknowledge the increasing interdependence between the three strategic areas of public policy—energy, industry, and trade. Tensions and trade-offs between the goals of energy and industrial policies mean that getting trade policy measures right is essential for clean energy transitions (IEA 2024a). This perspective offers a renewed understanding of the challenges facing industrial policies, and of how these can be effectively tackled. The issues raised by the energy transition clearly expose the complexity of industrial policy action, fundamentally calling into question its ability to bring about real structural change in economic activity in relation to key public interest goals. This draws attention to the need to thoroughly understand the mechanisms that govern the functioning of industrial policy, acknowledging, as highlighted in the recent debate on the subject, that "there is an inherent difficulty in ascertaining the causal effects of industrial policy since, by design, policy intervention is nonrandom and targets certain industries for a mix of economic, political, or administrative reasons that cannot be perfectly observed" (Juhász, Lane, and Rodrik 2024, p. 214). The emerging approach to industrial policy has shifted from a narrow reliance on subsidies or trade protection to a more holistic approach, integrating diverse instruments with strong governance and coherence with the political and economic context. According to Juhász, Lane, and Rodrik, three features are central to this transformation. First, industrial policy today requires more sophisticated governance: institutions must be able to monitor and evaluate programs, adjust policies as they unfold, and ensure transparency and accountability, while resisting short-term political pressures. Second, the range of available tools has broadened considerably. Beyond subsidies, governments now deploy fiscal incentives, credit facilities, infrastructure investment, R&D support, training policies, place-based interventions, regulatory instruments, and measures to foster value chains and technology diffusion. Third, modern industrial policy must reckon with the reality of deindustrialization. This means moving beyond attempts to recreate past manufacturing structures and instead adapting to a global economy shaped by new technologies, rapidly changing costs, intense international competition, and complex global value chains. In such a context, the focus shifts toward high-tech industries, advanced producer services, and strategies that integrate environmental sustainability and climate challenges.

In light of the recent literature on industrial policy, the shortcomings of the European approach become immediately evident. By concentrating narrowly on specific technologies and prioritizing strategic autonomy in the energy transition, EU initiatives risk overlooking the broader governance, institutional, and structural dimensions that the literature highlights as crucial for long-term effectiveness.

6.5 Rethinking the EU's Productive Structure (and Economic Governance)

As Hausmann and Auhja argue (2023, p. 159), once it is recognized that "Europe is a large net importer of energy" and that "it lacks the renewable resources to engage in zero-carbon energy-intensive industrial production", the development of a credible green industrial policy must go beyond the objective of global decarbonization, also fostering a fundamental rethinking of the region's productive structure—reassessing what should be produced, how, and where, in light of resource constraints, technological capabilities, and long-term strategic resilience. This could imply reconsidering the role of energy-intensive industries within the industrial base, while simultaneously capitalizing on the growth of a global decarbonized economy to boost sectors where Europe holds a stronger comparative advantage, as is the case with environmental and energy services, which are occupying an increasingly central position in the context of the energy transition. At the same time, it would be advisable to assess which relatively mature clean energy technologies require targeted support to enhance their competitiveness and secure market advantages (Auhja and Hausmann 2025). A telling example in this regard is solar panel manufacturing: while China currently maintains undisputed supremacy in the sector, production should nonetheless be concentrated in countries with lower labour costs to remain competitive, making Europe unable to rival this industry.

In this scenario, Europe could seek to strengthen its innovation capacity—particularly in digital technologies—while also further developing the internal market, aiming to reduce disparities among Member States. The overarching goal is to tackle the critical challenges highlighted by the energy crisis by initiating a virtuous cycle of innovation across the entire production system, aligned with decarbonization objectives. Launching this cycle would represent a key first step toward overcoming the so-called "medium-tech trap" which has confined Europe to medium-low technology sectors (such as automotive), limiting industrial innovation potential, reducing the effectiveness of public R&D as a growth driver, and contributing to a gradual erosion of technological competitiveness relative to the United States and China (Fuest et al. 2024).

Moving in the direction of reshaping Europe's productive structure also demands a profound overhaul of the EU's institutional economic governance—a transformation that has yet to materialize. As the most recent European green industrial policy strategies reveal, an approach overly reliant on the presumed allocative efficiency of the market persists. This significantly constrains the scale of public investment needed to revitalize the production system, as evidenced by the recent launch of the Competitiveness Compass, which foresees the creation of a European competitiveness fund only starting in 2028, within the framework of the next Multiannual Financial Plan. This timeline, combined with the fund's modest scale—due both to the EU's limited budget and potential conflicts with other policy priorities—renders the measure inadequate given the urgency and magnitude of the challenges ahead (Korolec 2025).

What should be considered instead is the adoption of a sort of energy transition plan based on the issuance of common debt, similar to the Next Generation EU initiative (set to expire in 2026) but specifically tailored to the critical demands of the energy transition and anchored in a credible financial base. Such an instrument should be made permanent, as proposed by Guerrieri and Padoan (2024), and embedded within a broader strategy for the structural transformation of the productive system, possibly establishing synergies with tools like the Horizon programme—devoted to scientific and technological research and the promotion of innovation—which itself should be coherently renewed and strengthened.

Coordinating an energy transition-focused recovery plan with a robust research and innovation strategy would also help to avoid the so-called "STI-only trap"[5] characterized by an exclusive emphasis on technological innovation policies that fail to encompass the broader ambitions of a genuinely mission-oriented approach (OECD 2023; Larrue 2022). Concurrently, it is imperative to implement targeted instruments that distinctly

---

5   Science, Technology, and Innovation (STI).

address diverse innovation objectives, differentiating between commercialization-driven research and frontier research, the latter having been persistently underfunded (Fuest et al. 2024). Such an approach would enhance policy effectiveness by bolstering the competitiveness of relatively mature technologies where they demonstrate optimal efficiency, while simultaneously fostering radical innovation in emerging fields—as in the case of energy-intensive sectors, where decarbonization technologies are most in their infancy.

This renewed mechanism for financing public investment could be further supported through a more flexible application of the Stability and Growth Pact, allowing Member States to implement active policies—especially where structural weaknesses in national production systems risk undermining the energy transition and exacerbating divergences across the Union. In this regard, the introduction of a "golden rule"—aimed at excluding strategic investments from deficit calculations, as suggested by Saraceno (2017)—specifically applied to investments negotiated at the EU level and devoted to the energy transition, with the inclusion of research and development expenditure, would provide essential fiscal space and serve as an additional lever to boost innovation in the energy sector.

A reform of the EU's fiscal frameworks along these lines could mark the beginning of a new coordination of economic and industrial policies capable of strategic foresight and future orientation, while also allowing greater flexibility in shaping international cooperation frameworks—as envisioned in the global energy transition process—and enabling timely and targeted policy adjustments necessary to effectively manage the unfolding transformation.

References

Ahuja, K., and R. Hausmann (2025) "Industrial Policy for Competitiveness in the Energy Transition", in H. Grabbe and S. Tagliapietra (eds), *Green Intersections. The Global Embedding of Climate Change in Policy*. Brussels: Bruegel, pp. 53–74, https://growthlab.hks.harvard.edu/sites/projects.iq.harvard.edu/files/bruegel_blueprint_34_0.pdf

Alvarez, J., et al., "Fragmentation and Commodity Markets: Vulnerabilities and Risks", in International Monetary Fund (ed.), *World Economic Outlook: Navigating Global Divergences*. Washington, DC: IMF, pp. 71–92, https://doi.org/10.5089/9798400235801.081

D'Amato, A., A. Pronti, S. Paleari, G. Romaldi, S. Speck, S. Tagliapietra, and R. Zoboli (2024) "Investment Needs and Gaps for the Sustainability Transition in Europe: Rethinking the European Green Deal as an EU Industrial Strategy", *ETC CE Report* 8, 1–117, https://hdl.handle.net/10807/299176

Draghi, M. (2024) *The Future of European Competitiveness*. Brussels: European Commission, https://commission.europa.eu/topics/eu-competitiveness/draghi-report_en

European Commission (EC) (2000), "Green Paper: Towards a European Strategy for the Security of Energy Supply", COM(2000) 769 final, https://eur-lex.europa.eu/EN/legal-content/summary/green-paper-on-the-security-of-energy-supply.html

EC (2006) "Green Paper. A European Strategy for Sustainable, Competitive and Secure Energy", COM(2006) 105 final, https://eur-lex.europa.eu/EN/legal-content/summary/green-paper-a-european-strategy-for-sustainable-competitive-and-secure-energy.html

EC (2014) "A Policy Framework for Climate and Energy in the Period from 2020 to 2030", COM(2014) 15 final, https://eur-lex.europa.eu/legal-content/EN/TXT/?uri=celex:52014DC0015

EC (2015) "Energy Union package, A Framework Strategy for a Resilient Energy Union with a Forward-Looking Climate Change Policy", COM(2015) 80 final, https://eur-lex.europa.eu/legal-content/EN/TXT/HTML/?uri=OJ:C:2018:204:FULL&from=LV

EC (2016) Clean Energy For All Europeans, COM(2016) 500 final, https://eur-lex.europa.eu/legal-content/EN/TXT/HTML/?uri=CELEX:52016DC0860

EC (2019a) "European Green Deal", COM(2019) 640 final, https://eur-lex.europa.eu/legal-content/EN/TXT/?uri=celex:52019DC0640

EC (2019b) "The European Green Deal Sets Out How to Make Europe the First Climate-Neutral Continent by 2050, Boosting the Economy, Improving People's Health and Quality of Life, Caring for Nature, and Leaving No One Behind", 11 December, https://ec.europa.eu/commission/presscorner/detail/en/ip_19_6691

EC (2024) "Regulation (Eu) 2024/1735 of the European Parliament and of the Council of 13 June 2024 on Establishing a Framework of Measures for Strengthening Europe's Net-zero Technology Manufacturing Ecosystem and Amending Regulation (EU) 2018/1724", https://eur-lex.europa.eu/eli/reg/2024/1735/oj/eng

EC (2025a) "An EU Compass to Regain Competitiveness and Secure Sustainable Prosperity", 29 January, https://ec.europa.eu/commission/presscorner/detail/en/ip_25_339

EC (2025b), "EU-wide Assessment of the Final Updated National Energy and Climate Plans Delivering the Union's 2030 Energy and Climate Objectives", COM(2025) 274 final, https://eur-lex.europa.eu/legal-content/EN/TXT/?uri=celex:52025DC0274

Fattouh, B. (2025), "Green Industrial Policy's Increasingly Complex Trade-offs", *Oxford Energy Forum* 143, 5–15, https://www.oxfordenergy.org/wpcms/wp-content/uploads/2025/02/OEF-143.pdf

Fuest, C., D. Gros, P.-L. Mengel, G. Presidente, and J. Tirole (2024) "EU Innovation Policy—How to Escape the Middle Technology Trap. A Report by the European Policy Analysis Group", https://iep.unibocconi.eu/sites/default/files/media/attach/2Report_EU%20Innovation%20Policy_upd_240514.pdf

Furfari, S. (2024) "Rapporto Draghi: Una visione errata del futuro energetico Europeo", *Energia* 4, 48–53.

Guerrieri, P., and P. C. Padoan (2024) "Industrial Policy and Security. The European Union and the Double Challenge: Strengthening Competitiveness and Enhancing Economic Security", in F. Cerniglia and F. Saraceno (eds), *Investing in the Structural Transformation: 2024 European Public Investment Outlook*. Cambridge: Open Book Publishers, pp. 135–147, https://doi.org/10.11647/OBP.0434.09

Guerrieri, P., and P. C. Padoan (2024) *Sovereign Europe. An Agenda for Europe in a Fragmented Global Economy*. Brookfield, VT: Edward Elgar.

Hausmann, R., and K. Ahuja (2023) "A More Globally Minded European Green Industrial Policy", in S. Tagliapietra and R. Veugelers (eds), *Sparking Europe's New Industrial Revolution. A Policy for Net Zero, Growth and Resilience*. Brussels: Bruegel, pp. 153–165, https://www.bruegel.org/system/files/2023-08/Bruegel%20Blueprint%2033%20080823%20 web.pdf

IEA (2023) *Overcoming the Energy Trilemma* (G7). Paris: IEA, https://www.iea.org/reports/ overcoming-the-energy-trilemma-secure-and-inclusive-transitions

IEA (2024a) *Energy Technology Perspectives 2024*. Paris: IEA, https://www.iea.org/reports/ energy-technology-perspectives-2024

IEA (2024b) *Government Energy Spending Tracker*, https://www.iea.org/data-and-statistics/ data-tools/government-energy-spending-tracker-policy-database

Ilyina, A., et al., 2024, "Industrial Policy Is Back but the Bar to Get It Right is High", *IMF Blog*, https://www.imf.org/en/Blogs/Articles/2024/04/12/ industrial-policy-is-back-but-the-bar-to-get-it-right-is-high

Juhász, R., N. Lane, and D. Rodrik (2024), "The New Economics of Industrial Policy", *Annual Review of Economics* 16, 213–242.

Jugè, M., U. Kellauskaitè, B. McWilliams, S. Tagliapietra, and C. Trasi (2025) "Clean Industrial Transformation:Where Does Europe Stand?", 24 February, *Bruegel Analysis*, https://www. bruegel.org/analysis/clean-industrial-transformation-where-does-europe-stand

Korolec, M. (2025) "Europe's Competitiveness Compass Points in the Wrong Direction", 10 March, *Project Syndicate*, https://www.project-syndicate.org/commentary/ eu-competitiveness-compass-misunderstands-challenges-facing-bloc-by-marcin-korolec-2025-03

Krugman, P., (1994) "Competitiveness: A Dangerous Obsession", *Foreign Affairs* 73.2, 28–44.

Larrue, P. (2022) *Do Mission-Oriented Policies for Net Zero Deliver on their Many Promises?* Paris: OECD, https://www.oecd.org/content/dam/oecd/en/publications/reports/2024/11/ mission-oriented-innovation-policies-for-net-zero_842360c5/5efdbc5c-en.pdf

Mazzucato, M. (2013) *The Entrepreneurial State: Debunking Public vs. Private Sector Myths*. London: Anthem Press.

Mazzucato, M (2018) *Mission-oriented Research & Innovation in the European Union—A Problem-solving Approach to Fuel Innovation-led Growth*. Brussels: Publications Office, https://data. europa.eu/doi/10.2777/360325

Mazzucato, M. (2021) *Mission Economy: A Moonshot Guide to Changing Capitalism*. London: Allen Lane.

Mazzucato, M. (2024) "Policy with a Purpose", September, *Finance and Development Magazine*, pp. 40–43.

McCarthy C. (2024) "Not Made in China: The US$6 Trillion Cost of Shifting the World's Clean-tech Manufacturing Hub", 12 February, *Wood Mackenzie*, https://www.woodmac. com/news/opinion/not-made-in-china-the-us$6-trillion-cost-of-shifting-the-worlds-clean-tech-manufacturing-hub/

Milanovic, B. (2025) "How the Mainstream Abandoned Universal Economic Principles (but Forgot to Mention It)", 8 January, https://branko2f7.substack.com/p/ how-the-mainstream-has-abandoned

Milne, R. (2025) "Northvolt Failure Raises Stakes for Europe's Battery Industry", May 22, *Financial Times*, https://www.ft.com/content/63b16b6a-e143-4e2c-ac27-5d3f7a89a41f

OECD (2023) "Driving Low-Carbon Innovations for Climate Neutrality", *OECD Science, Technology and Industry Policy Papers* 143, https://www.oecd.org/en/publications/driving-low-carbon-innovations-for-climate-neutrality_8e6ae16b-en.html

Paleari, S. (2024), "The Role of Strategic Autonomy in the EU Green Transition", *Sustainability* 16, 2597, https://doi.org/10.3390/su16062597

Rodrik, D. (2024) "A New Trilemma Haunts the World Economy", 9 September, *Project Syndicate*, https://www.project-syndicate.org/commentary/new-trilemma-of-climate-change-global-poverty-rich-countries-middle-classes-by-dani-rodrik-2024-09

Rodrik, D., and J. E. Stiglitz (2024), "A New Growth Strategy for Developing Nations", Harvard University, https://drodrik.scholars.harvard.edu/sites/g/files/omnuum7106/files/dani-rodrik/files/a_new_growth_strategy_for_developing_nations.pdf

Saraceno, F., "Nuovo mondo: Europa senza bussola", 7 March, *ISPI*, https://www.ispionline.it/it/pubblicazione/nuovo-mondo-europa-senza-bussola-202040

Saraceno, F. (2017) "When Keynes goes to Brussels: A New Fiscal Rule for the EMU", *Annals of Fondazione Luigi Einaudi* 51.2, 131–157.

Tagliapietra, S., et al. (2023) "Rebooting the European Union's Net Zero Industry Act", 22 June, *Bruegel*, https://www.bruegel.org/policy-brief/rebooting-european-unions-net-zero-industry-act

Tagliapietra, S., and Trasi, C., (2024) "Northvolt's Struggles: A Cautionary Tale for the EU Clean Industrial Deal", 11 December, *Bruegel*, https://www.bruegel.org/analysis/northvolts-struggles-cautionary-tale-eu-clean-industrial-deal

Veugelers, R., Tagliapietra, S., and Trasi, C. (2024) "Green Industrial Policy in Europe: Past, Present, and Prospects", *Journal of Industry, Competition and Trade* 24.4, 1–22, https://doi.org/10.1007/s10842-024-00418-5

World Energy Council (2010) *Energy Sustainability / Trilemma Index*, https://www.worldenergy.org/publications/entry/world-energy-trilemma-2010-pursuing-sustainability-assessment-of-country-energy-and-climate-policies

Youngs, R. (2021) "The EU's Strategic Autonomy Trap", 8 March, *Carnegie Europe*, https://carnegieendowment.org/research/2021/03/the-eus-strategic-autonomy-trap?lang=en&center=europe

Zachman, G. (2024) "Draghi's Pitch to Improve the Competitiveness of Energy-Intensive Industry", 12 September, *Bruegel*, https://www.bruegel.org/first-glance/draghis-pitch-improve-competitiveness-energy-intensive-industry

7. Energy Transition and Industrial Competitiveness in the EU

Mirko Armiento[1] and Andrea Villa[2]

The energy transition in the European Union is shaped by complex technological, economic, and geopolitical interdependencies. A coherent policy approach must account for the interaction between efforts to decarbonize the energy mix and measures that support the adoption of end-use clean technologies, in particular in the industrial sector. Photovoltaic and battery storage systems face structural challenges in Europe, including elevated production costs and limited upstream integration. Heat pumps, while more mature, would require demand stimulation and workforce skill development to fully realize their potential. Concurrently, industrial electrification presents considerable technical potential, especially for low- and medium-temperature heat processes, but progress remains constrained by infrastructure gaps, regulatory barriers, and cost competitiveness. Moreover, manufacturing industries are highly exposed to international competition, making them particularly sensitive to trade policies. A comprehensive policy framework should prioritize effective use of EU funds and ensure stable regulatory conditions. Key actions involve developing clean technology gigafactories, securing critical raw materials, supporting circular economy practices, expanding recycling capabilities, and fostering R&D collaboration. Complementary fiscal incentives, green finance mechanisms, and workforce upskilling are essential to reduce external dependencies, advancing Net-Zero Industry Act (NZIA) targets, and generating socioeconomic and environmental benefits. To bolster EU industrial competitiveness, accelerating the deployment of renewables, facilitating access to long-term instruments such as power purchase agreements, and establishing a coherent EU-wide framework to support industrial electrification are imperative. In particular, hard-to-abate manufacturing sectors will require targeted incentives—whether in terms of capital expenditures (CAPEX) or operational ones (OPEX)—to bridge the cost gap with fossil fuel-based reference technologies.

---

1   Enel Foundation.
2   Enel Foundation.

          https://doi.org/10.11647/OBP.0499.07

7.1 Setting the Stage: Energy Transition Strategic Technologies and Supply Chains to Boost EU Industrial Competitiveness

The European Union (EU) and its Member States are urged to act swiftly to develop and implement a renewed strategic vision aimed at accelerating the energy transition. Energy transition strategies are intrinsically linked to geopolitical dynamics, and a nuanced understanding of how international trade and geopolitics intersect with energy policies is essential for shaping global frameworks that ensure a fair, secure, and sustainable energy future.

Recent geopolitical developments have exposed the significant vulnerabilities of global energy markets, particularly their volatility and its direct effect on economic stability, industrial competitiveness, and the well-being of citizens. The ongoing conflict between Russia and Ukraine has had a profound impact in this regard, leading to a dramatic surge in energy prices and jeopardizing the EU's economic resilience and industrial competitiveness. These events have emphasized the unsustainability of Europe's dependence on external energy sources—particularly imported natural gas—thereby elevating energy security to a strategic priority.

Nonetheless, these challenges also offer a pivotal opportunity to recalibrate and strengthen the EU energy strategy. Accelerating the deployment of renewable energy sources (RES) emerges not only as a pathway to sustainability and energy security, but also as a critical means to mitigate the adverse effects of energy price volatility by reducing reliance on imports. Beyond their benefits for the climate, renewables represent a tangible lever for improving competitiveness and energy independence.

Insights from historical energy transitions offer valuable guidance. As examined in Kander, Warde, and Malanima (2014), past energy shifts—such as the transition from coal to oil and electricity between the First and the Second Industrial Revolutions—were instrumental in driving economic growth. These transitions provided cheaper energy to people and industry and a more efficient use of power through machines and infrastructure, spurring productivity. Nevertheless, they were neither rapid nor straightforward as they unfolded over decades, shaped by socioeconomic transformations, technological innovation, and significant infrastructural investments.

Similarly, Fouquet (2010) highlights that historical energy transitions have often been slow, uneven processes, driven by a complex interplay of economic, technological, and policy factors. His analysis reveals that significant changes in energy systems typically do not occur only through market forces, but they would need policy interventions. These findings highlight the importance of active, long-term governance to accelerate the current transition toward decarbonization.

Today's transition is arguably more ambitious: it seeks not only to switch fuels but to essentially restructure the energy system to align it with net-zero objectives. Innovation in clean technologies and digitalization are essential enablers, helping to reduce costs, expand access, and improve efficiency. Yet, as in the past, this transition will be complex and prolonged, requiring visionary policymaking, substantial investments, and broad societal support.

In this context, the EU must implement comprehensive policies that foster RES deployment and that support low-carbon innovative technologies that are critical for the energy transition. These key technologies would require targeted investment to strengthen their value chains and innovative policy frameworks to unlock their potential. Building robust, localized supply chains is essential not only to maintaining a competitive advantage but also to reducing strategic dependencies in an increasingly uncertain geopolitical context.

On the one hand, the widespread deployment of clean energy technologies has helped to reduce the energy system's vulnerability by decoupling it from fossil fuels price fluctuations. On the other hand, to fully reap the benefits, the EU must build out the entire clean energy value chain, addressing technological and material dependencies on third countries. Strategic sectors such as photovoltaics, battery storage systems, and heat pumps must be supported through the creation and integration of EU-wide industrial and technological supply chains, delivering socioeconomic and environmental benefits for both businesses and citizens.

Within this framework, a study conducted by Enel Foundation and The European House—Ambrosetti (2023) , in collaboration with Enel, focused on these three core technologies and assessed how Italy and Europe can achieve the targets set by Net-Zero Industrial Act (NZIA) by 2030. In fact, these supply chains are heavily concentrated outside Europe, particularly in China, which accounts for approximately 65% of global capacity on average. To address these structural imbalances, the EU put forward the NZIA in 2023, aiming to produce at least 40% of the annual domestic demand for clean technologies within Europe by 2030.[3]

The largest increase in the installed power capacity in Italy and in Europe is expected for photovoltaics (PV)—the cheapest power generation technology—followed by wind. Simultaneously, demand for batteries is expected to increase more than tenfold by the end of the decade, as storage systems are essential for integrating variable renewables, accelerating uptake of electric vehicles, and responding to evolving electricity demand patterns. Nevertheless, the production of PV panels and storage systems within Europe remains significantly more expensive than in China. This cost differential is driven by various factors, including higher capital investment requirements, longer lead times for establishing manufacturing plants, higher energy prices, limited specialization in upstream activities, and insufficient integration in the raw materials and refining stages of the value chain.

To strengthen local value chains, available financial resources—such as those allocated through the National Recovery and Resilience Plans—should be strategically

---

3   Europe should reach 30 GW per year of production capacity for all stages of the photovoltaic value chain, as well as at least 550 GWh of manufacturing capacity for the battery value chain and 31 GW for heat pumps.

deployed to expand and scale-up photovoltaic and batteries manufacturing capacities. Moreover, Europe's domestic production processes, which are often more sustainable in both environmental and social terms compared to those in China, must be better coordinated and integrated across EU Member States. In parallel, European research centres require increased funding and strategic alignment to compete with China's well-organized and heavily subsidized R&D ecosystem. Particularly in the battery sector, further investments and targeted research are necessary to enhance recycling capacity and reduce supply chain vulnerabilities.

Heat pumps represent a distinct case. As a mature technology that can be adapted to a wide range of climate conditions, they offer a compelling combination of technological readiness and low total cost of ownership; in addition, they can substantially reduce energy consumption for heating and cooling in buildings. Although the EU accounts for less than 20% of global production capacity, it meets nearly 80% of its domestic demand for heat pumps. Notwithstanding that, the market remains in an early stage of development. It is unclear whether demand forecasts—driven by EU policies aimed at reducing gas dependence—will be matched by actual market uptake. The sector continues to face several obstacles, including a shortage of skilled installers, uncertain demand trajectories, and price volatility, which collectively hinder the full conversion of the boiler value chain. In the long term, recycling strategies can play an important role in addressing issues related to the scarcity of raw materials and price fluctuations.

On the demand side, industrial electrification remains one area that has seen relatively little progress. The shift from fossil fuels-based systems to electricity-driven technologies—both direct and indirect electrification—has progressed slowly, despite its clear potential to reduce emissions and increase energy efficiency. This stagnation raises important questions regarding the technical, economic, and regulatory barriers that continue to impede the widespread adoption of electric solutions in industrial applications.

Addressing these barriers will require a holistic approach that targets both the supply and the demand sides of the electrification challenge. On the supply side, increased investments in the development of clean technologies—such as solar PV, heat pumps, and energy storage systems—are essential. On the demand side, policy interventions should incentivize industrial actors to adopt electrification technologies. A well-balanced strategy that addresses both fronts will not only accelerate industrial decarbonization but also facilitate a more rapid and resilient transition to a sustainable energy system. Policies promoting the growth of renewables must therefore be complemented by efforts aimed at dismantling barriers to industrial electrification.

A comprehensive and coordinated policy framework, backed by targeted investments, is essential for ensuring that the EU meets its climate goals while reinforcing industrial competitiveness and geopolitical resilience. Achieving these objectives will require an integrated strategy encompassing both supply-side and demand-side measures, underpinned by a deep understanding of the geopolitical dynamics shaping the global energy landscape.

In the end, the EU and its Member States must firmly embrace a forward-looking strategic vision aimed at building a competitive, European-wide decarbonization industry. This vision should be anchored in integrated and well-coordinated value chains for key technologies. Timely and decisive action from both EU and national institutions is imperative. In a global context marked by rising competition and declining international trust, the development of a resilient, sovereign clean energy industry in Europe stands as one of the most urgent challenges that will shape the future of its citizens and businesses.

7.2 Technical and Economic Analysis of the Potential for Industrial Electrification

The availability of low-cost electricity from renewable sources, along with the emergence of new technologies for producing heat both directly and indirectly from electricity—such as heat pumps—paves the way for the decarbonization of industrial processes that, until now, has not taken place.

Eurostat data shows the daunting task of the challenge associated with decarbonizing industrial sectors in the EU. Manufacturing industries account for more than 50% of EU's primary energy demand. Within this domain, the chemical and petrochemical sector represents more than 75% of energy used, primarily due to feedstocks. Other energy-intensive sectors include metallurgy (iron and steel), non-metallics minerals (aluminium), food and beverages, and paper and pulp, each contributing between 3% and 8% of total manufacturing energy use.

According to the latest Eurostat greenhouse gas (GHG) emissions data from 2021, manufacturing industries accounted for approximately 27% of the EU's total emissions. The chemical and petrochemical, metallurgy, and non-metallic minerals sectors together represent about 80% of the manufacturing industry's emissions.

In terms of energy carriers used in the different sectors, Eurostat data reveal that only 33% of the energy consumed by manufacturing industries, excluding feedstocks, was electrified in 2021, whereas almost 50% was derived from conventional fossil fuels (natural gas, solid fuels, oil and petroleum products). This data highlights that without a coherent and ambitious industrial decarbonization plan, it will be impossible to achieve 2040 and 2050 EU climate goals.

Decarbonization and competitiveness are closely linked and critically important for ensuring a sustainable and resilient European economy. Decarbonization—through the adoption of cleaner energy sources and technologies—is essential to meet the EU's climate goals and to mitigate the long-term risks associated with climate change. At the same time, production of electricity from RES could foster competitiveness by lowering electricity costs. In addition, by investing in low-carbon technologies, improving energy efficiency, and modernizing infrastructure, the EU can reduce its dependence on imported fossil fuels, create high-quality jobs, and stimulate industrial innovation. By aligning decarbonization efforts with economic competitiveness, the EU can be a global leader in the clean energy transition, thereby strengthening its strategic autonomy and economic security amidst increasing geopolitical volatility.

A study carried out by the Enel Foundation, Compass Lexecon, and ERCST (2024) has analyzed the potential for direct and indirect electrification of European industrial processes. In order to assess this potential, the study first identified the technical potential of electrification technologies (direct or indirect) applicable to specific industrial processes. Only after establishing technical viability did the study consider economic factors and additional non-economic barriers. A study carried out by Fraunhofer ISI (2024) has identified the technologies that could be deployed for direct electrification of industrial process heat. Based on 2019 data, process heating accounts for approximately 60% of the total energy demand within manufacturing industries, with half of that demand associated with high-temperature processes (above 500°C). Process heating applications in manufacturing industries have been relying on fossil fuel consumption for 75% of the demand, driven by the temperature level and energy density requirements of the raw material industries.

Among the different sectors, metallurgy, chemicals, and non-metallic minerals represent the bulk of industrial energy demand for process heating. Existing technological systems such as large furnaces and kilns meet the current need for high temperatures and energy density by relying predominantly on natural gas and coal. Even sectors with lower temperature requirements have historically been relying on fossil fuels. In order to satisfy these energy needs, a wide array of technologies has been identified as promising alternatives to fossil fuel-based process heating solutions. These technologies span both low- and high-temperature applications, enabling electrification across a diverse range of industrial processes. For low- to medium-temperature needs—common in sectors such as food processing, paper, and textiles— electric boilers and high-temperature industrial heat pumps are already technically mature. Current industrial heat pumps operate up to 250°C with capacities reaching 100 MW, while electric boilers can achieve up to 500°C with capacities around 75 MW. Resistance heating technologies can reach temperatures of 1800°C with capacities up to 80 kW/m^2.

These systems exhibit high efficiency and can be powered by renewable electricity, contributing to substantial emissions reductions. For high-temperature processes, technologies such as electric arc furnaces, resistance heating, induction heating, and plasma torches are either under continuous development and scale-up or are already commercially deployed in specific sectors like steelmaking and glass production. While some of these high-temperature applications remain at pilot or early commercialization stages, ongoing innovation is progressively enhancing their feasibility.

Considering the main manufacturing sectors—food and beverage, paper and pulp, plastics, chemicals and petrochemicals, metallurgy, and non-metallic minerals—direct electrification solutions are technically available across the board by 2040. In addition, indirect electrification technologies, such as hydrogen could further support industrial decarbonization efforts. For this reason, many studies have shown that the technical potential for industrial electrification in European manufacturing sectors could exceed 90% by the mid-2030s.

Once the technical potential for industrial electrification is assessed, it is possible to evaluate the competitiveness of low-carbon process heating solutions with respect to incumbent fossil-based technologies. Enel Foundation study constructed a bottom-up model simulating greenfield investments, using publicly available data to estimate CAPEX, OPEX, and other non-energy costs for electrified solutions. The total costs were then compared with those of incumbent fossil-based technologies, which include CO_2, CAPEX, OPEX, and other non-energy costs: the cost differential represented the decarbonization cost gap. In order to simplify the calculations, the study assumed fixed prices over the 2025–2045 period of 150 €/ton CO_2, 40 €/MWh for natural gas, 120 €/MWh for electricity, and 5 €/kg for green hydrogen.

Under these assumptions, the study demonstrates that different technologies are economically viable for decarbonizing specific manufacturing sectors. In particular, food and beverage and paper and pulp show clear opportunities for electrification in the short term. On the other hand, aluminium, glass, and cement—classified as "hard-to-abate" —will have viable alternatives only after 2035–2040. In this regard, the study further confirms that competitiveness of the different technologies depends on temperature requirements. In addition, hard-to-abate sectors—especially high temperature chemicals and aluminium—are more exposed to international competition. Therefore, it is important to consider this implication when the EU defines trade policies and sector-specific decarbonization pathways.

Despite its promising technical feasibility and economic potential, the widespread adoption of industrial electrification across Europe faces a complex set of additional barriers. These hurdles vary by sector and process, and span technological, economical, regulatory, infrastructural, and organizational dimensions. A major barrier is the technological readiness of electric alternatives for high-temperature processes, such as those used in cement, steel, and glass production. While low- and medium-temperature applications (up to 500°C) are generally well served by mature technologies like electric boilers and heat pumps, processes exceeding 1,000°C still lack commercially proven and reliable solutions, limiting immediate electrification potential in some of the most carbon-intensive sectors.

Economic barriers also play a central role. Electrification often requires significant upfront capital investment, not only in new equipment but also in retrofitting or redesigning industrial facilities to accommodate new technologies. Additionally, operational costs may be higher in regions where electricity prices are not yet competitive with fossil fuels, particularly if electricity taxation and levies are disproportionately high compared to fossil energy sources. This situation is compounded by carbon pricing uncertainty; while higher carbon prices could improve the cost-competitiveness of electric processes, volatile or insufficient carbon markets reduce the predictability essential for long-term investments. From an infrastructural perspective, the existing electricity grid is not always equipped to handle the increased and more variable load that would result from widespread electrification. Many industrial sites are located in areas with limited grid capacity or outdated infrastructure, requiring substantial grid upgrades and coordination with transmission system operators. Regulatory inconsistencies across EU Member States—such as differing levels of incentives, permitting procedures, and grid access rules—further complicate planning and implementation.

Finally, organizational and structural barriers persist. Smaller companies often lack the internal expertise and financial capacity to evaluate or adopt electrification technologies. Moreover, industrial technology shifts typically align with investment cycles that span decades; delays or missed opportunities can entrench fossil fuel dependencies for extended periods. Overcoming these multifaceted barriers will require a coordinated approach—combining financial incentives, regulatory reforms, infrastructure investments, and robust support for innovation and skills development— to make industrial electrification a central pillar of Europe's green industrial future.

7.3 Policy Recommendations to Overcome the Main Barriers to Electrification

A strategic policy framework is critical to unlock the full potential of electrification and achieve long-term sustainability goals. To accelerate the energy transition and enhance European industrial competitiveness, the EU must swiftly implement a coherent set of policies including both demand- and supply-side aspects, supported by stronger governance and coordination across Member States. These policies should reinforce European value chains for key clean technologies and advance electrification of industrial processes, thereby removing systemic barriers and fostering industrial competitiveness and more resilient and integrated energy systems.

On the demand side, efforts should focus on narrowing the cost differential between European and foreign—particularly Chinese—products, using fiscal instruments such as tax incentives or exemptions. On the supply side, key priorities include incentivizing capital and operational expenditures (CAPEX and OPEX), streamlining permitting procedures, and prioritizing strategic projects at the national level. Ensuring efficient and predictable administrative processes will be critical to accelerate deployment. A comprehensive policy framework must ensure an effective use of the existing EU funding instruments, stable regulatory and fiscal frameworks, and the promotion of circular economy and sustainable production models. Timely implementation of these measures would help close the gap between current production levels and the targets set by the NZIA, while reducing dependence on third-country supply chains. This shift would also yield substantial socioeconomic and environmental benefits, including GDP growth, skilled job creation, and enhanced energy price stability for businesses and consumers—an urgent issue in light of recent market volatility.

Specific actions include the development of gigafactories for photovoltaics and batteries, backed by competitive incentives to bridge cost gaps with Asia; guaranteed installation contracts and fiscal support for heat pump deployment; and targeted support for the conversion of traditional boiler value chains. Ensuring access to critical raw materials through strategic international partnerships and expanding domestic recycling capacity will also be vital. To mobilize private capital, the creation of green finance mechanisms should be pursued. Parallel investments in workforce development, including tax credits for training and hiring, will help ensure a skilled labour pool aligned with industrial transformation. It would also be important to distribute the value generated by local supply chains—e.g., through VAT exemptions for EU-made technologies—and foster R&D collaboration among Member States. Additional support should target both mature and emerging technologies, with ESG compliance embedded in all funded clean technology imports and installations.

On the supply side, it should be noted that electrification offers a strategic opportunity to enhance the competitiveness of Europe's industrial sector in a rapidly evolving global geopolitical context. Recent technological advancements—such as the increased affordability and efficiency of heat pumps—demonstrate that low-carbon solutions can already compete with fossil-based alternatives in several industrial applications. Innovation will remain a key enabler on this path but must be supported by an enabling regulatory and financial environment. In fact, to fully unlock the potential of industrial electrification, it is essential to address not only economic factors but also regulatory, infrastructural, and social barriers. There is no one-size-fits-all solution, and the diversity of industrial processes calls for a tailored and coordinated response. This includes the creation of a new dedicated cluster within the Innovation Fund to support electrification across both large enterprises and small and medium-sized enterprises (SMEs).

Electricity price volatility remains a major concern. To mitigate the impact of gas prices on electricity markets, Member States must accelerate the implementation of the Electricity Market Design and the Renewable Energy Directive (RED III). Long-term market signals and enhanced access to Power Purchase Agreements (PPAs), supported by guarantee mechanisms and dedicated platforms, are necessary to provide certainty for industrial actors. Moreover, accelerating the deployment of renewables and strengthening electricity grids is vital. Grids must be upgraded with anticipatory investments and designed to support flexibility, resilience, and RES integration. Programs such as demand response should be promoted to enhance system efficiency.

Ensuring a level playing field requires stable ETS-CBAM frameworks, adequate compensation for indirect costs, and fiscal parity between electricity and gas. At the same time, a European-level strategy—such as the "Clean Shift Initiative"—could provide common investment guidelines and funding mechanisms, including competitive auctions and an "Auctions-as-a-Service" approach for national resources. Future revisions of EU State Aid Guidelines should explicitly support industrial decarbonization, including investments in clean production technologies, leveraging on market-based tools such as Carbon Contracts for Difference (CCfDs), Electricity CfDs, and targeted tax incentives. Finally, strengthening domestic supply chains through green public procurement—by reserving quotas for European industrial products powered by renewables—would enhance EU industrial sovereignty, especially in sectors most exposed to global competition. In conclusion, the electrification of industry must be positioned at the heart of Europe's energy and industrial policy. With the right combination of innovation, regulatory foresight, and financial support, it can serve as a catalyst for sustainable growth, energy security, and climate neutrality.

References

Enel Foundation, Compass Lexecon, and ERCST (2024) "Reviving Europe's Industrial Power: How to Boost Competitiveness through Energy", December, https://www.enelfoundation.org/topics/articles/2024/11/potential-and-benefits-direct-indirect-electrification-eu-industry

The European House—Ambrosetti, Enel Foundation and Enel SpA (2023), "Energy Transition Strategic Supply Chains. Industrial Roadmap for Europe and Italy", September, https://www.enelfoundation.org/topics/articles/2023/09/energy-transition-strategic-supply-chains

Fouquet, R. (2010) "The Slow Search for Solutions: Lessons from Historical Energy Transitions by Sector and Service", *Energy Policy* 38.11, 6586–6596, http://8020vision.com/wp-content/uploads/2010/07/BC3WP201005.pdf

Fraunhofer ISI (2024) "Direct Electrification of Industrial Process Heat. An Assessment of Technologies, Potentials and Future Prospects for the EU", *Agora Industry*, https://www.agora-industry.org/fileadmin/Projects/2023/2023-20_IND_Electrification_Industrial_Heat/A-IND_329_04_Electrification_Industrial_Heat_WEB.pdf

Kander, A., P. Warde, and P. Malanima (2014) *Power to the People: Energy in Europe Over the Last Five Centuries*. Princeton, NJ: Princeton University Press.

8. Research and Innovation Policy for the Energy Transition in the EU

Francesco Pasimeni,[1] Willem Klok,[2] and Floor Alkemade[3]

The European Union's energy transition has entered a new phase, where the focus of research and innovation (R&I) policy must shift from advancing individual renewable technologies to enabling their systemic integration. This chapter draws on sustainability transitions literature to analyze the evolving demands on the EU's energy innovation system, emphasizing the need for coordinated governance, societal engagement, and institutional reform. A systems-based R&I approach is essential to address the complexity of integrating renewables, managing sociotechnical change, and ensuring economic and social sustainability. Special attention is given to the role of small and medium-sized enterprises (SMEs), energy communities, and sustainable finance mechanisms as critical drivers of bottom-up innovation and structural transformation. The chapter also engages with recent EU-level strategic reflections, including competitiveness and innovation agendas, to highlight how climate objectives, economic resilience, and social cohesion are increasingly interconnected. It offers recommendations for policymakers seeking to realign R&I strategies in support of a transformative, inclusive, and competitive European energy transition.

8.1 Introduction

The European Union (EU) has witnessed remarkable advancements in renewable energy technologies over the past two decades, giving an important boost to the energy transition process. Innovations in solar photovoltaic (PV) systems, wind energy, and energy storage have driven down costs and expanded the possibilities for decarbonizing the energy system. As these technologies mature, the focus of research and innovation (R&I) policy must evolve. The challenge is no longer only about

---

1   Technology, Innovation and Society Research Group, Department of Industrial Engineering and Innovation Sciences, Eindhoven University of Technology, The Netherlands.

2   Technology, Innovation and Society Research Group, Department of Industrial Engineering and Innovation Sciences, Eindhoven University of Technology, The Netherlands.

3   Technology, Innovation and Society Research Group, Department of Industrial Engineering and Innovation Sciences, Eindhoven University of Technology, The Netherlands.

https://doi.org/10.11647/OBP.0499.08

improving individual technologies but about integrating them into complex energy systems: systems that must be technically coherent, economically viable, and socially acceptable (Gallagher et al. 2012).

This evolution demands a systemic approach to innovation: one that goes beyond siloed technological improvements to address the coordination of infrastructure, institutions, markets, and users. The societal dimension of innovation emerges as a critical factor, particularly as energy systems co-evolve with new governance models such as energy communities and bottom-up initiatives. Successfully managing intermittency, aligning supply and demand, and ensuring digital connectivity requires robust, multi-level governance and the active participation of users as co-creators, not just consumers.

At the same time, the green transition is core to the EU's ambitions for both climate leadership and global competitiveness. Recent analyses (European Commission DG RTD et al. 2024; Draghi 2024) emphasize the systemic nature of these challenges, highlighting how competitiveness, innovation, climate policy, and social welfare are increasingly intertwined. Central to this is the role of small and medium-sized Enterprises (SMEs), which represent the backbone of the EU economy but face persistent barriers in scaling, financing, and adopting clean technologies.

Drawing on sustainability transitions literature, this chapter explores the multifaceted barriers constraining the EU's energy transition, from consumer technology diffusion and SME engagement to systemic financial obstacles and entrenched technological lock-ins. It highlights the need for a comprehensive, integrated R&I policy framework capable of driving transformative change by addressing these challenges holistically (Schot and Steinmueller 2018). In particular, the chapter highlights how R&I policy can unlock systemic transformation by empowering bottom-up, community-led initiatives to build societal legitimacy and readiness; overcoming institutional and infrastructural lock-ins to open space for innovative pathways; embedding SMEs into a supportive ecosystem that facilitates scaling and finance; and reshaping financial systems to align capital flows with long-term sustainability goals.

By focusing on these strategic levers, the chapter aims to inform policy interventions that foster inclusive, resilient, and environmentally grounded energy systems, ensuring the EU's leadership in the clean energy transition while advancing social equity and economic renewal.

8.2 A Systems Perspective on Energy Innovation

Innovation is not a linear process of research leading to technological breakthroughs, followed by market adoption. Instead, it is a systemic and co-evolutionary process involving diverse actors: universities, companies, regulators, users, and more frequently civil society. Such complexity necessitates a broader analytical lens that can capture interdependencies across technological, institutional, and societal domains.

Energy innovation is not exempt from this view. A systemic approach to energy innovation has to consider the full lifecycle of technologies, from basic research to deployment and societal embedding, passing through the regulatory landscape (Kim and Wilson 2019). A systemic approach to energy transition policy is required to have a comprehensive, inclusive, and integrated strategy that addresses the complexities and interdependencies of key dimensions of energy systems.

The technological dimension includes the development of low-carbon technologies and digital infrastructure which guarantee the smart and efficient operation of the energy system. The societal dimension, which includes public values, trust, and active participation, helps shape energy futures in line with the bottom-up spirit. The institutional dimension concerns the regulatory frameworks enabling mission-oriented coordination among all actors involved (Anadon 2012).

Recent years have seen sustained growth in renewable electricity generation. Wind and solar have become the fastest-growing energy generation technologies in history. Globally, renewable electricity surpassed 30% of total generation, and in the EU, nearly 50% of electricity came from renewable sources in 2024 (IEA 2024b; IRENA 2024). This growth is increasingly market-driven rather than reliant on subsidies. However, the rapid proliferation of distributed renewables poses challenges for the financial viability and operational logic of traditional electricity grids. While tensions between centralized and distributed systems are a global phenomenon, they play out differently in different countries and bring different energy justice concerns.

As clean energy technologies approach maturity and achieve cost competitiveness, the central challenge has moved from cost reduction to system integration. Electrification of end-use sectors (like heating and transport) is essential to reduce carbon emissions. Yet this requires overcoming deeply embedded technological, institutional, and behavioural lock-ins.

The EU energy system remains deeply path dependent, shaped by historical investments in centralized, fossil fuel-based infrastructure. This legacy has created significant carbon lock-in, as long-lived assets and institutional structures resist rapid change (Eitan and Hekkert 2023). Infrastructural lock-in tends to dominate for decades while technological and economic lock-ins arise because incumbent technologies enjoy established supply chains, large economies of scale, and well-aligned institutions, making them cheaper but also politically entrenched. In such an institutional lock-in, regulations, market rules, and subsidies co-evolve to favour the status quo, often reinforcing the market power of existing utilities and fuel suppliers. Behavioural and cultural lock-in enforces consumer habits and routines, making alternative energy futures unfamiliar, risky, or unattractive. Thus, path-dependence is not only a historic phenomenon but an ongoing dynamic: past choices continue to narrow future energy options and create institutional barriers that are hard to reverse.

The EU's energy system is still largely structured around centralized energy models, characterized by such lock-ins. Large-scale power plants, national monopoly utilities, and entrenched unsustainable consumption patterns have historically dominated, often driven by regulatory frameworks designed around incumbent interests. However, systemic forces are driving a shift toward decentralization (Hoicka et al. 2021), trying to overcome lock-ins and escape path dependency. Technological innovations, such as renewable energy generation, battery storage, and digital control systems, are enabling smaller, modular, and more distributed energy solutions. Market liberalization and environmental policy are also empowering bottom-up innovation (Markard and Truffer 2006), allowing new actors to challenge incumbents with flexible, community-based business models.

As a result, traditional top-down governance is being disrupted, giving rise to more varied and context-specific energy strategies. While this increases innovation and local resilience, it also introduces systemic challenges. Bottom-up innovations require not only technology solutions but also good governance, such as inclusive planning and new ownership models. The EU's energy transition thus faces a core tension between the inertia of technological path dependency and the transformative potential of decentralized, bottom-up approaches that promise more resilient, flexible, and low-carbon energy futures.

8.3 Energy Transition Barriers

8.3.1 Barrier for the Diffusion of Consumer Technologies

The levelized cost of energy from renewables is, in many cases, now competitive compared to fossil fuel-generated energy. As wind and solar energy are available at no cost, they benefit from a structural cost advantage over fossil fuels, and ongoing technological learning continues to improve their economic viability. For instance, the IEA (2024a) projects that by 2025, solar photovoltaic systems combined with battery storage will outperform the cost of coal-fired power in China and newly built gas-fired plants in the United States. However, systemic barriers continue to slow the diffusion of renewable technologies, particularly at the consumer level.

A critical structural barrier lies in the market design itself. In many countries, renewable energy prices are linked to fossil fuel prices. Specifically, under marginal pricing natural gas is often price setting. In the EU, for example, even though natural gas only generated 20% of electricity in 2022, it was responsible for setting the market price of electricity 63% of the time (Draghi 2024). This decouples electricity pricing from the true cost of renewable production, thereby diminishing consumer incentives to adopt technologies such as heat pumps, electric vehicles, and even rooftop solar or grid-scale renewables. Although operational costs for these technologies are typically lower than for fossil-based alternatives, their high capital costs create a significant barrier to widespread adoption.

Overcoming this barrier requires a systemic policy mix that addresses not only cost structures but also behavioural and institutional dynamics (Kern et al. 2019). Historical experiences in the energy sector demonstrate the pivotal role of government intervention in enabling consumer adoption. For example, rural electrification programs, like the one in the US of the 1930s, have played a key role in expanding household electricity access through subsidies and cooperative utilities (Haanyika 2006; Kitchens and Fishback 2015; Peters et al. 2009). In Germany, as well as in other European countries, the introduction of feed-in tariffs in the early 2000s created attractive returns for households, farmers, and cooperatives, accelerating consumer-level adoption of renewable technologies (Lauber and Jacobsson 2016; Pyrgou et al. 2016). More recently, Sweden's successful transition to heat pumps was facilitated by a combination of carbon taxation on heating oil and the availability of low-cost electricity. Another leverage point is minimum energy performance standards for buildings, such as those implemented in the EU and Canada (Schleich et al. 2021), particularly when timed with moments of natural building turnover, such as property sales. These interventions help ensure that renewable supply keeps pace with energy demand, especially in sectors like housing and cooling, where energy-efficient alternatives are available at comparable prices (like air conditioning).

In addition to financial and regulatory tools, non-financial drivers at the household level are often underestimated yet crucial. These include health co-benefits from better-insulated homes and the replacement of gas-fired stoves, as well as the desire for energy independence or autonomy. These motivations are also key to preventing people from switching back to the old technology. Recognizing and integrating these drivers into R&I and policy frameworks is critical, not only for adoption, but also for long-term behavioural lock-in and technology reliability.

Since the EU is experiencing rapid renewable energy growth, it is essential to complement supply-side advances with demand-side interventions. This includes supporting electrification across sectors and investing in enabling infrastructure, such as modernized electricity grids and charging networks. Encouraging household-scale energy autonomy (through rooftop solar, battery storage, or local energy communities) can reduce grid congestion and further align consumer behaviour with national energy goals.

8.3.2 Barrier for SMEs to Engage with the Energy Transition

SMEs play a pivotal role in anchoring technology innovation to household needs and bottom-up, user-led initiatives. SMEs serve as important intermediaries between local needs and broader innovation goals, due to their deep embeddedness in domestic and regional contexts across Europe (Burch et al. 2016; Hervás-Oliver et al. 2021). This proximity allows SMEs to adapt solutions to specific socioeconomic contexts and to translate local specializations into innovation pathways aligned with the EU's R&I agenda, particularly in sustainability and energy transition.

SMEs represent 99% of the EU firms and are crucial in the economic landscape of Europe and central in sustainable transitions and green industrial change (Chatzistamoulou and Tyllianakis 2022). The high potential to embed new practices and localize green innovation makes SMEs instrumental in enabling the EU to meet its climate targets, enhance energy security, and maintain global competitiveness.

However, despite their critical role, SMEs face persistent and systemic challenges that limit their ability to scale, innovate, and contribute to sustainability transitions. Many SMEs struggle to commercialize innovations and secure late-stage funding, particularly in clean technology sectors (Lee et al. 2015; Radicic and Pugh 2017). These issues are compounded by structural barriers such as the EU's fragmented capital markets, regulatory complexity, and the underdeveloped ecosystem for growth finance.

The urgency of addressing these barriers is amplified by the competitive pressures of the global clean-tech race. While the EU has a strong base in clean technology innovation, its companies often lack the scale-up support seen in more integrated markets like the United States or China. Between 2008 and 2021, 32 out of 147 EU-founded unicorns relocated to the US, primarily to access more favourable financing conditions (Testa et al. 2022). This trend represents a considerable loss of intellectual capital, job creation, and strategic autonomy for the EU.

In addition to financing challenges, EU SMEs are affected by rising energy prices, regulatory and administrative burdens, and technology adoption gaps. For example, according to the 2024 edition of the bulletin on digitalization in Europe, Eurostat data indicate that in 2023 only 7% of SMEs had adopted cloud computing compared to 30% of large enterprises, and just 8% of all the EU enterprises had adopted artificial intelligence technologies (Eurostat 2024). These disparities hinder SMEs' ability to engage with the digital and green transitions simultaneously and reduce their overall adaptability in the face of rising energy costs and regulatory demands.

To mobilize the transformative potential of SMEs, targeted support mechanisms are needed. These include tailored financing instruments, simplified regulatory procedures, and capacity-building programs that facilitate both technological and organizational innovation. Support should be designed to recognize the unique needs and constraints of SMEs, while embedding them more deeply into innovation ecosystems. Without such interventions, the EU risks sidelining a vital segment of its economy from the energy transition and weakening its ability to deliver a just, inclusive, and innovation-led climate agenda.

8.3.3 Barrier within the Financial System

A critical yet often overlooked barrier to the energy transition lies in the financial system itself, whose underlying logics and incentive structures structurally favour short-term, extractive investments such as fossil fuels. Insufficient financing restricts both the diffusion of consumer technologies and the potential of SMEs to contribute to transformative innovation.

Realizing the full potential of the energy transition requires not just incremental changes in capital allocation but a fundamental transformation of the financial system (Bergek et al. 2008; Crockett 2011; Naidoo 2020). Current global investment patterns remain far below the levels needed to meet agreed sustainability targets (UNEP 2022, 2023a). Despite growing commitments, investment in fossil fuels far exceeds the amount that could keep global warming within 1.5°C reach (IEA 2023). At the same time, the global annual financing gap to meet the Sustainable Development Goals (SDGs) has expanded from $2.5 trillion in 2015 to $4 trillion in 2020 (OECD 2022; UN 2024).

Some scholars argue that the focus on short-term financial profit makes modern capitalist finance and sustainability incompatible (Foster 2001; Jäger and Schmidt 2020; Lagoarde-Segot 2019). This view is echoed by major institutions, which agree that a deep transformation of financial systems is necessary to limit warming to 1.5–2°C and to adapt to changing global climate conditions (European Commission DG FISMA 2018; IMF 2022; IPCC 2022; NGFS 2019; UNEP 2022).

In response, the field of sustainable finance has emerged as a broad umbrella term encompassing practices that integrate Environmental, Social, and Governance (ESG) criteria into financial decision-making (European Commission 2024). This includes climate finance, green bonds, ethical banking, and Socially Responsible Investing (SRI). However, there is no universally agreed definition of sustainable finance, and its implementation varies widely across actors and jurisdictions (Sisodia et al. 2023).

Despite these definitional challenges, sustainable finance is gaining global traction (Crona et al. 2021; González Martínez 2021). More than half of the global banking sector has now adopted sustainability principles (UNEP 2023b), and over US $30 trillion in sustainable assets were estimated globally by 2022 (GSIA 2022). While sustainable finance practices can effectively mobilize capital for a sustainable economy (Crona et al. 2021; Hafner et al 2020), their capacity to trigger system-wide transformation required for long-term sustainability remains unknown (Ahlström and Monciardini 2022).

When analyzing the transformative potential of sustainable finance, recent work has emphasized the importance of discerning its underlying motivations or logics (Starks 2023; Klok 2025). Financially motivated approaches to sustainable finance incentivizes sustainable investment primarily through risk–return considerations. While this can support short-term investment in renewable energy, it ultimately reinforces financial structures and incentives that privilege short-term, extractive behaviour. By contrast, when the underlying motivations are non-financial (such as moral satisfaction, identity expression, or emotional "warm glow") sustainable finance challenges the contemporary logic. As such, only non-financially motivated sustainable finance holds the potential to move beyond the artificial redirection of investment flows and enable a genuine transformation of the financial system toward sustainability (Masini and Menichetti 2013).

Despite competing with the dominant financial logic (Yan et al. 2019), empirical studies observe a growing appetite for nonfinancial returns. Institutions such as Triodos Bank (Netherlands), GLS Bank (Germany), and The Co-operative Bank (UK) are experiencing faster growth than conventional banks (Weber and Remer 2014; Krause and Battenfeld 2019). Similarly, the rise of the so-called "green premium" (or "greenium"), where investors accept lower financial returns in exchange for environmental or social impact, signals a shift in investment priorities (Pástor et al. 2022; Pietsch and Salakhova 2022). Recently, the largest European pension fund (ABP) started to divest from fossil fuel assets because of both financial risk and ethical considerations (Reuters 2022), reflecting similar trend among institutional investors (Dyck et al. 2019).

Despite these promising developments, current sustainable finance policies remain primarily driven by financial incentives. While such mechanisms can contribute to greening the economy in the short term, they ultimately perpetuate an unsustainable system of capital allocation. A more transformative shift toward nonfinancial motivations is needed to align financial systems with the broader goals of a sustainable future. This includes rethinking fiduciary duty, redefining risk, and incorporating ethical imperatives into financial regulation and governance.

8.4 Implications for Research and Innovation Policy

EU R&I policy has evolved to focus more explicitly on enabling large-scale, transformative change, reflecting a growing recognition of the systemic and interconnected nature of innovation. Technology plays a central role in this transformation (European Commission DG RTD et al. 2023). On the one hand, it offers the promise of economic renewal, improved quality of life, and solutions to pressing global problems. On the other hand, it has also contributed to exploitative practices, biodiversity loss, ecosystem collapse, irreversible pollution, and accelerated atmospheric warming. This dual impact highlights the urgent need for a comprehensive governance framework that ensures technology serves the public good while respecting ecological boundaries (Raworth 2018).

Technology governance, therefore, must be both proactive and strategic, involving multiple layers of decision-making across local, national, regional, and global levels. It must be adaptable to the geopolitical realities of increasing competition for scarce resources and the rapid development of "next" technologies, many of which carry significant uncertainties (European Commission DG RTD et al. 2024). The EU should strengthen its capacity for strategic intelligence, enabling early identification and assessment of emerging technologies' risks and opportunities (OECD 2024). Without such anticipatory capabilities, the EU risks falling behind global competitors like the United States and China in critical areas such as artificial intelligence, quantum computing, and green technologies (Favino et al. 2025).

The scope of R&I governance must extend beyond the application of technology to include the earlier stages of research and knowledge creation, especially in domains with potentially irreversible or planetary-scale impacts. This requires embedding ethical, environmental, and societal considerations from the outset (Jenkins et al. 2018, Sovacool et al. 2020). Furthermore, achieving deep and inclusive structural change in energy systems demands coordinate interventions to unlock co-benefits across sectors and drive behaviour change, thereby helping to realize a whole-systems transformation.

Ultimately, the goal of technology governance is to guide R&I in ways that promote social well-being within the Earth's ecological limits. This includes fostering collaboration across disciplines, sectors, and scales; attracting financial and human capital; and developing dynamic, anticipatory capabilities that allow societies to confront uncertainty and build resilience. Effective governance must be holistic, combining clear rule-setting with strong enforcement mechanisms to ensure that technological development is ethical, inclusive, and aligned with long-term sustainability goals.

8.5 Implications for Research and Innovation Policy

EU R&I policy has evolved to focus more explicitly on enabling large-scale, transformative change, reflecting a growing recognition of the systemic and interconnected nature of innovation. Technology plays a central role in this transformation (European Commission DG RTD et al. 2023). On the one hand, it offers the promise of economic renewal, improved quality of life, and solutions to pressing global problems. On the other hand, it has also contributed to exploitative practices, biodiversity loss, ecosystem collapse, irreversible pollution, and accelerated atmospheric warming. This dual impact highlights the urgent need for a comprehensive governance framework that ensures technology serves the public good while respecting ecological boundaries (Raworth 2018).

Technology governance, therefore, must be both proactive and strategic, involving multiple layers of decision-making across local, national, regional, and global levels. It must be adaptable to the geopolitical realities of increasing competition for scarce resources and the rapid development of "next" technologies, many of which carry significant uncertainties (European Commission DG RTD et al. 2024). The EU should strengthen its capacity for strategic intelligence, enabling early identification and assessment of emerging technologies' risks and opportunities (OECD 2024). Without such anticipatory capabilities, the EU risks falling behind global competitors like the United States and China in critical areas such as artificial intelligence, quantum computing, and green technologies (Favino et al. 2025).

The scope of R&I governance must extend beyond the application of technology to include the earlier stages of research and knowledge creation, especially in domains with potentially irreversible or planetary-scale impacts. This requires embedding ethical, environmental, and societal considerations from the outset (Jenkins et al. 2018, Sovacool et al. 2020). Furthermore, achieving deep and inclusive structural change in energy systems demands coordinate interventions to unlock co-benefits across sectors and drive behaviour change, thereby helping to realize a whole-systems transformation.

Ultimately, the goal of technology governance is to guide R&I in ways that promote social well-being within the Earth's ecological limits. This includes fostering collaboration across disciplines, sectors, and scales; attracting financial and human capital; and developing dynamic, anticipatory capabilities that allow societies to confront uncertainty and build resilience. Effective governance must be holistic, combining clear rule-setting with strong enforcement mechanisms to ensure that technological development is ethical, inclusive, and aligned with long-term sustainability goals.

Recommendation 1: Support and Scale Bottom-up, User-centric Innovations

Bottom-up initiatives, such as community energy projects and grassroots innovations, should be supported and scaled, as they have crucial role in driving system-wide transformation and community legitimacy (Seyfang and Haxeltine 2012; Hargreaves et al. 2013). Civil society plays a vital role in legitimizing new energy technologies and practices, also because public resistance to infrastructure projects, such as wind farms or new transmission lines, is a growing concern (Hirsh and Sovacool 2013). Therefore, grassroots initiatives and community energy projects are key to building societal support and generating trust in emerging systems. Active participation can reduce uncertainty and create a sense of shared purpose.

In the energy transition, users are not simply passive recipients of new technologies but active participants in shaping how these technologies are adopted, adapted, and embedded into daily life. Their existing routines are shaped by decades of infrastructure, regulation, and social norms that favour unsustainable practices. So, transitioning to new energy systems requires more than technological innovation. It demands a reconfiguration of user habits, expectations, and social meanings around energy use (Alkemade et al. 2024).

Moreover, users are instrumental in shaping the meanings and practices associated with new technologies (Geels et al. 2018). As they incorporate innovations into their routines, they develop new ways of using them, assign symbolic value, and contribute to defining what is desirable or acceptable. This process of appropriation shows that consumption is active and creative, rather than simply a matter of market choice (Schot et al. 2016).

To harness this potential, energy and R&I policies must adopt a more user-centric perspective (Moallemi and Malekpour 2018; Peuckert and Kern 2023). This includes supporting user-led innovation, fostering platforms for collaboration, and incorporating user insights into the design and rollout of energy solutions. By recognizing users as co-creators of sustainable systems, rather than obstacles to change, R&I policy can drive a more inclusive, adaptive, and effective energy transition (Voulvoulis et al. 2022).

Therefore, technological innovation without societal buy-in can stall or fail altogether, making the concept of Societal Readiness Levels (SRLs) highly relevant. SRLs measure the extent to which society is prepared to adopt and engage with new technologies. Societal readiness should not be treated as a downstream issue but rather integrated into the design and governance of R&I agendas from the outset. Embedding SRLs in R&I programs can help anticipate barriers and improve the design of technologies that align with public values, hence strategic instruments to guide R&I priorities and stakeholder engagement.

Recommendation 2: Address Existing Lock-ins and Prevent the Formation of New Ones through Systems-based Governance

Existing lock-ins should be addressed and the risks of new lock-ins mitigated. To reconcile the inertia of technological lock-ins with the transformative potential of decentralized, bottom-up approaches, the EU R&I policy must adopt a systems-based governance perspective that embraces complexity, uncertainty, and long-term societal transformation. The EU R&I policy has a strong research foundation and ambitious climate targets, but its energy transition efforts remain constrained by transformation failures. These go beyond traditional market or system failures (Weber and Rohracher 2012; Woolthuis et al. 2005): transformation failures include misalignments between policy domains and fragmentation across governance levels (European Innovation Council 2025), but also, they include institutional practices that privilege incumbent technologies and actors (Lindberg et al. 2019). Such transformation failures undermine the EU's ability to realize large-scale, just, and sustainable change.

Transformative policy interventions are needed to address such transformation failures (Raven and Walrave 2020). On the one side, a more transformative approach calls for integrated governance that bridges national, regional, and EU-level R&I efforts, enabling shared learning, reducing duplication, and making space for different possible futures. This means not only supporting the creation of new, sustainable technologies, but also actively phasing out those that reinforce carbon-intensive systems, through mechanisms such as delegitimating, redirecting investment, and dismantling outdated policy support structures (Bento et al. 2025). At the same time, transformation cannot succeed without grounding innovation in societal contexts. People are not passive consumers of energy technologies. They have creative agency and capacity to catalyze broader system shifts via bottom-up initiatives, such as community energy projects. These grassroots innovations often surface ahead of policy yet rarely benefit from structured support or integration into mainstream R&I agendas.

Governance in the EU energy transition needs to be framed beyond technology deployment (Avelino et al. 2016). A transformative and systems-based approach reduces the risk of missing the opportunity to shape trajectories at their source. Less inclusive R&I strategic decisions made during early stage can embed certain pathways and preclude alternatives. Failing to govern at this stage risks lock-ins that may prove difficult or undesirable to undo later (Unruh 2000; Seto et al. 2016).

The systems-based approach to energy governance invites a shift in mindset: from managing discrete technologies to orchestrating transformations in how systems are imagined, governed, and lived. Transformative policy should give policymakers the framework to move beyond prediction toward anticipation and adaptation. In doing so, the EU can position itself not merely as a regulator or driver for technology innovation but can also bring people together to shape the future collectively. This means guiding transitions that are not only technologically advanced, but socially legitimate, environmentally grounded, and structurally transformative.

Recommendation 3: Integrate and Empower SMEs through a Systemic, Multi-level Policy Framework

In this context, the energy transition must be supported by a systemic, multi-level policy framework that actively integrates SMEs into its strategic vision. This includes a revitalization strategy embedded within a transformative R&I policy that addresses persistent bottlenecks, particularly financing gaps and innovation scale-up. Public and private financial instruments need to be strengthened to support clean-tech SMEs, especially in overcoming barriers related to intangible asset valuation and fragmented demand (Mazzucato and Semieniuk 2018; Aphecetche 2025).

Strategic interventions must also target the removal of regulatory obstacles, the enhancement of cross-border market access, and the provision of targeted funding to facilitate innovation uptake and technological deployment (Fawcett and Hampton 2020). This calls for a reorientation of the EU innovation policy, moving beyond traditional market failure logic to steer innovation towards societal missions, such as decarbonization, strategic autonomy, and sustainable competitiveness (European Commission JRC et al. 2024).

In comparison to its global competitors, the EU's clean-tech ambitions are constrained by structural disadvantages. China's state-led industrial policy provides extensive subsidies and benefits from resource abundance and massive economies of scale. The US similarly leverages a unified market, strong venture capital ecosystems, and proactive policy support to attract and retain innovative firms. A transformation of the finance system to target long-term societal values is key here.

To remain competitive, the EU must embed sustainability transitions within its industrial and innovation policy. R&I must serve as a foundation for building an economy that is not only innovative and productive, but also resilient, fair, and environmentally sustainable. This necessitates explicit policy mixes that align competitiveness with ecological limits, incorporate environmental and social costs, and prioritize sufficiency-based models of decentralized, low-carbon systems (Dasgupta and Levin 2023; Vezzoni 2023).

References

Ahlström, H., and D. Monciardini (2022) "The Regulatory Dynamics of Sustainable Finance: Paradoxical Success and Limitations of EU Reforms", *J. Bus. Ethics* 177, 193–212, https://doi.org/10.1007/s10551-021-04763-x

Alkemade, F., B. de Bruin, A. El-Feiaz, F. Pasimeni, L. Niamir, and R. Wade (2024), "Social Tipping Dynamics in the Energy System", *Earth System Dynamics* 15.2, 485–500,https://doi.org/10.5194/esd-15-485-2024

Anadón, L. D. (2012) "Missions-oriented RD&D Institutions in Energy between 2000 and 2010: A Comparative Analysis of China, the United Kingdom, and the United States", *Research Policy* 41.10, 1742–1756, https://doi.org/10.1016/j.respol.2012.02.015

Aphecetche, T. (2025) *Investment Barriers to Sustainable Finance: How to Enable the Transition in G20 Economies*, Economic Brief 083. Luxembourg: Publications Office of the European Union, https://data.europa.eu/doi/10.2765/50647

Avelino, F., J. Grin, B. Pel, and S. Jhagroe (2016) "The Politics of Sustainability Transitions", *Journal of Environmental Policy and Planning* 18.5, 557–567, https://doi.org/10.1080/1523908X.2016.1216782

Bento, N., A. Nunez-Jimenez, and N. Kittner (2025) "Decline Processes in Technological Innovation Systems: Lessons from Energy Technologies", *Research Policy* 54.3, 105174, https://doi.org/10.1016/j.respol.2025.105174

Bergek, A., S. Jacobsson, B. Carlsson, S. Lindmark, and A. Rickne (2008) "Analyzing the Functional Dynamics of Technological Innovation Systems: A Scheme of Analysis", *Res. Policy* 37, 407–429, https://doi.org/10.1016/j.respol.2007.12.003

Burch, S., M. Andrachuk, D. Carey, N. Frantzeskaki, H. Schroeder, N. Mischkowski, and D. Loorbach (2016) "Governing and Accelerating Transformative Entrepreneurship: Exploring the Potential for Small Business Innovation on Urban Sustainability Transitions", *Current Opinion in Environmental Sustainability* 22, 26–32, https://doi.org/10.1016/j.cosust.2017.04.002

Chatzistamoulou, N., and E. Tyllianakis (2022) "Commitment of European SMEs to Resource Efficiency Actions to Achieve Sustainability Transition. A Feasible Reality or an Elusive Goal?", *Journal of Environmental Management* 321, 115937, https://doi.org/10.1016/j.jenvman.2022.115937

Crockett, A. (2011) "What Financial System for the 21st Century", 26 June, *Bank for International Settlements*, https://www.bis.org/events/agm2011/sp110626.htm

Crona, B., C. Folke, and V. Galaz (2021) "The Anthropocene Reality of Financial Risk", *One Earth* 4, 618–628, https://doi.org/10.1016/j.oneear.2021.04.016

Dasgupta, P., and S. Levin (2023) "Economic Factors Underlying Biodiversity Loss", *Philosophical Transactions of the Royal Society B* 378, 20220197, https://doi.org/10.1098/rstb.2022.0197

Draghi, M. (2024) *The Future of European Competitiveness*. Brussels: European Commission, https://commission.europa.eu/topics/eu-competitiveness/draghi-report_en

Dyck, A., K. V. Lins, L. Roth, and H. F. Wagner (2019) "Do Institutional Investors Drive Corporate Social Responsibility? International Evidence", *J. Financ. Econ.* 131, 693–714, https://doi.org/10.1016/j.jfineco.2018.08.013

Eitan, A., and M. P. Hekkert (2023) "Locked in Transition? Towards a Conceptualization of Path-dependence Lock-ins in the Renewable Energy Landscape", *Energy Research & Social Science* 106, 103316, https://doi.org/10.1016/j.erss.2023.103316

European Commission (2024) "Overview of Sustainable Finance", https://finance.ec.europa.eu/sustainable-finance/overview-sustainable-finance_en

European Commission DG FISMA (2018) "Financing a Sustainable European Economy. Final Report 2018 by the High-Level Expert Group on Sustainable Finance", https://finance.ec.europa.eu/publications/high-level-expert-group-sustainable-finance-hleg_en

European Commission DG RTD, B. Cavicchi, O. Peiffer-Smadja, J. Ravet, and A. Hobza (2023) *The Transformative Nature of the European Framework Programme for Research and Innovation—Analysis of Its Evolution between 2002–2023*. Luxembourg: Publications Office of the European Union, https://data.europa.eu/doi/10.2777/73000

European Commission DG RTD, K. Richardson, A. Renda, F. Alkemade, R. Walz, et al. (2024) *Embedding Anticipatory Governance in Europe's Transitions*. Luxembourg: Publications Office of the European Union, https://data.europa.eu/doi/10.2777/3778181

European Commission JRC, S. Schwaag-Serger, L. Soete, and J. Stierna (2024) *Scientific Report—For an Innovative, Sustainable and Fair Economy in Europe*. Luxembourg: Publications Office of the European Union, https://data.europa.eu/doi/10.2760/0336180

European Innovation Council (2025) "EIC Board Calls for National and Regional Synergies to Boost Deep Tech Innovation", *European Innovation Council and SMEs Executive Agency*, 12 May, https://eic.ec.europa.eu/news/eic-board-calls-national-and-regional-synergies-boost-deep-tech-innovation-2025-05-12_en

Eurostat (2024) "Digitalisation in Europe—2024 Edition", https://ec.europa.eu/eurostat/web/interactive-publications/digitalisation-2024

Favino, R., N. Conte, A. De Maleville, E. Garcia Monreal, E. Montanari, A. Paganini, M. Sangiorgi, and C. Sfalagkiaris, C. (2025) *Emerging Risks and Opportunities for EU Internal Security Stemming from New Technologies*. Luxembourg: Publications Office of the European Union, https://data.europa.eu/doi/10.2760/9617320

Fawcett, T., and S. Hampton (2020) "Why and How Energy Efficiency Policy Should Address SMEs", *Energy Policy* 140, 111337, https://doi.org/10.1016/j.enpol.2020.111337

Foster, J. B. (2001) "Ecology Against Capitalism", *Mon. Rev.* 53, 1–15, https://doi.org/10.14452/MR-053-05-2001-09_1

Gallagher, K. S., A. Grübler, L. Kuhl, G. Nemet, and C. Wilson (2012) "The Energy Technology Innovation System", *Annual Review of Environment and Resources* 37.1, 137–162, https://doi.org/10.1146/annurev-environ-060311-133915

Geels, F. W., T. Schwanen, S. Sorrell, K. Jenkins, and B. K. Sovacool (2018) "Reducing Energy Demand through Low Carbon Innovation: A Sociotechnical Transitions Perspective and Thirteen Research Debates', *Energy Research & Social Science* 40, 23–35, https://doi.org/10.1016/j.erss.2017.11.003

González Martínez, C. I. (2021) "Overview of Global and European Institutional Sustainable Finance Initiatives", *Banco de Espana Article* 30, https://ssrn.com/abstract=3937147

GSIA—Global Sustainable Investment Alliance (2022) *Global Sustainable Investment Review 2022*, https://www.gsi-alliance.org/wp-content/uploads/2023/12/GSIA-Report-2022.pdf

Haanyika, C. M. (2006) "Rural Electrification Policy and Institutional Linkages", *Energy Policy* 34.17, 2977–2993, https://doi.org/10.1016/j.enpol.2005.05.008

Hafner, S., A. Jones, A. Anger-Kraavi, and J. Pohl (2020) "Closing the Green Finance Gap—A Systems Perspective", *Environ. Innov. Soc. Transit.* 34, 26–60, https://doi.org/10.1016/j.eist.2019.11.007

Hargreaves, T., S. Hielscher, G. Seyfang, and A. Smith (2013) "Grassroots Innovations in Community Energy: The Role of Intermediaries in Niche Development", *Global Environmental Change* 23.5, 868–880, https://doi.org/10.1016/j.gloenvcha.2013.02.008

Hervás-Oliver, J. L., M. D. Parrilli, A. Rodríguez-Pose, and F. Sempere-Ripoll (2021) "The Rivers of SME Innovation in the Regions of the EU", *Research Policy* 50.9, 104316, https://doi.org/10.1016/j.respol.2021.104316

Hirsh, R. F., and B. K. Sovacool (2013) "Wind Turbines and Invisible Technology: Unarticulated Reasons for Local Opposition to Wind Energy", *Technology and Culture* 54.4, 705–734, https://dx.doi.org/10.1353/tech.2013.0131

Hoicka, C. E., J. Lowitzsch, M. C. Brisbois, A. Kumar, and L. R. Camargo (2021) "Implementing a Just Renewable Energy Transition: Policy Advice for Transposing the New European Rules for Renewable Energy Communities", *Energy Policy* 156, 112435, https://doi.org/10.1016/j.enpol.2021.112435

IEA (2023) *World Energy Outlook 2023*. Paris: IEA, https://www.iea.org/reports/world-energy-outlook-2023

IEA (2024a) *Renewables 2024*. Paris: IEA, https://www.iea.org/reports/renewables-2024

IEA (2024b) *World Energy Outlook 2024*. Paris: IEA, https://www.iea.org/reports/world-energy-outlook-2024

IMF—International Monetary Fund (2022) *Crisis Upon Crisis*. Washington, DC: IMF, https://www.imf.org/external/pubs/ft/ar/2022/

IPCC (2022) *Climate Change 2022: Mitigation of Climate Change. Contribution of Working Group III to the Sixth Assessment Report of the Intergovernmental Panel on Climate Change*, P.R. Shukla, J. Skea, R. Slade, A. Al Khourdajie, R. van Diemen, D. McCollum, M. Pathak, S. Some, P. Vyas, R. Fradera, M. Belkacemi, A. Hasija, G. Lisboa, S. Luz, J. Malley, (eds.). Cambridge, UK: Cambridge University Press, https://doi.org/10.1017/9781009157926

IRENA (2024) *World Energy Transitions Outlook 2024: 1.5°C Pathway*. Abu Dhabi: IRENA, https://www.irena.org/-/media/Files/IRENA/Agency/Publication/2024/Nov/IRENA_World_energy_transitions_outlook_2024.pdf

Jäger, J., and L. Schmidt (2020) "Global Green Finance and Sustainability: Insights for Progressive Strategies", *J. Für Entwicklungspolitik* 36, 4–30, https://doi.org/10.20446/JEP-2414-3197-36-4-4

Jenkins, K., B. K. Sovacool, and D. McCauley (2018) "Humanizing Sociotechnical Transitions through Energy Justice: An Ethical Framework for Global Transformative Change", *Energy Policy* 117, 66–74, https://doi.org/10.1016/j.enpol.2018.02.036

Kern, F., K. S. Rogge, and M. Howlett (2019) "Policy Mixes for Sustainability Transitions: New Approaches and Insights through Bridging Innovation and Policy Studies", *Research Policy* 48.10, 103832, https://doi.org/10.1016/j.respol.2019.103832

Kim, Y. J., and C. Wilson (2019) "Analysing Future Change in the EU's Energy Innovation System", *Energy Strategy Reviews* 24, 279–299, https://doi.org/10.1016/j.esr.2019.04.012

Kitchens, C., and P. Fishback (2015) "Flip the Switch: The Impact of the Rural Electrification Administration 1935–1940", *The Journal of Economic History* 75.4, 1161–1195.

Klok, W. (2025) "The Limits of Sustainable Finance: A Systems Framework for Evaluating Transformative Change", https://papers.ssrn.com/abstract=5316711

Krause, K., and D. Battenfeld (2019) "Coming Out of the Niche? Social Banking in Germany: An Empirical Analysis of Consumer Characteristics and Market Size", *J. Bus. Ethics* 155, 889–911, https://doi.org/10.1007/s10551-017-3491-9

Lagoarde-Segot, T. (2019) "Sustainable Finance: A Critical Realist Perspective", *Res. Int. Bus. Finance* 47, 1–9, https://doi.org/10.1016/j.ribaf.2018.04.010

Lauber, V., and S. Jacobsson (2016) "The Politics and Economics of Constructing, Contesting and Restricting Socio-political Space for Renewables—The German Renewable Energy Act", *Environmental Innovation and Societal Transitions* 18, 147–163, https://doi.org/10.1016/j.eist.2015.06.005

Lee, N., H. Sameen, and M. Cowling (2015) "Access to Finance for Innovative SMEs since the Financial Crisis", *Research Policy* 44.2, 370–380, https://doi.org/10.1016/j.respol.2014.09.008

Lindberg, M. B., J. Markard, and A. D. Andersen (2019) "Policies, Actors and Sustainability Transition Pathways: A Study of the EU's Energy Policy Mix", *Research Policy* 48.10, 103668, https://doi.org/10.1016/j.respol.2018.09.003

Markard, J., and B. Truffer (2006) "Innovation Processes in Large Technical Systems: Market Liberalization as a Driver for Radical Change?", *Research Policy* 35.5, 609–625, https://doi.org/10.1016/j.respol.2006.02.008

Masini, A., and E. Menichetti (2013) "Investment Decisions in the Renewable Energy Sector: An Analysis of Non-financial Drivers", *Technological Forecasting and Social Change* 80.3, 510–524, https://doi.org/10.1016/j.techfore.2012.08.003

Mazzucato, M., and G. Semieniuk (2018) "Financing Renewable Energy: Who Is Financing What and Why It Matters", *Technological Forecasting and Social Change* 127, 8–22, https://doi.org/10.1016/j.techfore.2017.05.021

Moallemi, E. A., and S. Malekpour (2018), "A Participatory Exploratory Modelling Approach for Long-term Planning in Energy Transitions", *Energy Research & Social Science* 35, 205–216, https://doi.org/10.1016/j.erss.2017.10.022

Naidoo, C. P. (2020) "Relating Financial Systems to Sustainability Transitions: Challenges, Demands and Design Features", *Environ. Innov. Soc. Transit.* 36, 270–290, https://doi.org/10.1016/j.eist.2019.10.004

NGFS—Network for Greening the Financial System (2019) *A Call for Action: Climate Change as a Source of Financial Risk*, https://www.ngfs.net/system/files/import/ngfs/medias/documents/ngfs_first_comprehensive_report_-_17042019_0.pdf

OECD (2022) *Global Outlook on Financing for Sustainable Development 2023*. Paris: OECD, https://doi.org/10.1787/fcbe6ce9-en

OECD (2024), "Framework for Anticipatory Governance of Emerging Technologies", *OECD Science, Technology and Industry Policy Papers* 165. Paris: OECD, https://doi.org/10.1787/0248ead5-en

Pástor, L., R. F. Stambaugh, and L. A. Taylor (2022) "Dissecting Green Returns", *J. Financ. Econ.* 146, 403–424, https://doi.org/10.1016/j.jfineco.2022.07.007

Peters, J., M. Harsdorff, and F. Ziegler (2009) "Rural Electrification: Accelerating Impacts with Complementary Services", *Energy for Sustainable Development* 13.1, 38–42, https://doi.org/10.1016/j.esd.2009.01.004

Peuckert, J., and F. Kern (2023) "How User Innovation Communities Contribute to Sustainability Transitions. An Exploration of Three Online Communities", *Environmental Innovation and Societal Transitions* 49, 100785, https://doi.org/10.1016/j.eist.2023.100785

Pietsch, A., and D. Salakhova (2022) "Pricing of Green Bonds: Drivers and Dynamics of the Greenium", ECB Working Paper 2022/2728, https://doi.org/10.2139/ssrn.4227559

Pyrgou, A., A. Kylili, and P. A. Fokaides (2016) "The Future of the Feed-in Tariff (FiT) Scheme in Europe: The Case of Photovoltaics", *Energy Policy* 95, 94–102, https://doi.org/10.1016/j.enpol.2016.04.048

Radicic, D., and G. Pugh (2017) "R&D Programmes, Policy Mix, and the 'European Paradox': Evidence from European SMEs", *Science and Public Policy* 44.4, 497–512, https://doi.org/10.1093/scipol/scw077

Raven, R., and B. Walrave (2020) "Overcoming Transformational Failures through Policy Mixes in the Dynamics of Technological Innovation Systems", *Technological Forecasting and Social Change* 153, 119297, https://doi.org/10.1016/j.techfore.2018.05.008

Raworth, K. (2018) *Doughnut Economics: Seven Ways to Think like a 21st Century Economist*. White River Junction, VT: Chelsea Green Publishing.

Reuters (2022) "Dutch Pension Giant ABP Set to Sell Laggards as Sharpens Climate Focus", 23 December, *Reuters*, https://www.reuters.com/business/finance/dutch-pension-giant-abp-overhaul-portfolio-sustainability-drive-2022-12-23/

Schot, J., L. Kanger, and G. Verbong (2016) "The Roles of Users in Shaping Transitions to New Energy Systems", *Nature Energy* 1.5, 1–7, https://doi.org/10.1038/nenergy.2016.54

Schot, J., and W. E. Steinmueller (2018) "Three Frames for Innovation Policy: R&D, Systems of Innovation and Transformative Change", *Research Policy* 47.9, 1554–1567, https://doi.org/10.1016/j.respol.2018.08.011

Schleich, J., A. Durand, and H. Brugger (2021) "How Effective Are EU Minimum Energy Performance Standards and Energy Labels for Cold Appliances?", *Energy Policy* 149, 112069, https://doi.org/10.1016/j.enpol.2020.112069

Seyfang, G., and A. Haxeltine (2012) "Growing Grassroots Innovations: Exploring the Role of Community-based Initiatives in Governing Sustainable Energy Transitions", *Environment and Planning C: Government and Policy* 30.3, 381-400, https://doi.org/10.1068/c10222

Seto, K. C., S. J. Davis, R. B. Mitchell, E. C. Stokes, G. Unruh, and D. Urge-Vorsatz (2016) "Carbon Lock-in: Types, Causes, and Policy Implications", *Annual Review of Environment and Resources* 41.1, 425–452, https://doi.org/10.1146/annurev-environ-110615-085934

Sisodia, A., and G. C. Maheshwari (2023) "Exploring Sustainable Finance: A Review and Future Research Agenda", *Vision*, https://doi.org/10.1177/09722629231209177

Sovacool, B. K., D. J. Hess, S. Amir, F. W. Geels, R. Hirsh, L. R. Medina, C. Miller, C. A. Palavicino, R. Phadke, M. Ryghaug et al. (2020) "Sociotechnical Agendas: Reviewing Future Directions for Energy and Climate Research", *Energy Research & Social Science* 70, 101617, https://doi.org/10.1016/j.erss.2020.101617

Starks, L. T. (2023) "Presidential Address: Sustainable Finance and ESG Issues—Value versus Values", *The Journal of Finance* 78.4, 1837–1872, https://doi.org/10.1111/jofi.13255

Testa, G., R. Compano, A. Correia, and E. Rückert (2022) *In Search of EU Unicorns—What Do We Know about Them*. Luxembourg: Publications Office of the European Union, https://publications.jrc.ec.europa.eu/repository/handle/JRC127712

UN—United Nations Research Institute for Social Development (2024) *Report of the Inter-Agency Task Force on Financing for Development 2024. Financing for Sustainable Development Report: Financing for Development at a Crossroads*. New Yor: United Nations Publications, https://doi.org/10.18356/9789213588635

UNEP—United Nations Environment Programme (2022) *Emissions Gap Report 2022: The Closing Window — Climate Crisis Calls for Rapid Transformation of Societies*. Nairobi: UNEP, https://www.unep.org/emissions-gap-report-2022

UNEP—United Nations Environment Programme (2023a) *Emissions Gap Report 2023: Broken Record—Temperatures Hit New Highs, Yet World Fails to Cut Emissions (Again)*. Nairobi: UNEP, https://doi.org/10.59117/20.500.11822/43922

UNEP—United Nations Environment Programme (2023b) *Responsible Banking: Towards Real-world Impact*. Geneva: UN, https://www.unepfi.org/wordpress/wp-content/uploads/2023/09/PRB-Second-Progress-Report-2023.pdf

Unruh, G. C. (2000) "Understanding Carbon Lock-in", *Energy Policy* 28.12, 817–830, https://doi.org/10.1016/S0301-4215(00)00070-7

Vezzoni, R. (2023) "Green Growth for Whom, How and Why? The REPowerEU Plan and the Inconsistencies of European Union Energy Policy", *Energy Research & Social Science* 101, 103134, https://doi.org/10.1016/j.erss.2023.103134

Voulvoulis, N., T. Giakoumis, C. Hunt, V. Kioupi, N. Petrou, I. Souliotis, and C. Vaghela et al. (2022) "Systems Thinking as a Paradigm Shift for Sustainability Transformation", *Global Environmental Change* 75, 102544, https://doi.org/10.1016/j.gloenvcha.2022.102544

Weber, O., and S. Remer (eds) (2014) *Social Banks and the Future of Sustainable Finance*. London and New York: Routledge.

Weber, K. M., and H. Rohracher (2012) "Legitimizing Research, Technology and Innovation Policies for Transformative Change: Combining Insights from Innovation Systems and Multi-level Perspective in a Comprehensive 'Failures' Framework", *Research Policy* 41.6, 1037–1047, https://doi.org/10.1016/j.respol.2011.10.015

Woolthuis, R. K., M. Lankhuizen, and V. Gilsing (2005) "A System Failure Framework for Innovation Policy Design", *Technovation* 25.6, 609–619, https://doi.org/10.1016/j.technovation.2003.11.002

Yan, S., F. Ferraro, and J. Almandoz (2019) "The Rise of Socially Responsible Investment Funds: The Paradoxical Role of the Financial Logic", *Adm. Sci. Q.* 64, 466–501, https://doi.org/10.1177/0001839218773324

9. On Grids:
The Backbone of the Energy Transition

Antonella Battaglini[1] and Catharina Sikow-Magny[2]

This chapter examines the central role of electricity grids in Europe's energy transition toward climate neutrality, energy security, and sustainability. Historically overlooked, electricity infrastructure has now emerged as a critical enabler of decarbonization, enabling the integration of renewable energy, electrification of end-use sectors, and cross-border power flows. The study analyzes EU regulatory frameworks—especially the National Energy and Climate Plans (NECPs) and the Trans-European Networks for Energy (TEN-E)—and identifies key investment needs, flexibility technologies, and optimization strategies. It argues for a shift toward integrated, demand-cum-supply planning to ensure cost-effective, resilient, and environmentally responsible grid development. The 2025 Iberian blackout highlights the risks of underinvestment and inflexibility (Financial Times 2025; ENTSO-E 2025; REE and REN 2025). The chapter also stresses the importance of public engagement, regional cooperation, and cross-sectoral coordination to unlock local benefits and accelerate permitting. Policy recommendations focus on improving cost-benefit analysis, recognizing distributed assets, and aligning investment with long-term system value. It concludes that well-designed grids are the backbone of a just, secure, and efficient European energy transition.

9.1 Introduction

The European energy landscape is undergoing a profound transformation, driven by the imperatives of decarbonization, digitalization, and decentralization. These interconnected trends align with the EU's overarching objectives of climate neutrality, energy security, environmental sustainability, and economic competitiveness. At the heart of this transformation lies the development of a robust, integrated, and flexible electricity grid.

> A central element in accelerating decarbonisation will be unlocking the potential of clean energy through a collective EU focus on grids. (Draghi 2024, p. 50)

---

1   Renewable Grids Initiative.
2   Renewable Grids Initiative.

https://doi.org/10.11647/OBP.0499.09

This grid must support growing shares of renewable energy, enable seamless cross-border electricity flows, empower consumers as active participants, and ensure the efficient use of natural and material resources. Moreover, the grid has to withstand physical and digital threats from extreme weather events or hostile attacks to be able to guarantee energy and system security (Myers Jaffe, Loch-Temzelides, and Lo Prete 2024).

Historically, electricity grids received little attention in energy transition strategies, often treated as passive infrastructure rather than dynamic enablers of change. More recently, grids have come to the forefront of political and policy agendas across Europe (European Commission, 2022b, 2025) and globally. This shift reflects a growing recognition of their indispensable role in realizing a sustainable and secure energy system that minimizes environmental impact and resource intensity. Only in 2013, the EU complemented the rules on the internal energy market with a comprehensive policy framework for European networks (Regulation (EU) No 347/2013).

This chapter explores how integrated demand-cum-supply policies—which target both energy consumption and production—are reshaping grid development and system planning in Europe. It examines the evolving role of grids in decarbonization, the EU's regulatory and planning frameworks (including National Energy and Climate Plans and the Trans-European Networks for Energy), investment needs and optimization strategies, and concludes with policy recommendations to ensure integrated grid planning and optimization of all resources become a primary lever for systemic and environmentally responsible optimization. This analysis draws on the Clean Energy for All Europeans Package,[3] aiming also to provide inspiration to countries outside of the European Union.

9.2 The Role of Grids in the Energy Transition

Electricity grids at all voltage levels are the connective tissue of the energy transition. They connect producers and consumers within and across regions and borders, enable the integration of renewable energy sources, most of which are variable (VREs) like solar and wind, and facilitate the decarbonization of end-use sectors such as transport, heating, and industry. At the same time, they must be developed in a way that minimizes land take, preserves biodiversity, and avoids overbuilding, supporting a circular and resource-efficient energy economy.

Massively expanding the share of renewable energy sources, especially wind and solar, is central to Europe's decarbonization strategy. These sources are domestically available, reduce import dependencies (Aquila Group 2023), stabilize prices, and enhance energy sovereignty in a geopolitically unstable world. However, the success of this strategy hinges on adequate grid capacity and connectivity. Without strong

---

3   The Clean Energy for All Europeans Package was adopted in 2019 and comprises eight legislative
    acts that update the EU's energy policy framework, promoting decarbonization, consumer rights, and
    innovation across energy systems.

infrastructure, renewable energy cannot be delivered to where it is needed, leading to curtailment, inefficiencies, and wasted resources (Beyond Fossil Fuels, IEEFA, E3G, EMBER 2025).

> Significant queues of solar, wind and storage projects waiting for grid connections have built up across Europe. In fact, the volume of renewable energy projects waiting to connect far outstrips the additional installation required to reach 2030 national energy and climate plan targets.

In this context, the electricity grid is a critical enabler, especially when combined with flexibility options such as demand-side management, energy storage, and intersectoral integration (e.g., power-to-heat or power-to-hydrogen) (IEA 2023). Grids are also a key factor for making it possible for consumers to become active participants in the market to benefit from low prices when renewable production is abundant and to offer their solar production to the market when not needed. Greater grid intelligence—through digitalization, automation, and real-time data management—is essential to manage increasingly complex and decentralized energy flows while optimizing the use of existing assets and limiting unnecessary expansion (CEER 2021).

Electricity grids also enhance system resilience and security of supply. By interconnecting national markets, they enlarge the area that can provide efficient backup when renewable production is low and hence reduce the risk of localized disruptions and support mutual assistance during crises. Well-planned grids minimize system costs, enhance inclusiveness, reduce environmental footprint, and support long-term sustainability.

Despite their essential role in system security, electricity grids are often opposed by communities where they need to be built (European Commission 2020). Local political support is often missing or controversial. Efforts to engage local communities should be intensified with the overall aim to reduce asymmetries between those who have benefits and those who suffer impacts. This requires new approaches delivering tangible and lasting local benefits whenever building new grid infrastructure, as often happens with other infrastructure projects (European Commission, ACER, RGI 2023).

9.3 EU Regulatory and Planning Framework

9.3.1 National Energy and Climate Plans (NECPs)

The National Energy and Climate Plans (NECPs) are the main strategic policy planning tool for Member States to describe how they will meet the objectives and targets set for 2030. They were introduced in 2018 by the Regulation on the governance of the energy union and climate action (Regulation (EU) 2018/1999).

The NECPs form the basis for grid planning. As their name says, they are focussed on national targets, policies, and measures and hence rarely integrate the neighbouring countries policies into the analysis (see Chapter 10 for EU-level planning). Furthermore, local grids, so called distribution grids, are not always well covered in the NECPs, despite their increasingly important role in a much more decentralized energy system.

The NECPs are updated and monitored regularly so as to stay on track to achieve climate neutrality and resilience by 2050. The NECPs aim at providing investment predictability and help to ensure that the EU's transition is socially just, provides energy security and affordability.

The NECPs consist of the following five dimensions and provide for actions on how each Member State intends to reach the objectives set for the short and longer terms:

- decarbonization;
- energy efficiency;
- energy security;
- internal energy market; and
- research, innovation, and competitiveness.

According to the process set in the Governance Regulation, Member States had to submit their draft NECPs covering the period 2021–2030 by end of 2018. The Commission was given the task to analyze the plans and to provide country-specific recommendations. Member States were then required to submit the final NECPs by end 2019, addressing the recommendations.

As part of the regular update of the NECPs, Member States were to submit the draft NECPs by mid-2023, following the guidance the Commission had published earlier to guide the process and scope of the update. By the end of 2023, the Commission completed the EU-wide assessment of the updated NECPs, together with individual assessments and country-specific recommendations.

The Commission's assessment (European Commission 2023) reveals that gaps remain in terms of reaching the EU targets, whilst Member States are on the right track towards the 2030 requirements. This is not surprising because the targets were increased as part of the "Fit for 55" package only very recently, leaving too little time for Member States to increase the ambition of the plans and investments.

9.3.2 Trans-European Networks for Energy (TEN-E)

Whilst well-integrated grids are an essential part of the internal market, one of the five dimensions of the NECPs, EU's grid planning is carried out as a separate exercise based on EU-level planning instead of national approaches. This process has been governed since 2013 by the TEN-E regulation, under which the European Network of Transmission System Operators for Electricity and Gas (ENTSO-E and ENTSOG), and more recently on The European Network of Network Operators for Hydrogen

(ENNOH), develop ten-year network development plans (TYNDP) based on common scenarios (ENTSO-E 2022).

The TEN-E process is based on the identification of strategic energy priority areas across the EU (and beyond) that reflect regional specificities and infrastructure challenges and bottlenecks. Technical criteria are then used to identify the necessary projects that can remove the bottlenecks in a cost-efficient manner.

The TEN-E regulation puts regional cooperation at the core of developing the European grids that are relevant for cross-border flows and trade. The cooperation brings together all the relevant parties—ENTSOs, project promoters, Member States' authorities including regulators and permitting authorities, ACER, the Commission, and stakeholders—to discuss the regional investment bottlenecks and gaps and the merits of different projects proposed to remove them.

The process to translate these strategic corridors into concrete projects, labelled "projects of common interest" (PCI), consists of the following steps:

- Every two years, project promoters submit their proposals for candidate PCIs, which must already be part of the ten-year network development plan (TYNDP). Since 2013, the TYNDP is accompanied by a cost-benefit analysis which serves two purposes: first, to analyze the resilience of the grid to different future situations and disruption scenarios and second, to assess how candidate PCIs contribute to removing the identified bottlenecks.

- The regional groups assess these proposals against technical criteria and indicators. These are derived from the energy and climate policy objectives and reflect the three pillars of energy policy: completing the internal market, enhancing competition, and ensuring security of supply and sustainability.

- The regional groups rank the proposals according to their contribution to the specific criteria of sustainability, security of supply and market integration and prices, taking into account also some additional qualitative criteria, such as cohesion and regional balance.

- Following stakeholder consultations on the list of candidate PCIs, the decision-making body of each regional group adopts the respective regional list, taking into account ACER's opination on cross-regional consistency. The decision-making body consists of the Member States covered by the priority corridor and the Commission.

- Finally, the Commission adopts the Union-wide PCI-list through the delegated act procedure. This list may contain fewer projects than the combined regional lists if the Commission considers that these contain a non-manageable number of projects.

The selected PCIs benefit from regulatory and financing instruments to support their implementation, including streamlined permitting procedure, cross-border cost sharing, regulatory incentives to address specific risks, better information for decision-making and innovative financial instruments. The regional groups monitor progress and take action to remove obstacles.

The first PCI-list was adopted in autumn 2013 and a new list has been adopted every two years since. The currently valid PCI-list is from 2023 and it includes 166 projects, of which electricity projects represent more than half (85), while 65 are hydrogen projects and 14 CO_2 projects. Natural gas was removed from the scope of the TEN-E regulation in the 2022 review (Regulation (EU) 2022/869) after evaluation showed that EU's gas grid was sufficiently robust and resilient given the expected consumption of gas in the future.

9.4 Investment Needs and Challenges

Modernizing Europe's electricity grids demands unprecedented investment. The European Commission estimates that over €584 billion will be needed by 2030 to upgrade and expand grid infrastructure (European Commission 2022b). Two thirds of this is expected to be needed at the local distribution grid, confirmed by ENTSO-E's estimation that projects that transmission system needs alone could require up to €174 billion (ENTSO-E 2022).

In addition, further investments are needed in the interface of transmission and distribution systems, at all voltage levels so as to make the whole system efficient and seamless, from production to consumption.

These investments serve multiple objectives:

- integrating renewables and electrifying end-use sectors;
- replacing ageing assets;
- expanding interconnection capacity; and
- enhancing digital capabilities and cybersecurity.

However, several barriers hinder progress:

- permitting delays (grid projects can take well over seven years to complete);
- workforce and material limitations (labour shortages and constrained supplies of copper and aluminium); and
- public opposition (concerns over land use, environmental impacts, and fairness).

Investment frameworks must be fit for purpose. This includes ensuring cost-effectiveness, incentivizing innovation, and blending public and private finance. Instruments like the Connecting Europe Facility (CEF), InvestEU, and the Modernization Fund play key roles, but further reform is needed to accelerate disbursement and de-risk private capital.

9.5 Ensuring Efficient Investments

Keeping electricity prices affordable needs to be a political priority both to sustain economic growth and acceptance. While this may be a daunting task, alternatives are not generally cheaper. Moreover, by adopting a flexible and integrated system perspectives, we may find low hanging fruits and new opportunities.

Optimization of investments in the whole energy system is a key to keep prices affordable. Even if grid tariffs form a limited part of the electricity price, with the level of investments required they are expected to increase. It is therefore essential to explore options to minimize costs, increase efficiency while at the same time achieving multiple goals beyond those strictly related to the infrastructure which is being built. Good planning and optimal timing of investments will help keep grid tariffs in check.

9.5.1 Optimization and Prioritization

Not all grid investments yield the same systemic benefits. Prioritizing investments that deliver the highest net value—in terms of RES integration, flexibility, and system resilience—is essential. Least-cost planning and holistic assessments must replace siloed investment models. Tools like Integrated Resource Planning (IRP) (Wilson and Biewald 2013) and grid-enhanced CBA can aid in this process. Additionally, IRP and grid planning should consider how to plan and optimize investments across all voltage levels leveraging the benefits of distributed resources (including flexibility assets and demand responds) and the additional advantages of having high voltage, national and cross borders grid expansion. This optimization should include geographical and temporal considerations thus delivering an understanding on the timeline of needed investments. With a more granular understanding of where and why bottlenecks in the system occur, it will be possible to reduce the costs of grid investments, give confidence to supply chains and increase predictability for industries.

Whenever we build something, we build it in nature and next to someone. Therefore, environmental sustainability, circularity, and local benefit creation should be embedded in the planning and related investment prioritization. By promoting grid projects that reduce emissions per euro spent, that are designed to withstand extreme weather events and cybersecurity attacks while also avoiding ecological harm, it will be possible to deliver sustainability in a systematic and large scale. Lifecycle resource assessments can support this by identifying infrastructure with the lowest material and spatial intensity.

9.5.2 Key Drivers: Electrification and Demand Growth

The expansion of renewables, and the related electricity grid build up, needs to be timed and coordinated with parallel efforts in increasing direct electrification and therefore demand for renewable electricity. In Europe we have seen stagnating demand and the expected increase has not yet materialized (Weiss et al. 2024). Yet, the electrification of transport (e.g., EVs), buildings (e.g., heat pumps), and industry (e.g., electrolyzers) will require massive investments in further renewables and eventually significantly shift load profiles, yet their exact timing is uncertain. This increases both the urgency and the complexity of investment decisions. It also puts more pressure on grid planning to ensure that grids are ready in time and in the right places ahead of mass deployment of new technologies in transport, building, and industry.

Meeting future demand with minimal environmental impact requires integrating both centrally located and distributed generation, enhancing energy efficiency, and leveraging circular economy principles. Electrification pathways must be accompanied by sustainable infrastructure siting and design.

9.5.3 Enhanced Cost-benefits Analysis and Regional Specificities

The NECPs and the TYNDP process are crucial tools to plan the grids at the European level. However, they must be complemented by planning tools to capture regional contexts and differences and incorporate local decentralized resources like flexibility services, and non-wire alternatives (e.g., storage or demand-side solutions). This is a challenge per se, as we do not yet have the necessary data, models, or algorithms to have a robust representation of distributed generation in grid modelling. To add to this challenge, the assessment frameworks should be improved to account for ecosystem services, land use impacts, and resource efficiency. Tools that monetize avoided emissions and biodiversity protection should complement financial metrics. In this case, methodologies are largely lacking, as well as the willingness to invest resources in addressing these challenges.

9.6 Involving the Public and Unlocking Local Benefits

Public acceptance is essential to the success of grid development. Yet acceptance is rarely just about the project itself—it is fundamentally about what the project is for. People are more likely to support infrastructure when it clearly contributes to goals they care about: reliable and affordable energy, energy security, local development, environmental protection, and climate goals. This makes strategic and transparent planning indispensable—not only for identifying the right projects, but for clearly articulating their purpose in a way that resonates with diverse communities and values.

Engagement practices must go beyond formal consultation or information provision. Done properly, public engagement should strengthen the legitimacy of infrastructure decisions, showing that local perspectives have shaped the outcome, that trade-offs have been weighed transparently, and that possible harmful impacts have been carefully minimized. The process matters as much as the outcome: when people are engaged early, consistently, and meaningfully, trust can be built—even when agreement is not guaranteed (IEA UsersTCP 2024).

At the same time, engagement should not be treated as an open-ended veto process. Once a robust and inclusive engagement process has taken place, and legitimate local concerns have been addressed, the project's legitimacy must be upheld. This includes ensuring that remaining opposition does not indefinitely block decisions that serve broader public interest—provided those decisions are grounded in fairness, transparency, and democratic participation.

After meaningful engagement and careful impact mitigation, attention should shift to working together with local citizens and players in developing local benefits. These benefits should not be viewed as compensation or transactional payoffs, but as part of a broader value-sharing process. They may include:

- financial participation (e.g., co-ownership models, community investment opportunities);

- local economic development (e.g., hiring and training schemes, infrastructure upgrades);

- environmental enhancements (e.g., biodiversity corridors, undergrounding lines in sensitive areas); and

- social initiatives identified through dialogue with residents and local authorities.

What matters most is that these benefits are tailored to local contexts, designed together with affected communities, and aligned with the purpose and values of the project.

Environmental concerns often underpin public resistance. Transparent assessments of ecological impacts and the inclusion of nature-positive design principles—such as biodiversity corridors or undergrounding lines in sensitive areas—can significantly enhance public trust and acceptance. However, the current policy debate on environmental deregulation risks undermining these efforts. Attempts by some politicians to weaken environmental safeguards may seem like a way to accelerate project delivery, but they run counter to the lived experience of many project developers. In practice, deregulation often leads to greater uncertainty, increased legal risk, and stronger local opposition. Instead of weakening environmental legislation, in particular the Birds and Habitats Directives, efforts should focus on streamlining their implementation, offering clarity and efficiency without compromising ecological standards.

The EU's permitting acceleration reforms under REPowerEU provide a starting point, and the Pact for Engagement offers valuable guidance for project developers. However, more clarity is needed on how to systematically deliver and finance local benefits, and how to reflect engagement-related costs in regulatory frameworks. A clear and flexible system for recognizing the full costs and benefits of participation is essential to encourage early, sustained, and meaningful engagement—not just procedural compliance.

In a time of growing societal scrutiny and spatial competition, embedding purpose, legitimacy, environmental integrity, and fairness into grid planning is not only good practice—it is a structural requirement for the energy transition. The question is not whether to engage, but how to do so in a way that builds trust and delivers durable outcomes for both local communities and the broader energy system.

9.7 Flexibility Technologies for Grid Optimization

Flexibility is central to the operation of electricity systems with high shares of variable renewable energy sources. As Europe continues to scale up wind and solar generation, the ability to match supply and demand across time and space becomes increasingly important—not only for system stability, but also for economic efficiency and sustainability (ENTSO-E 2024).

A range of technologies is already helping to deliver this flexibility from milliseconds to days. Battery storage, demand response systems, virtual power plants, and advanced grid management tools enable more dynamic and decentralized balancing of supply and demand. These solutions are essential for the system operators to manage complexity efficiently. By providing balancing, reserve, and congestion management services, these technologies can help lower system costs, better prioritize and design grid projects and limit the environmental footprint of the electricity sector. At the same time, they can also open space for more participatory models of grid operation, in which consumers and communities actively contribute to stability and reliability.

Yet some flexibility challenges remain unresolved. One of the most critical is the issue of *Dunkelflaute*—extended periods of low wind and solar generation, often during cold winter periods with high demand for heat. These events expose the limits of current flexibility resources and underscore the need for decarbonized long-duration storage, dispatchable renewable capacity, and robust interconnection across regions. Addressing these challenges is not only a technical task but also one of planning, investment, and coordination. It requires systemic thinking about adequacy, backup, and resilience but also of the risks that may be systemic or correlated.

The flexibility challenge highlights the danger of over-relying on any single flexibility solution. A resilient energy system must draw on a broad and diversified portfolio of technologies, supported by market signals, adaptive infrastructure, and behavioural adaptation (European Parliament 2025). Unlocking this potential requires regulatory frameworks that provide investment certainty, appropriately value flexible capacity, and enable a level playing field for non-traditional solutions.

As these technologies mature and scale, it becomes increasingly clear that flexibility must be embedded not just in operations, but in how we plan and govern the system itself. That is the focus of the following section.

9.8 Flexibility and Optimization Are King

Flexibility has become a defining principle of modern grid systems. It enables adaptation to variability, decentralization, and growing demand-side complexity. But flexibility alone is not enough. To deliver a system that is resilient, cost-effective, and aligned with public value, it must be accompanied by a consistent commitment to optimization—across infrastructure, technology, regulation, and planning (ENTSO-E 2023).

At the system level, flexibility allows for real-time balancing and greater use of variable resources. Optimization ensures that these resources are deployed where they deliver the greatest value. Together, they support better use of existing infrastructure, better planning and timing of investments, and lower the material and environmental costs of system expansion.

Optimization is equally crucial in grid design. Cross-border interconnectors facilitate geographic balancing and strengthen system adequacy, while distributed energy resources bring supply closer to demand and enhance local resilience. Hybrid system architectures—combining centralized and decentralized elements—offer the best of both worlds. Realizing this potential requires planning tools and investment frameworks that reflect whole-system value, evaluate non-wire alternatives, and consider both spatial and temporal dimensions.

Today's infrastructure assessments must go beyond commercial needs. They must fully capture avoided emissions, resource efficiency, system services, and contributions to resilience. Cost-benefit analyses, particularly in the context of the investment plans, need to be expanded and refined accordingly. This is not just a modelling challenge—it is a governance imperative.

Yet many regulatory and procedural systems remain out of step with these needs. National permitting processes are slow and fragmented, while cross-border coordination is often hampered by misaligned standards. Instead of managing complexity, regulation often tries to simplify it—resulting in inefficiencies, delays, and missed opportunities. Flexibility and optimization require governance that is itself flexible and optimized: harmonized where needed, adaptable where possible, and clear at every stage.

Environmental policy is a revealing example. Efforts to weaken EU nature legislation often do not accelerated projects but instead increase legal uncertainty and community resistance. Rather than deregulating, the better path is to streamline implementation: maintain high standards while making procedures predictable, science-based, and outcome-oriented. This allows environmental and energy objectives to reinforce each other.

Finally, optimization cannot succeed without social legitimacy. Public engagement that is inclusive, timely, and responsive improves both project quality and system performance. It enables local knowledge to shape design and helps align infrastructure with local priorities. Flexible, cooperative processes are not ancillary—they are foundational to successful and efficient grid delivery.

In short, flexibility enables energy systems to adapt. Optimization ensures they do so wisely. Together, they form the backbone of a future-ready electricity grid—capable of delivering on Europe's climate, security, and affordability goals in a way that is efficient, just, and politically sustainable. Flexibility and optimization are not afterthoughts—they are the strategic core of the energy transition.

9.9 Conclusion

Electricity grids are stretching across Europe and communities, from low voltage local grids to high voltage cross-border connections. Integrated planning at all levels and engagement of all the players in the process are essential to deliver the right grids in the right place at the right time.

European Members States' path to climate neutrality runs through its electricity grids. Electricity grids are the foundation of Europe's energy security, energy transition, and energy independence. To fulfil this role, grids must evolve into high-performing, resilient, and flexible infrastructures that are efficient in their use of materials, space, and capital.

To achieve this, we must recognize that building well is not optional—it is essential to earning public trust and securing the social license to operate. Grid projects must deliver tangible, visible benefits to the communities in which they are built. Local co-benefits—such as economic opportunities, nature-positive design, and improved energy access—should be systematically embedded in planning, permitting, and in costs recovery frameworks.

Affordability must remain a political priority in Brussels and in each Member State. Through efficient planning and coordinated investment, costs can be controlled while delivering infrastructure that is robust, future-proof, and climate-resilient. Optimization and systemic thinking must go hand in hand: every grid investment should support multifunctionality, circularity, and long-term value creation.

In a world of growing scarcity—of land, raw materials, and societal patience, among others—clarity is essential. Transparent planning, strong investment signals, and engaged citizens are not just facilitators but preconditions. Done right, electricity grids can become the backbone of a sustainable, secure, and inclusive European energy future.

Immediate actions should include:

- reforming regulatory incentives to reward long-term system value;
- ensuring integrated planning across sectors and governance levels;
- enhancing cost-benefit methodologies to capture distributed and non-wire solutions; and
- deepening public participation to align infrastructure with local priorities.

Without these reforms, grid bottlenecks could undermine the speed, security, and affordability of Europe's energy transition. With them, we can build the public and political momentum needed to deliver excellence at scale.

References

Aquila Group (2023). *European Power Sovereignty through Renewables by 2030*. Hamburg: Aquila Group, https://www.aquila-capital.de/fileadmin/user_upload/PDF_Files_Whitepaper-Insights/ExecutiveSummary_EU_Power_Sovereignty_through_Renewables_by_2023.pdf

Beyond Fossil Fuels, IEEFA, E3G, EMBER (2025). *How Europe's Grid Operators Are Preparing for the Energy Transition*, https://beyondfossilfuels.org/wp-content/uploads/2025/05/REPORT_FINAL.pdf

CEER (2021). *Dynamic Regulation to Enable Digitalisation of the Energy System*. Brussels: CEER.

ENTSO-E (2022) *Ten-Year Network Development Plan*. Brussels: ENTSO-E, https://tyndp.entsoe.eu/about

ENTSO-E (2023) *E-Vision: A Power System for a Carbon Neutral Europe*. Brussels: ENTSO-E, https://eepublicdownloads.entsoe.eu/clean-documents/tyndp-documents/entso-e_Vision_2050_report_221006.pdf

ENTSO-E (2024). *System Flexibility Needs for the Energy Transition*. Brussels: ENTSO-E, https://eepublicdownloads.blob.core.windows.net/public-cdn-container/clean-documents/Publications/System_Needs/entso-e_System_Needs_Energy_Transition_v10.pdf

ENTSO-E (2025). "28 April 2025 Blackout", 28 April, *ENTSO-E*, https://www.entsoe.eu/publications/blackout/28-april-2025-iberian-blackout/

European Commission, (2020), "Impact Assessment Accompanying a Proposal for a Regulation on Guidelines for Trans-European Energy Infrastructure", SWD(2020) 346, https://eur-lex.europa.eu/legal-content/EN/TXT/?uri=celex:52020SC0346

European Commission (2022a) "REpowerEU Plan", SWD(2022) 230 final, https://eur-lex.europa.eu/legal-content/EN/TXT/HTML/?uri=CELEX:52022DC0230

European Commission (2022b) "EU Action Plan for Grids", COM/2023/757 final, https://eur-lex.europa.eu/legal-content/EN/TXT/?uri=celex:52023DC0757

European Commission (2023) "EU Wide Assessment of the Draft Updated National Energy and Climate Plans", COM/2023/796, https://commission.europa.eu/system/files/2023-12/EU-wide_assessment_draft_updated_National_Energy_Climate_Plans_2023.pdf

European Commission (2025) "Clean Industrial Deal", https://commission.europa.eu/topics/eu-competitiveness/clean-industrial-deal_en

European Commission, ACER, RGI (2023) "EU Pact for Engagement", https://energy.ec.europa.eu/document/download/65ffb0ca-928e-4746-adac-74c8f918c7f3_en?filename=Pact%20for%20Engagement%202023.pdf

European Parliament, Directorate-General for Economy, Transformation and Industry (2025) "Increasing Flexibility in the EU Energy System", *Think Tank European Parliament*, https://www.europarl.europa.eu/thinktank/en/document/ECTI_STU(2025)769347

Financial Times (2025) "Power Prices Spike as Iberian Blackout Hits Grid Resilience", 8 May, https://www.ft.com/content/3875c630-215b-490b-a0a8-c6bcf3cfedc6

IEA UsersTCP (2024) "Impact Assessment of Case Studies. Assessing the Impacts of Public Engagement in Energy Infrastructure Projects", https://ieecp.org/wp-content/uploads/2024/02/D3-Impact-assessment-of-selected-infrastructure-projects_compressed.pdf

IEA (2023) *Electricity Grids and Secure Transitions*. Paris: IEA, https://iea.blob.core.windows.net/assets/ea2ff609-8180-4312-8de9-494bcf21696d/ElectricityGridsandSecureEnergyTransitions.pdf

Draghi, M. (2024) *The Future of European Competitiveness*. Brussels: European Commission, https://commission.europa.eu/topics/eu-competitiveness/draghi-report_en

Myers Jaffe, A., T. Loch-Temzelides, and C. Lo Prete (2024) "Geopolitics of Cross-Border Electricity Grids", 9 January, *Medium*, https://medium.com/nyuspscga/geopolitics-of-cross-border-electricity-grids-a-working-paper-db2422529956

REE (Red Eléctrica Española) and REN (2025) "Preliminary Analysis of System Failure", https://www.ree.es/en/press-office/news/press-release/2025/06/red-electrica-presents-report-incident-28-april-and-proposes-recommendations

"Regulation (EU) No 347/2013 of the European Parliament and of the Council", https://eur-lex.europa.eu/eli/reg/2013/347/oj/eng

"Regulation (EU) 2018/1999 of the European Parliament and of the Council of 11 December 2018 on the Governance of the Energy Union and Climate Action", https://eur-lex.europa.eu/eli/reg/2018/1999/oj/eng

"Regulation (EU) 2022/869 on Guidelines for Trans-European Energy Infrastructure (TEN-E)", https://eur-lex.europa.eu/eli/reg/2022/869/oj/eng

Weiss, A., D. Hernandez Diaz, and T. Gruenewald, with M. Subbu (2024) "Electricity Demand in Europe: Growing or Going?", 24 October, *McKinsey & Company*, https://www.mckinsey.com/industries/electric-power-and-natural-gas/our-insights/electricity-demand-in-europe-growing-or-going

Wikipedia (2025) "2025 Iberian Peninsula Blackout", 7 October, https://en.wikipedia.org/wiki/2025_Iberian_Peninsula_blackout

Wilson, R., and B. Biewald (2013) "Best Practices in Electric Utility Integrated Resource Planning", 21 June, *RAP*, https://www.raponline.org/knowledge-center/best-practices-in-electric-utility-integrated-resource-planning/

10. Investing in Critical Raw Materials for the Clean-Tech Transition in the EU

Roberto Zoboli[1]

The procurement of critical raw materials (CRM) could become a fundamental barrier to the development of clean technology and net-zero manufacturing in the EU, thus endangering the achievement of major objectives of EU self-sufficiency in the climate-energy transition. The EU policy framework includes several measures introduced in 2024 and 2025 to push both clean-tech manufacturing and security of supply of CRM in the framework of the EU Competitiveness Compass and the Clean Industrial Deal of 2025. Criticality of materials has been defined as a combination of "economic importance" and "supply risk". On the side of "economic importance", an increasing demand for CRM comes from net-zero energy technologies as well as from digital and military technologies. The EU shows a mixed picture in clean-tech sectors: it holds a leadership position in some areas, while in others it faces a high, and increasing, dependency on imports. Although significant investments are underway to boost manufacturing autonomy, these efforts may struggle to keep pace with rapidly rising demand and intensifying external competition, particularly from China. Therefore, the security of supply of CRM has a key role in providing robustness to EU clean-tech value chains. On the side of the 'supply risk', CRM have entered a phase marked by international tensions and conflicts, exposing the EU's high dependency on exporting countries that can quickly become unreliable. Responses and strategies include diversifying the portfolio of supplier countries, expanding domestic mining within the EU, increasing recycling efforts, and investing in research and innovation. All these approaches face distinct barriers, varying degrees of feasibility, and different implementation timeframes. The first consequence of the 2024 CRM policies has been the approval of forty-seven "strategic projects" within the EU and thirteen outside the EU. It is important that these projects are matched by additional investments in clean-tech manufacturing to keep a balanced development across the whole EU domestic value chain for the energy transition. However, a fundamental uncertainty now surrounds the CRM issue, at both the EU and global scale.

---

1   CRANEC—Università Cattolica del Sacro Cuore and Accademia Nazionale dei Lincei.

https://doi.org/10.11647/OBP.0499.10

10.1 Introduction

The transition induced by the EU climate policy target of net zero by 2050 implies a radical change of the EU energy and techno-economic system. Unlike the energy transitions of the two past centuries, which unfolded gradually within the "fossil energy paradigm" through substitution among dominant primary sources, the current transition requires a rapid and sharp departure from that paradigm (IEA 2021). This radical energy transition, driven by renewables, energy storage, electric mobility, energy efficiency technologies, carbon capture and storage, and other technologies we define as clean tech, is also a revolution for industrial materials. More than conventional energy technologies, clean tech require a large amount of materials that we are now considering as 'critical' or 'strategic', which are becoming a hot area of policy action, research and innovation, and industrial investments.

This chapter addresses the material implications of the energy transition, the development of clean-tech value chains, and the associated investment needs to secure CRM for the EU.

10.2 The EU Policy Framework

With the adoption of the target of net zero by 2050 within the European Green Deal (2019, 2020), the EU started a process of energy transition that offers large opportunities of industrial and economic transformation together with the achievement of higher levels of energy self-sufficiency to reduce dependency on risky energy superpowers (US, Russia, and the other countries of OPEC+).[2] While the energy transition has achieved significant progress, for example renewables accounting for 44% of EU electricity consumption, it continues to face barriers and investment gaps relative to its ambitions, in particular in the scaling of electric mobility and further deployment of renewables (D'Amato et al. 2024).

The second von der Leyen Commission, while confirming the key target of net zero, puts the energy transition or decarbonization in the broader framework of the competitiveness strategy indicated by the Draghi report (European Commission 2024a).[3] The strategic framework is now the EU "Competitiveness Compass" (CC) adopted in January 2025 (European Commission 2025a), of which the second pillar is a roadmap for decarbonization and competitiveness that includes the Clean Industrial Deal (February 2025), an "affordable energy" plan, and a plan for "energy intensive sectors". The CC also includes a third pillar focused on reducing external dependencies to achieve "open strategic autonomy" through a network of trade agreements that secure the supply of raw materials. These pillars complement the first pillar of the CC, which aims at closing the EU innovation gap in artificial intelligence and advancing

---

2   On OPEC+, see https://www.eia.gov/todayinenergy/detail.php?id=56420
3   The overall strategy and several commitments summarized in the text have been confirmed, and possibly strengthened, in the Letter of Intent sent by the Commission to the Parliament with the report on the State of the Union 2025 (September), see https://commission.europa.eu/strategy-and-policy/state-union/state-union-2025_en

quantum technologies, biotech, robotics, and space technology. All these sectors require Europe to have the capacity to procure and efficiently use industrial raw materials.

The Clean Industrial Deal (CID) (European Commission 2025b) includes different initiatives for the industrialist re-direction of the Green Deal.[4] The CID provides for, inter alia, the speeding up of the rollout of clean energy investments, the acceleration of electrification, the need to complete the internal energy market and to use energy more efficiently, while reducing import. Key instruments under the CID include a proposed "decarbonization acceleration act" and the mobilization of €100 billion to support clean manufacturing, a new "clean industrial state-aid framework", and the proposal for an industrial decarbonization bank to create the financial capacity for these initiatives, supported especially through the revenues from the Emission Trading System and the revision of InvestEU. On the external side, the CID promises a strategy for international security and access to materials by enabling European companies to aggregate their demands for CRM, a "Clean Trade and Investment Partnership", and the simplification of the Carbon Border Adjustment Mechanism. On the domestic side, it pursues the acceleration of the domestic circular transition with the objective of having 24% of materials circular by 2030.

The specific strategy of the EU for clean tech and CRM started already in 2023 with the Net-Zero Industry Act, then adopted by the Regulation 2024/1735, and the Critical Raw Materials Act, then adopted by the Regulation 2024/1252. Both regulations are very ambitious.

The Regulation 2024/1735 on Net-Zero Industry (European Commission 2024b) includes several provisions aimed at boosting investment in clean-tech sectors as represented by a large list of technologies for electricity production from renewables, carbon capture and storage, electric transports, hydrogen, nuclear fusion, and other families of technologies associated with the clean energy transition. The regulation sets a benchmark for at least 40% of the Union's deployment needs to be met through domestic supply by 2030, alongside a target to increase the EU's share of global production of relevant technologies to 15% by 2040. It also provides for streamlining administrative and permitting procedures, the designation of net-zero 'strategic projects' and Net-Zero European Platforms, the creation of CO_2 injection capacity, and the use of regulatory sandboxes to support the establishment of strategic energy technology plans within Member States.

The Critical Raw Materials Regulation 2024/1252 (European Commission 2024c) aims at responding to the risk of supply disruption of critical raw materials needed for the clean-tech transition, and also for the digital transition and now the "military transition". The starting point has been the identification of a list of "critical" and "strategic" raw materials. For these materials, "benchmarks" for domestic supply capacity by 2030 have been set: at least 10% of the EU's annual consumption from extraction; at least 40% from processing; at least 25% from recycling; no more than 65% from imports from one single third country. To

---

4   See the communication on implementation of 2 July 2025 at https://commission.europa.eu/publications/delivering-clean-industrial-deal-i_en

achieve these benchmarks, the regulation provides for streamlined permitting procedures for CRM projects and the designation of "strategic projects" by Member States, which can benefit from enhanced access to finance together with shorter permitting timelines. In addition, Member States will develop programmes for exploiting their geological resources and will push for a more extensive collection and better management of waste that is rich in CRM, like electric and electronic waste, to extract materials. The same applies to mining waste. On the international side, the regulation introduces actions to geographically diversify the Union's imports of raw materials. Actions include trade agreements to secure the diversification of supply, using the EU's Globe Gateway to deploy projects along the raw materials value chain, setting up an export credit facility to reduce the risk of investment abroad in the areas of materials.

It is interesting to look at the way the lists of "critical" and "strategic" raw materials have been selected. Article 4 of the regulation explains how the thirty-four CRM were selected by the Commission using a methodology adopted in 2017, which is the result of a long process that started in 2011 with the first list of CRM.[5] The methodology considers two fundamental dimensions of "criticality" both related to economic dimensions, instead of geological scarcity criteria: (1) "economic importance" of the specific materials in the EU industrial system, which can be a proxy of the economic impact of supply disruption (demand side); (2) "supply risk" or the probability of supply disruption, which depends on the concentration of supply as measured by global primary supply and the dependence of the EU on that global supply, articulated by countries, also considering the potential for substitution of that material in the EU (European Commission 2023).

According to Article 3, the seventeen "strategic" materials were selected on the basis of the relevance of a raw material for the green and digital transition as well as defence and aerospace applications, following three key criteria: (a) the amount of strategic technologies using a raw material as an input; (b) the amount of a raw material needed for manufacturing relevant strategic technologies; (c) the expected global demand for relevant strategic technologies.

Such an articulated, detailed, selective, and ambitious policy framework in between the CC, CID, Regulation 2024/1735, and Regulation 2024/1252 raises important questions of realism and feasibility, given the mounting barriers to investment across the EU's clean-tech and raw materials value chains (D'Amato et al. 2024). These barriers and risks can be seen following the two dimensions of the criticality framework, that is "economic importance" and "supply risk".

10.3 "Economic Importance": The EU's Clean-Tech and CRM Value Chains

According to the Draghi report (European Commission 2024a), the EU has significant competitive advantages in clean-tech industries, compared to its weak advantages

---

5   https://single-market-economy.ec.europa.eu/sectors/raw-materials/areas-specific-interest/
     critical-raw-materials_en

in digital technologies. This is because the different technological families that we classify as clean tech are closer, in terms of industrial competence, knowledge, and technological basis, to the present capacities of the EU industrial system. The EIB Investment Report (EIB 2025) highlights how Europe is dominating the international system of patents for clean tech and significantly increased its export of low carbon technologies in the period 2017–2023. However, the state of clean-tech industries in Europe clearly shows a more mixed picture.

Number of clean tech manufacturing facilities by country

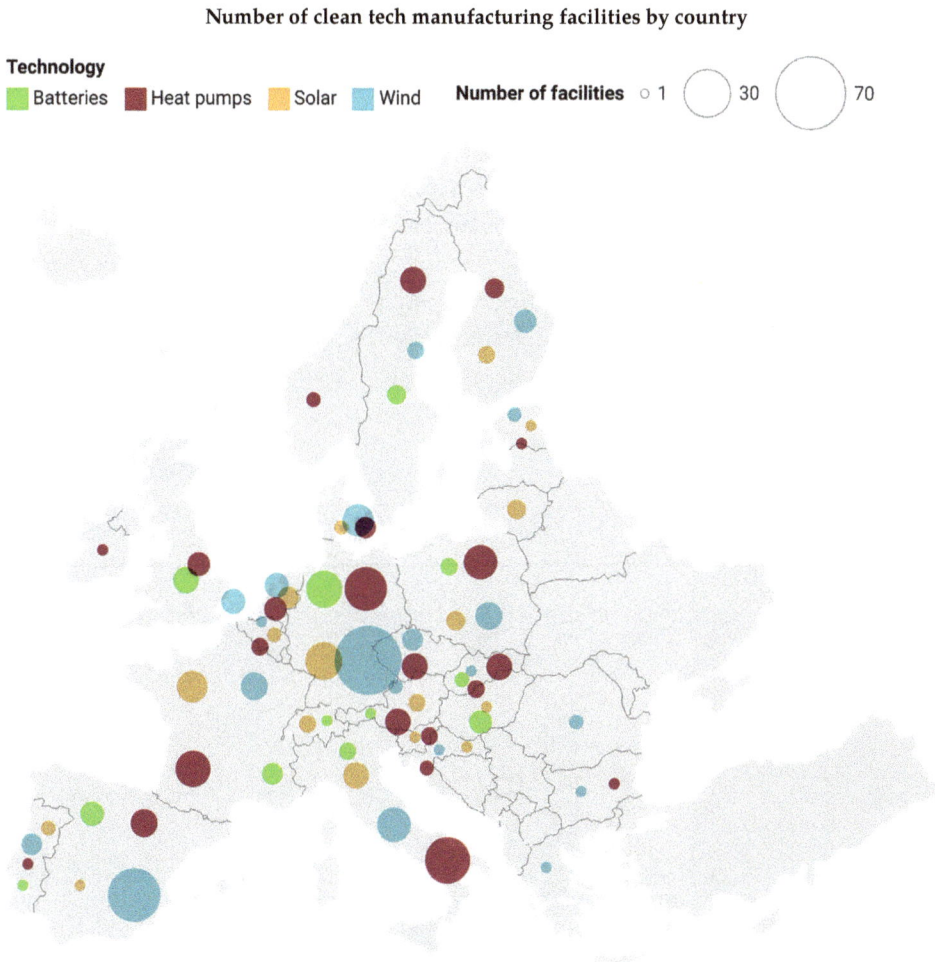

Europe refers to the EU27, Norway, and the United Kingdom. Note that the position of the dots is only indicative of the countries where the manufacturing facilities are located, not of specific cities. Currently, our maps only show the number of facilities. Future updates will include manufacturing capacities. To share capacity data, please email greeneconomy@bruegel.org.

Fig. 10.1 Location of clean-tech manufacturing in Europe. *Source:* Bruegel on European Heat Pump Association, Solar Power Europe, Transport & Environment and Wind Europe (https://www. bruegel.org/analysis/clean-industrial-transformation-where-does-europe-stand).

According to Bruegel's clean-tech tracker (Bruegel 2025), Europe has good positions in the production and net export of electric vehicles, at least for the moment, and of wind technologies, whereas it has a very weak position, including significantly increasing net imports, for batteries and solar technologies, for which there is a strong and increasingly dominant position occupied by China as a supplier of the global markets. Furthermore, domestic manufacturing capacity for the majority of clean tech is unevenly distributed across EU Member States, with a central role played by Germany and the neighbouring countries in Eastern Europe and the Nordic region. Southern Europe, in particular Spain and Italy, contributes in selected areas, such as heat pump production in Italy and wind technology in Spain (see Fig. 10.1).

When looking at the map of current investment and recently established clean-tech manufacturers, there is again a concentration in Germany and Eastern European countries, and partly in Nordic countries, with a limited role played by the rest of Europe (see Fig. 10.2). According to D'Amato et al. (2024), there are significant differences in the cost of capital across EU regions, and this can favour the localization of clean-tech manufacturing in some countries with respect to others. Eastern European countries have low cost of capital, which can make them attractive destinations for the localization of investments from Germany and other leading clean-tech countries.

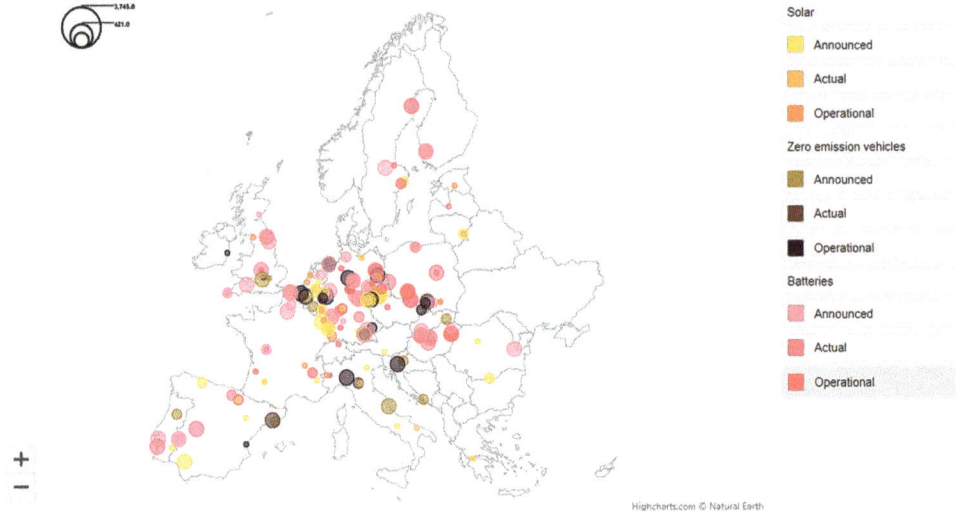

Note: Europe refers to the EU27, Norway, and the United Kingdom. The data displayed on the map are continuously being improved to ensure accuracy and completeness. If you identify any discrepancies or errors, please contact Bruegel. Your feedback is valuable in helping us enhance the quality of our dataset.

Fig. 10.2 Location of new investments in selected clean-tech industries in Europe. *Source:* Bruegel (Bruegel Clean Tech Radar 2025, https://www.bruegel.org/dataset/european-clean-tech-tracker).

The future development of EU clean-tech manufacturing and net-zero industries, as pursued by CC, CID, and the Net-Zero Industry Act, depends on the matching or mismatching between domestic deployment (demand) and the increasing global role of China and other competitors, which can weaken the relative competitiveness of European investments.[6] The scenarios for clean-tech manufacturing capacity (IRENA 2023) indicate that China is expected to experience substantial growth by 2030 across a range of technologies, including batteries, electric cars, solar PV, wind power and various intermediate products. While manufacturing capacity in the EU is also predicted to increase, its growth is likely to remain comparatively modest relative to China's expansion. Similarly, according to projections made by the International Energy Agency (IEA 2025), Europe might be outpaced by China's expanding capacity for solar photovoltaic systems, whereas it shows promising potential for growth in domestic capacities for wind technologies, batteries, electrolyzers, and heat pumps. Therefore, it cannot be taken for granted that the EU will be able to achieve a high degree of self-sufficiency in clean-tech manufacturing value chains.

These uncertain scenarios for EU domestic clean-tech can be seen in the general framework of estimated investment needs for the green transition. According to the overview presented in EEA (2023) and D'Amato et al. (2024), the additional investment needs to achieve the EGD targets are about €520 billion/year in the present decade with respect to the average level of the last decade, of which €392 billion/year are for climate and energy. For the period 2031–2050, the need is €660 billion/year (3.2% of EU GDP) for energy and €870 billion/year (4.2% of EU GDP) for transport. The largest investment gaps are in key transition sectors, like clean energy (renewables) and mobility. In the same report, the huge need of private investments is highlighted together with the different barriers to attract them, including the uneven cost of capital across Europe, as mentioned above.[7]

Clean tech and, in general, net-zero industries, together with sectors like digital and aerospace/military technologies, generate the EU's demand for critical raw materials. Detailed scenarios on the demand for CRM, produced by JRC (Carrara et al. 2023), indicate an unprecedented increase in the near future. Energy technologies essential for the net-zero transition are significantly more material-intensive than conventional energy systems. As demand for these technologies grows, even under scenarios of limited domestic self-sufficiency, the need for CRM is expected to rise sharply. At the same time, some materials that are classified as critical for the net-zero transition are similarly indispensable for the digital industry, aerospace and defence sectors. Therefore, it is expected that the EU will face substantial cumulative and competing demands for these materials, which could pose challenges to achieving its broader strategic objectives.

The EU's high external dependence on CRM—or the 'supply risk' that contributes to define their 'criticality'—could thus become the key bottleneck in achieving objectives

---

6   See also Le Mouel and Poitiers (2023).
7   On investment needs and the role of private investments see also Baccianti (2022).

for clean-tech and net-zero industries in Europe, thus endangering the success of CC, CID, and the Net-Zero Industry Act.

10.4 "Supply Risk": External Dependence within International Disorder

The EU has a high dependence on imports of CRM from major world producers, with an extremely high share of total imports from some of them. For example, the EU imports 40% of its consumption of palladium from Russia. From China, it imports 93% of its consumption of magnesium, 66% of scandium, 45% of titanium, 98–99% of light and heavy rare earths. The EU imports also 78% of its lithium consumption from Chile, 85% of niobium from Brazil, 62% of antimony from Turkey, 68% of cobalt from Democratic Republic of Congo.[8] These are just a few examples of the EU's high dependency of procurement from external suppliers, that can be reliable, politically stable, and "friendly", but in other cases can be unreliable and "unfriendly", or are simply strong competitors in the global green manufacturing value chains, like China.

The dependency of the EU reflects the concentration of global supply and the strategies of the dominant supplier in the global market. For example, in terms of value chain phases, the concentration of global supply is very high for the more advanced stages of processing, like manufacturing and assembly, as in the case of solar PV panels and batteries. For the same value chains, there is lower concentration of supply for the mining phase and, for batteries, in the material processing phase. However, not all the scenarios align or converge regarding the present and future geographical shape of the value chains. In any case, projections by IRENA (2023) suggest that supply concentration in both mining and refining is likely to increase in the future, for example, for materials such as lithium, nickel, and cobalt, with significant capacity expansions expected in Asia and Africa.

Supply risks are highly dynamic in the present disorder of the international system, where increasing tensions can translate risk into uncertainty. Leaving aside the role of the United States, Russia, and China, whose involvement in the CRM landscape is now entangled in broader global trade tensions triggered by the US, major producers of key CRM include countries such as Myanmar, Zambia, Gabon, Zimbabwe, and others, that can be subject to political instability. When looking at the World Governance Indicator, which is included in the EU measures of criticality, we see that some major suppliers of Europe perform very badly in the ranking, which suggests not only low ethical quality of governance but also a potential for political instability (Fig. 10.3). The same availability of CRM, in a world of procurements tensions, can stimulate political instability in weak-governance countries.

---

8   Among the many sources of this type of data, which are often not consistent one another, see Carrara et al. (2023).

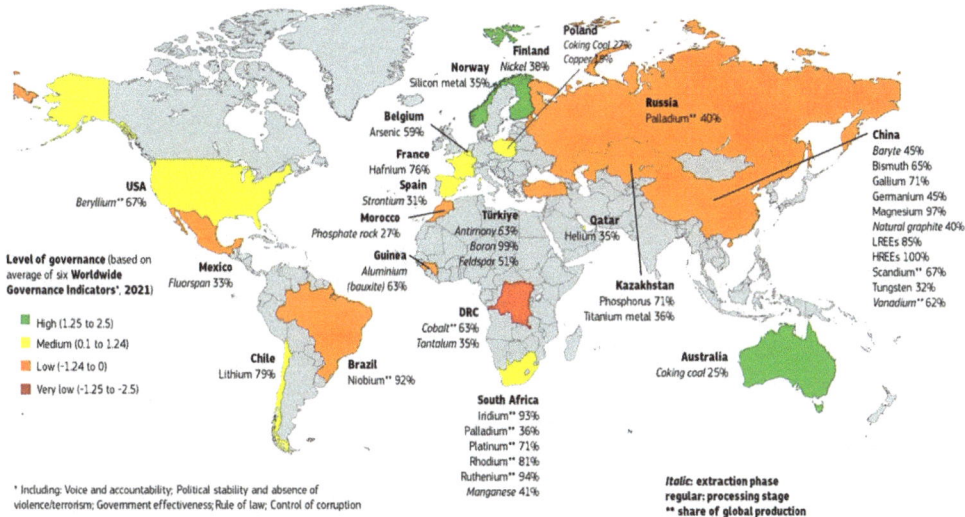

Fig. 10.3 Major EU suppliers of CRM (2023) and their quality of governance. *Source:* JRC (https:// rmis.jrc.ec.europa.eu/eu-critical-raw-materials).

In the present evolving situation, geopolitical risk analysis[9] is increasingly critical for understanding the EU's procurement uncertainties and for disentangling the truth from the many alarming narratives that fuel political and economic speculation. This is the case with Ukraine and Greenland, which have become focal points in recent US administration strategies. Ukraine is endowed with a significant amount of minerals and is actively seeking to leverage this by attracting international investments. However, it remains a relatively minor player in global CRM markets in terms of reserves.[10] The recent agreement between Ukraine the US appears to depart from the narrative promoted by the US administration and, based on available information, it is largely a joint venture whose actual impact will only become clear in a postwar scenario.[11] It is also worth noting that an agreement between the EU and Ukraine for critical raw materials has been in place since 2021.[12]

Greenland, according to the Greenland Mineral Resources Strategy (Greenland 2025) and US Geological Survey data, holds a relevant (though not extensive) known endowment of CRM and other mineral resources. While significant resources may lie under the ice cap, the mineral exploitation sector in Greenland remains underinvested.

---

9   See, for example, https://www.globalguardian.com/risk-map; https://www.policyuncertainty.com/ gpr.html; and https://www.52risks.com/2021/11/28/top-12-geopolitical-risk-resources/?srsltid=Af mBOophhHp5b9FQIK2534WBQWA3WgEabYa1VmV-VbfrWIIzFfRbo4tc

10   See https://www.geo.gov.ua/en/critical-raw-materials/

11   See   EuroNews   -   https://www.euronews.com/my-europe/2025/05/01/ washington-signs-historic-rare-earths-minerals-deal-with-ukraine

12   See https://uamap.org.ua/en/eu-and-ukraine-kick-start-strategic-partnership-on-raw-materials

The heightened attention from the US administration toward Greenland is largely political, tied to long-standing Arctic dynamics involving Russia, Europe, and the US. These dynamics, centred on strategic transportation routes, are now becoming more explicit with the increasingly aggressive US positioning.

The international tensions around CRM stimulated a recent proposal by a group of scientists for a Global Minerals Trust to create agreements on cooperative resource management, in which fair prices for both mineral suppliers and consumers can prevail, avoiding mining rushes in developing countries.[13] The proposal echoes the historical experience of the international funds for primary commodities launched in the 1950s, which ultimately failed due to persistent conflicts between consuming and producing countries, and due to the assertion of national sovereignty over natural resources, regarded as 'private goods' under domestic control.

Concerns about the scarcity of CRM are often amplified by dominant narratives, but these can be more accurately assessed by examining international price trends, such as those reflected in the World Bank's indexes of commodity prices (World Bank 2025). In the last few years, despite both actual and expected surges in demand, the international prices of critical materials used in net-zero technologies (such as nickel) have not shown significant increases, despite some huge spikes, in particular when looking at prices in real terms. The reason is that, looking at the world reserves, most CRM are not physically scarce: for instance, global lithium reserves are estimated to cover 250 years of consumption at 2020 levels. Then, supply can have a certain degree of price elasticity and has, so far, kept pace with the rising demand from expanding end-use sectors, such as electric vehicles. These markets tend to follow the typical cycles of internationally traded commodities that are subject to huge instability and speculation, but without significant upward trends in real prices. Therefore, according to the International Energy Agency's CRM market trends outlook (IEA 2024), the global market for key CRM has been $325 billion in 2023, with a decrease compared to the previous year. Prices for copper, lithium, nickel, and cobalt have returned to levels seen before the energy crisis of 2021–2023.

Even cleaning the global CRM picture from instrumental political narratives and market speculations fed by strategic information and expectations, the EU actually has a structural problem with supply security of CRM in an international system where geopolitics and competing industrial strategies can suddenly create scarcity and bottlenecks able to hinder the net-zero industrial transition.

10.5 Responses and Strategies

Different analyses converge on four strategic approaches to securing the EU's supply of CRM (Di Francesco et al. 2024; Specker et al. 2025; Carrara et al. 2023).

The first is diversification of procurement by activating trade relationships with alternative producing countries, so that a less risky suppliers portfolio can be achieved.

---

13   See https://www.science.org/doi/10.1126/science.adv9841

The second is to increase domestic supply capacity based on the redevelopment of mining sites in Europe, together with an increase in the manufacturing capacity at higher stages of the value chain. The third is to increase domestic recycling by exploiting what is known as "urban mining", as well as boosting the circular economy, to recover CRM from waste. The fourth is investing in innovation for both material efficiency and the substitution of CRM with materials that are not critical. These directions are already embodied in the policy framework defined by the CRM Regulation 2024/1252 as well as in the CID and the CC (see above).

The possible barriers to these four directions are different for each material, or families of materials, and vary for different countries in the EU. Furthermore, some of these four directions, for example domestic mining, are only viable in the longer term, requiring substantial investments to overcome significant barriers. Table 10.1 highlights the possible complexity of ex ante impacts of supply disruptions (quantities or prices) and of different responses in a realistic timeframe, also considering the expected differential environmental impacts of shocks and responses.

Table 10.1 Expected economic and environmental effects of a raw materials supply disruption and reactions to it. *Note:* I = importing countries; E = exporting countries; NE = new exporting countries; T = transit countries; ECSO = economic and social effects; ENV = environmental effects. *Source:* the author, see also adapted versions in Di Francesco et al. (2023) and Specker et al. (2024).

Type of expected effects without/with reactions	**Short term:** *Dominated by limited elasticity of supply in the world market and domestically (primary and secondary supply), limited elasticity of domestic demand (e.g., substitution), limited resource-saving innovations*	**Medium term:** *Dominated by good elasticity of supply in the world market (procurement shift) and possibly domestically (primary supply, if any, or secondary supply), possible reductions of domestic demand (e.g., substitution) and resource-saving innovations*	**Long term:** *Dominated by the importing country's possibility of strategic reaction based on self-sufficiency and re-shoring, reduction of domestic demand (e.g., full substitution), full deployment of resource-saving innovations, full circularity, new industrial policies and reshaping of domestic value chains (including secondary)*
Expected effects without reaction policies	I: **ECSO**: loss of value added and employment in using industries; input cost increase and inflation (if inputs costs passed on prices, depending on elasticity of demand) and loss of competitiveness; **ENV**: reduction of pressures		
	E: reduction of extraction; **ECSO**: loss of value added and employment; benefits from increase in selling prices; **ENV**: reduction of pressure		
	T: loss of transit benefits; **ECSO**: partial loss of value added and employment (if production phases in the transit country); possible gains from higher prices; **ENV**: reduction of pressures		T: possible shift to other Ts with no overall loss of transit benefits/costs (including ENV pressures); possible gains from higher prices

Possible reaction strategy by the Importing country	Attempt to geographically shift procurement (success depending on supply elasticity in world market, material specific); measures to alleviate price increases for final users (industry, consumers)	Partial geographical shift of procurement (good supply elasticity in world market); measures to alleviate price increases for final users (industry, consumers); possible measures to increase domestic supply (primary and secondary) and material savings	Full geographical shift of procurement; measures to exploit and increase domestic supply potential (primary and secondary); resource savings innovations fully deployed; adaptation of domestic value chains (new industrial policy); measures to alleviate price increases for final users (industry, consumers), including alleviating domestic price increases due to self-sufficiency; measures against NIMBY and oppositions
Expected effects with reaction strategies	**I:** Possible alleviation of **ECSO** effects (quantities and prices) **NE** (if available in the short term): **ECSO**: increase of value added and employment (quantity); benefits from increase in selling prices; **ENV**: increase of pressures	**I:** Alleviation of **ECSO** effects; alleviation of price increase; increase of domestic **ENV** effect if domestic supply increases; or decrease of **ENV** effects if circular economy deployed and if domestic technologies better than those of (old and new) exporter **NE**: **ECSO**: increase of value added and employment; benefits from increase in selling prices; **ENV**: increase of pressure	**I:** Alleviation of costs increase and inflation from international material prices, but likely higher domestic prices with self-sufficiency; change in industry mix and value chains; increase of **ENV** effects if domestic supply increases; decrease of **ENV** effects if circular economy and, at the global scale, if domestic technologies better than those of (old and new) exporter **NE** (if not full self-sufficiency): **ECSO**: increase of value added and employment; benefits from increase in selling price; **ENV**: increase of pressures

The direction of creating alternative new trading partnerships for CRM is the most urgent and, to some extent, more feasible in the shorter run considering the high mineral reserve potential at the global scale and the acceleration of economic tensions in the international system. One initiative aligned with this strategic direction is the establishment of a Critical Raw Material Club, as outlined in the EU's Critical Raw Materials Act (CRMA) of 2023. A relevant step forward came in 2024 with the launch of the Minerals Security Partnership Forum (MSP Forum), that includes fifteen MSP Partners and another fifteen critical mineral-producing and mineral-consuming countries (including Greenland and Ukraine).[14] To support this direction, international investments by EU operators in mining and refining activities could also be relevant, and such efforts are already underway through non-EU "strategic projects" promoted by the CRM Regulation 2024/1252 (see below).

In the medium run, there may be opportunities to develop a robust domestic recycling industry for certain CRM, though not for all. At present, recycling capacity is still underdeveloped for many specific CRM. The enabling condition is that the stock/flow of the material-containing products within the economy is sufficiently large to create a minimum critical size for profitable industrial-scale collection and recycling. However, in the case of lithium, for example, scenarios diverge on the feasibility of industrial recycling initiatives: some analyses anticipate a near-term surge in the availability of lithium-containing products (mainly batteries), sufficient to support industrial-scale recycling; others suggest that this minimum stock/flow will not be reached until 2040 or later.[15]

In the longer run, it is possible that a redevelopment of mining for CRM can take place in the EU. Already at present, several projects have been announced, for example, for lithium mining, but it is uncertain whether they can pass the test of economic and environmental sustainability and will be implemented. In addition to uncertainties in economic and environmental feasibility, the mining sector faces barriers related to the availability of suitable territories and communities willing to host new investments. This applies both to greenfield investments and the reopening of previously closed mining sites, many of which were shut down over past decades to favour alternative local models of development. Community opposition is likely to remain strong unless new approaches are adopted to share the benefits more equitably and demonstrate that mining can be good for local development. It is interesting to note that, according to Specker et al. (2025), mining activities in Europe can be more environmentally sustainable than in other regions, offering a global environmental net advantage if mining were reintroduced within the EU. However, this shift would relocate the environmental impact to European territories, which could intensify local opposition.

---

14   See   https://policy.trade.ec.europa.eu/help-exporters-and-importers/accessing-markets/raw-materials/minerals-security-partnership-forum_en

15   See   https://rmis.jrc.ec.europa.eu/analysis-of-supply-chain-challenges-49b749   and   https://eurometaux.eu/media/rqocjybv/metals-for-clean-energy-final.pdf

For the direction of innovation, the picture is very lively. According to a report of the European Parliament (2024), there are at present ninety-three projects on critical raw materials underway inside Horizon Europe, of which eleven are at the exploration stage, twenty at the extraction stage, and seventeen at the processing stage. Most of these projects concern catalytic technologies and batteries with no or low CRM content, and recycling. Most of them are based on cobalt, platinum, lithium, nickel, and manganese. Furthermore, excluding the exploration stage, European actors have a dominant role in international patents for CRM from refining to recycling, with the EU surpassing the United States and China (although China is fast growing). In between research and industry, relevant initiatives of the recent past have been co-funded, for example in the framework of the Important Projects of Common European Interest (IPCEI), with two big projects on batteries.[16]

Strategic Projects for the EU

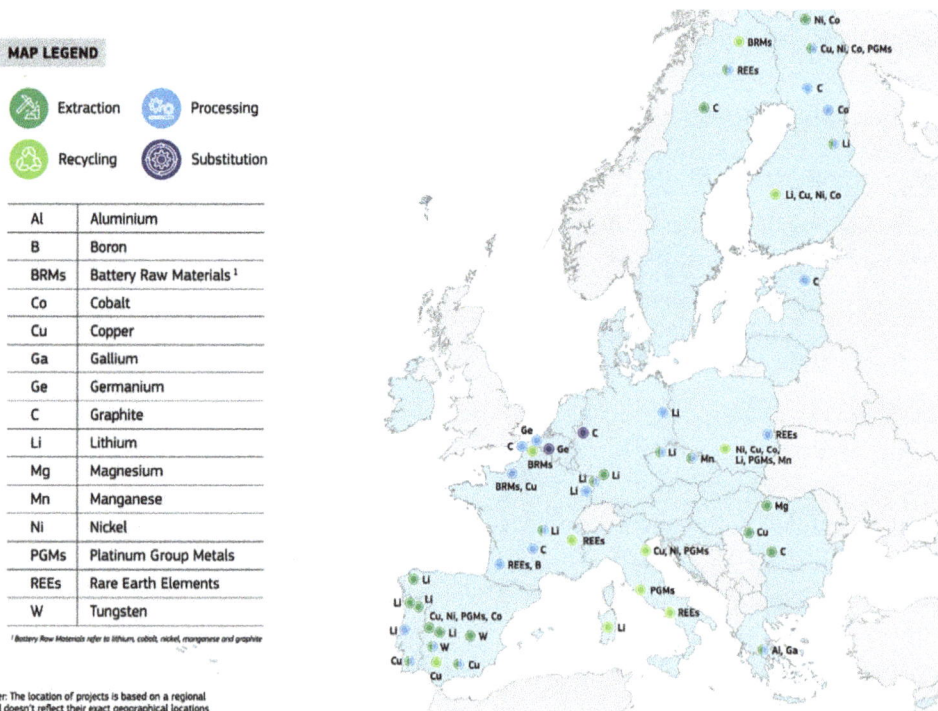

Fig. 10.4 Approved strategic projects on CRM in the EU. *Source:* https://ec.europa.eu/commission/presscorner/detail/en/ip_25_864

One of the first consequences of CRM Regulation 2024/1252 has been the implementation of its provisions on "strategic projects". With the first call of 2024, the European Commission approved forty-seven strategic projects in the EU and

---

16   See https://competition-policy.ec.europa.eu/state-aid/ipcei/approved-ipceis_en

thirteen strategic projects outside of the EU.[17] The projects inside the EU cover different stages of the value chain as well as recycling and substitution of lithium (twenty-two projects), nickel (twelve projects), cobalt (ten projects), manganese (seven projects), and graphite (eleven projects). Most of the forty-seven EU projects approved are in Germany, the Nordic Countries, and Eastern Europe, but several are in Spain and Portugal (Fig. 10.4). This geographical location just partially reflects the location of clean-tech manufacturing that demands CRM (see above), and the whole value chain made of clean-tech manufacturing and CRM must be seen at the EU scale and not nationally. The same applies to other sectors demanding CRM, like digital and military technologies.

According to the Commission:

> To become operational, the 47 Strategic Projects have an expected overall capital investment of €22.5 billion. These projects will be able to benefit from coordinated support by the Commission, Member States and financial institutions to become operational, notably regarding access to finance and support to connect with relevant off-takers. They will also benefit from streamlined permitting provisions, to ensure predictability for project promoters while safeguarding environmental, social and governance standards. In line with the CRMA, the permit-granting process will not exceed 27 months for extraction projects and 15 months for other projects. Currently, permitting processes can last from five to 10 years. (European Commission 2025c)

Of the thirteen approved "strategic projects" outside the EU, seven are in Canada, Greenland, Kazakhstan, Norway, Serbia, Ukraine, and Zambia, with whom the EU has a strategic partnership on raw materials. The others are in Brazil, Madagascar, Malawi, New Caledonia, South Africa, and the United Kingdom (see Fig. 10.5). According to the Commission:

> It is estimated that the 13 Strategic Projects outside of the EU need an overall capital investment of €5.5 billion to start operations. The Commission will also reinforce cooperation with the third countries concerned to ensure the development of those projects, especially through the Strategic Partnerships already concluded with some of these countries on raw materials value chains. (European Commission 2025d)

Although the EU's "strategic projects" for CRM, set to be replicated through a call in 2025, are an important step forward and address all four main strategic response directions, they require substantial financial resources. These projects are expected to be funded through a combination of EU, national, and private contributions, but full financing is not yet secured, leaving them exposed to industrial risks. In addition, even if demand for their products exists inside the EU—if not from clean-tech manufacturing, then from the digital and military sectors—domestically sourced CRM may not be cost-competitive compared to international suppliers. In any case, it is very relevant

---

17   See   https://single-market-economy.ec.europa.eu/sectors/raw-materials/areas-specific-interest/critical-raw-materials/strategic-projects-under-crma/selected-projects_en

that the EU path for clean-tech and net-zero industries, as promoted by the NZIA Regulation 2024/1735, will be stimulated to keep a balanced development of all the parts of the EU-level domestic value chain.[18]

Strategic Projects for the EU

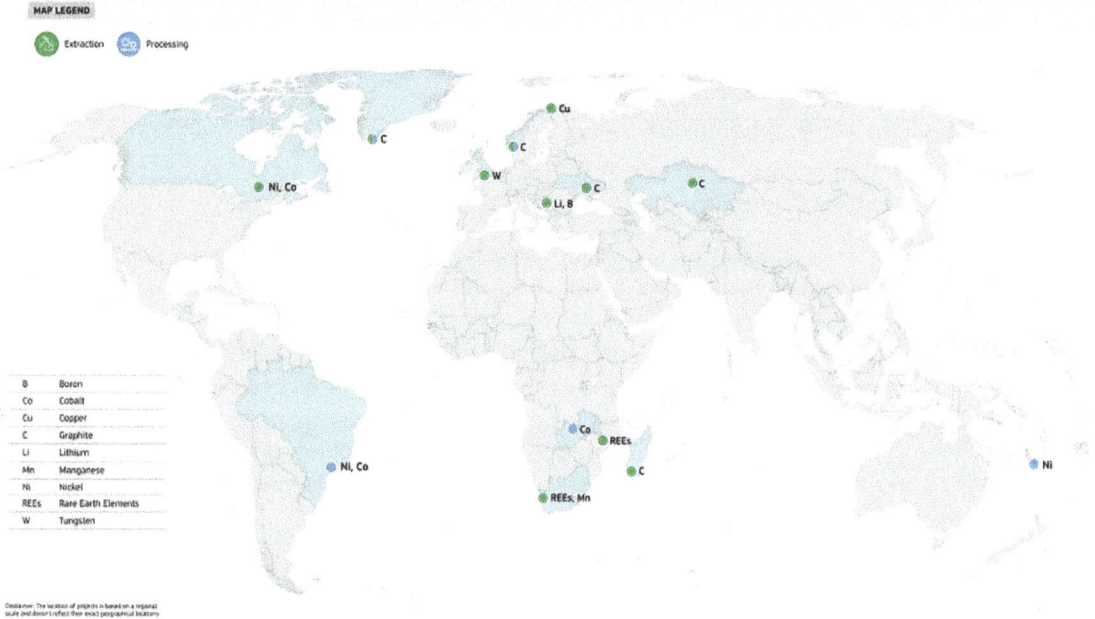

Fig. 10.5 Approved strategic projects on CRM outside the EU. *Source:* https://ec.europa.eu/commission/presscorner/detail/en/ip_25_1419

10.6 Conclusions: Keeping a Balanced Development of the EU Value Chain

The availability of CRM poses a fundamental challenge to the development of net-zero value chains, which are the backbone of the EU's transition towards its climate targets and greater energy self-sufficiency. The EU's current extreme dependency on supplier countries for CRM, some of which may prove unreliable, adds significant risk. Diversifying the portfolio of international suppliers, increasing domestic mining, increasing recycling and investing in innovation for materials efficiency and substitution are the key directions of response. The policy framework made by the regulations on net-zero industries and CRM adopted in 2024 supports these priorities and provides an important starting point. The regulation on CRM has already enabled

---

18   The call for net-zero technology manufacturing projects to become strategic projects under the Net-Zero Industry Act opened in June 2025, https://single-market-economy.ec.europa.eu/industry/sustainability/net-zero-industry-act/strategic-projects-under-nzia_en

the approval of forty-seven "strategic projects" inside the EU and thirteen projects outside the EU, including in countries with formal partnership agreements.

If these projects, as well as other projects, started or announced, will be feasible from financial and industrial perspectives and will deliver the expected outcomes, they will reinforce the upstream part of the net-zero industrial value chain alone. A question remains about the possibility of having a higher volume of investments in the clean-tech manufacturing sectors of the EU, which is the downstream part of the value chain. Despite relevant manufacturing initiatives taking place in the EU, significant investment gaps are emerging for these industries, which, in addition, are exposed to a strong industrial competition from international actors, in particular China. Without investments in clean-tech and net-zero technologies, the risk of a fundamental imbalance inside the EU value chain remains. This will impair the strategic objectives of the Competitiveness Compass and the Clean Industrial Deal, all aimed at achieving a competitive green industrial redevelopment of the EU. At the same time, EU digital and defence industries may become competitors of the clean-tech sector in CRM procurement, thereby contributing to weakening the net-zero industrial trajectory from the side of materials input availability and cost. In any case, at present, fundamental uncertainties surround the CRM issue at both the EU and global scale.

The new Commission's attitude towards state aid, also embodied in the new EU strategic framework described earlier, has the potential to boost investment in both clean tech and CRM, also in combination with "green" and "innovative" public procurement. However, this approach may also lead to growing divergence among Member States, especially where governments opt to take equity stakes in green industries rather than provide incentives.[19] When taking an overall EU perspective, this possible "specialization" of Member States can be non-negative or even positive, if there is a well-functioning, well-integrated single market.

References

Baccianti, C. (2022) "The Public Spending Needs of Reaching the EU's Climate Targets", in F. Cerniglia and F. Saraceno (eds), *Greening Europe: 2022 European Public Investment Outlook*. Cambridge, UK: Open Book Publishers, pp. 107–128, https://doi.org/10.11647/OBP.0328.08

Bruegel (2025) "European Clean Tech Tracker", https://www.bruegel.org/dataset/european-clean-tech-tracker

Carrara, S., S. Bobba, D. Blagoeva, P. Alves Dias, A. Cavalli, K. Georgitzikis, M. Grohol, A. Itul, T. Kuzov, C. Latunussa, L. Lyons, G. Malano, T. Maury, A. Prior Arce, J. Somers, T. Telsnig, C. Veeh, D. Wittmer, C. Black, D. Pennington, and M. Christou (2023) *Supply Chain Analysis and Material Demand Forecast in Strategic Technologies and Sectors in the EU—A Foresight Study*. Luxembourg: Publications Office of the European Union, https://doi.org/10.2760/386650

---

19   See the proposal of Teresa Ribera, Executive Vice President of the Commission, https://www.ft.com/content/f957bdf2-3624-441d-991c-368922549603

D'Amato, A., A. Pronti, S. Paleari, G. Romaldi, S. Speck, S. Tagliapietra, and R. Zoboli (2024) *Investment Needs and Gaps for the Sustainability Transition in Europe: Rethinking the European Green Deal as an EU Industrial Strategy*. Copenhagen: European Environment Agency, https://www.eionet.europa.eu/etcs/etc-ce/products/etc-ce-report-2024-8-investment-needs-and-gaps-for-the-sustainability-transition-in-europe-rethinking-the-european-green-deal-as-an-eu-industrial-strategy

Di Francesco, E., R. S. Gilli, P. Jensen, S. Manoochehri, G. Marin, A. Specker, S. Tagliapietra, and R. Zoboli (2024) *Environmental Impact of Material Supply Chain Disruptions*. Copenhagen: EEA, https://www.eionet.europa.eu/etcs/etc-ce/products/etc-ce-report-2024-3-environmental-impact-of-material-supply-chain-disruptionsl

EEA—European Environment Agency (2023) *Investments in the Sustainability Transition: Leveraging Green Industrial Policy against Emerging Constraints*. Copenhagen: EEA, https://www.eea.europa.eu/publications/investments-into-the-sustainability-transition

EIB (2025) *Investment Report 2024/2025: Innovation, Integration and Simplification in Europe*. Luxembourg: European Investment Bank, https://www.eib.org/en/publications/20240354-investment-report-2024

European Commission (2023) *Study on the Critical Raw Materials for the EU 2023*. Brussels: European Commission, https://op.europa.eu/en/publication-detail/-/publication/57318397-fdd4-11ed-a05c-01aa75ed71a1

European Commission (2024a) *The Future of European Competitiveness Part A | A Competitiveness Strategy for Europe (Draghi's Report)*. Brussels: European Commission, https://commission.europa.eu/topics/eu-competitiveness/draghi-report_en#paragraph_47059

European Commission (2024b) "Regulation (EU) 2024/1735 of the European Parliament and of the Council of 13 June 2024 on Establishing a Framework of Measures for Strengthening Europe's Net-zero Technology Manufacturing Ecosystem and Amending Regulation (EU) 2018/1724 (Text with EEA Relevance)," https://single-market-economy.ec.europa.eu/industry/sustainability/net-zero-industry-act_en

European Commission (2024c) "Regulation (EU) 2024/1252 of the European Parliament and of the Council of 11 April 2024 Establishing a Framework for Ensuring a Secure and Sustainable Supply of Critical Raw Materials and Amending Regulations (EU) No 168/2013, (EU) 2018/858, (EU) 2018/1724 and (EU) 2019/1020 (Text with EEA Relevance)", https://single-market-economy.ec.europa.eu/sectors/raw-materials/areas-specific-interest/critical-raw-materials_en

European Commission (2025a) "A Competitiveness Compass for the EU, Brussels, 29.1.2025", COM(2025) 30 final, https://commission.europa.eu/topics/eu-competitiveness/competitiveness-compass_en

European Commission (2025b) "The Clean Industrial Deal: A Joint Roadmap for Competitiveness and Decarbonization", Brussels, 26.2.2025", COM(2025) 85 final, https://commission.europa.eu/topics/eu-competitiveness/clean-industrial-deal_en

European Commission (2025c) "Commission Selects 47 Strategic Projects to Secure and Diversify Access to Raw Materials in the EU", 25 March, https://ec.europa.eu/commission/presscorner/detail/en/ip_25_864

European Commission (2025d) "Commission Selects 13 Strategic Projects in Third Countries to Secure Access to Raw Materials and to Support Local Value Creation", 4 June, https://ec.europa.eu/commission/presscorner/detail/en/ip_25_1419

European Parliament (2024) "The Role of Research and Innovation in Ensuring a Safe and Sustainable Supply of Critical Raw Materials in the EU", https://www.europarl.europa.eu/stoa/en/document/EPRS_STU(2024)762848

Greenland (2025) "Greenland Mineral Resources Strategy 2025–2029. A Sustainable Mineral Resources Sector", https://naalakkersuisut.gl/-/media/nyheder/2025/01/3101_ny_raastofstrategi/eng_greenland-mineral-resources-strategy-2025-2029.pdf

IEA (2021) *Net Zero by 2050. A Roadmap for the Global Energy Sector*. Paris: IEA, https://www.iea.org/reports/net-zero-by-2050

IEA (2024) *Global Critical Minerals Outlook 2024*. Paris: IEA, https://www.iea.org/reports/global-critical-minerals-outlook-2024

IEA (2025) *Energy Technology Perspectives 2024*. Paris: IEA, https://www.iea.org/reports/energy-technology-perspectives-2024

IRENA (2023) *Geopolitics of the Energy Transition: Critical Materials*. Abu Dabhi: IRENA, https://www.irena.org/Publications/2023/Jul/Geopolitics-of-the-Energy-Transition-Critical-Materials

Le Mouel, M., and N. Poitiers (2023) *Why Europe's Critical Raw Materials Strategy Has to Be International: In Ensuring Supplies of Critical Raw Materials, the European Union Cannot Rely on Domestic Measures Alone*. Brussels: Bruegel, https://www.bruegel.org/analysis/why-europes-critical-raw-materials-strategy-has-be-international

Specker A., S. Manoochehri, R. Gilli, G. Marin, R. Zoboli, P. Nuss, E. Pohjalainen, and P. Jensen (2025) *Environmental Impact of Material's Supply Chain Disruption. The Cases of Aluminium and Lithium*. Copenhagen: EEA—European Environment Agency, https://www.eionet.europa.eu/etcs/etc-ce/products/etc-ce-report-2025-5-environmental-impact-of-materials-supply-chain-disruption-the-cases-of-aluminium-and-lithium

World Bank (2025) "Commodity Markets", https://www.worldbank.org/en/research/commodity-markets

11. The EU Strategy for Green Hydrogen: More with Less (Public Investment)?

Rafael Fernández[1] and Clara García[2]

The EU's strategy for green hydrogen (GH2) reflects an evolving institutional logic that blends regulatory and investor-state tools to address the challenges of scaling up a nascent industrial value chain. While hydrogen is central to Europe's decarbonization agenda, its uptake is constrained by high capital costs, price risks, and uncertain demand. In response, the EU has moved beyond market design and financing mechanisms—hallmarks of the regulatory and investor states—by introducing a third layer of instruments targeting price and volume risks. Drawing parallels with the postwar development of natural gas, the chapter argues that although the EU is "doing more with less", the scale and coordination challenges of the hydrogen transition may exceed the capacity of current instruments. Without further fiscal innovation or quasi-planning coordination, Europe risks falling short of its hydrogen targets, undermining its wider ambitions for industrial transformation and climate neutrality.

11.1 Introduction

The European Union has set ambitious targets for "green hydrogen"[3] (GH2) as part of its strategy for climate neutrality. Under the REPowerEU Plan (COM/2022/0230), it aims to consume 20 million tonnes of GH2 by 2030, of which 10 million tonnes would be produced domestically.

Meeting these goals entails developing a nascent industrial value chain—from renewable energy generation and electrolyzer manufacturing to hydrogen storage, distribution, and end-use applications in heavy industry, transport, and electricity. The challenges of scaling up green hydrogen resemble those recently faced by renewables or in the postwar rollout of natural gas: large upfront investments in infrastructure and

---

1   Complutense Institute for International Studies (ICEI-UCM).
2   Complutense Institute for International Studies (ICEI-UCM).
3   Green or renewable hydrogen refers to hydrogen produced via electrolysis powered entirely by renewable electricity.

     https://doi.org/10.11647/OBP.0499.11

technology; price risks due to relatively high costs; and insufficient, uncertain demand, owing to high prices and the immaturity of end-use technologies.

Yet, unlike in the postwar period, these challenges are now addressed by what has been termed the EU regulatory state (Majone 1997), which emerged in the 1980s and has since evolved. Since the 2014 Juncker Plan—and especially following the COVID-19 pandemic—it has been complemented by elements of what Lepont and Thiemann (2024) describe as the investor state.

The regulatory state aims to perfect markets through technically designed regulations, often implemented by independent agencies. The investor state, in contrast, seeks to "do more with less", using limited public fiscal capacity to mobilize private capital and coordinate market actors. It layers (Prontera and Quitzow 2022) new goals and functions atop the regulatory framework, adding market-shaping ambitions (even market creation, see Mazzucato 2016)which requires long-run strategic investments and public policies that aim to create and shape markets, rather than just \"fixing\" markets or systems. Market creation has characterized the kind of mission-oriented investments that led to putting a man on the moon and are currently galvanizing green innovation. Mission-oriented innovation has required public agencies to not only \"de-risk\" the private sector, but also to lead the direct creation of new technological opportunities and market landscapes. This paper considers four key issues that arise from a market-creating framework for policy: (1, financial instruments, and political priorities to the technocratic market-fixing focus of the regulatory state.

This chapter presents the EU hydrogen strategy as a layered response to the distinctive challenges of a nascent industrial chain—investment intensity, price risks, and fragile demand. First, we argue that the strategy reflects a hybrid institutional logic combining regulatory and investor-type state roles. On the regulatory side, it involves the designing of a new market (Directive (EU) 2024/1788 and Regulation (EU) 2024/1789), based on technical criteria (ACER 2024), and includes mechanisms to internalize environmental externalities and enhance transparency. The investor state layer, in turn, adds political commitment to climate goals and aims to foster an industrial value chain by mobilizing private capital toward large upfront investments despite limited fiscal capacity.

Second, the chapter posits that the strategy introduces a further layer: instruments focused on price support and demand creation. Unlike the CAPEX-oriented tools of the investor state, this new layer targets revenue risks and guides energy end-uses, addressing the market's persistent demand weakness due to high costs.

Third, we evaluate how these layered instruments and goals constitute necessary yet evolutionary changes. Drawing parallels with postwar natural gas development, we contend this incremental strategy, centred on "doing more with less", may prove insufficient to scale up a high-risk, capital-intensive industrial transformation and ultimately secure Europe's clean energy future.

11.2 An Investor State for Hydrogen

To achieve its ambitious environmental and other goals—including green hydrogen—the EU relies on regulatory power to design new markets. It has established rules ranging from broad frameworks like the Taxonomy Regulation (EU) 2020/852 to hydrogen-specific measures[4] (European Hydrogen Observatory 2025), addressing market failures such as fossil fuel externalities (EU ETS Directive 2003/87/EC), economic concentration (e.g., Directive (EU) 2024/1788 for Transmission System Operators), and transparency gaps (RED II Delegated Acts). Renewable Energy Directive (RED III), Directive (EU) 2023/2413, even includes transitional rules to guide market development at a time when there is still minimal GH2 production or consumption.

Simultaneously, the EU has complemented its regulatory power with an investor approach to overcome its limited budget. To "do more with less", it has established financial mechanisms (Andersson et al. 2025), with some expanding public capacity, while most mobilize private financing. For hydrogen, these tools (few being sector-specific) help private companies undertake large upfront investments needed to establish a new industrial chain that remains nascent across all segments: production, transport, storage, and end uses.

The EU's primary mechanism to expand financial capacity has been capital market borrowing, enabling Next Generation EU to provide €800 billion in additional funding for 2021–2027. The second approach strengthened Europe's promotional banks (EIB and EBRD). By aligning their strategies with the Commission's—despite some overlaps (Clifton et al. 2025)—these banks have significantly expanded the EU's ability to finance private investments supporting strategic objectives.

In addition to these two large-scale alternatives, two other instruments may seem secondary but are nonetheless significant in the case of green hydrogen (Zabanova 2024). The first concerns the revision of state aid rules. Relaxing these rules, when aid targets investments of strategic EU interest, has allowed national budgets to provide additional financing for projects with European relevance. The second source of funding derives from revenues generated by the EU Emissions Trading System (ETS), which enabled the creation of the Innovation Fund, aimed specifically at supporting clean energy technologies, including hydrogen production, storage, and infrastructure.

In all cases—especially with Next Generation EU and promotional banks—these financial alternatives serve a dual purpose: increasing public resources for strategic investments and generating a crowding-in effect to attract, rather than displace, private funding, thereby producing a multiplier effect (catalytic, as in Prontera and Quitzow 2022) on private investment in productive assets.

---

4   According to the European Hydrogen Observatory (2025), thirty-two legislative initiatives—three cross-cutting, nine on production, five on transport, and fifteen on end-use—help define the rules of this emerging market.

This financial capacity is channelled through various funding programs and instruments not specifically dedicated to hydrogen, which can result in fragmented financial efforts. Among EU-level initiatives, only the Clean Hydrogen Partnership—a public-private initiative under Horizon Europe—is explicitly focused on GH2 development (European Hydrogen Observatory n.d.). It has a public budget of €1 billion, matched by an equivalent contribution from private partners (Zabanova 2024).

At the EU level, resources are spread across various programs targeting different areas or objectives, most of them managed by the European Climate, Infrastructure and Environment Executive Agency (CINEA, formerly INEA) under the European Commission.[5] Another portion of EU support is channelled through national governments, while promotional banks further complement available financing options (European Hydrogen Observatory 2025).

Programs managed by CINEA include the LIFE program, focused on climate change mitigation and adaptation; the Just Transition Fund, supporting regions and workers most affected by the shift to a climate-neutral economy; and the Modernization Fund, which aids energy system modernization and energy efficiency in thirteen low-income EU Member States, including renewable energy generation and use—such as renewable hydrogen. However, in the hydrogen field—particularly infrastructure development and large-scale demonstration projects—the two most important instruments are the Innovation Fund, financed by ETS revenues, and the Connecting Europe Facility-Energy (CEF-E).

The Innovation Fund has a projected €40 billion budget for 2020–2030 to support clean technology deployment. A significant share of funded projects to date involves hydrogen production. According to data from the 2023 and 2024 calls (European Commission n.d.), the Fund awarded €4.8 billion to eighty-five innovative projects, thirty-two of which—totalling about €1.5 billion—focus on hydrogen technologies. For large-scale projects, the Fund covers up to 60% of additional net costs (CAPEX and OPEX) during the first ten years of operation; for small-scale projects, it covers only capital expenditure (CAPEX).

The Connecting Europe Facility for Energy (Regulation (EU) 2021/1153) is an EU financial instrument supporting Projects of Common Interest (PCIs) that advance the Trans-European Networks for Energy (TEN-E), including cross-border renewable energy projects. In 2020, the Commission proposed a revision—adopted as TEN-E Regulation (EU) 2022/869—to extend support, under specific conditions, to hydrogen infrastructure, underground storage, certain electrolyzers, and smart gas grids. CEF-E has a €6 billion budget for 2021–2027, with at least 60% allocated to climate objectives and 15% to renewable energy.

---

5   In addition to CINEA-managed programs, some regions can use the Cohesion Fund and the Regional Development Fund—together accounting for nearly one third of the Multiannual Financial Framework—for hydrogen projects as part of their decarbonization strategies.

Alongside CINEA, Member State governments play a key role in managing EU climate and energy funding, as they channel resources from the Recovery and Resilience Facility (RRF) according to national objectives and needs. Financed through Next Generation EU, the RRF provides €386 billion in loans and €338 billion in grants, 37% of which must go to climate-related investments. This share may support projects involving green hydrogen production, transmission, distribution, and use in sectors such as transport and industry.

Given the varying strategic importance assigned to hydrogen across countries (though all Member States—except Greece, Latvia, Slovenia, Cyprus, and Malta— have published a national strategy), the use of RRF funds for hydrogen investments is also highly uneven (European Hydrogen Observatory 2025). According to their updated strategies, Spain (12 GW) and Germany (10 GW), followed by Portugal (5.5 GW), France (4.5 GW), Denmark (4–6 GW), and the Netherlands (3–4 GW), are setting ambitious goals far ahead other countries. These goals reflect differing national priorities that are expected to be supported through multiple instruments, including but not limited to the RRF, whose funds must be used by the end of 2026.

National governments complement their role in managing EU funds by financing Important Projects of Common European Interest (IPCEIs). Classified as state aid and funded through national budgets, IPCEIs offer discretionary support to selected companies for infrastructure and technology investment. The EU permits this exceptional aid—due to its alignment with climate goals—provided beneficiaries meet strict eligibility criteria. This allows Member States to use national fiscal resources to pursue productive transformation strategies while complementing the EU-wide approach to funding trans-European projects (Schmitz et al. 2025).

Of the ten IPCEIs approved since 2018, four focus on hydrogen: Hy2Tech, for developing renewable hydrogen technologies; Hy2Use, for infrastructure and industrial integration; Hy2Move, for hydrogen technologies in mobility and transport; and Hy2Infra, for hydrogen transmission and distribution networks. Together, these projects involve €19 billion in public funding (of €37 billion total) and €24.5 billion in private investment (of €66 billion total). However, only 21% of projects across the four IPCEIs have reached final investment decision (FID): 20% of projects in Hy2Tech, 9% in Hy2Use, 36% in Hy2Infra, and 23% in Hy2Move (Hydrogen Europe 2025).

Finally, the third pillar the EU relies on to generate and mobilize financing is the European promotional banks, particularly the European Investment Bank (EIB). As noted, these banks have increasingly financed investment projects aligned with climate goals, including the hydrogen industry. Their role in mobilizing capital toward these objectives has grown for three main reasons.

First, because of the development of blended finance mechanisms, which have increased these banks' involvement in co-financing EU programs managed by CINEA.

Second, because they serve as implementing partners for the InvestEU program, which uses the EU budget to guarantee €26.2 billion in loans. These guarantees—75%

to the EIB and 25% to national promotional banks—protect against financial risks tied to investments aligned with strategic priorities. The program aims to reduce risk, facilitate bank participation, and attract private capital, with a target of mobilizing up to €372 billion in total investment.[6] At least 30% of guarantees must support climate-related projects, 60% of which fall under the sustainable infrastructure window, where green hydrogen investments are eligible. However, the exact share supporting GH2 remains unclear.

Third, the role of these banks, especially the EIB, has been strengthened by its repositioning as the EU's climate bank (EIB, 2020), signalling a clearer strategic focus on climate and energy goals. In hydrogen, this is evident in the financing of thirty-eight projects related to green hydrogen production, transport, storage, distribution, and use in carbon-intensive sectors such as chemicals, steel, and heavy transport. Of these, twenty-eight have been approved since 2020, with twenty-five focused on investments within Europe (EIB n.d.). To support green hydrogen projects in developing economies, the EIB also launched the Green Hydrogen Fund in 2021, which currently holds €459 million in donor grant contributions.

In sum, scaling up a high-risk, capital-intensive industrial transformation involves numerous challenges. To address these—particularly the substantial CAPEX requirements—the EU has introduced a range of financial facilities. These may, to some extent, drive technological innovation and capital investment. However, as shown in the next section, the EU has complemented these efforts with additional instruments targeting price and demand risks.

11.3 Complementing the Investor State: Price Subsidies and Demand Targets for Hydrogen

Thus, the EU's shift from being solely a regulatory state to also acting as an investor state has enabled it to build significant financial capacity—despite its considerable fiscal limitations—to address the investment needs of the hydrogen industry in a context of uncertainty, where attracting private financing remains particularly difficult.

However, in an emerging industry like hydrogen, the issue is not only that private financing is held back by difficulty in assessing risks. More fundamentally, these risks are objectively very high. Some can be mitigated through collaboration between suppliers and consumers, enabling information sharing and coordinated decisions. Nevertheless, such alliances—like those promoted by the EU (e.g., the European Clean Hydrogen Alliance)—while beneficial, are not decisive in a context where

---

6   As of June 2024, the program had mobilized €280 billion in investment (70% private) with a €26.2 billion guarantee, though concerns remain over guarantee depletion, administrative burdens, and transparency (De Lemos Peixoto and Mazzocchi 2025).

hydrogen's availability, price, and demand remain not only uncertain but structurally disadvantageous.

For this reason, although the EU provides public funding for investments, scaling up requires addressing structural disadvantages and deep uncertainties. Recognizing this, the EU has complemented its role as an investor state with additional tools to reduce risks related to prices and demand volumes. This adds a layer that reinforces—rather than replaces—the investor role, aiming to steer the market toward strategic objectives. This additional layer includes, on the price side, instruments like the European Hydrogen Bank and emerging initiatives in key Member States. On the demand side, it includes lead markets, demand procurement, mandates, and national initiatives such as Carbon Contracts for Difference (CCfDs) targeting hydrogen-consuming industries.

Starting with high costs and price risk, this factor significantly deters investment regardless of financing costs. According to ACER (2024), the average cost of GH2 produced via electrolysis using grid electricity in the EU was about €8/kg, while production from direct renewable connections averaged €6/kg. In contrast, grey hydrogen from steam methane reforming (SMR) averaged €3/kg, and blue hydrogen (SMR with carbon capture) €4/kg.

This means green hydrogen costs are, on average, two to three times higher than hydrogen from natural gas. The disparity reflects not only technological factors but also input price trends—natural gas and CO_2 emission allowances for SMR, and electricity for electrolysis. For example, falling natural gas prices since mid-2023 and relatively low CO_2 prices (€52–€76 per tonne in 2024) have undermined the competitiveness of renewable hydrogen.

Looking ahead, 2030 projections suggest a significant reduction in green hydrogen production costs. The International Energy Agency (IEA 2024) estimates that, under the Net-Zero Emissions by 2050 Scenario, producing low-emission hydrogen from renewables could cost $2–$9/kg by 2030, narrowing the cost gap with unabated fossil hydrogen from $1.5–$8/kg today to $1–$3/kg by 2030.

There are already some non-hydrogen-specific regulatory elements that help mitigate high and uncertain costs, such as the EU Emissions Trading System (ETS) and Carbon Border Adjustment Mechanism (CBAM), which could be key to hydrogen's competitiveness. However, for now, the ETS has limited impact as a driver of rapid clean-technology adoption.

In this context, the EU created the European Hydrogen Bank (EHB) to intervene in pricing more directly and strategically. The EHB has an initial €3 billion capital, funded by the Innovation Fund and sourced from EU ETS revenues. Its aim is to stimulate investment by covering price risk through auction-based subsidies. In these auctions, project developers bid for a fixed premium over a maximum of ten years. This premium sets the subsidy for the winning bidder and is intended to cover part of the gap between production costs and the (estimated) market price. The remaining gap is borne by the developer, with the expectation that costs will fall post-investment and that part of the excess cost may be offset by passing on a green premium to consumers (Hydrogen Europe 2023).

In addition, Member States strengthen the system financially through the Auctions as a Service (AaaS) mechanism. After the most competitive projects are supported through the Innovation Fund, AaaS allows Member States to contribute additional resources to support specific projects among those submitted but not selected in the first round. For this second round of awards, participating countries may apply additional national criteria such as location-based priorities, industrial partnerships, or strategic sectors.

However, this pioneering EU-level initiative—while helping to market green hydrogen at a competitive price—does not fully eliminate price risks. In this regard, some Member States are testing additional instruments to complement the advantages offered by the European Hydrogen Bank (EHB), which the EU may adopt in the future.

The German foundation H2Global offers one such mechanism, where a publicly owned intermediary, Hintco, purchases products—generally more expensive than their carbon-intensive counterparts (such as hydrogen)—and resells them through an auction at a lower price. The funding gap created by this price difference is covered by public financing, though climate funds, private capital, or a combination of both can also support it.

A closely related option is a Contracts for Difference (CfD) scheme, where public support covers the gap between the strike price negotiated with the state and the market price agreed between seller and buyer. However, applying CfDs to hydrogen remains experimental due to the lack of a liquid, benchmark market price similar to that in the electricity sector (OIES 2024).

Regarding volume risk, long-term "take-or-pay" contracts—where buyers commit to purchasing a fixed annual quantity—do not always resolve the issue. While such contracts offer producers revenue certainty, buyers face binding commitments that intermediate industries like chemicals or steel are often reluctant to accept. Today, stakeholders seek to avoid such lock-ins due to uncertainty over hydrogen's price and availability, and anticipated consumer resistance to paying a significant premium for decarbonized products. Moreover, even if buyers were willing to pay a premium, they may be unable to provide producers with sufficient guarantees of future purchasing capacity.

To push intermediate industries to sign these types of contracts, providing certainty to suppliers, the EU has intervened with measures based not on price signals but on regulatory mandates. RED III, published in November 2023, stipulates that by 2030 at least 42% of hydrogen used in industry must be of renewable origin. By 2035, that share rises to 60%, although this is not strictly mandatory, as the directive allows relatively flexible deadlines for transposition into national regulations and permits countries to introduce exemptions or reduce the quota for various reasons (Ason and Dal Poz 2024)previously mainly known as financial hedging instruments, are increasingly seen as the method of choice for incentivising investment in clean energy technologies. In the power sector, the CfD mechanism has emerged as the preferred arrangement to provide the required revenue support and stimulate the construction of new renewable power generating facilities. Following the successful experience with renewable CfDs (in the UK and several other countries.

For transport, the mandates are less ambitious. A general quota of 1% is set for 2030, though the requirements are somewhat stricter for maritime and aviation. FuelEU Maritime (Regulation (EU) 2023/1805) sets a 2% quota for RFNBOs (renewable fuels of non-biological origin) in 2035, while ReFuelEU Aviation (Regulation (EU) 2023/2405) requires a 2% share of SAF (sustainable aviation fuel) in 2025 and 1.2% e-fuels in 2030, rising to 20% SAF and 5% e-fuels by 2035.

Overall, it is estimated that meeting these mandates would increase green-hydrogen demand by no more than 2 Mt, far below the 20 Mt (10 Mt domestic plus 10 Mt imports) foreseen in the REPowerEU plan for 2030 (Corbeau and Nassif 2025)like other regions, the EU is facing a demand issue as offtakers have been reluctant to sign offtake agreements given the high costs of renewable hydrogen. Renewable hydrogen is also part of a broader plan and series of directives aiming at increasing the share of renewable energies in EU's energy consumption. The latest iteration of the Renewable Energy Directive (RED III. Moreover, the main drawback of mandates is that they can place considerable pressure on consumer industries without offering compensatory measures or positive incentives.

In this respect, the EU is exploring two still-preliminary options to create lead markets. The first is to stimulate end-consumer demand through labelling standards and related regulations (e.g., the proposed RED III intended to ensure traceability and consumer confidence in "green" products—though this faces practical challenges in tracking feedstock origins across complex supply chains and harmonizing sustainability criteria across Member States. The second is to introduce non-price public procurement criteria, building on RED II/III, to reward renewable fuels of non-biological origin (RFNBO) in public tenders. More ambitiously, the Commission's Clean Industrial Deal would give preferential scoring to net-zero products like steel, cement, and chemicals, while Germany is reportedly considering binding quotas for these goods in federal procurement.

A third alternative—still not adopted by the EU—is the use of Carbon Contracts for Difference (CCfDs), as introduced by the German government (Klimaschutzverträge n.d.). Under these contracts, public funds compensate companies investing in decarbonization. A reference (strike) carbon price is set, and firms calculate the gap between the total cost (operating plus capital) of low-carbon production and the cost of conventional high-carbon production, including emissions priced at the strike level. Based on this, they bid for a premium, competing with other applicants. In return, winning firms must reimburse the state if forgoing the investment would have been costlier than adopting low-carbon technologies.

In sum, designing market rules and offering financial facilities is not enough to address the investment needs of the hydrogen industry. Uncertainty around price and demand volumes calls for additional policies that go beyond the typical instruments of either the regulatory or the investor state. As a result, a new layer of innovative measures has been put in place to de-risk not only financing but also production.

11.4 Doing More with Less (Public Investment)?

As discussed throughout this chapter, various regulations and policies address the challenges of scaling up green hydrogen: large upfront physical and technological investments for production, transport, and storage; price risks due to elevated costs; and insufficient and uncertain demand. However, it is arguable that the current pace of uptake is not matching what is needed to meet EU targets.

The EU target for Phase 1 (by 2024) was to deploy at least 6 GW of electrolizers capacity (approximately, 1 million tonnes per annum, mtpa), and 40 GW (10 mtpa) for Phase 2 (by 2030). But as of May 2025, the production capacity of renewable hydrogen operating projects in the EU is below 0.5 GW (50,000 tpa), and, including projects under construction, production capacity reaches no more than 3.2 GW (0.5 mtpa), less than 5% of the total pipeline of projects that have been announced to come online by 2030 (European Hydrogen Observatory n.d.). According to the Hydrogen Council (2025), the current estimated committed capacity by 2030 is of 4 GW (0.7 mtpa), below 10% of the EU target, and demand could reach 5 mtpa in the best possible scenario (25% of the EU target).

Although a more nuanced analysis would be required to explain the slow deployment of green hydrogen or to anticipate whether acceleration is likely, using the uptake of natural gas as a reference, we propose that existing instruments may need to be complemented with further efforts.

Europe's gas industry emerged in the 1960s and 1970s through a political decision and was structured around largely state-owned, vertically integrated companies. In countries without domestic reserves (most, except the Netherlands and the UK), gas firms contracted supply from foreign providers and built the infrastructure for import, transport, storage, and distribution.

The postwar state thus provided solutions to complex industrial development. It addressed the need for massive investment directly, channelling public capital into the physical and technological capacity required for growth. In trade, costs were passed on predictably through long-term, oil-indexed take-or-pay contracts. The risk of constrained end-demand due to high prices was mitigated through regulated tariffs for industry and households, and through public or publicly guided demand in sectors such as industry and electricity production.

Reform began in the mid- to late 1990s and introduced unbundling (separating production, transmission, and distribution), widespread privatization of state-owned utilities, and genuine supplier competition. At the same time, gas hubs emerged as trading points with spot and futures markets rather than fixed, oil-indexed contracts. Crucially, this shift only occurred after gas uptake had become a reality: the industrial chain was no longer nascent but mature, investment needs had declined, prices were relatively stable, and demand was secure. In contrast, the layering of regulatory, investor, and other instruments for hydrogen is happening in a context of virtually no production.

Reflecting the trajectory of natural gas development, it can be argued that even if the latest support mechanisms in some Member States were adopted EU-wide, policy support may still be insufficient to accelerate green hydrogen uptake.

First, several scholars question whether investor-state financing, even complemented with price and demand de-risking, can launch a new industrial chain. The amounts of funding available are insufficient for the investment required (Zabanova 2024). The EU Strategy will require, to reach its Phase 2 targets, €24–42 billion for electrolyzers, €220–340 billion for renewable energy generation, and €65 billion for distribution networks, totalling at least €320 billion (European Hydrogen Observatory n.d.). However, according to the Hydrogen Council (2025), the EU committed investment (post-FID) by 2030 is $19 billion, behind China (33) and the USA (23).

Some argue that the EU's fiscal limits are too restrictive for climate investment, proposing EU-level exemptions to enable green industrial projects (Gabor 2023; Griffith-Jones et al. 2022; Griffith-Jones and Naqvi 2021). Others advocate creating a permanent EU fiscal capacity through joint borrowing (Next Generation EU-style) to support large-scale decarbonization (Balakrishnan et al. 2022). Finally, some contend that public shareholdings in the energy sector should operate as mission-oriented investors—willing to accept longer return horizons or lower yields—rather than as passive financial investors (Lepont and Thiemann, 2024). Taken together, these proposals suggest that, even without reverting to a postwar-type state, new tools are needed to mobilize large amounts of capital along the GH2 value chain.

Second, hydrogen scale-up reflects a classic coordination failure (Andreoni and Chang 2019; Mazzucato and Rodrik 2023): there is no supply because there is no demand, and no demand because there is no supply. The European Court of Auditors (2024) reports limitations in the EU's ability to overcome this: insufficient coordination regarding translation of EU targets into binding national plans, permitting procedures, standards, or information on public-funding data and project pipelines. Beyond the soft coordination mechanisms of the catalytic state (Prontera and Quitzow 2022), the EU could create an effective sectoral platform to actively align stakeholders—regulators, grid operators, producers, and offtakers—around shared objectives. This platform would facilitate the alignment of national roadmaps while encouraging cross-sector partnerships to pool resources, expertise, and/or capital.

It could also enhance coordination by publishing binding milestones for electrolyzer capacity, pipeline build-out, and end-use demand; maintain a transparent data portal tracking project maturity; organize joint procurement to pool scale and attract investment; establish pooled guarantees to de-risk early projects; and harmonize technical and contractual standards (grid connections, offtake templates) to avoid regulatory fragmentation. By pooling resources and aligning incentives along the chain, the platform could overcome the "no supply/no demand" impasse without necessarily relying on state-owned firms.

A key question is whether strengthening fiscal capacity and introducing quasi-planning coordination mechanisms could be achieved simply by adding another layer to the regulatory state, or whether these measures would require a more fundamental paradigm shift in EU state model. If the latter, it may be more difficult to meet hydrogen scale-up targets. As a result, full decarbonization by 2050 could be jeopardized—as could the revival of legacy industries like steel or leadership in technological transitions in hard-to-abate sectors such as mobility.

References

ACER (2024) *European Hydrogen Markets. ACER Market Monitoring Report*. Ljubljana: ACER, https://www.acer.europa.eu/monitoring/MMR/european_hydrogen_markets_2024

Andersson, M., P. Köhler-Ulbrich, and C. Nerlich (2025) "Green Investment Needs in the EU and Their Funding", *ECO Economic Bulletin* 1, https://www.ecb.europa.eu/press/economic-bulletin/articles/2025/html/ecb.ebart202501_03~90ade39a4a.en.html

Andreoni, A., and H.-J. Chang (2019) "The Political Economy of Industrial Policy: Structural Interdependencies, Policy Alignment and Conflict Management", *Structural Change and Economic Dynamics* 48, 136–150, https://doi.org/10.1016/j.strueco.2018.10.007

Ason, A., and J. Dal Poz (2024) "Contracts for Difference: The Instrument of Choice for the Energy Transition", *OIES Paper* ET34, https://www.oxfordenergy.org/wpcms/wp-content/uploads/2024/04/ET34-Contracts-for-Difference.pdf

Balakrishnan, R., P. Medas, B. Barkbu, S. Weber, W. Lam, A. Shahmoradi, N. Arnold, L. Rabier, A. Lagerborg, C. Roehler, M. Spector, J. Otten, H. Davoodi, and J. Zettelmeyer (2022) "Reforming the EU Fiscal Framework", *Departmental Papers* 2022(014), 1.

Clifton, J., D. Díaz-Fuentes, A. L. Gómez, and D. Howarth (2025) "Overlapping Lending by the European Investment Bank and the European Bank for Reconstruction and Development", *Journal of Economic Policy Reform* 28.1, 97–101, https://doi.org/10.1080/17487870.2024.2312120

Corbeau, A.-S., and L. Nassif (2025) "Challenges and Opportunities Posed by the Eu's 42 Percent Renewable Hydrogen Target by 2030", *OIES Paper* ET42, https://www.oxfordenergy.org/wpcms/wp-content/uploads/2025/03/ET42-Challenges-and-Opportunities-Posed-by-the-EUs-42-Percent-Renewable-Hydrogen-Target-by-2030.pdf

De Lemos Peixoto, S., and R. Mazzocchi (2025) "Invest EU Programme: Functioning, Performance and Future Challenges", *Economic Governance and EMU Scrutiny*

Unit, https://www.europarl.europa.eu/RegData/etudes/IDAN/2025/764377/ ECTI_IDA(2025)764377_EN.pdf

EIB (n.d.) "All Projects—Finance and Global Impact Worldwide", https://www.eib.org/en/ projects/all/index

EIB (2020) *EIB Group Climate Bank Roadmap 2021-2025. European Investment Bank.* Luxembourg: EIB, https://www.eib.org/en/publications/the-eib-group-climate-bank-roadmap

European Commission (n.d.) "Innovation Fund Projects", https://climate.ec.europa.eu/ eu-action/eu-funding-climate-action/innovation-fund/innovation-fund-projects_en

European Court of Auditors (2024) "The EU's Industrial Policy on Renewable Hydrogen Legal Framework Has Been Mostly Adopted—Time for a Reality Check", *Special Report* 11/2024, https://www.eca.europa.eu/en/publications?ref=sr-2024-11

European Hydrogen Observatory (n.d.) "Financial Tools and Incentives", European Hydrogen Observatory, https://observatory.clean-hydrogen.europa.eu/hydrogen-landscape/ financial-tools-and-incentives

Europea Hydrogen Observatory (n.d.) "Many Datasets on the European Hydrogen Observatory", European Hydrogen Observatory, https://observatory.clean-hydrogen. europa.eu/media/news/many-datasets-european-hydrogen-observatory-are-now- updated-featuring-latest-available-0

European Hydrogen Observatory (n.d.) "EU Hydrogen Strategy under the EU Green Deal", European Hydrogen Observatory, https://observatory.clean-hydrogen.europa. eu/eu-policy/eu-hydrogen-strategy-under-eu-green-deal#:~:text=The%20Strategy%20 outlines%20investment%20needs,at%20least%20%E2%82%AC320%20billion

European Hydrogen Observatory (2025) "The European Hydrogen Policy Landscape", Extensive Update of the April 2024 Report, https://observatory.clean-hydrogen.europa.eu/ sites/default/files/2025-01/The%20European%20hydrogen%20policy%20landscape-%20 January%202025.pdf

Gabor, D. (2023) "The (European) Derisking State", *Stato e mercato* 1, 53–84.

Griffith-Jones, S., and N. Naqvi (2021) "Industrial Policy and Risk Sharing in Public Development Banks: Lessons for the Post- COVID Response from the EIB and EFSI", *Revista de Economía Mundial* 59, https://doi.org/10.33776/rem.v0i59.5258

Griffith-Jones, S., S. Spiegel, J. Xu, M. Carreras, and N. Naqvi (2022) "Matching Risks with Instruments in Development Banks", *Review of Political Economy* 34.2, 197–223.

Hydrogen Council (2025) "Global Hydrogen Compass 2025", Hydrogen Council, McKinsey & Co, https://compass.hydrogencouncil.com/wp-content/uploads/2025/09/Hydrogen- Council-Global-Hydrogen-Compass-2025.pdf

Hydrogen Europe (2023) "The European Hydrogen Bank: Kickstarting the European Hydrogen Market", Position Paper, https://hydrogeneurope.eu/wp-content/ uploads/2023/03/2023.03_Hydrogen-Bank_H2Europe_paper.pdf

Hydrogen Europe (2025) "Assessing the Implementation of Hydrogen IPCEIs: Challenges and Opportunities", *The Hydrogen Europe Quarterly Magazine* Q1 2025.

IEA (2024) *Global Hydrogen Review 2024.* Paris: IEA, https://www.iea.org/reports/ global-hydrogen-review-2024

Klimaschutzverträge (n.d.) "Carbon Contracts for Difference", https://www. klimaschutzvertraege.info/en/home

Lepont, U., and M. Thiemann (2024) "The European Investor State: Its Characteristics, Genesis, and Effects", *Competition & Change* 28.3–4, 381–396.

Majone, G. (1997) "From the Positive to the Regulatory State: Causes and Consequences of Changes in the Mode of Governance", *Journal of Public Policy* 17.2, 139–167.

Mazzucato, M. (2016) "From Market Fixing to Market-Creating: A New Framework for Innovation Policy", *Industry and Innovation* 23.2, 140–156.

Mazzucato, M., and D. Rodrik (2023) "Industrial Policy with Conditionalities: A Taxonomy and Sample Cases", *IIPP Working Paper* 2023/07.

Prontera, A., and R. Quitzow (2022) "The EU as Catalytic State? Rethinking European Climate and Energy Governance", *New Political Economy* 27.3, 517–531, https://doi.org/10.1080/135 63467.2021.1994539

Schmitz, L., T. Seidl, and T. Wuttke (2025) "The Costs of Conditionality. IPCEIs and the Constrained Politics of EUIndustrial Policy", *Competition & Change* 0.0, 1–25, https://doi. org/10.31219/osf.io/f63gd

Zabanova, Y. (2024) "The EU in the Global Hydrogen Race: Bringing Together Climate Action, Energy Security, and Industrial Policy", in R. Quitzow and Y. Zabanova (eds.), *The Geopolitics of Hydrogen*. Cham: Springer Nature, pp. 15–47, https://doi. org/10.1007/978-3-031-59515-8_2

12. The Power of Energy Communities for a Just Transition in Europe

Francesc Cots,[1] Jérémie Fosse,[2] and Diana Mangalagiu[3]

This chapter examines the evolving concept of Just Transition (JT) in Europe, emphasizing the shift from extractive, carbon-intensive economies to sustainable, community-centred energy systems. It analyzes the European Union's Just Transition Mechanism (JTM), highlighting its focus on coal-dependent regions and the sociopolitical, cultural, and economic challenges that impede transition. The chapter argues that, beyond technological and financial solutions, deeply rooted identities and local narratives must be addressed to ensure legitimacy and effectiveness. Energy communities are presented as catalysts for democratizing the energy transition, fostering local ownership, and overcoming resistance in regions historically reliant on coal. However, the development of genuine energy communities faces obstacles, including regulatory fragmentation and risks of corporate capture. The chapter concludes with policy recommendations to strengthen regulatory frameworks, safeguard community integrity, and promote citizen-led initiatives, positioning energy communities as pivotal actors in achieving a just and inclusive transition to a low-carbon future in Europe.

12.1 Understanding the Just Transition: Definitions, Mechanisms, and Regional Challenges

The concept of a Just Transition (JT) is increasingly recognized as necessary to ensure that the shift from extractive "brown" industries to sustainable "green" ones is equitable. Stark et al. (2023) highlight several definitions of JT. The UN International Labor Organization (ILO) defines JT as a "conceptual framework in which the labour movement captures the complexities of the transition toward a low-carbon and climate-resilient economy, highlighting public policy needs and aiming to maximize benefits and minimize hardships for workers and their communities in this transformation" (Rosemberg 2010). McCauley and Heffron (2018) define JT as a "fair and equitable

---

1   Eco-union.
2   Eco-union.
3   Neoma Business School.

https://doi.org/10.11647/OBP.0499.12

process of moving toward a post-carbon society", contending that the JT framework includes not only environmental but also energy and climate justice. In its simplest terms, the practice of JT is a way of linking dimensions of climate action with social fairness (Snell 2018). While historically associated with mining and energy transitions, the principles of JT are increasingly relevant to other high-emitting industries, such as animal agriculture, and are being extended to fields like food justice, green gentrification, and energy sovereignty.

In Europe, the Just Transition Mechanism (JTM), a policy framework developed by the European Union as part of the European Green Deal investment plan, has been established to address the social and economic impacts of the shift away from fossil fuels. With its budget of €55 billion over six years, the Just Transition Mechanism aims to disburse around €9 billion each year between 2021 and 2027. The JTM is a key component of the European Union's efforts to operationalize a transition to a climate-neutral economy in a manner that is equitable and inclusive, ensuring no disproportionate burdens on any segment of society. As such, the JTM currently and primarily focuses on regions characterized by high carbon intensity and a large proportion of the workforce employed in fossil fuel sectors, acknowledging the acute challenges these areas face. A significant number of the regions targeted by the JTM in Europe are those with a heavy reliance on coal, where economies, workforces, and even cultural identities are deeply intertwined with coal mining and related industries. The JTM, therefore, strategically targets these coal-dependent areas to mitigate the socioeconomic consequences caused by the shift to clean energy, and to facilitate their transition towards more diverse and sustainable economic activities. By supporting a diverse range of activities, including investments in renewable energy, energy efficiency, and new businesses, the JTM seeks to foster a sustainable and inclusive future for Europe's high carbon-dependent communities (European Commission 2019). EU funds are allocated to the identified regions based on their territorial just transition plans which outline how the funds will be used to support a just and equitable transition, including investments in renewable energy projects, that must be aligned with EU emission reduction targets for 2030 and on track to achieve net-zero emissions by 2050.

However, international climate policies frameworks such as the JTM often overlook the specific conditions and nuanced needs present at the regional and local level. As a result, they may produce misalignments between international or national goals and regional and local priorities. Such misalignments and disconnections can undermine the credibility of long-term goals that do not resonate with the immediate socioeconomic needs nor actual possibilities for transition existing at regional and local levels (Amundsen et al. 2018). These challenges are particularly acute in European carbon-intensive regions that must meet national and EU climate change targets but are economically dependent on extractive industries. Extractive regions frequently face a "resource curse", experiencing economic vulnerability, demographic instability, negative health and socioeconomic impacts, increasing geographic isolation, imbalances of scale and power with respect to extractive industries, and an absence of realistic alternatives for a more diversified development (Perdue and Pavela 2012). Such dependence means that extractive industries, like coal extraction and exploitation, are not only deeply entrenched in the region's economy but also in its culture.

While some contend that material resource limitations impede the transition to a low carbon economy, research shows that the primary obstacles to such a transition are sociopolitical (Taylor, Chong, and Röder, 2024). Entrenched interests, substantial investments in existing energy infrastructure, bureaucratic and political inertia, and citizens accustomed to long established ways of life create significant resistance and hinder the transition process (IRENA 2024). In coal-dependent regions, this resistance is often rooted in a deeply ingrained identity constructed around the "coal imaginary", a structural element that cannot be easily dismantled through incremental actions alone. A sense of place grounded in a shared industrial myth, along with associated place meanings, identities, and memories, has a profound influence on the possibilities to transition and lock-in mechanisms. For example, in Sardinia, the Carbonia region (literally "coal city") was established, due to its coal reserves, as the Italian national energy capital almost a century ago. Positive feedback loops between sense of place and structural factors of lock-in have legitimated the dominance of coal and carbon-intensive industries across time, impeding the recognition of the need for change and obscuring windows of opportunity for transition to low carbon (Biddau et al. 2024).

Successfully navigating transitions necessitates addressing not only technological innovation and lock-ins but also understanding and considering intangible cultural and perceptual factors that shape local visions and behaviours (Mangalagiu et al. 2025).

12.2 Energy Communities as a Catalyst of Change

Energy communities are grassroots initiatives that empower citizens to actively participate in the production, distribution, and supply of energy. In Europe, they have emerged through a combination of bottom-up grassroots initiatives and supportive policy frameworks. Many energy communities began as local, citizen-driven projects, relying on voluntary engagement of local citizens and aiming to foster community identity, energy democracy, and collective ownership of renewable energy resources. Evidence from countries like the Netherlands, Germany, and Denmark shows that community energy schemes were already growing organically before formal EU legislation, driven by local needs and social innovation (Williams 2024).

Energy communities, operating on principles of open participation, local ownership, and social benefit, foster a sense of collective agency and responsibility. Their primary goal is to deliver environmental, economic, or social benefits to their members or the local community, rather than to generate financial profits. This can lead to a fundamental shift in the energy landscape, where decisions are made, and benefits are shared, at the community level.

Building upon the foundational desire to democratize the energy system, the proliferation and rapid advancement of these community-led initiatives have been significantly propelled by concerted European and national policy interventions. The European Union's Clean Energy for All Europeans Package (2019) marked a pivotal moment, formally recognizing and defining distinct legal frameworks for Citizen Energy Communities (CECs) and Renewable Energy Communities (RECs). These frameworks, further nurtured by enabling policies at the Member State level, aim to empower collective citizen engagement in the ongoing energy transition. Specifically, RECs are characterized by more stringent conditions concerning geographical proximity among members, the autonomous nature of their operations, and the effective control exerted by local actors. Furthermore, the primary objective of RECs is the expansion of renewable energy sources, explicitly excluding other forms of energy generation. Conversely, CECs exhibit a broader scope, unconstrained by geographical limitations and applicable to any type of energy technology, including non-renewable sources. However, the operational domain of CECs is confined to the electricity sector, and their principal aim is to establish a level playing field for these community-based entities as emergent actors within the electricity market (Cots 2022a).

The supportive measures implemented by Member States, including the adaptation or creation of specific legislation, the establishment of dedicated funding streams, and the provision of tailored support structures, have been instrumental in facilitating the development of both RECs and CECs. These policies often built upon the existing momentum of grassroots projects, thereby not only fostering greater social acceptance of renewable energy deployment and empowering individual citizens but also unlocking access to crucial financial resources and cultivating the emergence of innovative, community-centric business models within the energy sector.

Ultimately, energy communities hold the potential to transform the energy landscape from one dominated by large companies towards a more decentralized and community-centric model. Therefore, energy communities can serve as a tool to overcome the multifaceted resistances often hindering energy transitions, like the ones in coal-dependent regions. However, the success of energy communities depends on multiple factors, including supportive policy frameworks, access to adequate funding and technical expertise, and the active engagement and collaboration of all stakeholders. With its commitment to the forthcoming Citizens' Energy Package, the European Commission presents a key opportunity to firmly place individuals and local communities at the core of the energy transition.

12.3 Community Engagement: Overcoming Resistance and Embracing Change

The enduring legacy of coal mining has deeply ingrained itself into the regional identities of many communities, creating significant obstacles to the transition towards a low-carbon economy. This phenomenon is evident in coal-dependent regions across Europe, a fact highlighted in the European Commission-funded research projects such as TIPPING+. Regions like Sulcis (Italy), Teruel (Spain), Jiu Valley (Romania), and Silesia (Poland), among others, show how the intertwined history of coal and community identity has profoundly influenced the regions' path and created a formidable barrier to change (Cots et al. 2024; Tabara et al. 2024). In such coal-dependent regions, the common memories, meanings, and sense of place associated with coal have hindered efforts to transition away from the coal extraction industry. This resistance is amplified by economic concerns, including potential job losses, the costs of abandoning existing infrastructure, and a perceived lack of readiness for alternative economic pathways (Della Bosca and Gillespie 2018). Such interconnected factors have limited these regions, and others similar regions, in their ability to imagine and embrace alternative futures, hindering their capacity to seize new opportunities. Cognitive and psychological factors, such as cultural traditions, language, identity, and senses of place, alongside judgments of the potential benefits and costs of change, significantly affect public communication and engagement processes regarding decarbonization (Cots et al. 2023). Compensatory policies alone, like early retirement packages for miners, are often insufficient to overcome this resistance. Unless these policies are accompanied by a more active and empowering component, stakeholders continue to perceive themselves as "losers" in the transition. A more empowering and place-based perspective is needed, involving local and community concerns, perceptions, and actors, to foster active participation and facilitate the adoption of a new, low-carbon economy (Cots et al. 2023). In fact, ignoring the deep connection between coal and community identity can undermine efforts to transition towards a low-carbon future. Attempts to transform coal-dependent regions risk being perceived as threats, leading to resistance from local stakeholders.

In this context, creating alternative narratives that resonate with local values and aspirations becomes key for generating legitimacy and mobilizing communities towards a just transition. This requires fostering a sense of shared purpose and collective agency, empowering communities to actively shape their future rather than simply being passive recipients of change. Energy communities can create such alternatives. By fostering local ownership and participation, energy communities have the potential to directly address entrenched interests and empower citizens to embrace new energy paradigms, potentially dismantling deeply ingrained "coal imaginaries" and reshaping place-based identities. In other words, the inherent political nature of energy communities is key to their transformative potential. By enabling active citizen participation in energy production and governance, they challenge traditional top-down energy structures.

This is particularly relevant in the context of the EU's JTM, where a risk exists that large-scale renewable energy infrastructure projects that often replace coal-fired plants may offer limited benefits to regional stakeholders beyond initial construction jobs, ongoing management, and standard business tax revenues. Indeed, the closure of coal plants and mines is frequently coupled with the development of these large renewable installations aiming to compensate for the lost energy generation capacity. However, this technological shift alone, without parallel efforts in economic diversification, the promotion of energy communities, and citizen empowerment, may fail to bring about genuine social change. Communities could remain reliant on a dominant economic activity, simply transitioning from coal to large-scale renewables, with the underlying power dynamics largely unchanged. In some instances, such as in Teruel (Spain), the very companies that owned the coal-fired plants are now the primary developers of these large renewable projects. This could result in most of the income leaving the region, rather than benefitting local communities. Increasingly, a more localized approach to deploying renewable energy is seen across Europe as a more effective way to ensure a just transition. For instance, a review of submitted Territorial Just Transition Plans (TJTPs) indicates significant interest among regional and local governments in implementing energy communities to promote the socially inclusive adoption of renewables (Hinsh 2023). This is evident in the TJTPs of regions like Hunedoara (Romania), Lower Silesia (Poland), Sulcis (Italy), and Ústí nad Labem (Czechia), among others, and demonstrates a promising trend, with many subnational authorities choosing to support the creation, scaling, and sustainability of local renewable energy projects.

12.4 The Transformative Power of Energy Communities in Just Transition Regions

The EU has been instrumental in advancing the development of energy communities. The Clean Energy for All Europeans Package (2019) established the concepts of CEC and REC, granting individuals and communities greater influence in the energy transition. The Directive on common rules for the internal market for electricity (2019/944) enables consumers and CECs to participate in various electricity market activities, while the revised Renewable Energies Directive (2018/2001/EU) strengthens the role of RECs, particularly in expanding renewable energy sources.

These communities can participate in a range of energy activities, including generation, distribution, supply, consumption, aggregation, energy storage, energy efficiency services, and electric vehicle charging, among others. Recent investment programs, such as the European Energy Communities Facility (European Energy

Communities Facility n.d.), further amplify this transformative potential by providing financial and technical support to emerging energy communities, accelerating the development of community-led renewable energy projects.

A relevant aspect of this transition involves moving from a consumer to a "prosumer" mentality, where citizens actively engage in energy production and management. This shift, incentivized by new European policies on energy communities, and the promotion of both collective and individual self-consumption, empowers individuals and communities to become actors in transforming just transition regions and accelerating decarbonization. By generating their own renewable energy, citizens become less reliant on coal and carbon-dependent energy sources, fostering a sense of ownership and responsibility for energy production, and motivating more sustainable energy practices. This also facilitates the decentralization of energy systems, reducing reliance on long-distance transmission and distribution, and making energy systems more resilient and less vulnerable to disruptions. By fostering a "prosumer" mentality, where citizens actively engage in energy production and management, energy communities can help dismantle the "coal imaginary" and create new narratives of community empowerment and sustainable development. As individuals and communities collaborate to generate and manage their energy, they develop new social networks and partnerships that can strengthen local economies.

According to the research conducted in the TIPPING+ project, energy communities have proven successful in generating collective imaginaries that drive local social-ecological systems towards sustainable trajectories (Apostoli Cappello 2024). They can address issues such as the lack of ownership and perceived injustice associated with top-down development strategies and help overcome negative cultural aspects and the stigma associated with being labelled "dirty energy regions". For instance, a compelling alternative narrative is emerging in Sulcis where local stakeholders envision a future energy system rooted in distributed generation, self-sufficiency, and self-consumption, with energy communities and energy districts playing a central role. This vision, championed by local professionals, technicians, and administrators, proposes a model of energy self-sufficiency based on renewable sources (wind and solar), coupled with energy efficiency and conservation. This nascent project, with its potential to transform the region, highlights the power of "cosmopolitan" thinking among local elites to envision and disseminate alternative energy futures and energyscapes, inspiring the community to embrace a more sustainable path (Apostoli Cappello 2024). The Jiu Valley in Romania, one of the European just transition regions hardest hit by the decline of the local coal industry with persistent high unemployment (Hinsch 2023), offers another example. In the Jiu Valley, six municipalities are cooperatively exploring the possibility of creating a renewable energy community based on solar photovoltaics on the site of a former surface mine. The produced electricity would be used for municipal needs, such as street lighting and social housing to lower electricity bills for vulnerable inhabitants. These measures are to be coupled with energy efficiency measures and building retrofits to maximize benefits to the community. Local skilled technicians would also be employed to build and maintain the project. Lepesant (2021) shows that regions with a history of reliance on carbon-intensive industries often face a decline in social cohesion and a loss of belonging as these industries decline. Energy communities offer an opportunity to maintain a shared identity by re-aligning it with the idea of citizens, local authorities, and businesses collectively producing, consuming, and sharing their own energy. The open and voluntary governance of most energy communities lends itself well to establishing jointly owned renewable energy projects which rely on and foster cohesion and a common identity (Hinsch 2023).

12.5 Navigating the Challenges of Energy Community Development

The European Commission's commitment to develop a Citizens' Energy Package (CEP) provides a pivotal opportunity to anchor people and communities at the very heart of the energy transition. Being developed alongside initiatives like the Clean Industrial Deal, the Competitiveness Compass, and the Action Plan for Affordable Energy, this forthcoming package offers a tremendous chance to place citizens and their local communities in direct control of their energy future. However, for the CEP to truly fulfil this promise and be credible, it must effectively dismantle persistent barriers hindering the growth of community energy projects. These obstacles include insufficient national regulatory frameworks, incomplete implementation of existing energy laws, and the significant threat of corporate takeover. A primary obstacle is the absence or deficient transposition of EU directives on CECs and RECs into national legislation. For example, despite a 2021 deadline, some countries, like Sweden, have not yet transposed the definitions of CECs and RECs into their national law. Other countries, such as Bulgaria and Romania, have only recently introduced these definitions, and their approach has been limited to directly copying the directive language, tasking their energy agencies with further defining barriers, potential, and legislative development (Cots 2024b).

Even where some regulatory progress has been made, many European Member States still lack coherent enabling frameworks and effective incentive schemes. In Spain, while definitions and general principles for CECs and RECs are in place, further regulatory development and a concrete enabling framework are still pending. Furthermore, even in countries that have made some progress in transposing the directives, the development of energy communities can be impeded by regulatory complexities. For example, in Lithuania, while an enabling framework exists, the process of obtaining energy community status from the regulatory body remains burdensome (Cots, 2024b). These factors, including inadequate or missing transposition and the presence of regulatory complexities, pose significant obstacles to the establishment and successful operation of energy communities, despite the growing interest and initiatives undertaken by citizens.

Also, in contexts where incentives for energy communities exist, the rise of energy communities has attracted interest from various actors, including large corporations, due to increasing public financial support. Governments and EU funds now offer assistance for project planning, implementation, and capacity building, which is essential for energy communities to be competitive in the electricity market. The EU's Clean Energy for All Europeans Package (2019), while intended to empower communities, has inadvertently incentivized corporate involvement due to its provisions for financial support and public backing. This raises concerns about the erosion of community ownership and control, particularly given the inherent power imbalances between corporations and local communities in a complex and capital-intensive market. When corporations appropriate these initiatives, they disrupt the fundamental creation of community bonds and citizen engagement that define genuine energy communities. These incentives have also led energy corporations to adapt their projects to align with the energy community model, raising concerns about potential corporate dominance. This poses a risk of sidelining the original goals of community-led initiatives, with large companies potentially exploiting public funding opportunities for their own agendas (Cots 2025).

Due to this situation, some countries are refining their regulatory approaches to address this risk. Germany, for instance, exempts certain community-led renewable energy projects from competitive auctions and made the requirements for defining eligible "citizen energy companies" more stringent to ensure genuine community involvement and local control. Similarly, Greece's 2023 energy law includes measures to prevent abuse of the energy community model, such as mandating a minimum number of members and limiting profit distribution for communities receiving grid priority access or financial support.

In this regard, it is essential that the transposition of the EU directives into national law reflects a strict adherence to the principles established in the Directive, namely: open and voluntary participation; effective control by local actors; proximity criteria; and democratic governance. This includes careful examination of how the prioritization of community benefits over financial profits is upheld or compromised; whether membership and engagement within energy communities are truly open and accessible to all; whether participation criteria are designed to promote genuine community involvement instead of favouring corporate interests; the extent to which decision-making power resides with local citizens or is unduly influenced by corporate actors; and the degree to which energy communities are independent of external influence and control, particularly from large energy companies (Cots 2025).

To ensure the integrity of the energy communities' development, a clear distinction between profit-driven corporate projects and genuine energy communities is essential, particularly regarding access to funding and incentives. Public funding and support mechanisms need to be specifically intended for initiatives that truly empower citizens and generate social and economic advantages, not only contributing to the expansion of renewable energies. It is therefore crucial to prevent the misuse of the "energy community" label by projects that fail to adhere to the core principles of community ownership, democratic governance, and local benefits (Cots 2025).

12.6 Conclusions and Recommendations

This chapter has explored the multifaceted role of energy communities in driving a just and equitable energy transition in Europe. Moving away from highly polluting, resource-extraction-based economies towards sustainable, low-carbon economies demands a fundamental rethinking of how energy is generated and consumed. These challenges are particularly acute in Europe's regions historically reliant on carbon-intensive industries, which endure the dual burden of past economic dependence on fossil fuels and the urgent need to meet ambitious climate targets. Indeed, many such regions face what's termed the "resource curse", marked by economic fragility, unstable demographics, detrimental health and social impacts due to high dependence on a single resource and sector. As we've seen in this chapter, in many cases, industries like coal extraction are not only central to these regions' economies but are also profoundly intertwined with their cultural identities.

To confront these difficulties, the European Union has established the JTM. Through specific TJTPs, carbon-intensive regions gain access to funding for projects aimed at supporting workers and communities impacted by the energy transition, encompassing investments in renewable energy and improving energy efficiency.

While some authors suggest that physical resource limitations impede a complete shift to renewable energy systems, a growing body of research increasingly points to sociopolitical factors as the primary hurdles. Deeply entrenched interests, significant investments in outdated energy infrastructure, administrative and political resistance, and populations accustomed to long-standing ways of life collectively create substantial opposition to change. In areas historically dependent on coal, this resistance is often rooted in a deeply embedded collective identity shaped by the "coal imaginary"—a structural element that cannot be easily overcome by small-scale actions alone. Successfully navigating this transformation therefore requires not only technological advancements but also thorough understanding and consideration of the intangible cultural and perceptual dimensions that shape local visions, behaviours, and stakeholder engagement, as shown by the TIPPING+ project.

Energy communities have emerged as a transformative force in overcoming these complex obstacles and accelerating a just transition. A robust European framework enhanced by the Clean Energy for All Europeans Package (2019), has been pivotal in empowering these grassroots efforts, officially recognizing CECs and RECs that enable individuals and localities to exert greater influence over energy sector shifts. This supportive regulatory environment allows citizens to actively engage in various aspects of the energy sector; instead of being passive consumers they become active "prosumers". Such proactive involvement, where people and communities collectively manage energy production, consumption, and distribution, fosters a strong sense of ownership and shared responsibility. This directly encourages the adoption of more sustainable energy practices and facilitates the decentralization of energy systems. Moreover, energy communities uniquely address the social and cultural dimensions of the energy transition by cultivating new narratives of local empowerment and sustainable development, effectively dismantling outdated perceptions tied to industrial heritage and strengthening local economies and social bonds.

However, the effective establishment of energy communities encounters several significant impediments. These include the absence or inadequate integration of EU directives into national laws, a widespread lack of supportive national frameworks and assistance measures, and the pervasive risk of being taken over by large corporations. Companies often seek to exploit financial incentives, potentially undermining the genuine purpose of these initiatives and eroding the very citizen ownership and control they are designed to promote.

To ensure that energy communities can truly catalyze a just energy transition across Europe, a collaborative effort among policymakers, regulators, and energy sector actors is essential. To achieve this, the following key recommendations are put forth, aiming to cultivate authentic, citizen-led initiatives.

Strengthen Regulatory Frameworks

EU Member States must prioritize the full and prompt transposition of EU directives into national legislation. This should include clearly defined and coherently integrated definitions of renewable and citizen energy communities, with a strict adherence to the core principles of open and voluntary participation, effective local control, proximity criteria, and democratic governance. Comprehensive enabling frameworks should also be developed, providing clear regulations, streamlined procedures, and effective support mechanisms.

Safeguard Community Integrity

Policymakers should implement measures to prevent the appropriation of energy communities by large corporations. This includes developing robust definitions of "effective control", establishing strict eligibility criteria for membership, ensuring transparency, and designing financial support schemes that prioritize community-led initiatives.

Promote and Support Citizen-led Initiatives

Public funding and support mechanisms should be specifically targeted towards initiatives that truly empower citizens, foster social cohesion, and generate a range of social and economic advantages that extend beyond simply expanding renewable energy capacity.

Foster Collaboration and Knowledge Sharing

Collaboration and knowledge sharing among energy communities at the local, regional, and European levels should be actively encouraged to facilitate the exchange of best practices, build capacity, and promote the development of innovative solutions.

Integrate Energy Communities into Just Transition Plans

Promote and incentivize the inclusion of energy communities in TJTPs as a strategic tool to foster citizen engagement, strengthen community bonds, and facilitate the transition away from coal-dependent identities towards new, sustainable imaginaries. This approach can help ensure that the benefits of the energy transition are distributed equitably and contribute to the long-term social and economic well-being of affected communities.

References

Biddau, F., V. Rizzoli, and M. Sarrica (2024) "Phasing-out 'Coal Tradition' in Favour of 'Renewable Colonialism': How the Press Contributes to the Discursive (De)legitimization of Coal and Renewables in a Coal Region in Transition", *Sustain Sci* 19, 381–402, https://doi.org/10.1007/s11625-023-01420-2

Cots, F. (2022a) "Engaging Citizens and Local Communities in the Solar Revolution: Rooftop Solar PV Country Comparison Report", Climate Action Network (CAN) Europe, https://caneurope.org/content/uploads/2022/05/Rooftop-Solar-PV-Country-Comparision-Report-2.pdf

Cots, F. (2024b) "Engaging Citizens and Local Communities in the Solar Revolution: An Update", Climate Action Network (CAN) Europe, https://caneurope.org/content/uploads/2024/04/Rooftop-Solar-PV-Report-Update_April-2024.pdf

Cots, F. (2025) "Corporate Capture of Energy Communities: A Threat for a Citizens Energy Transition in Europe. Report Commissioned by Friends of the Earth Europe, with the Support of the European Union and Elaborated by ECOUNION", https://friendsoftheearth.eu/wp-content/uploads/2025/04/Report-Corporate-Capture-on-Energy-Communities.pdf

Cots, F., J. Fosse, J. D. Tàbara, and V. S. Michas (2023) "Cultural, Identity, Behavioural and Demographic Issues in Public Engagement and Energy Community Transformations", Policy Brief #03, TIPPING+ Project, https://tipping-plus.eu/policy-briefs

Cots, F., J. D. Tàbara, J. Fosse, and G. Codina (2024) "Exploring the Role of Identities and Perceptions of the Future in a Post-coal Mining Region: The Demolition of Andorra Coal-fired Cooling Towers (Spain) as a Tipping Point", in J. D. Tàbara, A. Flamos, D. Mangalagiu, and S. Michas (eds), *Positive Tipping Points Towards Sustainability*. Cham: Springer Climate, pp. 193–209, https://doi.org/10.1007/978-3-031-50762-5_10

Cappello, E. A. (2024) "Situated Knowledge and Energy Transformations: A Socio-anthropological Exploration", in J. D. Tàbara, A. Flamos, D. Mangalagiu, and S. Michas (eds), *Positive Tipping Points Towards Sustainability: Understanding the Conditions and Strategies for Fast Decarbonization in Regions*. Cham: Springer, pp. 237–258, https://doi.org/10.1007/978-3-031-50762-5_12

Della Bosca, H., and J. Gillespie (2018) "The Coal Story: Generational Coal Mining Communities and Strategies of Energy Transition in Australia", *Energy Policy* 120, 734–740, https://doi.org/10.1016/j.enpol.2018.04.032

European Commission: Directorate-General for Communication (2019) *Just Transition Mechanism—The European Green Deal*. Brussels: Publications Office, https://data.europa.eu/doi/10.2775/31328

European Energy Communities Facility (n.d.) "LIFE23-CET-ENERCOM-FACILITY/101167230", https://webgate.ec.europa.eu/life/publicWebsite/project/LIFE23-CET-ENERCOM-FACILITY-101167230/european-energy-communities-facility

Hinsch, A. (2023) "Enabling Energy Communities: A Toolkit for Just Transition Regions", European Commission, https://ec.europa.eu/regional_policy/sources/funding/just-transition-fund/toolkit-enabling-energy-communities.pdf

IRENA (2024) *World Energy Transitions Outlook 2024: 1.5°C Pathway*. Abu Dhabi: IRENA, https://www.irena.org/-/media/Files/IRENA/Agency/Publication/2024/Nov/IRENA_World_energy_transitions_outlook_2024.pdf

Mangalagiu, D., J. Lieu, F. Biddau, A. Martinez Reyes, and B. Witajewska-Baltvilka (2025) "Enabling Sustainable Transitions in Coal and Carbon-Intensive Regions", *Global Environmental Change*. 93, https://doi.org/10.1016/j.gloenvcha.2025.103022

McCauley, D., and R. Heffron (2018) "Just Transition: Integrating Climate, Energy and Environmental Justice", *Energy Policy* 119, 1–7, https://doi.org/10.1016/j.enpol.2018.04.014

Perdue, R., and G. Pavela (2012) "Addictive Economies and Coal Dependency: Methods of Extraction and Socioeconomic Outcomes in West Virginia, 1997–2009", *Organization & Environment* 25, 368–384, https://doi.org/10.1177/1086026612464767

Taylor, D., K. Chong, and M. Röder (2024) "Designing Biomass Policy: The Political Economy of Renewable Energy for Net Zero", *Wiley Interdisciplinary Reviews: Energy and Environment* 13.2, p.e512.

Snell, D. (2018) "'Just transition'? Conceptual challenges meet stark reality in a 'transitioning' coal region in Australia", *Globalizations* 15.4, 550–564, https://doi.org/10.1080/14747731.2018.1454679

Stark, A., F. Gale, and H. Murphy-Gregory (2023) "Just Transitions' Meanings: A Systematic Review", *Society & Natural Resources* 36.10, 1277–1297, https://doi.org/10.1080/08941920.2023.2207166

Rosemberg, A. (2010) "Building a Just Transition: The Linkages between Climate Change and Employment", *International Journal of Labour Research* 2.2, 125–161, https://labordoc.ilo.org/discovery/fulldisplay/alma994615923402676/41ILO_INST:41ILO_V1

Tàbara, J. D. (2024) "The TIPPING+ Project Journey", in J. D. Tàbara, A. Flamos, D. Mangalagiu, and S. Michas (eds), *Positive Tipping Points Towards Sustainability*. Cham: Springer, pp. 1–9, https://doi.org/10.1007/978-3-031-50762-5_1

Williams, A. (2024) "Clean Air Task Force Clean Energy from the Ground Up: Energy Communities in the European Union", 18 March, *CATF*, https://www.catf.us/resource/clean-energy-ground-up-energy-communities-european-union/

13. Making the ETS2 Socially Acceptable through Carbon Revenue Redistribution and Investments

Andreas Eisl[1] and Phuc-Vinh Nguyen[2]

The introduction of a CO_2 price for housing and mobility is a key measure to ensure that the EU will be able to achieve its climate objectives. However, without adequate accompanying compensation and investment measures, additional costs for citizens will not be socially acceptable and might lead to a reversal of climate policies. This chapter thus sets out to make recommendations on how to best design accompanying policies in the context of the introduction of the ETS2, which will broaden the scope of the European Emissions Trading System to new economic sectors (road transport, buildings, and small industries). To draw lessons from already existing instruments, this chapter studies the carbon taxation schemes of France, Germany, and Austria as well as their accompanying redistribution and investment measures. Based on this analysis, it highlights the importance of strict earmarking of ETS2 revenues and the visibility of support measures, and discusses how to best target citizens through redistributions mechanisms and balance compensation with investment tools.

13.1 Introduction

In 2027, the second carbon market on buildings, road transport, and small industries is expected to enter into force. This European ETS2 (Emissions Trading System) will make fossil fuels significantly more expensive for many citizens across EU Member States. The key objective of ETS2 is to induce behavioural changes, switching from carbon intensive uses (fossil fuel boilers, internal combustion engine cars) to decarbonized ones (heat pumps, electric vehicles). However, without targeted support mechanisms to trigger these behavioural changes, the cost of decarbonization may disproportionately fall on the most vulnerable households, who lack the financial capacity to transition on their own. For instance, the impact assessment from the European Commission

---

1   Jacques Delors Institute (JDI) and Institut d'Etudes Politiques de Paris—Sciences Po.
2   Jacques Delors Institute (JDI).

    https://doi.org/10.11647/OBP.0499.13

estimated that with a €48 price as for 2030 fuel prices would increase by 11ct/l (petrol) to 13ct/l (diesel) (European Commission 2021).

By design, the Social Climate Fund (SCF) should fulfil this role. It was created alongside the ETS2 as a social safeguard and solidarity measure, channelling financial support towards the most affected Member States (Eastern Europe) and ensuring a fair redistribution of ETS2 revenues to vulnerable households and micro-enterprises to facilitate political buy-in. However, its limited temporal scope (2026–2032) and capped funding envelope of €86.7 billion constrain its capacity to properly help foster social acceptance regarding carbon pricing. Of this amount, up to 65 billion will stem from the auctioning of emission allowances—€50 million from ETS1 and 150 million from ETS2—while the remaining 25% is expected to be covered through mandatory national co-financing.[3] As a result, complementary use of broader ETS2 revenues will be indispensable to meet the scale of investment required to achieve a just transition.

With a conservative CO_2 price of €45 over the 2026–2032 period, the ETS2 would generate more than €170 billion for Member States (Eden et al. 2023). A €60 CO_2 price, which appears to be the central scenario, would generate more than €250 billion, while a €100 CO_2 price would generate more than €480 billion (Jüngling et al. 2025). The ETS2 revenues that belong to Member States would have to be allocated to climate action and social measures. Combined with the SCF spending, and under several conditions (discussed within the recommendation section), the remaining ETS2 revenues offer a unique opportunity to turbocharge investments and mitigate the social impacts of carbon pricing while driving the transition by supporting the uptake of cleaner alternatives. In that regard, the introduction of different carbon pricing systems in France, Germany, and Austria together with their respective social redistribution and climate investment programs provide valuable lessons on how to effectively design carbon revenues uses.

13.2 The French Carbon Tax

In 2014, France introduced a progressive carbon tax on fossil fuels based on their carbon content (see Table 13.1). The tax covers around 40% of French emissions, e.g. the transport, residential, and service sectors, as well as industries outside of the ETS1, and is paid directly by households and companies. Initially it was supposed to reach €100/tCO_2 by 2030. Until 2017, the gradual increase of France's carbon tax remained largely unperceived by citizens, as it was offset by favourable international market dynamics. Specifically, geoeconomic shifts triggered a sharp drop in global oil prices— with Brent crude falling from $111 per barrel in June 2014 to $31 in January 2016— cushioning the fiscal impact at the pump following the introduction of the carbon tax. However, this equilibrium was disrupted in 2018, sparking social protests known as

---

3   See https://eur-lex.europa.eu/legal-content/FR/TXT/PDF/?uri=CELEX:32023R0955

the "Yellow Jacket movement". The surge in fuel prices—a rise of 21ct/l (INSEE 2025b) for diesel and 8ct/l (INSEE 2025a) for petrol between November 2017 and November 2018—stemmed from a convergence of three factors. First, the carbon tax increased significantly, from €30.5/tCO_2 to €44.6/tCO_2, accounting for roughly half of the rise. Second, global oil prices rebounded, with the average Brent price in 2018 rising by over 30% compared to 2017, amplifying the cost burden on households. Third, a tax adjustment, initiated in 2015, aimed at having petrol and diesel prices converge, led to a 2.6c/l increase in 2018.

Table 13.1 Overview of the French CO_2 price. *Source:* Authors work, based on figures from the Ministry of Energy, French Court of Auditor, and I4CE. *Note:* * The carbon tax remains subject to VAT. ** The 2030 target price was set within the 2015 Energy Transition Law alongside a €56/tCO2 target for 2020. The latter was amended within the 2018 Budget Law and raised at €65.4/tCO_2, but the raise was frozen following the Yellow Jacket movement. This still hints that the €100/tCO_2 target for 2030 would probably have been updated had the tax not been frozen. *** Revenues from the carbon tax are an estimation as the carbon tax is a calculation method, not a full-fledged levy.

Year	2014	2015	2016	2017	2018	2019	2020	2021	2022	2030
CO_2 price*	€7/t	€14.5/t	€22/t	€30.5/t	€44.6/t	€44.6/t (frozen)	€44.6/t (frozen)	€44.6/t (frozen)	€44.6/t (frozen)	Replaced by ETS2?
						€55/t (initially expected)	€65.4/t (initially expected)	€75.8/t (initially expected)	€86.20/t (initially expected)	€100/t (initially expected)**
CO_2 price revenues***	0.3 bn	2.3 bn	3.8 bn	5.4 bn	9 bn	8 bn	7.2 bn	8.2 bn	7.7 bn	TBD

This triple shock was perceived as unfair by French citizens especially as the revenues from the tax were neither being redistributed nor directly allocated to investments related to the green transition, following the French principle of universal budgeting (Moysan 2017) that prevent an explicit earmarking of the revenues to a dedicated spending item, unless a specific exemption were to be made. Ultimately, the government's lack of consideration for carbon revenue redistribution as a tool to foster social acceptance led to the rise of the Yellow Jacket movement in November 2018.

Originally, France's carbon tax was conceived less as a climate tool than as a fiscal one, designed to fund tax relief for businesses (De Perthuis 2013) rather than the energy transition. In other words, since its inception, the question related to carbon revenue redistribution was left outside of the equation by policymakers. Against that backdrop, in 2016, out of the €3.8 billion in revenues raised through the carbon tax, €3 billion facilitated—even though no direct affectation was made—the financing of the Competitiveness and Employment Tax Credit (CICE), a flagship measure to reduce labour costs. It wasn't until 2017 (DGEC 2017) that a shift began: €1.7 billion out of €5.4 billion in carbon tax revenues were earmarked—as an exception to the principle of budgetary universality (Beaufils 2019)—for a special account dedicated to the energy transition, primarily to support renewable energy deployment. Still, both the absence of public awareness and dedicated communication regarding the special account in addition to the lack of significant and direct redistribution schemes, contributed to fuel the Yellow Jacket argument that the carbon tax was set up to increase budget earnings at the expense of households. As a matter of fact, this discourse was reinforced when, despite the 2018 price increase that generated an additional €3.7 billion revenues compared to 2017, only €181 additional million were allocated to compensatory measures through either an energy voucher or a conversion bonus (ADEME 2021).

These empirical observations confirm the findings from recent public opinion polls and academic literature—notably Carattini et al. (2017)—which highlight earmarking as the most effective strategy to build public support for carbon pricing. In the French case, earmarking was too little and too late in addition to being too poorly advertised. The upcoming implementation of the EU ETS2, which targets a similar scope as the carbon tax (and could eventually substitute it) presents a unique opportunity to apply the lessons learned from these past shortcomings. Given that the ETS2 price is expected to exceed that of the former carbon tax (€60/tCO_2 vS €44.6/tCO_2), it will generate substantial revenues for France, estimated at €7.2 billion yearly on average (Cour des Comptes 2024) over the 2027–2030 period in addition to around €1.2 billion coming yearly from the SCF. With households bearing 62% of the carbon tax in 2022 (Ministère de la transition écologique 2025) redistribution schemes will have to target them as a priority, especially low-income ones and residents of rural and suburban areas that will be the most exposed to the new carbon price.

In that regard, a French public opinion poll by ADEME (2024), that is updated yearly, documents that support for a carbon tax (51% in 2024, +6% compared to 2023) significantly increases (69% in 2024, +4% compared to 2023) provided that "this does not penalize the purchasing power of households in the middle and lower classes, and that the revenues from the tax are used to finance ecological transition measures, particularly in territories". Against that backdrop, a 2022 opinion poll (DREES 2024) highlighted that more than six out of ten residents in France were in favour of an increase of the carbon tax if a redistributive, fiscal, or environmental measure were to be implemented in return. Yet, that support was lower among residents of rural communities whatever the compensation mechanism was, with "the creation of local transport, jobs and services" being the favoured option by the respondents. This signals that particular attention should be paid to that segment of the population, especially given the fact that it represented, together with the suburban population, the beating heart of the Yellow Jacket movement. This observation could give food for thought to French policymakers when designing their compensation and investment schemes. Indeed, while these are complex instruments that sometimes take time to materialize, as illustrated by the upcoming German case study, their effectiveness relies on obtaining a broad consensus among the population.

13.3 The German Klimageld

In 2021, Germany introduced a national emissions trading system for heating and transport, which, however, largely corresponds to a CO_2 price (see Table 13.2). For the period 2021–2025, the country has set an annual price, increasing from 25€/t to 55€/t. In 2026, the system will gradually move towards a market-based system but will be kept in a corridor between 55€/t and 65€/t. Due to the increasing CO_2 price, its revenues have almost doubled since its introduction, going up from €7.2 billion in 2021 to roughly €13 billion in 2024. This increase is also based on the gradual extension of the covered fuels and emissions sources (see the note in Table 13.2). The revenues of the national CO_2 price do not flow into the general budget, instead filling up the country's climate and transformation fund (KTF), which can finance actions towards climate neutrality and sustainability, and compensate for additional costs caused by climate measures.

Since the introduction of the CO_2 price, politicians have repeatedly discussed the establishment of a direct redistribution mechanism of the revenues, a so-called Klimageld. In their 2021 coalition agreement, the Socialdemocratic SPD, the Greens and the liberal FDP stated that they would "develop a social compensation mechanism [...] in order to compensate for a future price increase and ensure acceptance of the market system" (Koalitionsvertrag 2021). But while this and other public announcements by policymakers suggest broad support for such a measure across party lines and among various stakeholders (Deutschlandfunk 2024), the Klimageld has, however, not materialized until today (Bauchmüller and Hulverscheidt 2024). This has been due to various budgetary, political, and administrative reasons.

Table 13.2. Overview of the German CO_2 price and related spending. *Source:* Umwelt Bundesamt (2025), Verbraucherzentrale Bundesverband (2023), Interview BMWK (2025). *Note:* Until 2022, only gasoline, diesel, petroleum, LNG, and gas were included in the CO_2 price. Since 2023, all other fuels, such as coal, are also covered, and since 2024, also the emissions of waste incinerators.

Year	2021	2022	2023	2024	2025	2026
CO_2 price	€25/t	€30/t	€30/t	€45/t	€55/t	€55/t – €65/t (Corridor)
CO_2 price revenues	€7.2 bn	€6.4 bn	€10.7 bn	€13 bn	...	...
EEG levy spending	€18.7 bn	€5.0 bn (€19.8 bn[est])	€14.1 bn (-€3.64 bn[est])	€18.5 bn (€10.6 bn[est])	€17.2 bn[est]	€17.2 bn[est]

First, the KTF, which is fed by the ETS1 and national CO_2 price revenues, did, until 2025, not possess sufficient resources for providing funding for a large financial compensation mechanism. KTF expenditures were already earmarked for numerous subsidy schemes when the German Constitutional Court, at the end of 2023, annulled the government's plan to reallocate €60 billion of credit authorizations from a pandemic response package to the KTF, deeming it incompatible with the German constitution (Bundesverfassungsgericht 2023). This caused major problems for the

KTF's capacities, especially as the government had also decided that the levy to support renewable energies (EEG-Umlage) would not be paid by consumers directly anymore, but would be financed through the KTF instead. With EEG-related costs amounting to €18.5 billion in 2024 alone, this strongly hampered the ability of the KTF to finance a direct Klimageld. To avoid cutting other subsidy schemes, the German economy and climate protection minister Robert Habeck subsequently argued that the abolition of the EEG levy actually constituted a compensation mechanism towards residents, already fulfilling the function of a Klimageld.

Second, administrative difficulties have repeatedly been mentioned as hindering the rapid introduction of the Klimageld. When the national CO_2 price was introduced in 2021, no national state agency in Germany, in contrast to other countries, possessed the necessary information to carry out payments to all concerned residents (Bohmann et al. 2025). It took until 2025 for the German government to put such a system in place, linking the individual tax-ID database to bank account data (Deutsche Bundesregierung 2024; Deutschlandfunk 2024).

Public opinion polls on the German CO_2 price and a potential redistribution mechanism of its revenues conducted over the course of the last years paint a differentiated picture, depending on the posed questions and the broader political context. A 2022 poll found that while 33.9% of respondents found the German CO_2 price to be effective, only 22.1% considered it to be fair. In contrast, 45.2% of the population found the CO_2 price to be ineffective, while 52.8% thought it to be unfair (Holzmann and Digulla 2024, p. 12). When asked about a policy bundle consisting of a CO_2 price and a compensation mechanism (Klimageld), support for the CO_2 price increases, as shown by Bohmann et al. (2025, p. 75). The opinion poll they conducted tested different combinations of CO_2 prices and compensation payments. They found that 48% of citizens would support a CO_2 price at €45/tCO_2 bundled when 80% of the CO_2 price revenues would be used for compensation (with 52% still not supporting such a model). When asked about higher CO_2 prices and lower compensation levels, respondents' support decreases. This highlights the need for socially acceptable CO_2 prices and generous compensation levels.

The conservative and social democratic coalition that formed in 2025 addressed a few of the key problems of the KTF with a modification of the Constitution to bypass the existing German fiscal rules without risking another repeal by the German Constitutional Court. This allows the government to endow the fund with an additional €100 billion in the coming years. In addition, EEG-related costs will not be covered by the KTF anymore but instead will have to be paid through the general budget (Greive et al. 2025). This will significantly increase the capacity of the fund to support a redistribution mechanism. However, the new coalition agreement no longer explicitly mentions a Klimageld. Instead, it mentions measures to redistribute CO_2 price revenues towards citizens and enterprises through unbureaucratic and socially adapted support for housing and mobility, and through electricity price reductions and investment support towards climate neutrality (Patermann and Rathai 2025). A more general Klimageld approach could thus potentially be substituted by a more targeted but complex system, in contrast to the Klimabonus, a general compensation mechanism that was in place in Austria from 2022 to 2024.

13.4 The Austrian Klimabonus

In 2022, Austria introduced a national CO_2 price, accompanied by a mechanism to redistribute the expected revenues to citizens, the so-called Klimabonus (climate bonus). These measures were part of the eco-social tax reform, a major reform effort to remodel the national tax system towards the green transition. The reform was initiated by a coalition government of Conservatives (ÖVP) and Greens, that led the country since the 2019 parliamentary elections.

The national CO_2 price was set at €30/tCO_2, starting to apply by October 2022, and supposed to rise based on annual pre-fixed increases until reaching €55/tCO_2 in 2025, moving to a market-based price in 2026 (see Table 13.3). The accompanying Klimabonus was designed to compensate citizens for increased costs, while incentivizing the adoption of zero- or low-carbon alternatives to fossil fuel-based heating and transport. To do so, the Klimabonus consisted of an annual cash payment to each Austrian resident, adding a regional component to account for differences in the availability of fossil fuel-free alternatives up to doubling the base payment.

The regional component of the Klimabonus was based on two variables, a measure for the urbanity-rurality of a given locality and a measure for the quality/availability of public transport. Taken together, these allowed for the construction of four categories to regionally differentiate between localities in terms of access to public transport but indirectly also to heating-related offers, such as district heating (Fig. 13.1). The full amount of the Klimabonus was paid out to each adult, while every person under eighteen received half the amount.

Along the increasing national CO_2 price path, the legislation also laid out the criteria to raise the Klimabonus every year to ensure a full compensation of the additional costs. However, due to the design of the Klimabonus, but also for political reasons, the annual costs were generally higher than the associated revenues (see Table 13.3). For 2023 and 2024, the gap between revenues and expenses was around €500 million annually, with another gap expected for 2025. In addition, the gap reached almost €4 billion in 2022, when the CO_2 pricing was started later than originally planned, leading to lower revenues, and the Klimabonus was strongly increased to respond to the inflation shock related to the energy price crisis. Instead of €100 (in the base version), the Klimabonus was increased to €250 for every adult citizen (without any regional adaptation), with an additional €250 paid out as an anti-inflation bonus. Citizens thus received €500 in 2022 through the Klimabonus instrument.

This temporary and structural revenue provided by the Klimabonus, however, likely undermined its political and budgetary acceptability and blurred the link of the

Klimabonus with the national CO_2 price. Following the 2024 legislative elections, coalition talks between parties focused heavily on the budget and how to cut expenditures, as a prolonged recession following the energy price crisis had created a significant public deficit, finally reaching -4.7% in 2024. Due to its size, the Klimabonus rapidly became a focal point for expenditure-cutting measures, especially as the initial coalition talks took place between the right-wing populist FPÖ and the conservative ÖVP, with the former having heavily campaigned on cutting the Klimabonus as well as the national CO_2 price.

Table 13.3 Overview of the Austrian CO_2 price and Klimabonus. *Source:* BMK (2025), ORF (2025). *Note:* * The originally set CO_2 price for 2023 was €35/t, but the price increase was halved due to the activation of a price stability mechanism in response to strongly increasing fossil fuel prices. ** In 2022, CO_2 pricing started only in October, leading to comparatively low annual revenues. *** In 2022, the Klimabonus was increased to €250 for every citizen, without any regional differentiation and further doubled through an anti-inflation bonus, thus reaching €500.

Year	2022	2023	2024	2025	2026
CO_2 price	€30/t	€32.5/t (€35/t)[*]	€45/t	€55/t	Market price
CO_2 price revenues	0.27 bn[**]	1.05 bn	1.4 bn	(1.7 bn)[est]	tbd
Klimabonus spending	4.07 bn[***]	1.47 bn	1.96 bn	(2.0-2.3 bn)[est]	tbd
Klimabonus base level	€250 + €250 (€100 - €200)[***]	€110 - €220	€145 - €290	…	

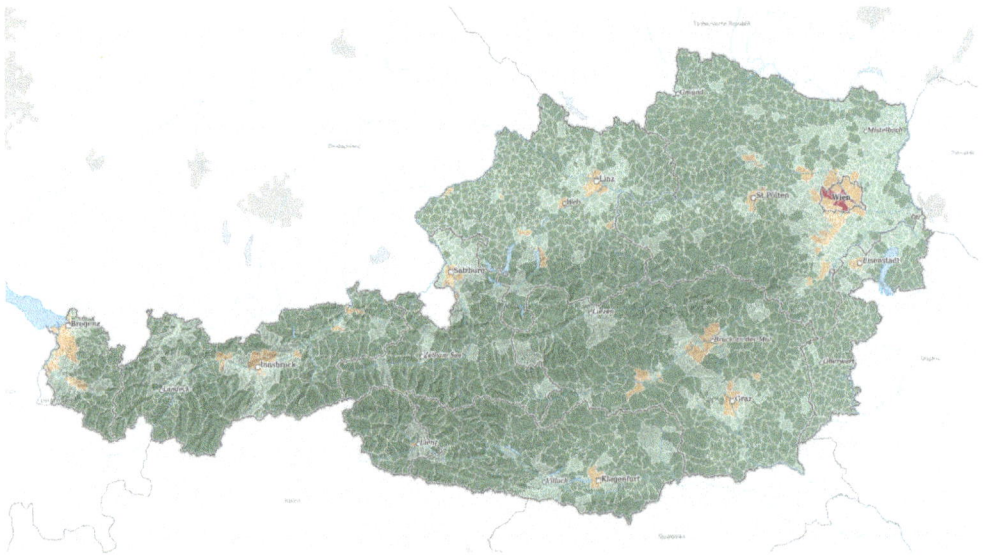

Fig. 13.1 Regional differentiation of the Austrian Klimabonus. *Source:* Statistik Austria (2025). *Note:* The areas in red, covering only parts of the Austrian capital Vienna, received only the base-level Klimabonus. Areas in orange (mainly urban centres beyond Vienna) received an additional 33%, areas in light green (mainly smaller town and peri-urban areas) received an additional 66%, while areas in dark green (rural areas with little access to public transport) received an additional 100%.

The Klimabonus seemed to be a relatively easy target as opinion surveys highlighted little attachment to it (Hager 2024). In a survey published at the end of 2024, 41% of respondents called for a "social differentiation" of the Klimabonus, 36% supported its abolition, and 13% wanted it to be used for other purposes. In addition, only 4% saw it as the best measure of the outgoing government, in comparison to 38% for the abolition of the income tax bracket creep, 21% for the Klimaticket (an annual ticket for all public transport) and 16% for the electricity price brake (Hager 2024).

When the initial coalition talks collapsed, however, ÖVP, SPÖ, and the liberal NEOs resumed negotiations, originally aiming to reform rather than remove the Klimabonus. As the budgetary data for 2024 and forecasts for 2025 continuously worsened, the three parties, however, finally decided to completely cut the Klimabonus to reduce the public deficit, while keeping the CO_2 price in place. For 2025, the abolition of the Klimabonus alone accounts for about one third of the country's fiscal consolidation of €6.3 billion. The new government justified the complete abolition of the Klimabonus based on a broader narrative of stopping the "over-subsidizing" and "over-compensation" provided by the public budget since 2020 (Kern and Winter 2025). To at least partly compensate for the discontinuation of the Klimabonus, the new government plans to triple the existing, and already generous, commuter tax allowance (Pendlerpauschale). In practice, this, however, basically constitutes a fossil fuel subsidy, as it also supports the use of oil-powered cars, which still dominate the Austrian car market (Kontext 2025).

Beyond the size of its spending, the Klimabonus was also criticized for its design. First, the Klimabonus was originally paid out independently of the revenues of recipients. While this meant that people with lower incomes received a proportionally higher percentage than people with higher incomes, it was nevertheless questioned whether residents with high incomes would need to receive any compensation (Burtscher 2024). To at least partly respond to this critique, the Klimabonus became taxable income in 2024 for annual gross incomes above €66,612.

Second, many administrations, organizations and citizens criticized various aspects of the regional differentiation mechanism of the Klimabonus (Österreichischer Städtebund 2024; Burtscher 2024). Some considered that the Klimabonus was insufficiently differentiated, as the availability of public transport could vary strongly also inside individual municipalities, which was not taken into account even if more granular data would have been available (Pilch 2024). Another line of criticism concerned the fact that while a higher dependence on individual car-based transport needs was acknowledged for rural areas, requiring more support to ensure sufficient compensation, higher housing prices in cities were not considered as a criterion (Österreichischer Städtebund 2024). This argument is related to a broader questioning of the design of the Klimabonus, stating that the regional differentiation mechanism actually favoured climate-harming behaviour, overcompensating for higher fossil fuel costs especially in rural areas (TU Wien 2024). The Klimabonus could thus be constructed as an instrument fostering housing sprawl and the use of individual transport instead of more climate-friendly behaviour. Finally, the design of the Klimabonus was also criticized because the exclusive focus on redistribution did not allow for sufficient support for directly promoting climate transition. The Austrian Association of Cities and Towns claimed that while the federal government was promoting car-oriented mobility behaviour through the Klimabonus, cities and urban regions were lacking around €1 billion annually to support the expansion of public transport towards the achievement of climate targets (Österreichischer Städtebund 2024). Overall, criticism of the regionally differentiated version of the Klimabonus was more pronounced than of the undifferentiated 2022 version (BMK 2025).

13.5 Policy Recommendations

13.5.1 Strict Earmarking

The three country case studies highlight the value of clearly and visibly earmarking CO_2 price revenues for measures that compensate residents and provide support for investment in clean technologies for housing and mobility. First, it is important that there is a clear link (from a budgetary to the communication perspective) between the size of CO_2 price revenues and climate/redistribution-related spending. In the French case, the lack of this link aggravated the rise in living costs for lower-income citizens in the late 2010s. A redistribution mechanism, whose payouts would automatically increase with growing CO_2 price revenues, could have potentially avoided a backlash that also resulted in a freezing of the French CO_2 price.

To the contrary, redistribution payments beyond actual CO_2 price revenues can at least partly undermine climate policies, as shown in the Austrian case. Given the perception of "over-subsidizing", the Klimabonus became a politically opportune spending item to cut in a period of budgetary difficulties. While the national CO_2 price was kept in place, the missing redistribution mechanism makes the carbon instrument more vulnerable to political dismantling. To make matters worse, the CO_2 price revenues will partly serve to finance climate-harming behaviour through a reinforcement of the commuter tax allowance. In other words, if another energy price spike were to occur, similar to the one initiated by the summer 2021 gas shock (Nguyen and Pellerin-Carlin 2021), the carbon revenue redistribution scheme should not act as the vehicle of choice to shield consumers as it would risk conveying the image of "over-subsidizing".

In Germany, finally, a national redistribution mechanism hasn't become a reality until today as the national CO_2 price revenues were not directly accompanied by a Klimageld. Earmarking revenues for the KTF ensured that (a majority of) funds would be used to finance climate-related investments, but the inclusion in a broader scheme with multiple revenue sources and spending objectives created complications for the financing of a redistribution scheme and targeted investment support for citizens.

To address these issues in the context of the introduction of ETS2, we thus recommend that Member States put into place a dedicated fund that covers all national and SCF-based revenues and that serves exclusively to finance compensation and clean investment mechanisms, in line with the criteria set out by the SCF Regulation for the respective share of SCF funding. This means that as the price goes up, which is expected to happen, especially starting 2029 onwards, the amount of redistributed carbon revenues from the fund must correspond fully to the exact price increase observed on the market.

13.5.2 Visibility

The visibility of policy measures supporting the green transition is not solely a communication issue—it is central to social acceptability. While Member States might be tempted to draw on already existing redistributive schemes to spend parts of national or SCF-based ETS2 revenues, this strategy could hinder citizens' ability to clearly identify the schemes as being financed by these revenues. Indeed, if support measures cannot clearly be linked to the CO_2 price, it might lower the social acceptability of the latter. If the public perceives that the burden of carbon pricing is not offset by transparent and targeted support, especially for the most vulnerable ones, opposition could arise. Eventually, setting up new redistributive schemes or rebranding existing ones under a new name, in addition to increasing them, would create more visibility, highlighting their use to offset additional costs for citizens.

To reinforce the visibility of earmarking of ETS2 revenues for compensation and clean investment measures, Member States should create a public platform that tracks and presents the use and spending of ETS2 revenues in an easily accessible manner. This would increase transparency, trust and social acceptance towards the ETS2. It would also help ensure that strict earmarking is followed through and not watered down over time.

In addition, public opinion polls conducted in late 2024/early 2025 in Germany, France, Italy, Poland, and Spain show that "a reduction in electricity bills" is the most favoured item by citizens when asked how CO_2 tax revenues should best be used (Arregui et al. 2025). In that regard, direct action on electricity bills might be a relevant solution to ensure the visibility of the redistribution scheme, therefore increasing social acceptance of carbon pricing while offering the possibility of targeting vulnerable households, which is part of the following policy recommendations.

13.5.3 Targeting of Redistribution Mechanisms

How to best design the targeting of redistribution mechanisms is a key issue to address for any CO_2 price system. For instance, should the universality principle that implies that every citizen (including children) benefits from a redistribution scheme be applied or not? Or should we rather consider that only carbon price payers (de facto excluding children) are eligible?

Regardless of the exact system, we believe that vulnerable citizens (excluding small industries in the context of this chapter) who face financial difficulties in rapidly switching from fossil fuel heating and mobility to decarbonized options should be fully compensated for CO_2 price increases. But while the SCF rules are geared towards this approach, for some countries the size of the allocated funds and the gradually decreasing 37.5% limit for redistribution instruments included in national social-climate plans will not suffice to adequately compensate all vulnerable households. Thus, in addition, funding from the national ETS2 revenues will be needed.

In practice, however, it might be difficult to adequately identify vulnerable households and to compensate them individually according to their level of vulnerability. First, this might be due to difficulties in available data, as precise targeting would require knowing not only information about revenues but also cross-matched data on fossil fuel dependence for housing and mobility. Second, even if a country would possess individual data for these variables, there might, however, be difficulties in easily paying out support to them, as highlighted by the German case. The result of such practical difficulties has been that actual redistribution mechanisms have been based on less precise or little targeting or could not be put into place at all.

One of the simplest approaches to deal with problems in data availability is to pay out a lump sum to each resident, which would correspond to a certain amount of CO_2 emissions. While this is, in principle, an untargeted approach, as higher-income households typically have higher CO_2 emissions, it is, in practice, regressive (IEA 2023). This means that when set at the right level, lower income households would be fully compensated for a CO_2 price while higher income households only get partial compensation. This was the case for the Austrian Klimabonus in 2022. This approach can then be made more regressive by capping compensation to specific income levels or making it taxable from a specific income level onwards. The latter was applied in Austria in 2024.

More targeted approaches can try to take into account specific vulnerabilities, e.g., regarding fossil fuel mobility. This has been the case for the Austrian Klimabonus from 2023 onwards, putting into place a regional differentiation. However, this incomplete targeting approach, not considering the housing sector, was criticized strongly by various organizations and citizens, which felt that it did not adequately reflect real vulnerabilities and would reduce incentives to move towards climate-friendly alternatives to fossil fuels (Österreichischer Städtebund). In the Austrian case, the 2022 version of the Klimabonus, providing the same amount of compensation for each resident was criticized considerably less (BMK 2025), raising the question of model preferability.

Based on these observations, we make the following recommendations regarding the targeting of redistribution mechanisms. First, while precise targeting would be the preferred option, in the absence of sufficiently granular data, a non-targeted generic lump sum payment might be the best initial option by default. Indeed, given the expected entry into force of the ETS2 in 2027, time is running out and partial targeting measures might undermine the legitimacy of redistribution mechanisms, an issue which repeatedly came up in the Austrian case. But even an untargeted mechanism requires a country's administrative capacity to actually identify and pay all eligible residents in a quick and easy manner. It should be an absolute priority for all Member States to put such systems in place, which can also serve more broadly in crisis situations, through distinct instruments, to provide financial support to citizens, as highlighted by the COVID-19 and energy price crises.

Second, in countries where sufficient data is available, we recommend directly providing more targeted support to residents, taking into account key aspects of the housing and mobility sectors. The concrete design should be based on in-depth consultations with key stakeholders to identify potential criticisms and ensure that the applied targeting is considered socially acceptable and fair. For those Member States that lack the necessary comprehensive and cross-matched data on residents, we recommend them to start out with a more general scheme, but then move towards a more targeted one in a second step.

13.5.4 Avoiding Mismatches in Transition Incentives through CO_2 Prices

When implementing a CO_2 price for citizens, it is crucial to ensure that it can actually create incentives to invest in the clean transition. One potential mismatch between price signal and incentives exists for rental households where the owner of the flat, and thus of the heating system, would not have to bear the costs of increasing heating costs, which are instead paid by the renter. While the renter would have a strong interest in changing from a fossil fuel heating system to a decarbonized one or to improve insulation, he or she cannot influence the landlord's choices on these matters. If the renter bears the full costs of a CO_2 price, the landlord has little interest in switching to a less polluting heating system or better insulating the flat.

To address this problem, it is important to accompany a CO_2 price with accompanying measures to avoid incentive mismatches. An interesting example in this regard is the German distribution scheme of CO_2 price costs between landlords and renter. Since 2023, the German CO_2 price system includes a mechanism to share heating-related costs according to the landlords' and renter's areas of responsibility and influence on a building's CO_2 emissions. Depending on the amounts of emitted CO_2 per m² (taking into account energy consumption, the size of the flat, and the type of used fossil fuel), landlords and renters must pay varying shares of CO_2 price-related costs. The less climate-friendly a heating system, the higher the share the landlord has to pay.

This system can help to reduce transition incentive mismatches in the housing sector but needs to be accompanied by additional measures to work well. First, regulatory rules need to ensure that landlords cannot simply increase rents to move CO_2 price costs onto renters. And second, additional support for landlords such as cheap credit lines for decarbonized heating systems and insulation might be a cost-efficient means to allow landlords to reduce and smooth expenditures across time.

13.5.5 Compensation Schemes and Investment Support

The final key issue is how to best balance redistribution mechanisms that protect vulnerable citizens from rising CO_2 prices with investment support that helps citizens move away from fossil fuel heating and mobility towards decarbonized options. Indeed, any type of CO_2 price compensation could, in the long run, be assimilated to a fossil fuel subsidy if it were to only be used to compensate for the price increase instead of also helping to finance the switch to low-carbon alternatives. It is not necessary to consecrate 100% of ETS2 revenues for redistribution to residents to compensate for CO_2 price costs for large parts of the population due to differences in CO_2 emissions between poor and rich households. There is, thus, significant space to provide investment support, for example, by co-financing leasing and purchasing schemes for electric vehicles and heat pumps.

To accelerate the green transition in the housing and mobility sectors, investment support should be frontloaded. First, as the SCF is supposed to enter into force in 2026, one year prior to the start of the ETS2, the initial dotation should be dedicated fully to investment support as no compensation scheme would yet be required to compensate for higher CO_2 costs. Second, investment support during the early years of the ETS2 could be further strengthened by bringing more of the expected revenues forward through a limited public debt instrument (see Agora 2024; EPICO and Frontier Economics 2025; T&E 2025), with repayment being strictly linked to the ETS2. Doing so would also require Member States to quickly and fully transpose the ETS2 into national law given that, as of early June 2025, only eleven countries effectively did so. It would prevent Member States from arguing for a postponement of the entry into force of the carbon pricing system in January 2027.

Bringing all of these elements together would considerably help improve the social acceptability of the ETS2 and make it less vulnerable to dismantling, as the carbon pricing system remains a crucial tool for meeting the 2030 climate target. However, broader changes (for instance, to avoid the occurrence of too many price spikes due to excessive volatility) to the ETS2 will be required to ensure that it survives the political battles expected for the upcoming months.

References

ADEME (2021) "Analyse des conditions de reprise d'une valeur équitable du carbone", July, https://comptecarbone.cc/wp-content/uploads/2022/10/valeur-carbone-equitable_202207.pdf

ADEME (2024) "Les représentations sociales du changement climatique—25ème vague du baromètre", 7 November, https://librairie.ademe.fr/

societe-et-politiques-publiques/7728-les-representations-sociales-du-changement-climatique-25eme-vague-du-barometre.html

Baccianti, C., M. Buck, O. Sartor, and C. Schröder (2024) "Investing in the Green Deal: How to Increase the Impact and Ensure Continuity of EU Climate Funding", *Agora Energiewende*, 9 December, https://www.agora-energiewende.org/publications/investing-in-the-green-deal

Beaufils, Cyrille (2019) "Le cadre juridique de la fiscalité environnementale", February, https://www.ccomptes.fr/system/files/2019-09/20190918-rapport-particulier2-CPO-fiscalite-environnementale.pdf

Bauchmüller, M., and C. Hulverscheidt (2024) "Energiepolitik. Warten auf das Klimageld. Süddeutsche Zeitung", 16 January, https://www.sueddeutsche.de/politik/energiepolitik-klimageld-robert-habeck-christian-lindner-1.6333805

BMK (2025) "Klimabonus: Einführung eines CO2-Preis-Ausgleichsmechanismus", March 2025.

Bohmann, S., L. Felder, P. Haan, C. Kemfert, M. Kücük, L. Schmitz, and J. Schupp (2025) "Mehr Klarheit schaffen: Klimageld als sozialer Ausgleich bei höheren CO2-Preisen", *DIW Wochenbericht* No. 6/2025, https://www.diw.de/documents/publikationen/73/diw_01.c.935740.de/25-6-1.pdf

Budgetdienst (2022) "Ökosoziale Steuerreform 2022. Analyse des Budgetdienstes. 10.01.2022", https://www.parlament.gv.at/dokument/budgetdienst/analysen-zu-gesetzen/BD_-_Oekosoziale_Steuerreform_2022.pdf

Bundesverfassungsgericht (2023) "Judgment of 15 November 2023", https://www.bundesverfassungsgericht.de/SharedDocs/Entscheidungen/EN/2023/11/fs20231115_2bvf000122en.html

Burtscher, Leonard (2024) "Warum es in Österreich schon heute Klimageld gibt. Umweltinstitut München. Interview mit Johannes Wahlmüller", 24 July, *Umwelt Institut*, https://umweltinstitut.org/energie-und-klima/meldungen/interview-klimabonus/

Carattini, Stefano, Maria Carvalho, and Sam Fankhauser (2017) "How to Make Carbon Taxes More Acceptable", Grantham Research Institute on Climate Change and the Environment Policy Report, https://www.lse.ac.uk/GranthamInstitute/wp-content/uploads/2017/12/How-to-make-carbon-taxes-more-acceptable.pdf

Cour des Comptes (2024) "La place de la fiscalité de l'énergie dans la politique énergétique et climatique française. Exercices 2012-2022", 27 March, https://www.ccomptes.fr/sites/default/files/2024-09/20240906-S2024-0646-Place-fiscalite-energie-dans-politique-energetique-et-climatique-francaise_0.pdf

Direction Générale de l'Energie et du Climat (2017) "Rapport de la France—Actualisation de 2017", March, https://tinyurl.com/272ww4td

De Perthuis, Christian (2013) "Travaux du comité pour la fiscalité écologique. Rapport du Président", https://www.vie-publique.fr/files/rapport/pdf/134000547.pdf

Direction de la recherche, des études, de l'évaluation et des statistiques (2024) "Taxe carbone: une moins grande adhésion à sa hausse dans le milieu rural, quelle que soit la mesure sociale ou fiscale en contrepartie", *Etudes et Resultats*, 1296, https://drees.solidarites-sante.gouv.fr/publications-communique-de-presse/etudes-et-resultats/taxe-carbone-une-moins-grande-adhesion-sa

Deutsche Bundesregierung (2024) "Antwort der Bundesregierung auf die Kleine Anfrage der Fraktion der CDU/CSU. Umsetzungsstand zur Einführung und Auszahlung eines

Klimageldes. Deutscher Bundestag. 20. Wahlperiode", *Drucksache* 20/13587, https://dserver.bundestag.de/btd/20/138/2013865.pdf

Deutschlandfunk (2024) "CO2-Preis. Wann kommt das Klimageld?", 3 February, *Deutschlandfunk*, https://www.deutschlandfunk.de/klimageld-102.html

Eden, A., J. Cludius, N. Unger, V. Noka, K. Schumacher, A. Vornicu-Chira, P. Gutowski, and K. Glowacki (2023)"Putting the ETS2 and Social Climate Fund to Work", Adelphi Policy Report, https://adelphi.de/system/files/document/policy-report_putting-the-ets-2-and-social-climate-fund-to-work_final_02.pdf

EPICO and Frontier Economics (2025) "Strengthening the EU ETS2 through Revenue Frontloading", Policy Report, June, https://epico.org/uploads/files/EPICO-Defending-the-EU_250605.pdf

European Commission (2021) "Impact Assessment Report", Commission Staff Working Document, https://eur-lex.europa.eu/resource.html?uri=cellar:7b89687a-eec6-11eb-a71c-01aa75ed71a1.0001.01/DOC_1&format=PDF#page=122

Fiedler, S., S. Meemken, S. Greifoner, and S. Bach (2025) "Regionales Klimageld in Deutschland. Potenziale, Herausforderungen und Verteilungswirkungen", https://www.nachhaltigkeitsrat.de/wp-content/uploads/2025/03/20250314_DIW_FOES_RNE_Studie_Regionales_Klimageld_in_Deutschland.pdf

Gagnebin, M. (2025) "Why Early Action by Five Countries Is Key to ETS2 Success", 20 March, *Agora Energiewende*, https://www.agora-energiewende.org/news-events/why-early-action-by-five-countries-is-key-to-ets-2-success

Greive, M., J. Hildebrand, and J. Olk (2025) "KTF. Bund fördert mit sieben Milliarden Euro den Heizungstausch", 25 March, *Handelsblatt*, https://www.handelsblatt.com/politik/deutschland/ktf-bund-foerdert-mit-sieben-milliarden-euro-den-heizungstausch/100116328.html

Holzmann, S., and F. Digulla (2024) "Klimapolitik für Akzeptanz", *Focus Paper* 25, https://www.bertelsmann-stiftung.de/fileadmin/files/user_upload/W_Focus_Paper__25_Klimapolitik_fuer_Akzeptanz.pdf

IEA (2023) "Energy-related CO2 Emissions per Capita by Income Decile in Selected Countries and Regions, 2021", February, *IEA*, https://www.iea.org/data-and-statistics/charts/energy-related-co2-emissions-per-capita-by-income-decile-in-selected-countries-and-regions-2021

Insee (2025a) "Prix moyens mensuels de vente au détail en métropole - Supercarburant sans plomb, indice d'octane 95", https://www.insee.fr/fr/statistiques/serie/000849411

Insee (2025b) "Prix moyens mensuels de vente au détail en métropole—Gazole", https://www.insee.fr/fr/statistiques/serie/000442588#

Jüngling, E., G. Sgaravatti, S. Tagliapietra, and G. Zachmann (2025) "Making the Best of the New EU Social Climate Fund", April, *Bruegel*, https://www.bruegel.org/policy-brief/making-best-new-eu-social-climate-fund#footnote13_2lks01e

Hager, Johanna (2024) "KURIER-OGM-Umfrage: „Klimabonus hatte fast keine Relevanz"", 29 December, *Kurier*, https://kurier.at/politik/inland/kurier-ogm-umfrage-klimabonus-einsparungen-arbeiten-im-alter-2025/402992526

Kern, J., and J. Winter (2025) "Kogler kämpft für den Klimabonus—mit einer Falschbehauptung", 26 January, *Profil*, https://www.profil.at/faktiv/kogler-gruenen-klimabonus-fpoe-oevp-budget/403002042

Koalitionsvertrag (2021) "Mehr Fortschritt wagen. Bündnis für Freiheit, Gerechtigkeit und Nachhaltigkeit", Koalitionsvertrag 2021-2025 zwischen der sozialdemokratischen Partei Deutschlands (SPD), Bündnis 90/die Grünen und den freien Demokraten (FDP), https://www.spd.de/fileadmin/Dokumente/Koalitionsvertrag/Koalitionsvertrag_2021-2025.pdf

Kontext (2025) "Budget und Klima: Menschen in Österreich für kluge Einsparungen statt Förderkürzungen", 14 May, *Kontext Pressemitteilung*, https://kontext-institut.at/presse/budgetrede-klima-umfrage-/

Ministère de la Transition Ecologique (2025) "Fiscalité environnementale—Extrait du Bilan environnemental 2024", https://www.statistiques.developpement-durable.gouv.fr/fiscalite-environnementale-extrait-du-bilan-environnemental-2024

Moysan, Emilie (2017) "Les indispensable du droit des finances publiques—Fiche 8. Le principe d'universalité", *Plein Droit*, https://droit.cairn.info/les-indispensables-du-droit-des-finances-publiques--9782340022997?lang=fr

Nguyen, P.-V., and T. Pellerin-Carlin (2021) "The European Energy Price Spike", October, Jacques Delors Institute, https://institutdelors.eu/en/publications/flambee-des-prix-de-lenergie-en-europe-2/

Österreichischer Städtebund (2024) "Städtebund/TU Wien: Klimabonus—Etikettenschwindel ohne Lenkungseffekt", 12 September, https://www.staedtebund.gv.at/services/aktuelles/aktuelles-details/staedtebundtu-wien-klimabonus-etikettenschwindel-ohne-lenkungseffekt/

Patermann, S., and E. Rathai (2025) "Klimageld 2025. Wann kommt die CO2-Preis-Entlastung und wie hoch fällt diese aus?", 11 April, *Wirtschaftswoche*, https://www.wiwo.de/politik/deutschland/klimageld-2025-wann-kommt-die-co2-preis-entlastung-und-wie-hoch-faellt-diese-aus/29605390.html

Pilcher, G. (2024) "Unfaire Verteilung? Kurz vor Klimabonus-Auszahlung wird erneut Kritik laut", 28 August, *Kleine Zeitung*, https://www.kleinezeitung.at/steiermark/18799162/kurz-vor-klimabonus-auszahlung-wird-erneut-kritik-laut

Reguant, M., U. Arregui, and S. Martin Belmonte (2025) "Energy and Just Transition with the Social Climate Plan", June, *Revo Presperidad Sostenible*, https://www.revoprosper.org/wp-content/uploads/2025/06/Revo-Energia-transicion-report-English-v2.pdf

Salzburger Nachrichten (2025) "Ersatzlose Streichung von Klimabonus trifft Ärmere stärker", 31 March, *Salzburger Nachrichten*, https://www.sn.at/politik/innenpolitik/ersatzlose-streichung-klimabonus-aermere-176062477

Schuster, Barbara (2025) "Klimabonus: Für sozialen Ausgleich der CO2-Steuer notwendig", 16 January, *Momentum Institut*, https://www.momentum-institut.at/news/klimabonus-fuer-sozialen-ausgleich-der-co2-steuer-notwendig/

Statistik Austria (2025) "Regionale Staffelung des Klimabonus", 15 May, *STATatlas*, https://www.statistik.at/atlas/?mapid=topo_urt_oev

T&E (2025) "How to Turn ETS2 Implementation into a Success", June, *T&E Report*, https://www.transportenvironment.org/uploads/files/ETS2_implementation_report_03062025.pdf

TU Wien (2024) "Robert Kalasek im Interview: Kritik an der aktuellen Verteilung des Klimabonus", 23 September, https://www.tuwien.at/ar/srf/aktuelles/news-detail/news/robert-kalasek-im-interview-kritik-an-der-aktuellen-verteilung-des-klimabonus

Umwelt Bundesamt (2025) "Einnahmen aus dem Emissionshandel erneut auf Rekordniveau. Über 18,5 Milliarden Euro für Klimaschutz, Technologieförderung und sozialen Ausgleich in Deutschland", 7 January, *Umwelt Bundesamt*, https://www.umweltbundesamt.de/presse/pressemitteilungen/einnahmen-aus-dem-emissionshandel-erneut-auf

Verbraucherzentrale Bundesverband (2023) "Einnahmen aus der CO2-Bepreisung der Jahre 2021 bis 2023 als Klimageld rückerstatten. Position des Verbraucherzentrale Bundesverbands (vzbv) zur Verwendung der Einnahmen aus der CO2-Bepreisung", 15 January, https://www.vzbv.de/sites/default/files/2023-12/23-12-15_Position_vzbv_Klimageld_final_barrierefrei.pdf

Woerner, A., T. Imai, D. P. Pace, and K. M. Schmidt (2024) "How to Increase Public Support for Carbon Pricing with Revenue Recycling", *Nature Sustainability* 7, 1633–1641.

14. (How) Can the Energy Transition in Europe be a Just Transition?

Bela Galgóczi[1] and Andrew Watt[2]

In order to ensure that benefits and burdens of the transition to a net-zero economy are shared in a just and balanced way—which is a precondition for accepting the needed changes—effective and inclusive governance structures in both private and public spheres are essential. Given sluggish growth and increasing competition for resources from other policy goals, especially defence, the challenges of achieving a just transition, and with it political acceptance, not to mention political and social stability, will also intensify. We examine four key dimensions of a just energy transition: employment transitions, distributional effects of energy transition, accessibility and affordability of clean energy, and the participation of social partners and stakeholders. Analysis of the EU instruments in place—in particular the Just Transition Fund (JTF) and the nascent Social Climate Fund (SCF)—reveals serious gaps behind large headline numbers. Amongst other issues, JTF disbursement has been very slow. The SCF imposes Just Transition principles on only a small proportion of the revenue to come from the expanded emissions trading scheme, leaving much to the Member States. The chapter closes with policy proposals.

14.1 Introduction

The green energy transition holds significant promise: not only in averting climate-related risks, but also in delivering other environmental benefits such as less pollution, and in unlocking social and economic gains through potentially unlimited sources of domestically produced energy with low marginal costs. However, it is an important feature of this transition that, while it has significant frontloaded costs in terms of the needed investments and the disruption to existing forms of production and employment, there is a delay before many of the positive effects are felt. In order to ensure that benefits and burdens are shared in a just and balanced way—which is a precondition for acceptance of the needed changes—effective and inclusive governance structures in both private and public spheres are essential.

---

1   ETUI—European Trade Union Institute.
2   ETUI.

    https://doi.org/10.11647/OBP.0499.14

Meanwhile, the dominant narrative within the EU institutions regarding energy transition is shifting. In 2019, fighting the climate crisis was one of the top priorities on the EU agenda, with broad political support. But this has come under challenge from geopolitical and domestic social developments in complex ways. Russia's invasion of Ukraine has made a fast-track transition to renewables a key condition of energy security. At the same time, the subsequent fossil-energy price increases have highlighted the importance of the social dimension of this transition, raising the risk of a backlash against transition-related burdens on households. Equally, the Russian threat, coupled with the risk of US-decoupling from Europe under Trump, has led to calls for a massive increase in defence expenditure, threatening to squeeze out climate-related (and social) investment. A final element is that the current framing of the energy transition has increasingly focused on competitiveness; here again, against the background of the Trump presidency, but, more importantly, in light of the increasingly evident Chinese dominance in key transition-related sectors. The collapse of Europe's "Great Battery Hope", Northvolt, symbolises this concern (Geschwindt 2025).

Amidst this changing and complex context, the pace of energy transition is expected to continue to intensify, as it must if net-zero targets are to be met. This will require far more resources, not least because the low-hanging fruit in terms of reducing emissions has already been picked. On the other hand, the benefits of past investments—notably the appreciable increase in the supply of electricity from renewable sources—will start to make themselves felt. Given sluggish growth and competing policy goals, the challenges of a just transition and thus ensuring political acceptance, not to mention political and social stability, will also intensify, with inequality and employment changes at their heart. Appropriate governance structures to oversee the EU's energy transition and steer it in line with concepts of social and environmental justice, territorial cohesion, and fair participation are needed more than ever. Both are important: the attainment of socially just outcomes (output legitimacy) and establishing processes that meaningfully involve workers and communities in decisions that will affect them (input legitimacy).

14.2 The Concept of a Just Energy Transition and the Main Challenges

Just transition is about how social justice with fair burden-sharing can be applied in the context of managing and limiting climate change. Here we examine the four key dimensions of a just energy transition:

- employment transitions in a decarbonizing economy;
- distributional effects of energy transition;
- accessibility and affordability of clean energy; and
- participation of social partners and stakeholders.

First, a just energy transition requires adequate funding to finance and subsidize necessary investment to deploy renewables at scale and establish the necessary network infrastructure to transfer the energy to the place of consumption. Several studies have pointed to the "investment gap", defined as the difference between actual yearly investments and the investment needed necessary to reach the EU 2030 targets. The European Commission (2021) calculated that, to achieve the European Green Deal (EGD) objectives, an additional investment of €520 billion per year would be needed. This compares to the annual €406 billion calculated by the Institute for Climate Economics (I4CE 2024) on top of the actual investments of €407 billion realized in 2022.

The energy transition takes place at different levels, each having specific "just transition" characteristics.

14.2.1 Power Generation

The starting point for the energy transition is movement away from energy generation based on fossil fuels and towards the use of renewable energy sources to generate power. To achieve this at the required speed and scale demands huge investments (both public and private) and creates jobs across the economy. The necessary equipment (wind turbines, solar panels, etc.) must be manufactured. And then it must be installed, both in large stand-alone sites and in households and user firms at local level. Employment transitions are a key part of this, requiring not only employment or social policies, but also regional and industrial policies.

From an ecological perspective, the necessary hardware can be imported, but a just transition requires that much of the deployed technology be sourced from a European manufacturing base, both to redirect workers displaced from fossil-fuel industries into gainful employment and to ensure that new jobs in the renewable energy sector offer comparable quality to the ones lost.

14.2.2 Power Distribution

Power generation is only the first step: power must be distributed to consumers and industrial users. An important feature of renewable energy sources is their intermittency. Accordingly, the transition from fossil fuels to renewables requires a new energy infrastructure to ensure the stable provision of low-cost energy where and when it is needed. The most important requirement is a modern electricity grid that enables multiple interconnections between markets so as to maximize the use of renewable electricity generated, minimizing the need for fossil-based backups while ensuring grid stability. An important additional element is investment in various forms of electricity storage. Beyond that, a clean industry infrastructure (e.g., hydrogen networks) or charging stations for electric vehicles are needed. Because of coordination and collective action problems, these investments will require public-sector support in one form or another. A 'just transition' approach to power distribution should address inequality across Member States and regions in financing the establishment of such networks, to avoid leaving disadvantaged regions behind.

14.2.3 Energy Use

Finally, much needs to be done in the spaces where energy is consumed, in households and user firms. Some issues are primarily regulatory, e.g., the design of electricity markets. Smart metering systems and pricing mechanisms, for different types of users that encourage a rational use of the available energy, seeking to match demand and (variable) supply more closely, will be the key issues to address here. From a just transition perspective, the distributional question is paramount. Without sacrificing efficiency, metering and pricing systems must be such that the adjustment burden is not unduly placed on the shoulders of those least able to bear it, forcing them into energy poverty.

The four dimensions of a just energy transition appear in each of the three different levels of the energy transition, with different characteristics.

14.3 The Main Dimensions of a Just Energy Transition

Climate policies are having, and will continue to have, a major effect on the world of work. Millions of new jobs are being created in the transition to a net-zero carbon economy, but millions of jobs will also disappear. The majority of jobs will go through a fundamental transformation. This unprecedented wave of restructuring will have unequal effects on people depending on factors such as skills, gender, age, economic activity, and region.

14.3.1 Employment Transitions in a Decarbonizing Economy

Describing employment transitions during the green transformation, in particular within the framework of established statistical classification, proves to be huge challenge. Various studies and statistical approaches have attempted to identify products and services that meet one of several criteria for a green economy.

The European Commission (2021a) makes a distinction between four categories of structural change in the labour market linked to the green transformation:

- job creation: new jobs emerge to reduce environmental pressures or increase resource efficiency or to develop circular business models;

- job substitution: shift in economic activity within or across sectors from resource-intensive activities to more circular activities (the automotive sector is a good example, as jobs in combustion engine related segments are disappearing, while jobs in software development and battery manufacturing emerge);

- job destruction: job loss with no direct replacement (fossil-fuel extraction and power generation); and

- job redefinition: existing jobs change their day-to-day skillset, work methods, and profiles as part of the transition (e.g., in construction).

In its 2024 Employment Outlook (OECD 2024) the OECD distinguishes between "green-driven occupations" and "greenhouse gas (GHG) intensive occupations", where the former category includes: 1. occupations that emerge due to the green transition and that didn't exist before (for example, wind turbine service technicians); 2. green-enhanced skills occupations (not new, but whose skills and tasks are changing due to the green transition); and 3. green-increased demand occupations (not being green but providing inputs to the green economy; for example, workers in lithium mining).

The report stresses that while GHG-intensive occupations are those where most job losses are expected, they often share similar skill requirements with green-driven occupations, suggesting that transitions out of these jobs are possible with targeted retraining. It adds, however, that the move towards emerging green-driven occupations is more challenging for workers in low-skilled positions than for those in high-skilled positions—a clear case for just transition policies. As regards estimates for the distribution of jobs, the report finds that between 2015 and 2019, around 20% of workers in OECD countries were employed in green-driven occupations, but the overwhelming majority of these jobs were existing ones and only 14% (within the 20%) were "green new or emerging occupations".

Policymakers frequently claim that the green transformation will be a win-win game with a net positive overall employment effect. According to projections by the European Commission (2021b), the green transition is expected to have a moderately positive impact on total jobs in the EU: reaching the 2030 climate policy targets would result in a net employment increase of up to 884,000 in the EU27. A study by Ernst and Young (2021) carried out a sectoral analysis of investment projects under the EU Next Generation Recovery Fund devoted to the green economy (covering energy, transport, buildings, industry, and land use) and found that these projects represent an aggregate investment of €200 billion and could create 2.3 million jobs. With the announcement of the Green Deal Industrial Plan (European Commission 2023), the Commission's factsheet stated that the green transition could create up to 1 million additional jobs in the EU by 2030, in particular in the solar and battery sectors.

These very optimistic forecasts are mostly based on the assumption that the huge investments necessary to achieve decarbonization targets will be made and a strong job creation effect will follow in Europe. They do not account for industrial, trade, and investment policy repercussions and regard the developments in isolation from the rest of the world. The main message is that the evolving transition would be smooth and create a win-win situation for all.

Evidence from the recent past does not always support these optimistic assumptions. While jobs have indeed been created, the rate of job creation is muted and uneven. What is more, jobs in some key clean-technology sectors were actually falling in the period between 2018 and 2022.

According to a data-base developed by the Bruegel thinktank (Jugé et al. 2024), as of 2022, there were 347,000 jobs in solar energy at EU27 level, 273,500 in wind and 416,200 in heat pumps (a total of just over one million). These jobs are concentrated in ten Member States, Germany having the highest number of jobs in solar and wind power (87,000 and 86,000 respectively), while Italy has the most jobs in heat pumps (135,000) followed by France (80,000).

It is important to note that Germany, Italy, and Denmark all saw job losses in the respective sectors compared to 2017. Based on the Bruegel database, manufacturing employment in the German wind energy sector had fallen from 140,800 in 2017 to 86,600 by 2022; over the same period, it fell from 34,200 to 22,400 in Denmark. Italy, the leader in heat pumps with 85,000 jobs in 2022, had lost 6,000 jobs by that year, while Spain saw a loss of jobs in heat pumps from 68,000 in 2018 to 32,000 by 2022, and in Portugal the number fell from 80,000 in 2019 to 25,000 by 2022.

These losses point to challenges in terms of both the investment activity that determines the rate of deployment (the demand side for manufacturing) and the market share of European manufacturers in satisfying this demand. The negative employment trend in key clean manufacturing segments is very concerning, suggesting that Europe's transition to net-zero emissions is unlikely to contribute to employment, and risks leading to increasing import dependence rather than the development of a strong domestic production base generating quality jobs.

Irrespective of the net aggregate employment effect, just transition approaches focus on the need to design low-carbon transitions in ways that support workers to cope with these labour market transitions, for instance through retraining programmes, employment protection and procedural justice (i.e., worker participation) in anticipating and managing change (Galgóczi 2020).

Turning from quantity to quality, newly created jobs in the renewable energy sector should at least be of comparable quality to the ones lost, but this is not always the case. A study by the European Trade Union Institute (Zwysen 2024) found that jobs in more polluting sectors, are generally characterized by having relatively *good* conditions, with an above-average likelihood of being covered by a collective agreement as well as above-average union density and access to worker representation. An IG Metall (2024) survey on wind industry jobs in Germany conducted among works councils in the sector found that 63.6% of plants in the sector had no collective bargaining coverage. A study by the Somo Institute (Merk et al. 2024) provides an insight into the bleak reality of battery jobs in Hungary, one of the key locations for the EU's emerging battery manufacturing sector. Details of the wage structure and highly flexible working-time schedules reveal the high pressure put on workers. Hungary's battery industry also exposes workers to significant health and safety hazards.

These examples caution that there is absolutely no reason to believe that new "green" jobs are automatically of better quality than old "brown" jobs. Policy measures will be needed, among other things to promote collective bargaining in new industries. One promising initiative is the Quality Jobs Roadmap (QJR) announced by the European Commission (2025a) at the launch of the Clean Industrial Deal in early 2025, which is to be presented by the end of 2025. According to the Commission, the QJR should support Member States and industry in providing decent working conditions by providing a non-legislative framework on just transition and anticipation of change, with the aim of early intervention in restructuring cases with a strengthened information and consultation framework. The ETUC (2025) demands a legally binding framework that includes a Just Transition Directive.

14.3.2 Distributional Effects of the Energy Transition

Market-based climate policy instruments such as carbon or energy taxes or emission trading schemes, as well as subsidies for low-carbon technologies have, unless they are offset by a significantly progressive system of returning revenues to households, regressive distributional effects, i.e. placing higher (relative) burdens on poorer than on richer people (Büchs et al. 2021).

14.3.2.1 Energy Poverty

According to Eurostat, in 2024, energy poverty in the EU27 has remained at a high level with 9.2% of the total population, as shown by Figure 14.1: 41.1 million people in the EU27 were unable to afford to heat their homes adequately, roughly the same as in 2022, but 6 million less than in 2023 when energy prices peaked. Furthermore, 19.7% of those at risk of poverty in the EU (i.e., whose household income was 60% or less of the median) were unable to maintain their homes at an adequate temperature; in Greece and Cyprus more than 40% of poor households suffered energy poverty. Inequality in exposure to energy poverty was particularly high in Slovakia, Croatia, Hungary, and the Netherlands, where those at risk of poverty were three times more likely to suffer from energy poverty than the total population.

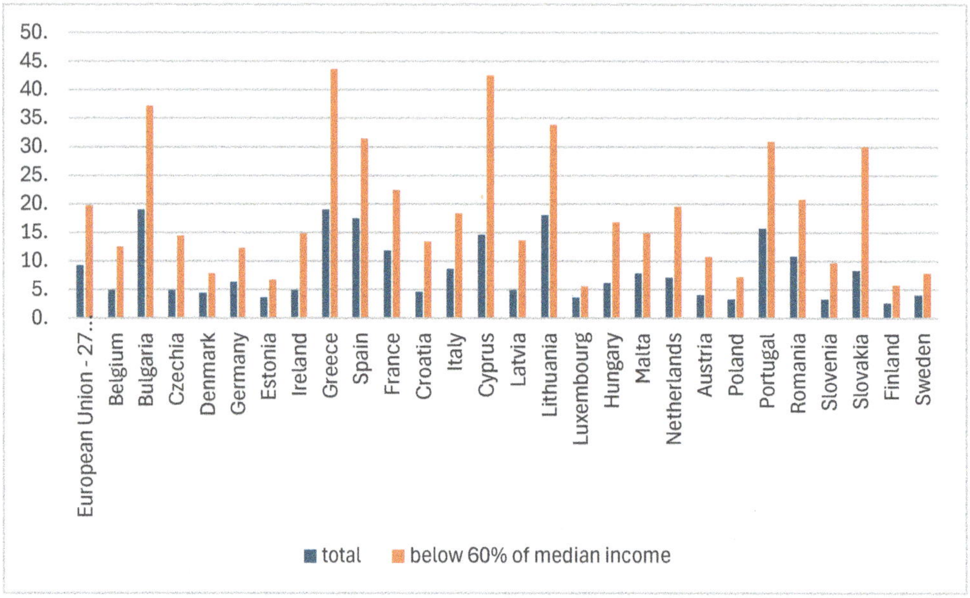

Fig. 14.1 Energy poverty—share of population unable to keep their home warm, for total population and for those at risk of poverty (%, 2024). *Source:* Eurostat (2025).

Data for Figs. 14.1–14.4 are available at
https://hdl.handle.net/20.500.12434/9ed6e276

With more than 40 million Europeans facing energy poverty, a fair distribution of the burdens of the energy transition and the costs of operating the energy system among different types of consumers is even more important.

Looked through a distributional lens, the apparent "level playing field" of an EU-wide carbon price in critical sectors with a direct impact on consumers can have huge effects on inequality—both between and within Member States. Feed-in tariffs with higher electricity prices to finance investments into renewables, for example, have a regressive effect, as low-income households are hit hardest. Although market mechanisms that set price signals to market actors—such as those under the newly created emissions trading system for transport and buildings—are essential to changing investment and behavioural patterns, these market signals have significant regressive distributional effects (IEEP 2022).

Data on household expenditure on heating energy reveals that in the lowest-income households in low-income countries, more than 10% of expenditure goes on heating. A carbon tax levied on these fuels would impose a large burden on these households. Data published in a policy brief by Bruegel (Jüngling et al. 2025) also suggests significant inequality between countries. The households with the highest incomes in low-income countries spend, on average, higher shares of their incomes on heating energy than the households with the lowest incomes in rich countries. This is influenced by divergence in incomes across countries and in the quality of buildings, resulting from the materials used in construction or age of the building stock (Gevorgian et al. 2021).

The cited study by Bruegel also reveals that lower-income households are particularly affected by the rising costs of petrol and diesel. As about 70% of national transport emissions across the EU arise from traffic in areas outside the major cities, rural populations will be more strongly affected by the fuel price increase induced by the prospective ETS2. Based on the differences in driving patterns and incomes across different settlement types, the share of income spent on the fuel price increase varies significantly. Those in rural areas that lack public transport risk being disadvantaged. Assuming a €60/tonne CO_2 price, the calculated fuel price increases for rural households in both Germany and Poland would be more than double than for urban ones. Relative to their incomes, however, rural households in Poland would still spend twice as much as German rural households. This example shows that the distributional effects of market-based instruments to induce change have different dimensions, including unequal effects between and within Member States, as well as spatial characteristics; a detailed study for Germany is Endres (2023).

To the extent that such instruments are relied upon to induce change (and they have some advantages compared to regulatory approaches), a critical question becomes how the revenue from market-based measures is returned to households in the form of transfers and/or the revenue is used to fund investments. This aspect will be dealt with in Section 14.4, that deals with policy instruments.

14.3.2.2 Energy Price

A further distributional effect of the energy transition is how energy system costs are borne by different type of consumers. Electricity prices are a contentious issue for both industry and households. For the former they are regarded as a key component of competitiveness, whereas for the latter they are an essential part of the cost of living. To what extent final electricity prices reflect the electricity generation and distribution costs incurred by different type of consumers is a matter of regulatory choice. Only one third of the average retail electricity price paid by EU households in 2021 was related to the cost of energy generation; the other two thirds were made up of taxes, which also have a regressive element in that taxes have a higher weight in the final price paid by consumers when the volumes of electricity contracted are smaller (McWilliams et al. 2024). National governments decide how these elements of the final electricity price should be split between groups of consumers, using instruments that include tax exemptions, reduced levies, and compensatory mechanisms, with such diversity undermining the notion of an Energy Union.

Figure 14.2 shows electricity prices for both households and energy-intensive industries (those with a yearly consumption above 20 GWh) across the Member States. For example, a household in Germany pays almost five times as much as a comparable household in Hungary. For energy-intensive industries, the price of electricity in the Netherlands is four times the price paid by a comparable firm in Sweden or Finland. In Belgium, households pay three times as much as energy-intensive industries. In most Member States households pay electricity prices that are significantly higher than those paid by energy-intensive industries. While electricity prices are seen as a key factor of competitiveness (and by extension for keeping industrial jobs), the result is that households (including those under the poverty line) are financing the energy transition and subsidizing heavy industry.

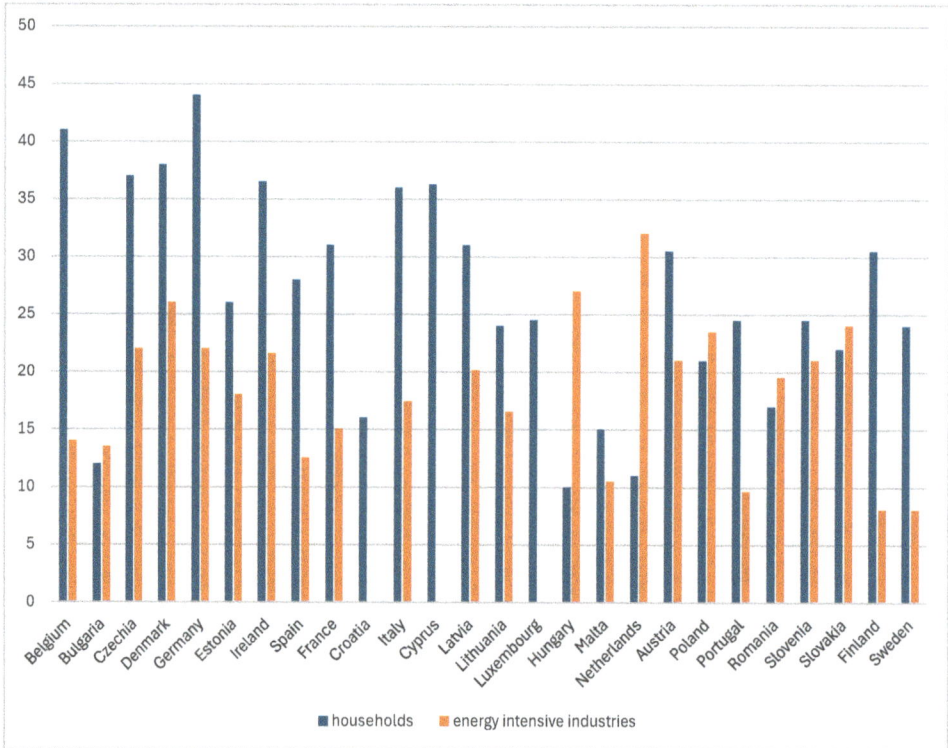

Fig. 14.2 Electricity price for households and for energy-intensive industries (above 20 GWh/year) in EU Member States (second half, 2023, cents/kWh). *Source:* Eurostat and Sgaravatti (2024). *Note:* No data for Greece; no data for energy-intensive industries in LU, HR, and CY. The Eurostat data are biannual, hence the reference to S2.

Data for Figs. 14.1–14.4 are available at
https://hdl.handle.net/20.500.12434/9ed6e276

14.3.2.3 Accessibility and Affordability of Clean Energy

Poorer households also have less capacity to adapt, since while low-carbon products (electric vehicles, rooftop solar panels, and so on) may have low operating costs, they tend to have high, upfront capital costs—presenting a hurdle for households lacking access to cheap capital. Consumers on lower incomes also often have insufficient information about available low-carbon alternatives. Furthermore, those in a precarious situation have a short-term planning horizon and so discount potential, long-term cost savings. Large redistributional effects are also likely between those in urban areas and people living in the countryside. This results in very different levels in the ability of households to invest in low-carbon products and technology.

14.4 What Are the Available Instruments and How do They Work?

After the challenges flagged up in the previous sections, here we present some evidence on the existing supporting measures.

Some of the dedicated just transition instruments have a dual climate and social focus, linked to the EGD and explicitly intended to promote a just transition *that leaves no one behind*, while others have mixed objectives with a more indirect just transition relevance.

The first of these is the Just Transition Mechanism, an EU framework which secures €55 billion between 2021 and 2027 to address the socioeconomic effects of the transition in the "most affected regions", which in practice mainly means coal regions. The pivotal mechanism is the Just Transition Fund (JTF), which is part of the EU cohesion policy framework. To unlock funds, Member States have to submit Territorial Just Transition Plans (TJTPs) for Commission approval. As a reporting and allocation mechanism, these plans are an important governance tool in ensuring a just transition.

Another mechanism is the Social Climate Fund (SCF). This will provide €86.7 billion between 2026 and 2032 to deal with the social impacts of the new emissions trading scheme for buildings and road transport (ETS2, starting in 2027) on vulnerable households, micro-enterprises, and transport users. It is one of the ways that the revenue from the ETS is recycled. Member States must submit Social Climate Plans (SCPs) identifying how they intend to use the funds. This can include measures or investments to increase the energy efficiency of buildings or decarbonize heating and cooling, or to provide temporary direct income support. The revision of the main emissions trading scheme (ETS1) also envisages a

Modernization Fund for thirteen Member States that can be used for just transition objectives, among others.

Alongside the dedicated just transition instruments, there are also other governance tools that are less explicit but in practice equally important for delivering just transition. The Next Generation EU programme and its cornerstone, the Recovery and Resilience Facility (RRF), have contributed both directly and indirectly to just transition governance. The RRF is a funding instrument intended to address the consequences of the pandemic[4] and requires Member States to submit extensive national Recovery and Resilience Plans (RRPs) outlining measures across six priority pillars, including green transition and social and territorial cohesion. These plans were an important step towards more systemic policies. However, studies have shown that, despite some of the funds being used to ensure that people are not left behind in the green transition, the link between social and green objectives is often not made explicit and is not required in the reporting (Galgoczi 2024).

Below we discuss the main recipients of the funds, their priorities, and how the resources are allocated.

14.4.1 Just Transition Fund

The areas where the JTF will be implemented are defined in "territorial just transition plans", which are agreed during talks with the European Commission. A total of sixty-seven plans covering ninety-three areas have been approved.

Each plan includes an analysis of the anticipated economic and social impacts of the green transition, such as job losses, and also of how pollution from production processes will be reduced. Member States are under pressure to use the money quickly. A total of 70% of the total JTF allocation is concentrated in the first two annual tranches of the operational programmes through which the funding will be used, and these need to be spent by 2025 and 2026 respectively.

To be eligible for the funding allocated under the Just Transition Mechanism, EU Member States were required to negotiate territorial just transition plans for regions identified as likely to suffer negative socioeconomic impacts from the transition to a carbon-neutral economy. This process lasted from the launch of the Just Transition Fund Regulation in June 2021 until the European Commission's approval of the plans, which had to be completed by 31 December 2022. Apart from Germany, the main beneficiaries are mostly Central and Eastern European (CEE) Member States that have relatively low GDP per capita levels, higher carbon intensity and a higher concentration of affected regions. Even twenty years after the "big bang" EU enlargement, their economic catch-up process is still ongoing—and the JTF is an instrument that will support their green transformation in this context.

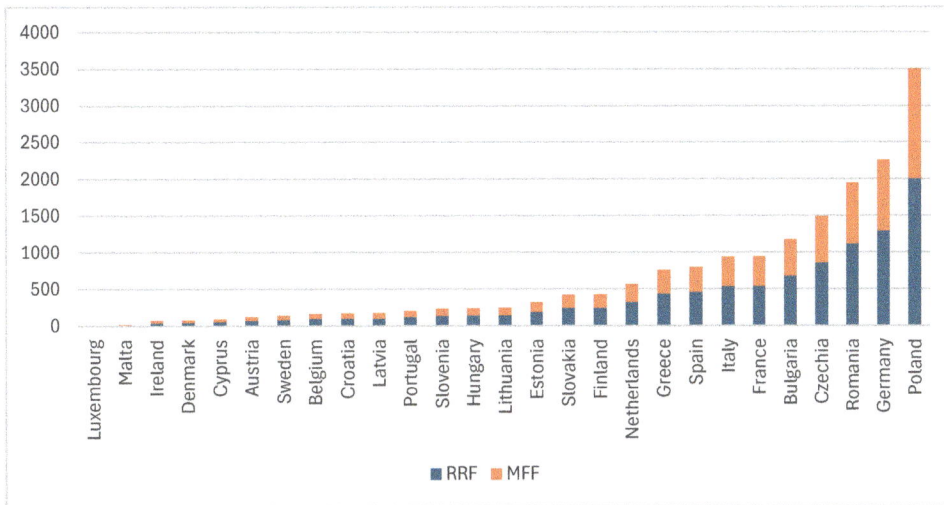

Fig. 14.3 Just Transition Fund allocations for Member States, with source of funding (million euros). *Source:* EU Monitor (2021). *Note:* RRF = Recovery and Resilience Facility; MMF = Multiannual Financial Framework.

Data for Figs. 14.1–14.4 are available at https://hdl.handle.net/20.500.12434/9ed6e276

Based on twenty-eight Territorial Just Transition Plans developed for regions within eight Central and Eastern European countries, CEE Bankwatch analyzed fund allocations by policy area and funding priority (Dobre and Stepien 2024). The study shows that the Fund is allocated between three policy categories: economic, environmental, and social. The economic category covers investments in employment, retraining and upskilling, small and medium-sized enterprises, business incubators, and large enterprises, including research, development, and innovation. The environmental category covers investments in renewable energy sources and related infrastructure, energy communities, energy efficiency, land recultivation, waste management, mobility, and climate adaptation. The social category covers social services, care for children and older people, research, development and innovation in the public sector, education, and small-scale community initiatives.

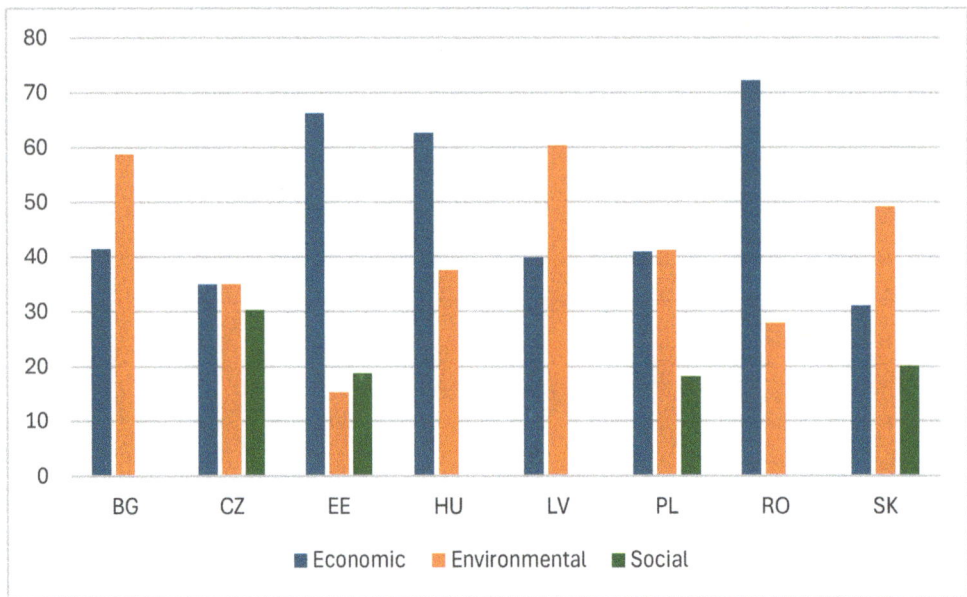

Fig. 14.4 Just Transition Fund allocations by policy category. *Source:* CEE Bankwatch (2024).

Data for Figs. 14.1–14.4 are available at
https://hdl.handle.net/20.500.12434/9ed6e276

Funding priorities for the just transition vary significantly across the eight countries. While the Czech Republic demonstrates a balanced approach, allocating resources almost equally across economic, environmental, and social policies, Romania heavily prioritizes economic policies to the detriment of environmental and social initiatives.

Overall, economic and environmental policies receive the most funding and are seen as top priorities by most countries. The social impacts of the just transition receive far less funding or are even ignored entirely, such as in Bulgaria, Hungary, Latvia, and Romania.

The huge gap in funding for social measures (beyond job losses in transitioning industries) indicates that the broader social impacts of the just transition will likely require additional support from other funds, such as the European Social Fund or the Social Climate Fund. All eight countries chose to direct funds towards employment or retraining/upskilling. Poland, Bulgaria, and Romania are the countries expected to be most affected by job losses in the coal industry so they will invest most in these types of interventions.

Allocating funds aimed at covering the gaps created by job loss is crucial to a successful just transition. In most carbon intensive regions, the focus is on workers in the polluting industry, and doesn't include the wider community and vulnerable groups.

However, JTF absorption rates raise concerns about the capacity of countries to implement policies swiftly. By March 2025, only 3% of funding was actually spent, and confirmed budget allocations were also well below the 70% target set for 2026 (Yeung 2025).

14.4.2 Social Climate Fund

The second important instrument, the Social Climate Fund (SCF), was introduced with the primary objective of correcting the detrimental social side effects of the decision to use a market mechanism, the ETS2, to reduce GHG emissions in two main sectors that have underperformed in terms of emissions reduction: buildings and transport.

As mentioned in Section 14.2, data on household expenditure on heating energy reveals a significant degree of inequality both within and across Member States. After the introduction of the ETS2, fuel prices will rise as producers pass their cost increases on to consumers. Keliauskaite et al. (2024) estimated price fluctuations between €60 and €200 per tonne of CO_2, depending on the success of decarbonization efforts. At an ETS2 price of €60 per tonne of CO_2, standard use of a gas boiler would incur additional heating costs of €162 per year, whereas users of a coal-boiler would see their costs increase by €350 per year. Naturally, with rising carbon prices, the price effect increases proportionately. The combined effect of these factors can lead to a significant increase in inequality. Poor households that cannot afford to modernize their heating systems and insulate their flats might fall into fossil fuel traps from which they cannot escape, as high running costs constrain further their ability to invest in renewable-based alternatives or energy efficiency.

To address these distributional concerns, some ETS2 auctioning revenues will be redistributed, including through the establishment of the SCF, which will pool €65 billion from total ETS2 revenues. This fund is intended to address within-country inequality by supporting the most vulnerable households and SMEs, and to address between-country inequality by helping the most-affected countries more.

In order to access funding, Member States must have submitted Social Climate Plans (SCPs) that detail the use of the SCF funding, by the end of June 2025. As of September 2025, the dedicated website of the European Commission (2025b) does not (yet) provide information about the number and content of the submitted national plans. The NGO CANEurope (2025) has stressed that progress by Member State in drafting their SCPs is uneven, while only seven have organized public consultations and the involvement of social partners was generally weak.

The main challenge for policymakers is to direct the funds effectively to vulnerable groups. Evidence from the energy crisis showed that many countries struggled to effectively target households with necessary support (Galgoczi 2024).

For the period 2027–2032, total ETS2 revenue is estimated to amount to between €342 billion and €570 billion depending on the actual price of CO_2 allowances. Out of this, €65 billion will directly be absorbed by the Social Climate Fund. The rest will be distributed among Member States based on their historical emissions between 2016 and 2018. Member States top up the SCF by €22 billion to reach its total budget of €87 billion. The remaining €255–€483 billion funds are for additional measures at the national level. This is a significant resource to finance national measures to tackle both emissions and distributional concerns.

The spending of this money is less strictly regulated than the SCF funding. According to the regulation, measures should target vulnerable households or contribute to the reductions of emissions. However, the increased discretion for governments means that they might prioritize different political objectives. For each measure in the SCPs, milestones and targets must be defined, with SCF payments to the countries only made after they are reached. The measures themselves must aim to alleviate the additional financial pressure ETS2 puts on vulnerable households and SMEs. Only a maximum of 37.5% of the total costs of the SCPs may be allocated to temporary direct income support.

The money pooled in the SCF is distributed among countries according to an allocation formula that takes into account total population, population at risk of poverty living in rural areas, the percentage of households in utility bill arrears, gross national income per capita in purchasing power standard, overall greenhouse gas emissions and CO_2 emissions from fuel combustion by households. Out of the total €87 billion EU funding to support Social Climate Plans in the 2026–2032 period, Poland would receive the most (ca. €15 billion), while Germany would receive ca. €7 billion, and Belgium, the Czech Republic, and Slovakia ca. €2 billion each. When taking into account the number of (vulnerable) households in each country, Greece will have the highest amount available per vulnerable household followed by Bulgaria, Croatia, Romania, and Poland. A paper by Bruegel (Jüngling et al. 2025) has calculated that if these resources were concentrated on the first income decile of households, those in Greece could receive a support of €1,800 in a year (for Poland, ca. €1,600). If the two poorest income deciles were to be targeted, support for such households in Greece could be just under €1,000, in Poland ca. €800.

The SCF thus offers substantial support, but as this example has shown, proper targeting will be crucial. The other concern is about the absorption rate, how Member States can mobilize available resources. If the SCF were to suffer from a similarly low absorption rate than the JTF, vulnerable households and SMEs would be exposed to the ETS2-induced price increase without benefitting from the SCF resources for years. Given the bigger weight of the SCF over the JTF, both in terms of funding (€87 billion vs €27 billion, including national cofinancing) and coverage (all EU vs ninety-six territories), it is crucial that the EU and Member States have in place a strong structure for policy design and implementation.

14.5 What Are the Risks and Where Are the Gaps

This chapter provided insight into the complexity of what would be needed to render an energy transition "just". There are several layers and dimensions that must be dealt with. The above analysis suggests that doing so is very challenging for policymakers and there are grounds for scepticism that, without a change of approach and substantial additional commitment of funds—which could come from a bigger allocation from ETS 2 to the SCF—Europe will struggle to realize its Just Transition ambitions:

- Industrial, trade, employment, and social policies are all relevant in achieving a balanced and fair energy transition, these need to be properly co-ordinated in a volatile and complex international environment.

- The investment gap, both public and private, to reach climate targets remains huge and the current fiscal environment is not favourable.

- Policy targeting is a huge challenge, as experience with the anti-inflation measures suggests. The performance of the Member States varies substantially on this metric.

- The absorption rate of funds in the JTF is very low. Unless improvements are implemented, the deployment of the significantly larger sums under the SCF will also be delayed. For transition to be perceived as just, compensatory measures must be available when burdens are being shouldered, not years later.

Governance of a just energy transition is critical to ensuring that the benefits of the transition are shared equitably and to minimizing the social and economic burdens placed on vulnerable workers and communities. Existing EU mechanisms provide an initial framework but these instruments have significant limitations, including a lack of coordination, insufficient resources, and in the case of the JTF low absorption rate. It is critical that the SCF that starts its initial phase from 2026 improves this poor disbursement record. Targeting the available resources toward the most vulnerable will also be key for its success.

A strengthened, systemic just transition governance framework will be essential in order to overcome these challenges and ensure that the principles of transparency, accountability, and inclusiveness are embedded in the transition process. More granular data collection, awareness-raising policies, more binding obligations, improved coordination between social and environmental policies, and greater involvement of all stakeholders, including workers, civil society, and local communities will be important supportive factors. Apart from improving funding, the EU can leverage positive change by applying clear social and environmental conditionalities in EU policy processes, such as state aid, investment support, or public procurement. The initiative of the European Commission for a Quality Jobs Roadmap is a good starting point, but it should be based on a legally binding framework that includes a Just Transition Directive.

References

CANEurope (2025) "Media Briefing: Social Climate Plans", Brussels, https://caneurope.org/content/uploads/2025/06/MEDIA-BRIEFING-SOCIAL-CLIMATE-PLANS-CAN-Europe.pdf

Dobre, D, and M. Stepien (2024) "Following the Money from the Just Transition Fund: Just Transition", 29 April, *Just Transition*, https://www.just-transition.info/following-the-money-from-the-just-transition-fund/

Endres, L. (2023) "Verteilungswirkung der Co2-Bepreisung in den Sektoren Verkehr und Wärme mit Pro-Kopf Klimageld", *IMK Policy Brief* 161, https://www.imk-boeckler.de/fpdf/HBS-008757/p_imk_pb_161_2023.pdf

Ernst and Young (2021) "A Clean COVID-19 Recovery: The Global Opportunity", https://www.ey.com/en_cn/insights/strategy/a-clean-covid-19-pandemic-recovery-the-global-opportunity

EU Monitor (2021) "Annexes to COM(2020)22—Just Transition Fund", https://www.eumonitor.eu/9353000/1/j4nvirkkkr58fyw_j9vvik7m1c3gyxp/vl5bgb7s1szs

European Commission (2021a) "Greening of the Labour market—Impacts for the Public Employment Services", https://op.europa.eu/en/publication-detail/-/publication/a5ce471b-f0dd-11eb-a71c-01aa75ed71a1/language-en

European Commission (2021b) *The Future of Jobs Is Green*. Luxembourg: Publications Office, https://publications.jrc.ec.europa.eu/repository/handle/JRC126047

European Commission (2025a) "Quality Jobs Roadmap", https://ec.europa.eu/info/law/better-regulation/have-your-say/initiatives/14707-Quality-Jobs-Roadmap_en

European Commission (2025b) "Social Climate Fund", https://climate.ec.europa.eu/eu-action/carbon-markets/eu-emissions-trading-system-eu-ets/social-climate-fund_en

ETUC (2025) "ETUC Demands for the Quality Jobs Roadmap", https://www.etuc.org/en/document/etuc-demands-quality-jobs-roadmap

Galgóczi, B. (ed.) (2024) *Response Measures to the Energy Crisis: Policy Targeting and Climate Trade-offs*. Brussels: ETUI, https://www.etui.org/sites/default/files/2023-11/Response%20measures%20to%20the%20energy%20crisis-policy%20targeting%20and%20climate%20trade-offs_2023.pdf

Geschwindt, S. (2025) "After Northvolt, Europe's Battery Path Leads to China—or New Tech Frontiers", 21 March, *TNW*, https://thenextweb.com/news/after-northvolt-europe-eyes-new-battery-frontiers-beyond-china

Gevorgian, A., S. Pezzutto, S. Zambotti, S. Croce, U. F. Oberegger, R. Lollini, L. Kranzl, and A. Müller (2021) *European Building Stock Analysis: A Country by Country Descriptive and Comparative Analysis of the Energy Performance of Buildings*, Bolzano: Eurac, https://webassets.eurac.edu/31538/1643788710-ebsa_web_2.pdf

I4CE (2024) "European Climate Investment Deficit Report", 20240222-i4ce3859-Panorama-EU_VA-40p.pdf

IEEP (2022) "Can Polluter Pays Policies Be Progressive?", Research Report, Institute for European Environmental Policy, https://ieep.eu/publications/can-polluter-pays-policies-be-progressive

IG Metall (2024a) "Umfrage unter den Betriebsräten der Windindustrie ausgewählte Ergebnisse der Umfrage im Jahr 2023", https://kueste.igmetall.de/dam/jcr:2e8eacc9-d9bf-4daf-80c6-c3a515576c73/DMASSET_21580.pdf

Jugé, M., et al. (2024) "European Clean Tech Tracker", 3 September, *Bruegel*, https://www.bruegel.org/dataset/european-clean-tech-tracker

Jüngling, E., G. Sgaravatti, S. Tagliapietra, and G. Zachmann (2025) "Making the Best of the New EU Social Climate Fund", 3 April 2025, *Bruegel*, https://www.bruegel.org/policy-brief/making-best-new-eu-social-climate-fund

Keliauskaitė, U., B. McWilliams, G. Sgaravatti, and S. Tagliapietra (2024) "How to Finance the European Union's Building Decarbonisation Plan", Policy Brief 12/24, *Bruegel*, https://www.bruegel.org/policy-brief/how-finance-european-unions-building-decarbonisation-plan

McWilliams, B., G. Sgaravatti, S. Tagliapietra, and G. Zachmann (2024) "Europe's Under-the radar Industrial Policy: Intervention in Electricity Pricing", *Policy Brief* 01/2024, Bruegel, https://www.bruegel.org/system/files/2024-01/PB%2001%202024_3.pdf

OECD (2024) "OECD Employment Outlook 2024: The Net-Zero Transition and the Labour Market", https://www.oecd.org/en/publications/oecd-employment-outlook-2024_ac8b3538-en.html

Sgaravatti, G. (2024) "Electricity Tariffs Dashboard", Bruegel, https://www.bruegel.org/dataset/electricity-tariffs-dashboard

Yeung, P. (2025) "Where Is the Money the EU Promised Workers to Go Green?", 5 June, *Context*, https://www.context.news/just-transition/where-is-the-money-the-eu-promised-workers-to-go-green

Zwysen, W. (2024) "Green Transition and Job Quality: Risks for Worker Representation", *ETUI Technical Brief* 2, https://www.etui.org/sites/default/files/2024-02/Green%20transition%20and%20job%20quality-risks%20for%20worker%20representation_2024.pdf

Contributor Biographies

Floor Alkemade is a Full Professor of Economics and Governance of Technological Innovation at Eindhoven University of Technology. Her key areas of expertise include innovation, clean tech, and sustainability. She received an ERC Consolidator grant (2022), a Vidi grant (2014), and a Veni grant (2008) to work on research projects on innovation for sustainability. Floor received her PhD in Agent Based Evolutionary Economics, from TU/e in 2004. Her PhD work was done at the Dutch National Centre for Mathematics and Computer Science (CWI). She holds an MSc in Artificial Intelligence from VU University Amsterdam. Floor is Associate Editor of the *Journal of Environmental Innovation and Societal Transitions*.

Ignacio Alvarez has been Secretary of State for Social Rights of the Government of Spain between January 2020 and November 2023. With a PhD in International Economics from the University Complutense of Madrid, he is currently Associate Professor of Applied Economics at the Autonomous University of Madrid. He has been Visiting Researcher at the University Paris VII-Denis Diderot, at the Lisbon School of Economics and Management, and at the University of South-Eastern Norway, and has participated in several European Union research projects. His research currently focuses on the study of the relationship between income distribution, demand, and economic growth.

Mirko Armiento is an economist with almost twenty years of professional experience in the energy sector. Currently, he is Senior Researcher at the Enel Foundation, where he regularly publish articles in international journals and authors studies on energy transition and renewable energy technologies, exploring future scenarios and helping to define policy and regulation opportunities.

Giovanni Barbieri is a Research Fellow at CRANEC at Università Cattolica del Sacro Cuore. He holds a PhD in Institutions and Policies (2017, Università Cattolica del Sacro Cuore, Milan). He was previously Adjunct Professor of History of International and Commercial Institutions at the University of Palermo (DEMS) and Visiting Scholar at Scuola Normale's "Istituto Ciampi" in Florence (2022). His main expertise are International Relations Theory and International Political Economy (IPE).

Antonella Battaglini is the CEO and founder of the Renewables Grid Initiative—RGI (https://renewables-grid.eu), established in 2009. Under her leadership, RGI has become a pioneering collaboration between NGOs and transmission system operators (TSOs) across Europe, driving transparent and environmentally responsible grid development to accelerate the integration of renewable energy and the energy transition. Beyond RGI, Antonella has contributed her expertise as a member of the World Economic Forum's Global Future Council (https://initiatives.weforum.org/global-future-council/) on Clean Electrification and the European Commission's Interconnection Target Group. She also spent many years as a Senior Scientist at the Potsdam Institute for Climate Impact Research—PIK (https://www.pik-potsdam.de/en/), where she deepened her engagement with climate and energy issues.

Tom Bauermann is Head of the Unit "Macroeconomics of the Social-Ecological Transition" at the Macroeconomic Policy Institute (IMK), which is part of the Hans Böckler Foundation. He holds a PhD in economics from the Ruhr University Bochum, with research stays at the New School for Social Research (New York) and the Université Sorbonne-Paris-Nord. From 2020 to 2022, he worked as a policy advisor for the state of Bremen in the areas of economics and employment, digitalization, (sea) ports, energy, and climate protection. He also contributed to the work of the Enquete Commission "Climate Protection Strategy for the State of Bremen". At IMK, his work focuses on climate change, energy economics, infrastructure investments, industrial policy, and measures to promote a just transition. His recent projects have addressed the potential costs of Germany's future power grid, support measures for the heat transition, and the impact of the Inflation Reduction Act (IRA) on the American energy supply, the clean-tech industry, and its implications for Europe.

Andrea Brasili is a Senior Economist at the European Investment Bank (EIB, Luxembourg) where his research interests are both micro (firm level) data analysis and macroeconomic developments, in particular those related to fiscal policy. He received his PhD in Public Economics from the University of Pavia (Italy). Before joining the EIB, he worked in the private sector (in Italian banks and asset management companies) as a research economist, whilst still collaborating within academia.

Floriana Cerniglia is a Full Professor of Economics at Università Cattolica del Sacro Cuore (Milan) and Director of CRANEC (Centro di ricerche in analisi economica e sviluppo economico internazionale). She is the Co-Editor-in-Chief of *Economia Politica* (*Journal of Analytical and Institutional Economics*). She received her PhD from the University of Warwick (UK) and her research interests are in public economics and in macroeconomic policies. She has published in leading international journals and she has coordinated and participated in a number of peer-reviewed research projects.

Francesc Cots is a lawyer holding a PhD in Environmental Policy and Law. He brings almost twenty-five years of professional experience dedicated to climate change, energy, environmental policy, and sustainable development. Currently, his work at Eco-union focuses on coordinating European Horizon projects on climate change and energy, such as INCITE-DEM and TIPPING+, in addition to other national projects. His expertise extends to serving as an ambassador for the European Commission's Just Transition Platform and as an expert advisor and member of the Stakeholder Reference Group for the Horizon project KNOWING, which is dedicated to climate change. He is the lead author of Climate Action Network (CAN) Europe's report "Engaging Citizens and Local Communities in the Solar Revolution" (published in May 2022 and updated in June 2024) and Ecounion and Friends of the Earth Europe's report "Corporate Capture of Energy Communities: A Threat to a Citizen-Led Energy Transition in Europe", and has contributed to numerous reports on energy communities, with the most recent being "Community Engagement and Fair Benefit Sharing of Renewable Energy Projects". Furthermore, he is a co-author of book chapters published by Earthscan, Springer, and Cambridge University Press, and articles in journals like *Environmental and Planning C*. From 2015 to 2022, he worked as a lawyer for the renewable energy cooperative SOM ENERGIA SCCL. He is also currently a Professor at Universitat Oberta de Catalunya (UOC), teaching the subject of Energy and Sustainable Consumption. His experience across diverse environments—academia, consultancy, and the public sector—equips him with a deep and cross-cutting understanding of all relevant aspects involved in guiding communities toward sustainability.

Andreas Eisl is a Senior Research Fellow in European Economic Policy at the Jacques Delors Institute and Associated Researcher at Sciences Po. As a comparative political economist, his expertise is centred on EU economic governance, macroeconomic and budgetary policies, as well as industrial policymaking, with a particular focus on the financing of the green transition. Currently, he works on the development of key instruments for a clean EU industrial policy and the implementation of the reformed European fiscal framework. Eisl holds a PhD in political science from Sciences Po and the Max Planck Institute for the Study of Societies (MPIfG)/University of Cologne, as well as a Master's degree in geography from the University of Salzburg. He has taught at Sciences Po and the Sorbonne Nouvelle.

Rafael Fernández holds a PhD in Economics from the Complutense University of Madrid (UCM) and a degree in Political Science from UNED. He is currently a Professor at UCM's Faculty of Economics, and serves as an independent board member of the Instituto de Crédito Oficial (ICO). His research focuses on industrial policies for the energy transition. He has directed the World Political Economy Research Group (UCM), and is a member of the Labour and Structural Transformations in Spain and the EU (LAST) Research Group, the CLACSO Energy and Sustainability Working Group, and the Self-Steering Committee for Sustainability of the UnaEuropa Alliance. Additionally, he is a Researcher at the Complutense Institute of International Studies (ICEI) and a Fellow at the Research Institute for Sustainability (RIFS). At UCM, he has held leadership roles including Vice-Dean of Research and Doctorate, Coordinator of the Master in International Economics and Development, and Coordinator of the

Economics and Double Degree in Economics and Mathematics programs. He currently teaches Political Economy of Energy in the Master of International Economics at UCM and contributes to the Bachelor in Sustainability, a joint European degree.

Jérémie Fosse is an international expert on green and blue economy transitions in the Euro-Mediterranean region. He is Co-founder and President of Eco-union, an independent environmental think-and-do tank based in Barcelona, and a board member of several Civil Society organizations including Climate Action Network (CAN) Europe, European Environmental Bureau (EEB) and the Mediterranean Information Office for Environment, Sustainable Development and Education (MIO-ECSDE). His work bridges policy, research, and stakeholder engagement, supporting public institutions, NGOs, and multilateral bodies such as UNEP, OECD, the European Commission, and the World Bank. He has contributed to over thirty international reports and international research projects, notably on sustainable economy, energy transitions, and participatory democracy (e.g., PROSEU, TIPPING+, INCITE-DEM). He is also the initiator of multi-stakeholders initiatives such as the Blue Tourism Initiative and the Eco Forum. Fosse holds an MSc in Industrial Engineering (INSA Lyon), an Executive MBA (ESADE Business School), and is currently enrolled in the Global Executive Master (GEM) at the European University Institute (2024–2026). His academic and advisory activities focus on environmental governance, sustainability strategies, and socioecological transitions across Europe, North Africa, and beyond.

Bela Galgóczi is Senior Researcher at the European Trade Union Institute, Brussels, since 2003, working on capital and labour mobility in the EU. His current research focus is a just transition towards a carbon neutral economy with focus on fair labour market transitions and on distributional effects of climate policies. He has been conducting studies on the energy transition, on the transformation of carbon-intensive sectors (automotive, chemical, and steel), also mapping regional effects. His research also considers the cumulative effect of multiple transformations including decarbonization and digitalization in a changing geopolitical context. He has a degree in engineering and holds a PhD in Economics.

Clara García holds a PhD in Economics from the Complutense University of Madrid (UCM), where she is Professor of Political Economy. She has been a Visiting Researcher at the Political Economy Research Institute (University of Massachusetts-Amherst), the Center for China Studies, the Berkeley Roundtable for the International Economy, the Haas School of Business (University of California-Berkeley), and the Research Institute for Sustainability (GFZ-Potsdam). Her research examines the political economy of productive development, with a focus on energy transitions and industrial policies. She has conducted empirical studies on East Asia—especially China—and on the European Union. Dr. García's work appears in leading journals, including *Journal of Economic Policy Reform, Structural Change and Economic Dynamics, Cambridge Journal of Economics, Energy Policy, and Governance*. She co-leads the Complutense University LAST research group (Labor and Structural Transformation in Spain and the EU) and serves as Editor-in-Chief of *Revista de Economía Mundial*. She has been Deputy Coordinator of UCM's PhD Programme in Economics and has served as an independent board member at the Official Credit Institute (ICO). Currently, she sits on the boards of Enagás S.A. and Spain's National Productivity Council.

Francesco Gracceva is Head of the Analysis and Scenarios of the Energy and Economic System Section at ENEA (the Italian National Agency for New Technologies, Energy and Sustainable Economic Development). He has over twenty years of experience in energy market analysis and in the development of models and scenarios for the energy system, both for research purposes and in support of decision-makers. He served as a National Expert seconded to the Energy Security Unit of the Joint Research Centre (JRC) of the European Commission. Since 2016 he has been responsible for the publication *ENEA Quarterly Analysis of the Italian Energy System*. He is the author of approximately one hundred publications on energy-related topics.

Willem Klok is a Doctoral Candidate in Industrial Engineering and Innovation Sciences at Eindhoven University of Technology, in the Technology, Innovation, and Society group. His research examines how the financial system can transform to support sustainability, rather than undermine it. Taking a transitions perspective, he explores what kind of systemic change is needed to move beyond short-term, profit-driven incentives and toward a more resilient and responsible alternative. His work combines conceptual analysis with computational modelling to better understand pathways for aligning finance with long-term social and ecological goals.

Bertrand Magné is a Senior Economist in the Economics Department of the European Investment Bank. In 2023, Bertrand was appointed co-rapporteur of the EU Platform on Sustainable Finance and co-led the Subgroup on Monitoring Capital Flows to Sustainable Investments. He specializes in the green transition and policy assessment. He worked previously as Senior Economist and Energy Specialist in various international organizations (including the IEA, the OECD, and the UN). He is an Expert Advisor for the World Economic Forum. Bertrand holds a PhD from Toulouse School of Economics.

Paul Malliet is a Senior Economist at the French Economic Observatory (OFCE), where he works on macroeconomic modelling of climate and energy transition policies. He is part of the team responsible for developing the THREEME model (a multisectoral macroeconomic model for evaluating environmental and energy policies) in collaboration with the French Environment Agency (ADEME). He contributes to the improvement of modelling tools used for policy evaluation in a forward-looking approach, whether for the national carbon emission reduction strategy or for labour market developments. His latest research focuses on the macroeconomic evaluation of energy pricing, the redistributive effects of climate and energy policies, and carbon accounting principles.

Diana Mangalagiu is a leading interdisciplinary scientist specializing in the intersection of artificial intelligence, sustainability, and strategic foresight, advancing research on sustainability transitions, risk governance, and long-term policy planning. With a dual background in natural and social sciences, holding a PhD in Artificial Intelligence (Ecole Polytechnique), MSc in Physics, MSc in Sociology, and MSc in Management, she brings over two decades of experience spanning academia, policy, and advisory work. Her expertise is widely recognized through leadership roles such as Co-Chair of the Sixth Global Environment Outlook for the pan-European region and Coordinating Lead Author of the IPBES Nexus Assessment. She has co-founded the Initiative for Science, Society and Policy Dialogue and serves as Co-Chair and Special Advisor to the World Energy Council and on scientific and advisory boards including the Global Climate Forum and the International Science Council. Diana has led projects with the World Bank, OECD, European Space Agency, and multiple UN agencies. A Romanian and French national fluent in seven languages, Diana is committed to bridging science, policy, and practice to foster systemic change in global sustainability. Recent publications include the IPBES Nexus Assessment on the Interlinkages among Biodiversity, Water, Food, Health and Climate, *Navigating New Horizons—A Global Foresight Report on Planetary Health and Human Wellbeing*, "Positive Tipping Points Towards Sustainability", and the special issue *Enabling Sustainable Transitions in Coal and Carbon-Intensive Regions: Interdisciplinary Social Science Perspectives in Global Environmental Change*.

Phuc-Vinh Nguyen is the Head of the Jacques Delors Energy Centre and a Research Fellow on French and EU energy policy at the Jacques Delors Institute. At the European level, his expertise is centred on the political dynamic surrounding the European Green Deal and more precisely, the carbon markets (ETS1 and ETS2) and the gas and electricity markets. At the French level, he works on the deployment of renewable energy sources and nuclear energy. Nguyen holds a Master's degree in European Business Law Business Law (Université Jean Moulin Lyon III) and a Master's degree in Energy Law (Université Paris I Panthéon-Sorbonne). He teaches European Energy Policy at Sciences Po Paris, HEC, and IRIS-SUP.

Ege Öndeş is a trainee at the European Investment Bank (EIB, Luxembourg) and holds an MSc in Economic and Social Sciences from Bocconi University. He previously interned at the European Bank for Reconstruction and Development (EBRD), co-authoring the Transition Report 2024–2025 chapter on regional inequality and special economic zones. His recent research focuses on industrial policy, development finance, and energy transition.

Daniela Palma is a Research Director at ENEA (the Italian National Agency for New Technologies, Energy and Sustainable Economic Development), in the field of Innovation Economics and Sustainable Development. She holds a PhD in Applied Economic Analysis from Sapienza University of Rome. She was a Visiting Research Fellow at the National Center for Geographic Information and Analysis (NCGIA) of the United States National Science Foundation, hosted by the University of California, Santa Barbara. She has coordinated the activities of the ENEA Observatory focused on Italy in the context of International Technological Competition.

Francesco Pasimeni is Assistant Professor in Economics of Technological Change at Eindhoven University of Technology. His research focuses on the economics of green innovation and modelling agent behaviour toward sustainable consumption solutions. Previously, he worked as an Associate Programme Officer at IRENA, a Scientific Policy Analyst at the JRC European Commission, and held positions in the private sector. He holds a BSc and MSc in Industrial Engineering from the University of Salento (Italy), as well as an MSc and PhD in Science and Technology from SPRU, University of Sussex (UK).

Mathieu Plane is a Deputy Director of the Analysis and Forecasting Department at the OFCE Research Center in Economics, Sciences Po, Paris. He is in charge of economic forecasts for the French economy and works on economic policy issues. He teaches at Sciences Po, Paris and at the University of Paris Pantheon-Sorbonne. He was, in 2013–2014, economic advisor to the Ministers of Economy, Industry, and the Digital Sector. He has recently published, in collaboration with other authors of the OFCE, *What Trajectory for France's Public Finances?*, *Uncertain Growth: Economic Outlook for the French Economy 2025–2026*, and *French Economy 2026* by Éditions La Découverte, Repères collection.

Andrea Pronti is Assistant Professor of Economics at Università Cattolica del Sacro Cuore (Milan), Department of International Economics, Institutions and Development and is a member of the interuniversity research centre SEEDS. He holds a PhD in Economics and Management of Innovation and Sustainability from the Universities of Ferrara and Parma. His research focuses on Environmental Economics, with particular attention to the economic impacts of climate change, eco-innovation, natural resource management, and green transitions. He teaches environmental and development economics at Università Cattolica del Sacro Cuore. He has published in peer-reviewed international journals and has participated in several European research projects in collaboration with the European Commission and the European Environment Agency.

Debora Revoltella has been Director of the Economics Department of the European Investment Bank (EIB) since April 2011. The Department comprises thirty economists and provides economic analysis and studies to support the bank in defining its policies and strategies. Before joining the EIB, Debora worked for many years at CESEE, was head of the research department in COMIT, and later worked as Chief Economist for CESEE in UniCredit. Debora holds a PhD in Economics and has also worked as Adjunct Professor at Bocconi University. She is a member of the Steering Committees of the Vienna Initiative and CompNet, an alternate member of the Board of the Joint Vienna Institute, and a member of the boards of SUERF and the Euro 50 Group.

Francesco Saraceno is Deputy Department Director at OFCE, the research centre in economics at Sciences Po in Paris, and Professor of Practice at LEAP-Luiss, Rome. He holds PhDs in Economics from Columbia University and the Sapienza University of Rome. His research focuses on the relationship between inequality, macroeconomic performance, and European macroeconomic policies. From 2000 to 2002 he was a member of the Council of Economic Advisors for the Italian Prime Minister's Office. He teaches international and European macroeconomics at Sciences Po, where he manages the Economics concentration of the Master's in European Affairs, and in Rome (Luiss). He is Academic Director of the Sciences Po-Northwestern European Affairs Program. He advises the International Labour Organization (ILO) on macroeconomic policies for employment and participates in IMF training programmes on fiscal policy.

Anissa Saumtally completed her PhD at the University of Bordeaux, after graduating from the London School of Economics with a BSc in economics. Her doctoral works focused on economic modelling in innovation and development economics, studying technological and economic catching up. She has previously worked at the French Directorate of the Treasury, where she worked on the Opale macroeconomic forecasting model used for the French budgetary laws. She is currently working at the OFCE (Sciences Po Paris) in the department of environmental economics where she contributes to the development of the ThreeME macroeconomic multisectoral model used for the analysis of environmental and energy policies.

Katharina Sikow-Magny is part-time Professor at Florence School of Regulation at European University Institute since 2024, European Coordinator for the Baltic synchronization project since 2025, and Adjunct Professor at Copenhagen School of Energy Infrastructure since 2025. In addition, she cooperates with several organizations dealing with energy policy and transition. Until 2024, Catharina worked at the European Commission where she held various positions since 1997, including Director responsible for Green Transition and Energy System Integration, Head of Unit in charge of Consumers, Local Initiatives, Just Transition and Head of Unit responsible for Networks and Regional Initiatives at the Directorate General for Energy. She has also worked on international transport, trans-European network policy and financing, internalization of external costs, and strategic policy research. Before joining the Commission, Catharina was a team leader and chief economist in the private sector in Finland. She has also worked for the United Nations Development Programme in Port-au-Prince, Haiti. She holds a Master's in Economics from the Aalto University, Finland.

Annamaria Tueske is an Economist at the Economics Department of the EIB. Her current work focuses on public investment, climate and energy economics and sustainable finance. Prior to joining the EIB, Annamaria worked at the University of Luxembourg, at the OECD and at the Fiscal Council of Hungary. Her academic training focused on industrial organization, networks, and transport economics, she graduated from the Toulouse School of Economics.

Jorge Uxó has a PhD in Economics by the University Complutense of Madrid. He is currently Associate Professor of Applied Economics at the Complutense University of Madrid and Vice-President of the Spanish Productivity Board. He has been visiting researcher at the University of Coimbra (Centre for Social Studies), University of Alcalá and the European Trade Union Institute (ETUI) and has participated in European Union and national research projects, mainly focused on Macroeconomics and Economic Policy in Spain and the EMU and Post Keynesian Economics. His academic articles have been published, among other journals, in *Cambridge Journal of Economics*, *Structural Change and Economic Dynamics*, *Review of Keynesian Economics*, *Review of Political Economy*, *International Labour Review*, *Journal of Post Keynesian Economics*, *Applied Economics*, and *Metroeconomica*.

Andrea Villa is an energy economist and policy advisor with extensive professional experience in Italy, the European Union, and South America. He currently leads the regulatory and legislative team at Elettricità Futura in Rome, the major Italian Association of Electricity Firms. Villa has published scholarly articles on electricity and gas markets and frequently speaks at international energy conferences.

Andrew Watt is General Director of the European Trade Institute, formerly Macroeconomic Policy Institute, Hans-Böckler Foundation. His research interests include European economic governance, collective bargaining and macroeconomic policy, comparative pollical economy, industrial policy, and the green transition.

Roberto Zoboli is Full Professor of Economic Policy and teaches "Economic Policies for Resources and the Environment" and "Economics of Natural Resources" at the Università Cattolica del S. Cuore, Milan. At the Cattolica, he has been Vice-rector for Research and Sustainability and Director of ASA—Graduate School on the Environment. In the past, he has been a researcher at Nomisma S.p.A., Cariplo Foundation for Scientific Research, and the Research Office of Montedison S.p.A. For twelve years, Roberto has been Research Director at the National Research Council, where, at present, he is Research Associate at IRCrES—Research Institute on Sustainable Economic Growth. He is Board member of SEEDS, the inter-university centre on "Sustainability, Environmental Economics and Dynamics Studies" that gathers environmental and innovation economists from twelve Italian universities. Roberto has been task leader in FP7 and Horizon 2020 projects, and project leader of about seventy research projects at the international, national, and regional level. Since 2001, he has been Task leader within different Topic Centres of the EEA—European Environment Agency, at present the ETC CE—European Topic Centre on Circular Economy and Resource Use (2022–2026). Roberto is author/co-author of about 170 publications in peer-reviewed journals and edited books, in English and Italian, and about seventy research papers and published research reports in the areas of environmental and resource economics, sustainable development, environmental policy, and the economics of eco-innovation.

About the Team

Alessandra Tosi was the managing editor for this book.

Adèle Kreager proof-read this manuscript.

Jeevanjot Kaur Nagpal designed the cover. The cover was produced in InDesign using the Fontin font.

Annie Hine typeset the book in InDesign.

Jeremy Bowman produced the paperback and hardback editions and created the EPUB. The main text font is Tex Gyre Pagella and the heading font is Californian FB. Jeremy also produced the PDF edition.

The conversion to the HTML edition was performed with epublius, an open-source software which is freely available on our GitHub page at https://github.com/OpenBookPublishers

Hannah Shakespeare was in charge of marketing.

This book was peer-reviewed by Professor Joan R. Rosés, London School of Economics (LSE), and an anonymous referee. Experts in their field, these readers give their time freely to help ensure the academic rigour of our books. We are grateful for their generous and invaluable contributions.

This book need not end here...

Share

All our books — including the one you have just read — are free to access online so that students, researchers and members of the public who can't afford a printed edition will have access to the same ideas. This title will be accessed online by hundreds of readers each month across the globe: why not share the link so that someone you know is one of them?

This book and additional content is available at
https://doi.org/10.11647/OBP.0499

Donate

Open Book Publishers is an award-winning, scholar-led, not-for-profit press making knowledge freely available one book at a time. We don't charge authors to publish with us: instead, our work is supported by our library members and by donations from people who believe that research shouldn't be locked behind paywalls.

Join the effort to free knowledge by supporting us at
https://www.openbookpublishers.com/support-us

We invite you to connect with us on our socials!

BLUESKY	MASTODON	LINKEDIN	INSTAGRAM
@ openbookpublish .bsky.social	@ OpenBookPublish @hcommons.social	open-book-publishers	@ openbookpublishers_

Read more at the Open Book Publishers Blog

https://blogs.openbookpublishers.com

You may also be interested in:

Transforming Conservation
A Practical Guide to Evidence and Decision Making
William J. Sutherland (editor)

https://doi.org/10.11647/OBP.0321

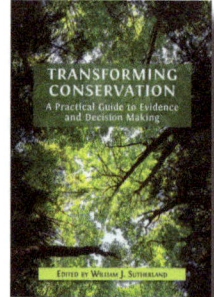

Models in Political Economy
Collective Choice, Voting, Elections, Bargaining, and Rebellion
Martin J. Osborne

https://doi.org/10.11647/OBP.0490

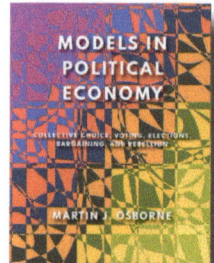

Allocation, Distribution, and Policy
Notes, Problems, and Solutions in Microeconomics
Samuel Bowles and Weikai Chen

https://doi.org/10.11647/OBP.0466

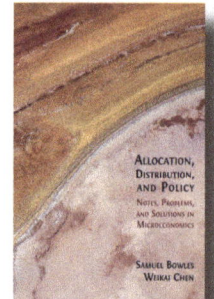

Having Too Much
Philosophical Essays on Limitarianism
Ingrid Robeyns (editor)

https://doi.org/10.11647/OBP.0338

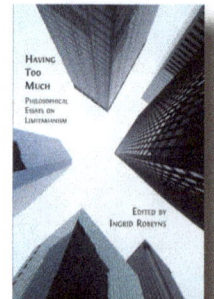

www.ingramcontent.com/pod-product-compliance
Lightning Source LLC
Chambersburg PA
CBHW050236220326
41598CB00044B/7411